SOCIAL POLICY RESEARCH

SOCIAL POLICY
RESEARCH

Edited by

Martin Bulmer

Lecturer in Social Administration
London School of Economics and Political Science

First published 1978 by
THE MACMILLAN PRESS LTD
London and Basingstoke
Associated companies in Delhi Dublin
Hong Kong Johannesburg Lagos Melbourne
New York Singapore and Tokyo

Printed and bound
in Great Britain by
REDWOOD BURN LIMITED
Trowbridge & Esher

British Library Cataloguing in Publication Data

Social policy research.
1. Decision-making 2. Great Britain –
Social policy
I. Bulmer, Martin
300'. 941   HN390

ISBN 0–333–23142–2
ISBN 0–333–23143–0   Pbk

Contents

Part Three

ACTION RESEARCH

Part Four

SOCIAL INDICATORS

Part Five

CONCLUSION

Preface

The mushroom growth of the social sciences in Britain in recent years has been remarkable. Within higher education, in the press and on radio and television, and in journal and book publishing, there is ample evidence of the rise and importance of sociology, political science, social psychology and related subjects. Much of this material is written or spoken by teachers in universities and polytechnics, interpreters of these new modes of thought to students, colleagues and the wider public.

There exists, however, another realm of British social science concerned with research. In higher education this overlaps to a considerable extent with teaching. But outside the' academic world and the media – and outside the limelight – there is an important body of social science being done, finding its way into a growing volume of research reports, and representing the efforts of several thousand people. In central government, local government, market research and polling organisations, independent research agencies and autonomous research institutes, there are probably more people employed to do social research than there are staff employed on research (as distinct from teaching) in higher education. Although many non-university researchers are social science graduates, they do not necessarily identify themselves in terms of their academic discipline of origin. More likely they identify in terms of their kind of work (for example, survey analysis) or their employer (for example market research organisation, government, etc.).

Much, though by no means all, of non-university social research is relevant to – and intended to be relevant to – social policies of all kinds, whether formulated and implemented by central and local government; proposed by political parties and pressure groups; or investigated by Royal Commissions or official committees. The growth of such policy research in Britain is a significant phenomenon, and the aim of this book is to examine some of the methodological issues which it raises. Despite the textbooks, syntheses and monographs that weigh down the shelves of academic bookshops, material on methods of social research – particularly of British origin – is much sparser. It is hoped that the present collection will fill a gap by examining problems in the _application_ of social research, and its uses and limitations in relation to policy.

Indirectly the book is a product of a year spent working in the civil service. The different view of the world which this provided helped to sharpen my appreciation of the difficulties there may be in Britain in utilising social science perspectives in the policy-making process. The substantive contributions of economics and demography and the technical skills of statistics and social survey research are recognised and well established inside central government. It is, however, somewhat curious that the contributions of other social sciences – such as sociology, political science, social psychology and social anthropology – are largely unrecognised despite their central focus upon society and social processes. Perhaps the chapters which follow may throw some light on this curious state of affairs and render it more intelligible.

Acknowledgements

For the preparation of the typescript, I am indebted to the invaluable secretarial assistance of Bridget Atkinson and Gay Grant at the London School of Economics. To former colleagues in the Office of Population Censuses and Surveys, I am grateful for providing a friendly and stimulating milieu in which to work, and for the benefits of first-hand acquaintance with policy-relevant research inside government. (All the views expressed here are, however, my own.) To fellow social scientists in O.P.C.S. and elsewhere in the civil service, I am particularly indebted for a series of discussions on subjects very close to the themes of this book. If I maintain the civil service convention of not identifying individuals, I hope nevertheless that those concerned will accept my thanks and carry on the fight. To the extent that this work has a dedication, it is for social scientists in government.

London, July 1977   MARTIN BULMER

Contributors

DR JACK BRAND is Senior Lecturer in Politics and Director of the Strathclyde Area Survey, University of Strathclyde, Glasgow. Previously he was Lecturer in the Politics of Education at the University of London, and has also taught at the Universities of Reading and Glasgow. His publications include *Political Stratification and Democracy* (1970) and *Local Government Reform in England 1888–1974* (1974).

MARTIN BULMER is Lecturer in Social Administration at the London School of Economics and Political Science. Previously he worked in the Population Statistics Division of the Office of Population Censuses and Surveys, London, and taught in the Department of Sociology and Social Administration at the University of Durham. His publications include *Working-Class Images of Society* (editor, 1975), *Sociological Research Methods* (editor, 1977), and *Mining and Social Change* (editor, 1977).

DAVID DONNISON is Chairman of the Supplementary Benefits Commission and Visiting Professor of Social Administration at the London School of Economics and Political Science. Previously he was Director of the Centre for Environmental Studies, London (1969–76), and Professor of Social Administration at the L.S.E. (1961–9). He was a member of the Milner–Holland Committee on Housing in Greater London (1963–5), the Plowden Committee on Primary Education (1963–6) and Chairman of the Public Schools Commission (1968–70). His publications include *Housing since the Rent Act* (1961), *The Government of*

Housing (1967), *London – Urban Patterns, Problems and Policies* (with D. Eversley, 1973), and *Social Policy and Administration Revisited* (jointly, 1973).

JOHN EDWARDS is Lecturer in Social Policy at Bedford College, University of London. Previously he was Research Fellow in the Department of Social Policy and Administration at the University of Leeds, where from 1972 to 1975 he was attached to the Urban Deprivation Unit of the Home Office carrying out an evaluation of the Urban Programme. His main teaching and research interests are in the fields of urban policy, policy formulation and social problem construction. His publications include *The Politics of Positive Discrimination* (with R. Batley, 1978).

DR DAVID EVERSLEY is a Senior Fellow at the Centre for Studies in Social Policy, London. Previously he was at the Centre for Environmental Studies (1972–6), Chief Planner (Strategy) at the Greater London Council (1969–72), and Professor of Population and Regional Studies at Sussex University. His publications include *Social Theories of Fertility and the Malthusian Debate* (1959), *The Dependants of the Coloured Commonwealth Population of England and Wales* (with F. Sukdeo, 1969), *London – Urban Patterns, Problems and Policies* (with D. Donnison, 1973), and *The Planner in Society* (1973).

DR A. H. HALSEY is Professor of Social and Administrative Studies, University of Oxford, and Professorial Fellow of Nuffield College. Previously he taught at the Universities of Liverpool and Birmingham. He was Adviser to the Secretary of State for Education, 1965–8. His publications include *Social Class and Educational Opportunity* (with J. Floud and F. M. Martin, 1956), *Education, Economy and Society* (with J. Floud and C. A. Anderson, editors, 1961), *The British Academics* (with M. Trow, 1971), and *Educational Priority* (editor, 1972).

DR KEITH HOPE has been University Lecturer in Methods of Social Research and Fellow of Nuffield College, Oxford, since 1968. From 1967 to 1968 he was a Research Officer in the Scottish Home and Health Department. His publications include *Methods of Multivariate Analysis* (1969), *The Analysis of Social*

Mobility (editor, 1972), *The Social Grading of Occupations* (with J. H. Goldthorpe, 1974), and articles on the analysis of social mobility.

SIR CLAUS MOSER has been Director of the Central Statistical Office and Head of the Government Statistical Service since 1967. He was Professor of Social Statistics at the London School of Economics and Political Science, 1961–70, and Director of its Higher Education Research Unit, 1964–7. His publications include *Survey Methods in Social Investigation* (1957, 1971), and *British Towns* (with W. Scott, 1961).

JENNIFER PLATT is Reader in Sociology at the University of Sussex, where she has taught since 1964. She is co-author (with J. H. Goldthorpe, D. Lockwood and F. Bechhofer) of *The Affluent Worker* series, and author of *Social Research in Bethnal Green* (1971) and *Realities of Social Research* (1976).

D. E. G. PLOWMAN is Professor of Social Administration at the London School of Economics and Political Science, and founder editor of the *Journal of Social Policy* (the journal of the Social Administration Association). His publications include *Small Town Politics* (with A. H. Birch and others, 1959).

L. J. SHARPE is University Lecturer in Public Administration and Fellow of Nuffield College, Oxford. He is currently Editor of *Political Studies* (the journal of the Political Studies Association of the United Kingdom). Previously he was Lecturer in Government at the London School of Economics (1962–5) and Director of Intelligence for the Royal Commission on Local Government in England (the Redcliffe–Maud Commission) (1966–9). His publications include *A Metropolis Votes* (1963), *Why Local Democracy?* (1965), and *Voting in Cities* (editor, 1967).

IAN SHAW is Lecturer in Social Work at University College, Cardiff, where he is currently doing research on the social background of applicants to social work training. His main teaching interests are in social work research and social policy research. His publications include contributions to *Towards a New Social Work* (ed. H. Jones, 1975) and articles in the *Journal of Social Policy*, *British Journal of Social Work* and other journals.

GEORGE A. N. SMITH is Lecturer in Applied Social Studies and Research Officer at the Department of Social and Administrative Studies, University of Oxford. Previously he was research officer on the West Riding Educational Priority Area project, 1969–72, and on the Liverpool and Birmingham Community Development Project research teams, 1972–7. His publications include *Educational Priority 4: The West Riding E.P.A.* (H.M.S.O., 1975), *Strategies of Compensation* (with A. Little, O.E.C.D., 1971), and *Action-Research in Community Development* (editor with R. Lees, 1975).

STEPHEN W. TOWN is on the staff of the Transport and Road Research Laboratory (Department of the Environment), Crowthorne, Berkshire, engaged on research into social aspects of transport planning. He previously held research fellowships at several universities. His chapter in this book is based on experience gained while working on the Community Development Project at Southampton University, and on the Dundee Educational Priority Area Project at Dundee University. His publications include *After the Mines: Changing Employment Opportunities in a South Wales Valley* (1977).

Part One

Introduction

---

1 Social Science Research and Policy-making in Britain

Martin Bulmer

Research for Social Policy

Social research in Britain in the last quarter of the twentieth century is a large-scale activity carried on by central government, local authorities, market research firms, independent research organisations and universities and polytechnics. Compared to the middle of the nineteenth or early years of the twentieth century, the character and organisation of social research has altered greatly. The well-documented history of the rise of empirical social research in Britain between 1800 and 1914 emphasises the role of reforming public servants who encouraged social inquiry, the significance of communication among a comparatively small elite drawn from the professional middle classes, the important role of both voluntary associations and private individuals of means, and the absence (until well into the twentieth century) of a base for much of their activity in the universities of the day.[1]

Within central government a degree of continuity has been provided by the General Register Office, responsible since 1837 for vital registration and conducting the decennial census and now part of the Office of Population Censuses and Surveys.[2]

From 1895 the London School of Economics, founded by a group led by Sidney and Beatrice Webb and devoted exclusively to the study of the social sciences, provided continuity and a focus for organised research.[3] But, in general, the contrasts between the late nineteenth century and the present are much greater than the similarities.

Why has so great an expansion in the scope and organisation of empirical social research come about? In the past, social research was done predominantly by socially-minded individuals. Now a great deal of research is done by or (indirectly and directly) for government. The growth of government activity overall, with increasing intervention in the social-policy field from the early twentieth-century social legislation onwards is very important. In central government, 'social' departments such as education, health and social security and employment account for a high proportion of government expenditure, channel resources to the majority of the population in one form or another, and employ hundreds of thousands of staff. Such growth has been reflected in the academic study of these areas. In social administration, for example,

> there have been consistent trends in research over many years, notably in the study of poverty, medical care, social security, welfare services and social work. Gradually, in response to changing social conditions and growing awareness of social problems or as a result of pioneering individuals' activities, other topics have entered – housing and physical environment, planning, educational administration, legal administration, race relations.[4]

The twentieth-century history of this growth is complex. Only a brief sketch can be provided here, though several points stand out. The effects of both world wars, the role of several key government inquiries and, latterly, the expansion of the social sciences in an expanding higher-education system are all significant. So is the time-scale. Cherns and Perry, for example, have documented the extent to which this growth in social science research has been a recent phenomenon, since the middle 1960s, though its small-scale origins go back at least to the Second World War.[5]

In central government, for example, demography was probably the first social science to be taken seriously by policy-makers. Social changes during the Second World War gave a push to applied psychology, economics, social statistics and social survey research. Two key institutional developments date from this period; the setting up of the Government Social Survey in 1941, and the establishment of the Government Statistical Service in 1946. At this time, too, economists first became closely involved in providing advice to central government.

These trends were consolidated by the Clapham Committee of 1946,[6] which recommended increased government support for social sciences in the universities. By the standards of the 1970s, post-war development was slow, and the size of the social science research community very small. In the early 1960s, for example, there were said to be as many university teachers of sociology in the whole country as there were university teachers of history at Oxford alone.

The situation was changed in the middle 1960s by the publication of the Robbins Report,[7] recommending substantial expansion in higher education as a whole, both in student and staff numbers and 'in the number of institutions of higher education. At the same time, the Heyworth Committee on Social Studies[8] recommended, in 1965, increased government support for the social sciences and the setting-up of a government-financed, though autonomous, Social Science Research Council (S.S.R.C.). The large expansion that followed in higher education in general and the social sciences in particular reflected not just the internal preoccupations of higher education, but demands for social research from policy-makers outside.

Clapham in 1946 and Heyworth in 1965 were in a sense simply recognising the increasing involvement of government in social policy, and the contribution which social science might make to the understanding and management of social services. By 1972, for example, social security, health and personal social services, education, and housing accounted for half total public expenditure. The 1971 census recorded that 2 million people were employed in the social services, including a high proportion of the country's highly qualified manpower.[9]

There was growing interest, too, in the *impact* of social and economic policies upon individuals and groups. It was no longer assumed that, if output grew, social conditions automatically got better. Were social services reaching those for whom they were intended? What were the unintended consequences of particular measures? How far was equity achieved in the provision of different services? Such questions required research to answer them, as well as being the subject of interpretation and argument.

More generally, there was a growing demand from an increasingly highly educated public and, particularly from a more sophisticated and specialised media, for understanding and enlightenment about current social trends. The Central Statistical Office publication *Social Trends*[10] was one attempt to meet this need; the expansion of social science book publishing another. By the 1970s, the audience for social science research was far different and much greater than it had been in the 1870s or even the 1920s.

A further difference between social science research in the past and today is the much greater degree of specialisation. The Webbs, for example, turned their hand to social history, political science, economics and sociology as appropriate to the subject in hand. In the present, however, specialisation is the rule. In the chapters which follow a number of different social science disciplines are represented. Sharpe (a political scientist) writes principally about economics, sociology and political science. To these we may add economic and social history and demography (Eversley), social psychology (Plowman), social anthropology and social statistics (Moser). Different disciplines make different contributions. They vary, too, in the closeness of their relationship to policy-making. The present collection is organised around a subject area – social policy and administration – which seeks to *integrate* different social sciences in the study of social policy, to apply different disciplines to substantive problems in society.

It is worth emphasising these specialisms to correct one view of the rise of empirical social research, which traces a line from the great nineteenth-century social reformers through the Webbs, Charles Booth and Seebohm Rowntree to certain mid-twentieth-century social-democratic university teachers. These figures are highly significant, but the 'great man' history of British social research tends to gloss over certain general and analytical issues. It is these that are discussed in the remainder of this chapter and the rest of the book.

It is first important to establish the different conceptions which exist of 'research': it may mean different things to different people. Then the role of theory in policy research needs to be examined closely, as do the place of values, and the relationship between research and political action. A discussion of the organisational context of contemporary British social research leads on to considering the institutionalisation of social research both within and outside universities, this being a necessary condition for its effective contribution to the policy-making process.

Typologies of 'research'
So far 'research' has not been defined. What does 'social research' encompass? Does it refer to discovering and recording social facts? To the analysis of such facts? To gaining understanding of social processes or issues? Or to explaining why certain events or conditions occur? In some classic early studies such concerns were often blended. Seebohm Rowntree's studies of poverty,[11] for example, sought to establish its incidence, analyse the concept of poverty itself, understand the conditions that produced it and explain its occurrence (introducing in the process such explanatory terms as the 'cycle of poverty').

Most academic social scientists would probably endorse the following definitions:

> The most important elements in science are the content of attested facts and the theories which give it form and structure and which facilitate further advances.[12]

Social sciences are characterised by their particular combinations of theory and data; by developing distinctive organising frameworks of ideas and by marshalling evidence about the world related to those ideas. Thus some economists, for example, construct theoretical models of market behaviour and then collect evidence about economic decision-making to test and refine these models. Different social sciences are distinguished less by their factual content than by the intellectual frameworks which are used to organise data. 'Social science' thus entails both empirical evidence *and* general propositions with which to make sense of the evidence.

It might seem that this would provide a sufficient definition of 'social research' as an activity within social science. In fact, particularly in research directed to policy matters, the formulation is not adequate. Contemporary empirical social research is not unitary. It differs, of course, in its problems and its methods, reflecting differences among and between various disciplines. But it also differs in the way in which 'research' is conceived, in its scope, generality and purpose. This must reflect in part the relative youth of the social sciences, and their failure to produce general laws in the manner of various natural sciences. It also reflects difficulties and problems in applying research to policy ends. And it reflects different expectations and demands made upon social scientists by policy-makers.

Since different types of research embody rather different assumptions about 'social science' and its methods, and impinge quite differently on the policy-making process, it is important to clarify several different types of research. A fivefold classification is proposed here, as follows:

(1) *Basic social science*, concerned with advancing knowledge whether through theory-building and testing or the satisfaction of curiosity. It is also the foundation of a social-scientific education. Such inquiry is not designed to have practical uses, although it may do so. Sharpe contrasts the contribution of economics, sociology and political science to British central government in terms of the acceptability to civil servants of basic research in each discipline.

(2) *Strategic social science*, grounded in an academic discipline or subject, but orientated towards a problem which has arisen in society without being aimed at prescribing a solution to it. The housing research described by Donnison in chapter 2 is a good example; it aimed at improving understanding of a practical problem without suggesting a solution to it. This lay with politicians and administrators. In turn, research would monitor the outcome of legislation.

(3) *Specific problem-orientated research*, carried out for a customer (most often a government or local authority department or commercial organisation) who provides a specification to the

researcher. The results of research are designed to help deal with a practical, operational, problem. Much 'in-house' social research in central government is of this type, for example, the work of the Home Office Research Unit and other units discussed later in this introduction.

(4) *Action research*, involving research as part of social programmes of planned social change. Such research is designed to study the effects of change as it happens. The most notable British examples are the Educational Priority Areas research and the Community Development Projects. Both are discussed in detail by Halsey, Town and Smith in chapters 7 to 9.

(5) *Intelligence and monitoring*, the collection of demographic, economic and social statistics in repositories of data that may be drawn upon, with expert guidance, by politicians and administrators to help in the formulation of policy. The Government Statistical Service has traditionally played this role in central government, but is now enlarging its role to encompass both the presentation of data to a wider audience (notably in *Social Trends*) and through more analytic work on social monitoring and social indicators described by Sir Claus Moser in chapter 10, and critically examined in chapters 11 to 13. In some respects public opinion polling, discussed in chapters 4 to 6, also performs an intelligence function, without seeking explanations of the patterns which it discovers.

This fivefold classification may be thought of as a continuum; the distinctions proposed are not absolutely clear-cut, although most policy research may be classified into one of the five types. A consequence of adopting such a classification is that 'social research' is in practice somewhat broader than 'social science' as defined earlier, since intelligence and monitoring activities (the fifth type) often lack any theoretical rationale. For example, conducting the decennial population census, maintaining records of births, marriages and deaths, or compiling monthly unemployment statistics, are not usually termed 'research'. The results of such inquiries may be used by others for research purposes – but they may also be used by politicians, administrators, planners and publicists for quite different purposes. As the Heyworth Committee noted, the difference between fact-finding and research is an exceedingly difficult distinction to make, as research may require, or alternatively emerge from, fact-finding exercises or surveys. We would not, however, regard as research either routine fact-finding, or fact-finding for specific administrative purposes . . .[13]

The justification for including 'fact-finding' as 'research' in this book is pragmatic: this is how research is quite often understood in the British policy context. Some of the problems that this raises are considered in the next section.

Why elaborate such a typology[14] when a more straight-forward dichotomy between basic and applied research is available? This appears in different forms: basic v. applied; pure v. utilitarian; strategic v. tactical; curiosity-orientated v. mission-orientated; fundamental v. applied, and so on, 'not so much descriptions of different parts of the same animal as different elevations of the beast'.[15] The most influential recent statement was Lord Rothschild's report (1971) on the organisation and management of central government research and development.[16] He distinguished between basic research (whose end product is an increase in knowledge) and applied R and D (whose end product is a process, a product or a method of operation).

Such a distinction is unsatisfactory. The Dainton Report on the future of the research council system, published at the same time as Rothschild, rejected the distinction. 'The adjectives "pure" and "applied" imply a division where none should exist and their use can be harmful.'[17] Supposedly theoretical research may have important practical consequences; supposedly applied research may have theoretical pay-off.

Moreover, the supposed method of working of the applied researcher, as described by Rothschild, is of doubtful applicability. According to Rothschild, using the model of technology, applied research has a practical application as its objective. The customer (usually a government department) says what is wanted, the contractor (usually an applied researcher) does it (if he can), and the customer pays.[18] As has often been pointed out, such a model is largely inapplicable to the social sciences. Few social sciences (other than economics) are in a position mechanistically to 'do what the customer wants' in a simple way.

Intervention in society (for example in the housing market[19]) is fraught with difficulty, because of the complexity of social processes. 'Applied' research refers to intention rather than outcome.[20] What is needed is a typology which reflects this diversity of outcome.

The distinctions proposed earlier between basic social science, strategic social science and problem-orientated research closely parallel the distinctions proposed by the Dainton Committee between basic science, strategic science and tactical science (summarised by Donnison on pages 51–2). Such a threefold classification is preferable to a simple pure/applied dichotomy. The virtue of recognising an intermediate type of research – strategic social science research – between basic and specific problem-orientated research, is that it gives due weight to a social science contribution which, though relevant to practical objectives on a broad front, is also firmly grounded in the underlying social scientific disciplines. It is precisely this dual capacity which makes economics useful in policy-making. If problem-orientated research is designed to provide rapid solutions to small-scale, short-term problems, strategic social science is designed to provide policy-relevant results of broader scope looking beyond the short term.

Theory, inquiry and policy
Different conceptions of 'research' imply different ideas about social science. Basic and strategic social science are firmly grounded in particular subject areas; intelligence and monitoring are much more atheoretical fact-gathering functions. Some of the confusion about the contribution of research to policy can be clarified if one considers the importance accorded to particular disciplinary perspectives, and the relative importance of theories and empirical data, in social policy research.

Economics clearly stands apart. It is the only social science discipline recognised as having a direct contribution to make to policy-making in central government; a contribution, moreover, which is based on theoretical ideas and not just a body of data or technical skills. Although the Government Economic Service was only formally established in 1964, the influence of economics within government may be traced back to the Second World War and particularly to Keynes. He helped to establish

economic policy . . . as a matter for economists, not only in
the sense that they are invited to provide expert advice on the
means to be employed to achieve specified ends – that would
apply to other social scientists in their respective spheres – but
arguing about the ends themselves.[21]

The contribution of economists to policy is founded on two
pillars. One consists of comparatively rigorous and sophisticated
techniques of empirical measurement, with greater capacity to
quantify variables which are susceptible to influence by policy-
makers. The other, more important, is that economics

> operates within a comprehensive theoretical system which, at
> any rate in principle, purports to cover the relationships
> between all the relevant phenomena in its field of study.[22]

It is the recognition accorded to economic theories (regardless of
the performance of economic advisers in practice) which legi-
timates the central role played by professional economists in
contemporary economic policy-making.

Is economics the exception among social sciences? One could
certainly not make for political science or sociology in Britain
today the famous claim made by Keynes for economics:

> The ideas of economists and political philosophers, both
> when they are right and when they are wrong, are more
> powerful than is usually understood. Indeed, the world is
> ruled by little else. Practical men, who believe themselves to
> be quite exempt from any intellectual influences, are usually
> the slaves of some defunct economist. Madmen in authority,
> who hear voices in the air, are distilling their frenzy from
> some academic scribbler of a few years back. I am sure that
> the power of vested interests is vastly exaggerated compared
> with the gradual encroachment of ideas.[23]

Shonfield has argued that if other social sciences seek to
emulate economics, they must sharpen their tools of measurement and develop improved social indicators. These issues are
considered in chapters 10 to 13. Such a line of argument clearly
has considerable force as the amount of resources devoted to

social indicators by governments and international bodies suggests. But in the British context it is arguable that there are other tendencies that help to explain why economics is an exception. In the discussion which follows, economics is specifically excluded from consideration.

Some of the obstacles facing other social sciences have been well summed up by Glennerster and Hoyle in discussing educational research.

Probably of all the fields of social policy, education has the richest background of international and policy-orientated research. Perhaps its greatest contribution has been to help create relatively well-informed and critical journalists, commentators, teachers and public. Even so, doubts remain about the current contribution of educational research. There are perhaps three main reasons for this. Firstly, social scientists have not yet adequately resolved the conflict between a disciplinary and a policy orientation. (For example, sociologists of educational organisations have been more concerned with testing general theory than with problems of streaming, curriculum change and school management.) Secondly, educational issues cannot as a rule be wholly explored from the standpoint of a single discipline. Thirdly, education has suffered from what might be called the non-disciplinary approach. Many examples of educational research use the tools of the social sciences – tests, surveys and so on – but have little theoretical basis. These studies are often useful at the level of description, but lack explanatory power.[24]

A strong disciplinary orientation implies a commitment to basic research over all else, and a corresponding weakening of its policy relevance. The development of *inter*-disciplinary research has on the whole been disappointing, despite its potential value for policy studies. The third tendency, what Glennerster and Hoyle call 'non-disciplinary' research has perhaps been most significant and most insidious. Whereas in economics, a fairly close and fruitful relationship has been developed between theory and inquiry, in other social sciences (particularly sociology and social administration) the two elements have tended to shift apart and become separate.

This is not new. What Noel Annan has called 'the curious strength of positivism' in English social thought[25] has a long and distinguished ancestry, and still appears to exercise a powerful hold upon the English intellectual climate. The view that 'the facts speak for themselves' is very strongly entrenched; such *empiricism* still characterises much social policy research in Britain, and partly accounts for the lack of impact of social science disciplines other than economics.

In addition to *empiricism*, another tendency undermining theoretical rigour has been the *political* involvements of social scientists, touched on by Donnison in chapter 2. Both tendencies are well exemplified in P. Abrams's account of British sociology around 1900. He shows how the development of the subject was hindered by fragmentation between philosophical, empiricist and political tendencies. Such continuity as there was in the early years of the twentieth century was at the level of empirical research, but this tradition was statistical rather than socio-logical.[26] Academic sociology was preoccupied with evolu-tionary philosophy and comparative anthropology,[27] 'while the ameliorist attitude for a policy science was being channelled more and more towards the Labour Party'.[28]

Both Booth and Rowntree, despite the importance of their contributions to policy research and improved survey methods, saw their work as contributing to an empirical social science untroubled by theory.[29] In the case of Rowntree this was coupled with an increasingly strong commitment to liberalism as the other side of the coin to social inquiry.[30]

Abrams contrasts early developments in social science in Britain and in America (which had consequences in the present considered by Sharpe in chapter 15). In America social science developed early, with a strong university base. The political system was relatively closed to academic social scientists, who therefore devoted more energy to building up their disciplines. Within the political system, welfare provision was slow to develop, limiting the demand for social science from govern-ment. In Britain, on the other hand, the reverse was the case. The universities were (initially) closed to social science whereas government and party politics were open. With the growth of welfare legislation, a demand for social scientists developed and there were close ties between policy-makers and leading social scientists. In this context it becomes intelligible why such a prominent figure as Rowntree should have become 'a victim of the Whig interpretation of history'.[31] 'The relative openness and malleability of the (British) political system, particularly after 1900, encouraged a persistent migration of energies. . . .'[32]

The history of empirical social research in Britain in the twentieth century is also markedly different from the situation in the United States. In Britain, a greater influence has come from research organisations outside universities – particularly the Government Social Survey and market research firms – than in the United States. Moreover, within higher education, the most common method of social research, the social survey, has tended to be the province of statisticians alone, from A. L. Bowley onwards. The major role played in survey research by academic sociologists, political scientists and social psychologists in the United States is very much less marked in Britain.

There is other evidence that supports this characterisation. Moser and Kalton's well-known textbook, for example, notes that

> many – perhaps most – of the social research surveys men-
> tioned in this book are fact-collecting inquiries, just as are the
> bulk of Government Social Survey or market research
> enquiries. Nor is the preoccupation of social scientists with
> descriptive, fact-finding enquiry anything to be ashamed of.[33]

It is, however, a very different conception of social research from that held by leading figures in American survey research in the tradition of Samuel Stouffer or Paul Lazarsfeld.[34]

A representative statement of the empiricist view of surveys as applied to social policy is to be found in Mark Abrams's *Social Surveys and Social Action* (1951), where he argues that social surveys are primarily utilitarian. They are directed to curing 'obviously pathological social conditions'. Occasionally surveys originate in an abstract desire for more knowledge about social structure, more frequently, however,

> they are carried out as an indispensable first step in measuring
> the dimensions of a social problem, ascertaining its causes and
> then deciding upon remedial action. Thus, we have surveys of

poverty, of overcrowding, of race conflict, juvenile delinquency, sickness, industrial strife, gambling, malnutrition,
loneliness in old age, the spread of illiteracy and the decline of
voluntary associations.[35]

This conception of survey research sees it as providing social
intelligence or as solving specific problems. The prime purpose
of such research is to tackle short-term problems, as an aid to
rational policy-making.

Social surveys have been used as a method by which society
could obtain precise information about itself and thus achieve
social change in a peaceful and coherent manner . . . We now
all realise that the modern community needs social engineering and that in such engineering the social 'survey is a
necessary and valuable preliminary to planning.[36]

Two years earlier, D. V. Glass had put forward similar arguments for the application of social research in town planning,
the provision of health services, housing and manpower policies.

Adequate provision should be made within the structure of
government for social research applied to the assumptions of
social policy and the implementation of social policy . . . the
larger the area of governmental responsibility in the field of
social policy, the greater the urgency for governmental action
to be based on and tested by social research.[37]

This conception of research has also held powerful sway over
that characteristic British institution, the Royal Commission or
Committee of Inquiry. Particularly in recent years, a good deal
of research has been carried out for such bodies, but with a few
exceptions it has tended to be of a fact-gathering kind. Shonfield
has suggested that such lay committees in Britain tend to be a
victim of the pragmatic fallacy:

just plunge into your subject; collect as many facts as you
can; think about them hard as you go along; and at the end
use your common sense and your *feel* for the practicable, to
select a few good proposals . . . This method derives from a

view of public affairs which puts the functions of an investigator on essentially the same footing as those of a common-law judge. Such a person is supposed to know all about the underlying theoretical assumptions of those whose affairs he is examining. All he needs is facts.[38]

Such watered-down versions of social 'science' almost entirely exclude theoretical matters from the scope of research, and by implication also diminish the stature of the social researcher, who tends to become a technical specialist providing information, the interpretation of which is carried out by others (often planners, administrators, or politicians). Or where theoretical issues *are* tackled, they are approached in an unsystematic and 'common-sense' manner. An instructive case study is provided by comparing the Plowden Report on primary education (1967) with the U.S. Coleman Report on Equality of Educational Opportunity (1966).[39] Considerable scientific controversy was sparked off by both reports, but it is notable how much more explicit and sophisticated was the level of theoretical argument about the Coleman Report than about the Plowden Report.

A comparison of these reports and other significant policy research in other areas of social policy – for example, Myrdal's classic *An American Dilemma* and its British imitator *Colour and Citizenship*[40] – supports Pinker's generalisation that

in (British) social policy and administration we begin with fact-finding and end in moral rhetoric, still lacking those explanatory theories which might show the process as a whole and reveal the relations of the separate problems to one another.[41]

These differences between Britain and America are explored further in chapter 15, but they have quite deep historical roots. The British tendency to interpret research as the gathering of facts – often indeed 'left-wing facts' and 'right-wing facts'[42] – owes a good deal to the greater openness of government to influence by social scientists. Abrams argues that it took the Second World War and five years of post-war Labour government to realise that 'social problems were more *fundamentally* problematic than they had yet been in British experience.'[43] In the United States, on the other hand, social reform was much slower. Simple political responses to social problems were less easily available and less plausible. A more analytic and theoretically-informed approach to policy research developed accordingly.

It is difficult to imagine, for instance, American social scientists taking seriously the naive conception of social administration propounded by T. S. Simey. Though making legitimate criticisms of the absurdity of value-free empiricism, he rejected any significant contribution from theory, which he regarded as too abstract and far removed from practical concerns. Instead he argued for a normative orientation as the guiding principle.

> What we want is both science to give us techniques and morals to give us a grasp of values. They are equally important, for without both we cannot know any sociology that is relevant to needs and situations . . . The objectives of social administration must embody components, established by evaluation, with which it is impossible to dispense. [44]

The limitations of both empiricist and normative conceptions of social policy research are emphasised in the following chapters.

In the discussion of public opinion polling, Platt in particular emphasises the necessity for clarity about theory and values in polling-type activities, and in their use to draw conclusions with practical implications. Shaw shows the difficulty of determining what is 'consumer opinion' on a particular issue. The important theoretical assumptions built into social indicators are also brought out, particularly by Brand and Hope.

The importance of being clear about values is also underlined. Brand, Edwards and Hope all emphasise the extent to which supposedly 'objective' statistical indicators may contain implicit value assumptions. The uses made of public opinion polls, too, may have normative consequences unrecognised by their practitioners.

> The social scientists concerned with the appraisal of voting intentions design questions concerned with aspects of the policies of political parties, which may not be at all those that the leaders of these parties would choose of their own accord

to throw into the discussion . . . By probing the deeper springs of popular political sentiment the researchers may have the effect of forcing decisions on issues that the political machines of all the parties in the contest might have preferred to evade or play down.[45]

No wonder, as Sharpe suggests, politicians suspect polls of usurping their representational function in the political process.

To a considerable extent the contribution from social science (other than economics) to British social policy-making has tended to be either statistical intelligence or specific problem-orientated research. This may be explained by the dominant empiricist conception of social research, together with the overtly political orientation of some academic researchers. There are signs, however, that both strategic social science and action research are now being taken more seriously and producing results of value. Both Donnison in chapter 2 on strategic research and Halsey in chapter 7 on action research emphasise a social science contribution grounded in analysis and theory, rather than over-simple presentation of 'the facts'. In understanding either the working of a housing market or the structural conditions that maintain poverty, a model of the social processes at work is essential.

How far can subjects such as sociology, political science or social administration be expected to contribute to policy-formulation in the future? In the immediate future it is unlikely that they will come to play a role analogous to economics and economists. This will be due in part to unrealistic expectations on both sides about what social scientists can contribute. On the part of policy-makers there has been insufficient recognition of the potential analytic contribution of strategic research or action research. On the part of social scientists, overoptimistic views of the possibilities for political intervention (itself a historical legacy) have weakened their impact. The fate of the Community Development Projects is perhaps a case in point.

It is due in part to external and internal obstacles to the development of a fruitful relationship. If the legitimacy of political scientists is not recognised by administrators, and if many sociologists champion the underdog and are suspicious of the State, then something of a vicious circle develops, where social scientists fail to contribute directly to policy deliberations (though they may have an important effect on the general climate of opinion), and this is then cited by policy-makers as a good reason for not involving them. The most hopeful sign is the growing interest within social administration in developing genuine applied sociology, applied political science and applied social economics, which take both the constraints of the policy process *and* the potential analytic contribution of social science seriously.

Unlike economics, other social sciences have yet to demonstrate effectively that they offer a body of theory sufficiently precise (and susceptible to measurement) to be of use even in the construction of social indicators. As a recent government statistical commentary noted:

> The selection of data for a publication such as *Social Trends* presents particular difficulties. In the economic field there is a set of coherent theories, linked conceptually by a common monetary unit and administratively by the Treasury as a central economic department. The social field has no such theoretical or administrative unity.[46]

Much social science no doubt appears to policy-makers like Alastair McIntyre's general theory of holes:

> There was once a man who aspired to be the author of the general theory of holes. When asked 'What kind of hole – holes dug by children in the sand for amusement, holes dug by gardeners to plant lettuce seedlings, tank traps, holes made by roadmakers?' he would reply indignantly that he wished for a *general* theory that would explain all of these. He rejected *ab initio* the – as he saw it – pathetically common-sense view that of the digging of different kinds of holes there are quite different kinds of explanations to be given; why then he would ask do we have the concept of a hole? Lacking the explanations to which he originally aspired, he then fell to discovering statistically significant correlations; he found for example that there is a correlation between the aggregate hole-digging achievement of a society as measured, or at least one day to be measured, by econometric techniques, and

its degree of technological development. The United States surpasses both Paraguay and Upper Volta in hole-digging. He also discovered that war accelerates hole-digging; there are more holes in Vietnam than there were. These observations, he would always insist, were neutral and value-free. This man's achievement has passed totally unnoticed except by me. Had he, however, turned his talents to political science, had he concerned himself not with holes, but with modernisation, urbanisation or violence, I find it difficult to believe that he might not have achieved high office in the APSA.[47]

British social policy research will only fructify if academic social scientists and policy-makers can adjust to each other. To expect the theories of, for example, Talcott Parsons to inform the work of the Central Statistical Office is merely bizarre. Much more fruitful is likely to be the application of more modest, middle-range social science theories to specific areas of governmental activity, such as employment, crime and deviance, or poverty and income maintenance. In all of these fields social scientists have made important contributions to the general climate of opinion, and in some cases to policy-formulation through their work on Royal Commissions and advisory committees.

To underline this point a few examples may be mentioned, purely for purposes of illustration. In the study of employment and labour markets, an officially sponsored O.P.C.S. large-scale survey and Martin and Fryer's sociological case-study, *Redundancy and Paternalist Capitalism*, provide an instructive contrast. Martin and Fryer's is much the more illuminating analysis, because they have a working model of the local labour market which enables them to explain the course and effects of factory closure. They can show why, for example, such a high proportion of workers are unwilling to leave the area (where no work is available) and move to other areas (where it is). In the fields of poverty and income maintenance, one may compare official descriptive statistics derived from the Inland Revenue and Family Expenditure Survey (F.E.S.) sources with the more theoretical approach adopted by Halsey in chapter 7 and by Townsend. The two are, of course, not mutually exclusive; it is simply that the latter enriches the interpretation of the former. In the study of inter-generational transmission of social disadvantage, any respectable social science analysis *must* come to grips with the difficult theoretical issues involved, as recent work by Rutter and Madge indicates.[48] Such analysis goes beyond a simple description of the facts of social inequality to an attempt to *explain* how such inequalities occur and why they persist.

Yet, as suggested earlier, there is considerable resistance in some quarters to recognising that social science has any valid theoretical contribution to make, even when theory is defined in such specific terms. Whether this potential contribution is recognised in the future will depend on the organisational framework and the models of the relationship between research and action that are held by policy-makers and academics.

Research, values and action

How does research influence action? How do social scientific findings affect what policy-makers decide to do? There are no simple answers to these questions, indeed they are a source of considerable friction and misunderstanding between policy-makers and social scientists. Even the techniques used by social scientists are fraught with value problems, let alone their research findings or the advice that they give. A neutered, value-less, social science is an impossibility. How far, and in what ways, values enter in is central to understanding; lack of awareness of the value dimension may have crippling effects.

This is not the place to review the important social science debate about objectivity and values, principally associated with the names of Max Weber, Karl Mannheim and Gunnar Myrdal.[49] One of the consequences of this debate has been to discredit several views of the relationship of research to policy as oversimple. Three such views will be considered briefly.

The first is that values can be excluded from social science by an exclusive reliance on 'hard', objective, quantitative data – 'social facts'. The idea that quantitative data have objective validity and truth-value not enjoyed by qualitative material is a powerful and enduring one. It is, therefore, salutary that both Brand and Hope point to some of the limitations of social indicators and the way in which value premises can enter in unnoticed. Eversley provides a more general critique of the position, and demonstrates effectively the necessary role which values play in social inquiry. Edwards in chapter 11 provides a pointed example from studies of urban deprivation. He emphasises that social indicators of deprivation – and the programmes of which they form a part – are necessarily the subject of value assumptions and value conflict.

A more elaborate but related view of value-freedom is that of social science as a value-free *theoretical* science. Even as developed a subject as economics embodies value-assumptions in its axioms and principles – indeed demonstrating this was how Myrdal first became involved in the problem of objectivity.[50]

A second solution, most sharply enunciated by Simey, is to recognise that social science itself is guided by normative principles. His argument draws on the critique of 'pure objectivity' by Weber and Myrdal, but he fuses with it a prescriptive element that is lacking in their work. Simey's approach to social policy in terms of asserting

> morality is as unhelpful as an uncritical belief in the detached objectivity of the scientist. To see the social scientist as a combination of philosopher and social engineer is merely naive. Few would nowadays agree that the ends of social research are normative in any simple sense, its long-term effects are more likely to make choice more complex, dilemmas more baffling and conflicts more stark.[51]

Indeed, the sheer intractability of many social problems is worth underlining, and the complexities of intervening in the political process. Social scientists themselves hold values and one of the dangers of the social scientist drawn to policy research is that he may fail to keep his own values in their proper perspective. The problem is less lack of commitment than a surfeit of it.

A third conclusion sometimes drawn from the value-permeated nature of social research is that policy research is of necessity tainted. The post-war optimism represented by D. V. Glass and M. Abrams sometimes seems to have been replaced, particularly among British sociologists, by a blanket scepticism about policy research on the grounds of disciplinary purism or moral distaste. Since all research is influenced by values, research for policy (it is argued) will be tinged by the values of policy-makers. Such research will tend to be a prop to the *status quo*, a tool of manipulation for those in power.

It is certainly true that since social research is often sponsored, conducted and used by the established sections of society, it tends to be applied to the problems perceived by those elites. In particular fields, notably social deviance and minority-group research, some groups of researchers may become identified with those in power – for example in British criminology[52] – and there may be intractable problems over control of research access.[53] It is argued by extension that research is controlled and used to further the ends of those in power. The relationship between the Establishment and social research is, however, much more subtle and complex than a conspiracy theory would allow.

> The various agencies that sponsor social research are not monolithically and relentlessly dedicated to the maintenance of the status-quo . . . One often finds an interest in social experimentation and a commitment to social change in the most unexpected quarters. As far as social scientists themselves are concerned, as a group, they hardly represent an entrenched group in the ruling class. To be sure, they are usually not members of the most deprived segments of society, and a subset of social scientists has in fact been moving close to the centres of power. Yet many social scientists are marginal within their own society and play the role of gadflies to the establishment. There is a strong tradition among social scientists of commitment to social critique and social reform.[54]

Nor do applied social scientists in positions of influence have their say without opposition. When D. P. Moynihan produced his 1963 report *The Negro Family: The Case for National Action*, informed by an analytic social science approach, it provided a highly critical response from fellow social scientists in the United States.[55] The recent U.S. debate about busing is another example of controversy over the policy conclusions to be drawn from research, where interpretations favouring the *status quo* were fiercely attacked in public debate.[56] As Hope suggests in chapter 13, there are few such debates in Britain. One of the reasons for it is a powerful current of radical pessimism, among sociologists in particular, about the contribution of social research to policy-making.[57]

Apart from the fruitfulness of the American debates on the black family and on busing, there are a number of reasons why pessimism is premature. One is that policy research is not all cast in the same mould. There is variety and innovation in its form. A new form, action research (discussed in chapters 7 to 9), emerged from a rather unlikely quarter. It is slightly ironical that the Home Office, *bête noire* of some prison researchers, should have been the home of the Community Development Projects, through which

> a new relation between social science and social policy (was) postulated. It asserts that political ends may be seriously pursued through social science experiment. The traditional political mode of reform has been to announce a nostrum which is held to be certain in its cure of the social ills to which it is addressed. The new idea acknowledges ignorance. The politician commits himself to trying a plan in an experi- mentally devised situation, but at the same time commits himself to abandoning it for another scheme if evaluation by the most valid social science techniques show that it does not work.[58]

Another ground for resisting pessimism is that social science research need not be social engineering. Morris Janowitz, for example, has contrasted what he calls the 'engineering model' of the relationship between sociology and social policy with what he calls the 'enlightenment model'.[59] In the engineering model, there is a sharp distinction between basic and applied research. The task of applied researchers is to collect empirical data to solve specific problems within an existing theoretical frame- work. The Columbia Bureau of Applied Social Research directed by Lazarsfeld would be an example. Those who favour the enlightenment model (including Janowitz himself) do not stress the basic/applied distinction. The 'applied' sociologist is not a technician acting as if he were external to society, but recognises himself as a member of it. He does not make a sharp distinction between theory and research, but attempts to place a particular and specific social problem in a broader context; his data must be set in a general and theoretical framework. While a specific answer is sought, the emphasis is on creating the right intellectual conditions for problem-solving, not just on technical solutions.

Finally, conducting policy research is not incompatible with moral commitment. The critical contribution of someone like Richard Titmuss to social policy, revealing the limitations of existing policies while striving to improve them, is one of the distinguishing characteristics of the study of social administration. But it is not the naive prescribing of values of Simey. As Martin Rein has recently argued, such an approach to policy critically questions morality rather than asserts it.

> At the centre of my concern is the question of social objectives, the purposes of policy, and the goals of welfare organisations. I start with the premise that defining coherent social purposes in public policy is an endemic problem ... the current conception of political process assigns to the social scientist the task of dispassionately assessing the social costs of alternative methods of achieving specific goals. In this way the expert usurps no political prerogatives. In practice, however, the analysis of means is seldom merely a technical question; it characteristically masks a more fundamental debate about ends. ... I am inclined therefore to treat debate about means as masked ideology and try to make explicit the fact that a review of alternative means can also embrace conflicting goals.[60]

The task of policy research is (in part) to examine such alternative means and goals in a value-critical way. There are competing paradigms among those who interpret policy, and no satisfactory way of resolving these differences.

> There is no central, abiding, over-arching guiding principle that can fill the gaps in understanding, resolve the quandaries of action, order the conflicts of human purposes or resolve the conflicting interpretations of action which competing frameworks pose. ... I am inclined to take the view that these dilemmas are desirable, because they pose moral choices and hence permit a debate about moral purposes. If there were no

dilemmas in social action, then there would be no opportunity for meaningful moral discourse on human affairs.[61]

The Organisation and Institutionalisation of Social Science Research

How are dilemmas about social facts and social theories, social values and social interventions, resolved in practice? How is social policy research organised and institutionalised, so that its results feed into the policy-making process? The way in which this happens today is likely to be very different from the pattern of personal contacts between members of the late-nineteenth-century upper-middle-class elite to which Beatrice Webb, Charles Booth, Seebohm Rowntree and L. T. Hobhouse belonged. In Britain it is important to look at the record carefully, because over the years the establishment of policy research has been characterised by failure as much as success, and by interrupted development due to serious obstacles as much as steady growth.

The picture is variable, depending on where one looks. Intelligence and monitoring in central government has the longest history. Data on population and medical subjects have been systematically collected since the early nineteenth century, starting with the first Census of 1801.[62] Most significant was the establishment of the General Register Office in 1837, responsible both for vital statistics of birth, marriage and death, and for the decennial census, and an important pioneer of socio-medical research.[63] The existence of the office of Registrar General provides a thread of continuity linking the nineteenth and twentieth centuries. Though much of the work was sheer data collection and storage, his staff contributed significantly to demographic and socio-medical research.

For other kinds of policy research, discontinuity is more characteristic. Some kinds of research – action research is one example – are of very recent origin in any case. Important methodological innovations, such as the social survey using probability sampling, are twentieth-century developments. Most serious was the failure before 1914 to institutionalise basic social research to provide a foundation for future developments.

In this respect it is instructive to compare sociology and political science at L.S.E. and at the University of Chicago in the early years of the twentieth century. In the latter it was poised for rapid and fruitful development, in the former merely embarking upon several decades of quiescence.

The roots of this failure must be traced back into the nineteenth century, and particularly to the lack of any framework for the integration of research results with theoretical social science. Abrams emphasises this in his account of the first effort to establish empirical sociology in Britain, and its collapse.[64] The dominant modes of research in the nineteenth century were characterised by empiricism, a desire for efficient administration and, above all, the aim of bringing about social reform.[65]

The organisation of research, too, was completely different. In the last century, social research was a leisure-time activity conducted by 'amateurs, ministers, physicians, civil servants and businessmen who were primarily interested in social reform'.[66] There was little professionalisation or specialisation, and no avenues for training and socialisation since social research had no base in the universities, from which it was excluded. No status of empirical researcher existed; therefore no-one thought of himself as an empirical researcher, and there were no channels of recruitment into empirical research. Probably most important was the failure to connect research to any systematic body of theory. 'Not only did they not have common theoretical problems but also they had no theory at all – common or individual.'[67]

Some reasons for the growth of social policy research in the twentieth century were indicated earlier. Here we are concerned with its *form*. Six main trends may be distinguished: the growth of university social science; the development of the professional social survey organisation; the expansion of the intelligence and monitoring function in central government; the rise of the academic expert; the establishment of S.S.R.C.; and the introduction of new research-based government programmes of social intervention.

The single most important transformation compared to the nineteenth century is the firm establishment of social sciences in British universities in the twentieth century. The process can perhaps be dated to the establishment of the London School of Economics and Political Science in 1895, the first institution of higher education in Britain devoted entirely to the study of the social sciences. For two generations, until the 1960s, it was the dominant centre for education – particularly postgraduate education – in British social science. Originally concentrating on economics and political studies, other social sciences such as social administration, sociology and social psychology gradually increased in importance. Since the rapid expansion of British higher education beginning in the 1960s, the position of the L.S.E. is much less pre-eminent. Social science teaching and research are now spread more widely· around the country, although in earlier periods, too, there had been important centres away from London, for example, Nuffield College, Oxford (founded as a postgraduate centre in 1947); the Manchester School of Social Anthropology under Max Gluckmann; Cambridge economics. In the 1960s such alternative centres became much more numerous.

The growth may be demonstrated statistically in a number of ways – by the increase in the number of universities, of social science departments within new and existing universities, in the number of staff teaching social science. For the present argument two indicators are of particular interest. The number of graduates in all subjects receiving honours degrees in British higher education increased by 152 per cent between 1959 and 1969: for the same period honours social science graduates increased by 206 per cent.[68] In particular subjects growth was even more rapid; the number of graduates obtaining first degrees in sociology and social anthropology jumped from 700 in 1967 to 1700 in 1970.[69] The number of current British full-time postgraduate students in sociology (defined broadly to include social administration and social science) increased from under 1000 in 1965 to over 2500 in 1975, an average rate of increase of ten per cent per annum.[70] Potentially, such graduates and postgraduates provided manpower for research posts. And Cherns and Perry have indeed documented the growth of research organisations which accompanied the expansion of higher education. Out of 160 research organisations in universities and polytechnics which they identified, 17 per cent had been founded before 1955, 22 per cent in 1955–64, and 61 per cent in 1965–72.[71] The present scale of British social science research is a comparatively recent development.

A second trend, largely apart from higher education in its organisation, has been the rise of the professional social survey organisation, providing technical expertise in the conduct of the sample survey, the research procedure most common in contemporary social research. In its present form, the social survey is based on probability sampling, first developed around 1912 by L.S.E. statistician A. L. Bowley.[72] Bowley's work received the warmest reception in the United States. 'His lead was very quickly followed by social researchers in the United States, and the development of a large and expanding market for consumer goods stimulated the application of Bowley's methods in marketing research.'[73]

In fact several distinct developments within the field may be noted. One of the earliest and most important was the wartime establishment (in 1941) within the Central Office of Information of the Government Social Survey (today the Social Survey Division of O.P.C.S.), to carry out factual inquiries into social questions on behalf of other government departments. The G.S.S. work has embraced a very large number of subjects. Its characteristic strengths are very high standards of technical competence in survey work, meticulous reports of objective conditions, and non-involvement in politically contentious issues. As a government department O.P.C.S. has to avoid public opinion polling type work, concentrating on inquiries into objective conditions. These include both specific *ad hoc* inquiries, usually requested by other government departments, and the large-scale continuous surveys such as the Family Expenditure Survey, General Household Survey and International Passenger Survey.[74]

Though sharing common techniques and methods of research, market research organisations (first established in Britain in the late 1930s) tend to be more concerned with market research into consumer products, carried out on a commercial basis for industrial firms. Market research is now a very large-scale activity which, however, does not impinge directly upon policy research.[75] Its closely associated partner, public opinion polling, does so directly. Polling members of the public for their opinions about voting intentions, political leaders and political and social issues of the day is now widely practised, and the results used by politicians, the media, government and academic political scientists.[76] How far such techniques are fruitful when applied to policy issues is debatable. Plowman's important critique in chapter 4 demonstrates some of the assumptions behind polling, while Brand in chapter 12 comments on subjective social indicators, an application of polling techniques in an attempt to measure satisfaction with the quality of life.[77] As Platt and Shaw in chapters 5 and 6 indicate, the application of such techniques to more complex social issues is fraught with difficulty.

A more recent development has been the use of independent research organisations, undertaking social research for academic and central and local government clients. Some of these are primarily research centres, which contract out their field work to specialist organisations. Examples include Political and Economic Planning, the Tavistock Institute, the Institute of Community Studies (whose work is discussed by Platt), and the Centre for Environmental Studies.[78] Others are primarily social survey organisations, of which Social and Community Planning Research is the most important.[79] In addition to conducting surveys for clients, it has contributed to methodology through work on sampling, response error and ethical problems of survey research.[80]

S.C.P.R. bears some resemblance (on a small scale) to an American research organisation such as N.O.R.C. in Chicago, although Rossi has compared N.O.R.C. to the Government Social Survey.[81] There are, however, at present no large university-based survey organisations in Britain such as the Bureau of Applied Social Research at Columbia or the Institute of Social Research at Michigan. In 1965 H. Selvin commented adversely on British provision in this respect.[82] A decade and more later the situation had actually deteriorated. Dr W. Belson's Survey Research Centre was no longer located at L.S.E., and the S.S.R.C. Survey Unit, opened in 1970 to promote survey research in higher education, closed in 1976 and was not replaced. The most significant academic centre for survey work (in 1977) was the S.S.R.C. Survey Archive at Essex University, a repository and not an organisation itself conducting surveys.

The growth of so much survey research, most of it separate from universities and not informed by disciplinary perspectives, reflects the demand for information from commercial, political, interest group, media, civil service and academic sources, all of which leads to more surveys being carried out. The same demands, most particularly from politicians and pressure groups, have also led to the expansion of government intelligence and monitoring functions.

The growth of the Government Statistical Service, formally recognised at the end of the Second World War, has been particularly rapid in the past ten years. In 1966, for example, there were less than 200 professional staff (that is professional statisticians as distinct from administrative support). By 1976 there were nearly 500, a growth rate of over ten per cent per annum. As Pite has shown, this was concentrated particularly in social statistics. Numbers working on social topics (as distinct from economic, defence and other subjects) doubled from 51 in 1969 to 106 in 1974, growing at 16 per cent per annum. In all, the Government Statistical Service now employs nearly 500 specialists and over 6000 administrative staff, the most formidable concentration of social research expertise (albeit of a rather narrow and particular kind) in the country.[83]

Though the Government Statistical Service exists primarily to serve ministers and civil servants, increasing resources have been devoted in recent years to making government statistical data more widely and attractively available. The production of *Social Trends* and *Population Trends*, for example, are models of their kind for the collection and presentation of quantitative data. Some of these same skills are employed also in the Joint Approach to Social Policy. [This was an initiative begun in 1975 to try to co-ordinate social policies between different central government departments.] Great emphasis was placed on presenting significant social trends to ministers in an intelligible fashion.[84] The first J.A.S.P. report examined the impact of demographic change (particularly the declining birth rate) on the social services.[85] The work of the Central Statistical Office on social monitoring and social indicators is discussed in chapter 10. It represents a significant extension of government activity in the field of social intelligence, which is itself part of an international effort being actively promoted by the Organisation for Economic Cooperation and Development (O.E.C.D.).[86]

The fourth quarter of the twentieth century is also distinguished from the nineteenth by the use of the academic expert, discussed by Donnison. Booth and Rowntree were businessmen, their twentieth-century counterparts are academics. 'However involved some of these people may be temporarily in the corridors of power, their strengths are drawn from the academic community to which they belong. . . . Most work, or have worked, as university teachers of social administration, sociology, statistics or economic and social history . . .'[87] (They are represented here by, for example, Donnison himself, Halsey, Eversley and Moser.) Such people have brought social sciences to the higher reaches of government in various ways, have done original research in fields such as income maintenance, housing, town planning and personal social services which has made an impact on opinion and those making policy. They have served as research advisers to important commissions – Moser to the Robbins Committee and Sharpe to the Maud Commission for example. More directly, they have played 'an active part in serious policy debates as members of public authorities or committees of inquiry, or as advisers to ministers or shadow ministers, their departments or party committees.'[88] Donnison's membership of the Plowden Committee and Chairmanship of the Public Schools Commission, and Halsey's role in 1965–68 as adviser to the Secretary of State for Education, are examples.

A further significant development sharply distinguishes the present from the past – the channelling of financial resources from government to academic social science through the semi-autonomous Social Science Research Council, established in 1965 in the wake of the Heyworth Report. The Council, a majority of whose (changing) members are academic social scientists, has distributed its budget between postgraduate training and research grants in the proportions shown in table 1.1. Both tables 1.1 and 1.2 show the rapid rate at which the S.S.R.C.'s budget has grown in recent years. Such expanding research activity (some of it through S.S.R.C.'s own research units) has been a further stimulus to the growth of the social sciences, although in terms of funding research the financial contribution of S.S.R.C. is not as great as some other sources.

Finally, organised social research has received a further impetus from research-based or research-linked government programmes for social intervention, notably the Educational Priority Area and Community Development Project programmes. These are fully discussed in chapters 7 to 9. They embody both a new conception of research and a commitment to *evaluate* the results of social action more directly than hitherto.

The present scale of organised social research in Britain may be gauged in various ways. Expenditure would be one indicator, but for various reasons precise figures are difficult to obtain. One estimate suggests that the total annual sum involved in the financing of social science R and D in the early 1970s was £20 million.[89] An earlier estimate suggested government expenditure, exclusive of University Grants Commission (U.G.C.) funds, of £5 million.[90] A third source states that direct central government expenditure on social research is in excess of the annual expenditure of S.S.R.C.[91]

By comparison with the United States, British expenditure on social research is very modest. A 1970 estimate suggested that in that year the U.S. Federal Government, with four times the population, spent thirty times as much on social research as British central government.[92] There are considerable problems of precise comparison here: whether to include university finance; whether to include research funds from private foundations (a much larger source in the United States); how to deal with commercial research expenditure. Such data as are available are not adequate to reach definite conclusions, save that although total social research expenditure in Britain has grown rapidly since the 1960s, it is still comparatively small either in comparison with other sciences in Britain (table 1.2, last column) or with social science in America.

The number of social research organisations and staff is perhaps a more satisfactory guide; here firmer data are available, principally from a major S.S.R.C. survey by Perry. Table 1.3 shows the number of social science research organisations doing research identified in his 1972 survey, with their distribution between sectors.

Nearly two-thirds of them were in an academic setting, but this exaggerates their importance for policy research, for two reasons. A proportion of academic research organisations would be engaged upon basic social science research without policy relevance. And if one looks at numbers of staff employed, and their concentration, the position is rather different. Central government, for example, was found in Perry's survey to employ

TABLE 1.1

The Growth of the Social Science Research Council Budget, 1967–76

£ millions

	1967–8	1968–9	1969–70	1970–1	1971–2	1972–3	1973–4	1974–5	1975–6
S.S.R.C. Expenditure on postgraduate awards during year	0.4	0.7	1.2	1.8	2.1	2.4	2.7	3.3	4.4
Value of S.S.R.C. research grants awarded during year	1.0	1.3	1.4	2.0	1.7	2.5	2.4	2.6	3.0

Source: *S.S.R.C. Annual Reports, 1966/67 to 1975/76*, London, H.M.S.O.

TABLE 1.2

The Growth Rate of S.S.R.C. 1967–72, Compared to other Research Councils

Research council	% growth over previous year in real terms					Size of parliamentary estimate in 1971–2
	1967–8	1968–9	1969–70	1970–1	1971–2	
Science Research Council	7	5	3	4	5	£56 million
Medical Research Council	15	5	7	8	4	£23 million
Natural Environment Research Council	20	13	20	10	5	£16 million
Social Science Research Council	47	48	26	30	16	£4 million

Source: 'The future of the research council system' (Dainton Report), in *A Framework for Government Research and Development*, Cmnd. 4814, 1971, p. 20.

526 research staff with an average of 11 staff per division. Commercial research firms had an average of 10 staff each, and independent non-commercial organisations (with 327 staff) an average of 9 staff each. University *research units* (with 995 staff) had an average of 7 staff each. Local government research departments had an average of 5 staff each, university and polytechnic *teaching departments* an average of 3 research staff each.[93] The largest concentrations of social research workers are thus in central government, market research firms and independent non-commercial research organisations. In all, there are several thousand staff currently employed to carry out empirical social research in Britain. A recent study of the employment of sociologists by C. S. Smith, for instance, suggested that in 1973 nearly 1000 were so employed.[69] This is only one group, more narrowly defined, within the more general framework of social science research.

TABLE 1.3

Organisations doing social science research in the United Kingdom, 1972

	Number of organisations	*Percentage of organisations*
University department	443	38
Polytechnic department	88	8
University research unit	160	14
Research Council units and other public sector	29	2
Central government division	70	6
Local government department	216	19
Independent non-commercial research organisation	42	4
Commercial research firms	56	5
Professional associations/ charities	52	4
Total	1156	100

Source: A. Cherns and N. Perry, 'The development and structure of social research in Britain', in E. Crawford and N. Perry (eds), *Demands for Social Knowledge*, London, Sage, 1976, p. 79.

Most of those researchers working in commercial organisations are employed in market research and public opinion polling. Those working in independent non-commercial organisations are more heterogeneous, including survey organisations like S.C.P.R., specialist research centres like the Institute of Community Studies, and broader-based research organisations like Political and Economic Planning, the Tavistock Institute, and the Centre for Environmental Studies.

In local government, many research staff are employed in planning and social service departments, with smaller numbers in housing, transport, health and education. In larger authorities some are grouped in centralised Research and Intelligence Units – for example in the G.L.C., where mixed teams of planners, economists, statisticians and sociologists examine aspects of urban structure relevant to local decision-making and corporate management. (They are referred to by Eversley in chapter 14.)

In central government the position is more complex. It will be discussed briefly because it illustrates many of the problems of utilising social science research in policy-making. Whatever links there may be between individual social scientists and politicians, if social science is to make a continuing contribution in a sustained manner to public policy-making, it must be made a part of the machinery of government in some way. Three main factors all diminish attempts so far to do this effectively. They are that social research, like social policy in general, is fragmented between departments. The role of social research is defined as being technical, providing intelligence or doing short-term problem-solving research. And social research workers in the civil service lack adequate occupational recognition as social scientists.

Although there is growing recognition of the need to co-ordinate social policy between government departments, the unit of organisation in Whitehall remains the individual department (for example D.H.S.S., D.o.E.), not the civil service as a whole. Unlike economic policy, there is no strong central department like the Treasury which can co-ordinate and control the direction taken by social policies in a particular area or for a particular group. If 'many of the most intractable problems affect more than one department' and there is a serious lack of information about many social problems, it is hardly surprising that 'there is no effective mechanism for determining coherent and consistent priorities in the field of social policy generally.'[94]

The recognition that economics enjoys in public administration derives in part from the centralisation and co-ordination of economic matters through the Treasury. Since *social* policy is neither unified nor coherent, it is hardly surprising that other social sciences do not receive the same recognition. Even when they are admitted, however, their role is a circumscribed one. In-house research in central government is concentrated in the Home Office, D.H.S.S., D.o.E., the Department of Employment, Civil Service Department, the Scottish Office, and a number of smaller units in other departments. Overall, the number of professional staff is small though not negligible. 'Research' is defined largely as either intelligence or specific problem-solving research. With very few exceptions, research staff are not asked to do strategic research (drawing on basic academic disciplines) nor to advise policy-makers in the manner of economists.

The impact of the social sciences is further weakened by occupational fragmentation. 'Research staff' may be found in any of seven different civil service occupational groups each of which is effectively, for purposes of recruitment and career, a closed caste; to move between them is exceptionally difficult. Administrators, Economists and Statisticians form the elite, and the influence of economics and statistics is recognised by the status of the heads of the Government Economic and Statistical Services as permanent secretaries. Scientific Officers and Psychologists also form separate classes. The majority of the former are natural scientists, but they include, for example, the administrative staff of S.S.R.C. The majority of social scientists are employed either as Social Survey Officers (employed exclusively in the Social Survey Division of O.P.C.S.) or as Research Officers. Research Officers are occupationally a residual category, lacking a clear identity and scattered through a number of departments. There is no unified social science class, no head of government social research, and until 1976 little co-ordination or movement of staff between one department and another. There are also very few even relatively senior posts. Hence there are few staff in a position to argue the case for social research from within the civil service.

Sir Henry Tizard's description of the position of natural scientists in government at the end of the Second World War no longer applies to natural scientists, but perhaps it applies with even greater force today to social scientists in government:

> Many (scientists) feel they are looked down on as a lower stratum, strange creatures who are brought out in times of emergency and cast back into obscurity to which they properly belong when the emergency has passed. So long as this state of affairs persists, I am convinced that the best will prefer either the 'splendid isolation' of academic life or the material rewards which industry is prepared to offer.[95]

Conclusion

How can the best use be made of social research in policy-making? Academics have produced a large literature on 'policy science', 'policy studies' and like terms, yet there remains considerable uncertainty as to what is the input from such work into policy-making. Unlike applied economics, 'policy research' sometimes seems a bit like a jelly. Its form is rather indefinite, and when examined more closely and approached, it wobbles and either changes its shape or breaks up. Hence the focus in this work on three specific types of research: public opinion polling, action research and social indicators.

The conclusions of the preceding discussion can now be drawn. These are that there are two parallel continua, one of types of research and the other of the organisational contexts in which research is carried out. The two continua are closely aligned, and certain points on one tend to be linked to certain points on the other. At one extreme, 'in-house' government research is primarily intelligence or problem-oriented research: at the other, research supported by the S.S.R.C. tends to be basic or strategic research.

'In-house' government research and intelligence activity is predominantly fact gathering or short-term problem solving. The theoretical or disciplinary element is slight, and there are strong administrative pressures discouraging any movement in this direction. In this activity statisticians are pre-eminent, with research officers playing the role of poor relation. Statisticians are called upon to present facts and interpret them, but neither they nor research officers are expected to provide advice or comment on the policy implications of their findings. One special case of 'in-house' research is the Social Survey Division of O.P.C.S., which is *sui generis*. The most important recent development in 'in-house' research is the social indicators movement, which as Brand and Hope indicate, retains a strong predeliction for hard data and a blind eye for theoretical and value issues.

In addition to in-house research, several government departments now commission a large amount of research from outside – notably the Home Office, D.o.E., D.E.S., D.E., D.H.S.S. and the Scottish Office. In commissioning such research there is greater willingness to be more adventurous – to support action research and strategic research as well as problem-orientated research and intelligence. In the wake of Rothschild, some departments now have their own internal structure for commissioning and evaluating research. In the D.H.S.S., for example, a new Chief Scientist now heads an elaborate committee structure on which outside academics sit to advise upon the research priorities of the Department. A greater receptivity to strategic research is also evident in initiatives such as the joint D.H.S.S./S.S.R.C. programme on transmitted deprivation. D.H.S.S. probably makes more use of external social research than most departments, and certainly makes more use of academic advisers.[96] Whether it provides a model for the rest of central government remains to be seen.

The Social Science Research Council, on the other hand, somewhat distanced from practical policy-making, is not concerned with specific problem-solving research but more with basic research. Its funds tend to be devoted to this and to strategic research, and it applies disciplinary and theoretical considerations in judging the allocation of research resources. Similarly, charitable bodies such as the Nuffield Foundation and the Rowntree Trusts tend to favour strategic research and social experiment rather than intelligence or problem-solving research.

Is policy research best carried on inside or outside government? Sharpe argues that the extent to which research leads rather than follows the policy consensus will depend on how much of it is pursued under conditions of academic freedom. Research in government or even an independent research organisation is under a degree of constraint not experienced by the academic. Cullingworth has drawn a similar conclusion. 'The higher purposes of government, of social science and of universities are best served by a major freely committed research element within universities. Though much research of value to all three can – and inevitably must – be undertaken outside universities, large shifts of effort in this direction, however justified in the short term, may have disastrous long-term consequences.'[97]

Nevertheless, it is useful to consider whether academics hold a stereotype of the conditions under which non-university researchers work. Perry concludes an extensive comparison based on first-hand research with the conclusion that non-university research organisations in the United Kingdom do not have the same degree of independence as the university department, and some were heavily client-orientated rather than knowledge-orientated. 'On the other hand, many non-university organisations had teaching and training functions; they had a good deal of participation in the choice of research projects and the structure of their research effort – the split between theory, methodology, and policy-orientation – was not dissimilar to the university. . . . university departments were not necessarily as "academic" as the sociological theories of science would predict, nor were other organisations as utilitarian and dull as their detractors would suppose.'[98]

There are also powerful pressures resisting the establishment of large-scale research organisations, particularly survey organisations, within higher education. Since a significant amount of market research, independent research and central government research is based on the social survey, this has led to a separation of non-university from university research, tending to cut the latter off from methodological developments in particular. Rossi has provided a plausible explanation of such trends:

There are undoubtedly many reasons why survey research did not develop inside the groves of academe, but among the most important reasons is the organisational set-up of academic departments. Essentially, an academic department

is a collection of scholars whose work is only minimally
integrated in a division of labour sense. . . . when an
academician refers to the independence of academic life, he is
usually referring to the fact that once he has met his teaching
obligations (over which he has a great deal of control) he is
free to pursue his own intellectual interests within the limits
set by local production standards and the amount of research
funds he is able to obtain. Indeed, so pleasurable is the lack of
a defined division of labour that any attempt to engage in
large-scale research enterprises has led to the grafting onto
university structures of organisational entities in which such a
division of labour is possible, rather than imposing such a
division of labour upon existing departmental structures.[99]

The impact of values on the policy-making consensus can be
uncomfortable and disconcerting. It is arguably this, more than
anything else, which distinguishes the academic contribution to
policy research from all others. If 'the purpose of research is to
bring political controversy closer to realities',[100] it is likely to
involve an examination of the goals of policy, the values implicit
in policy and the consequences for different groups of the
pursuit of particular lines of action. To raise such questions is to
steer perilously close to the preserves of politicians and
administrators.

Different audiences may treat social scientists differently. The
media and some politicians may not regard a degree of explicit
value commitment as out of the ordinary; a civil servant may be
profoundly suspicious. Donnison, for example, was once
reportedly described by a senior civil servant as 'a dangerous
doctrinaire'.[101] Advising ministers, shadow ministers or party
committees is one thing; advising permanent civil servants who
hold strongly entrenched constitutional doctrines about im-
partiality is another. New modes of thought seeking to contribute
to policy-making may face very severe obstacles from permanent
officials if they become too closely allied to politicians. The main
impact of Keynes's economic ideas seems to have come after he
converted the Treasury to his point of view.

The social networks described by Donnison on pages 54–9
are clearly important in facilitating contact between leading
social scientists and policy-makers, who 'inhabit a closely-knit

world of interlocking networks and institutions clustered in the single, overwhelmingly dominant centre of London'.[102] Although not a counterpart to the nineteenth-century 'intellectual aristocracy',[103] 'the considerable advantages that derive from the closely-knit world of the London clubs, Oxbridge colleges and the L.S.E. Common Room in supplementing more formal links between government and the university'[104] distinguish the British political scene from its counterpart in America. There is indeed no equivalent there to Webb's Fabian doctrine of 'permeation', still influential in practice today.

Since the attractions of this political embrace have been so strong in British social science, it may be salutary to conclude by remembering its limitations. Although 'permeation' connects leading social scientists and party politicians, it may actually hinder relations with civil servants and administrators, who are suspicious of overt commitment. In the process, professional social researchers in government tend to be entirely by-passed – or reduced to the technician role in which administrators also cast them. Let it be remembered that 'the interconnectedness of the upper level of British society – to foreign eyes like nothing so much as one great extended family – may have drawbacks for the maintenance of a creative, detached and critical academic community.'[105]

2 Research for Policy*

David Donnison

The more pervasive the influence of governments and the larger
their investment in research, the more urgent becomes our need
to understand the contributions which research can make to
policy. Much of the published doctrine available to guide those
who spend public funds on research has been derived from work
on the development and application of new technologies. To
this process, scientists are expected to contribute a flow of
knowledge, originating in 'pure' research, which is gradually
hammered into usable form through 'applied' research and
development. But decisions about policy (including technological policy) emerge from a different sort of process – a continuing debate, to which research workers contribute on equal
terms with many others, and in which they seldom apply the
findings of their research in a direct technological sense. Instead,
their studies equip them in various ways – often not foreseen
when they were planned – to contribute to the debate.

Research for Technological Innovation

If policies for research in the social sciences lean heavily on experience gained in industrial, military, medical and agricultural

* Reprinted from *Minerva*, **10**, 1972, pp. 519–36, with the permission of the
publishers and the author.

technology, that is not for lack of broader perspectives. An international committee convened by the Secretary-General of the Organisation for Economic Cooperation and Development (O.E.C.D.) to reassess science policies is only one of the more distinguished groups which has recently warned us that research must not be confined to a narrow, technological role. It recommends, for example, 'that the Organisation [the O.E.C.D.] take the leadership in stimulating the development of the social sciences as tools of policy on a multi-national basis, much as it has already done in the field of economic policy', and it calls on governments to 'ensure the central availability of a proportion of their research funds for longer-term investigations and studies, which will probe beyond the research programmes planned to meet well-formulated problems of departments and agencies responsible for particular sectors'.[1]

When it comes to spending the taxpayers' money, governments are naturally more interested in work which promises an early technological pay-off. Meanwhile, the few academics who have studied innovation and the contribution made to it by research have devoted more attention to the more easily identifiable and traceable innovations in technology than to innovations in policy. Hägerstrand, in his classic work, traced the dissemination of pasture grazing, methods for the control of bovine tuberculosis, soil mapping, postal checking services, the automobile and the telephone.[2] An American study, made for the National Science Foundation, traced the research and development work which produced magnetic ferrites, the video-tape recorder, the oral contraceptive pill, the electron microscope and matrix isolation.[3] The main findings of this important study can be briefly summarised.

The American investigations distinguished three kinds of work: 'non-mission research', 'mission-orientated research' and 'development and application'. The innovations examined originated from a long history of non-mission research in a variety of disciplines, conducted mainly in universities. The peak of relevant non-mission activities occurred 20–30 years before the innovation, and 10–20 years before anyone conceived of the possibility of the innovation eventually accomplished. About 70 per cent of the 'key events' leading ultimately to an innovation were non-mission research, and their practical implications could seldom have been foreseen when this research was being done. Fifteen years before the innovation, about 80 per cent of the non-mission 'events' were completed and 70 per cent of the mission-orientated research and development 'events' were yet to come: '... most inventors rely heavily on information created in the previous generation'.[4] Mission-orientated research and development work built up in the last decade before innovation, generating some new non-mission research which often proved crucial for the innovation. Communication between scientific disciplines and between scientists and technologists played an essential part in the story: 'Also important were the dynamic personalities of many of these scientists, exhibiting an enthusiasm that can only be communicated by personal contact'.[5]

These findings must give pause to anyone who believes he can offer any guidance to governments investing in research. They suggest that he can recommend applied studies and development work on a few problems for which most of the basic research has already been completed; but when it comes to non-mission research he will generally do better to leave the choice of projects to the scientists, for no-one can tell what outcomes will ultimately emerge or where they will lead.

It may not be surprising that Lord Rothschild,[6] in the most important British official report on research policies for many years, adopts an even simpler version of this technological model, using only two categories – 'basic research' and 'applied R and D'. Expenditure on the former should be more carefully rationed, and government departments should take a tighter grasp of the latter, acting as 'customers' specifying the problems to be studied and approving the methods to be used by research 'contractors'. Although he excluded the social sciences and social policies from his proposals, the government has not hesitated to apply them in these fields too, for this is a pattern they can understand.

Social Policy is Different: Three Instances

Decisions about technology deal with materials, machines and techniques. They cannot be infallibly distinguished from decisions about policy: what appears to be a question of policy (should we introduce a system of negative income tax?) may suddenly become a technical problem (have we got computers which would make the system work?), and what appears to be a technical problem (can we produce cheap contraceptive pills?) may suddenly become a question of policy (if cheap, why not distribute them free to unmarried women?). These may only be different ways of looking at the same issue – but significantly different, none the less. Decisions about policy deal with the allocation of benefits and penalties, and the values which characterise a society and shape the relationships between its members.

Innovations in policy pose special problems which must be explored before we consider the contribution research workers can make to them. Some features of policy issues are familiar. As in technology, innovators certainly 'rely heavily on information created in the previous generation' and on communication through 'personal contact' by 'dynamic personalities'. But policy innovations are often much less specific than innovations in technology. A century later, historians may still dispute when, or whether, they occurred. The most important of them are *ideas*, or a way of perceiving the world, derived from related assumptions, concepts and aspirations, and carried forward by political pressures. Innovations in policy may owe a good deal to past scientific discoveries and technical innovations, or they may not; but they often help to shape the *future* directions of research and technical innovation. The whole process is more diffuse, less linear.

Some illustrations will show what I mean. Policies for the maintenance and distribution of incomes lie at the centre of any government's social programmes. In Great Britain, as in many other countries, three major innovations have succeeded each other in this field. The principle of 'less eligibility', clearly expressed and widely disseminated in the 1832 report of the Royal Commission on the Poor Laws,[7] expressed the idea that the condition of those who accepted poor relief should be 'less eligible', or more uncomfortable, than that of the lowest paid independent labourer. From this development, derived from a set of related assumptions, concepts and aspirations, many other innovations followed: the central government's Poor Law Commission, the first major national inspectorate, the boards of guardians chosen by a uniform, nationwide system of local elections, 'test' workhouses to frighten malingerers – right down the line to workhouse cocoa, the content of which was exactly prescribed in a circular issued a hundred years later.[8] But the function and value of all these innovations depended on the original principle of less eligibility. Reject that idea – that way of seeing the world – and the status of many of the subsequent innovations becomes dubious.

The original principle was derived partly from the social theories and psychological assumptions of the Benthamites – a systematically elaborated intellectual tradition, if not exactly 'research'. But it owed at least as much to other influences, such as the demands of manufacturers for a mobile, disciplined labour force, no longer tied to the land or seduced from regular work habits by the old Poor Laws, the discontent of farmers and landed proprietors upon whom the crude fiscal procedures of the day loaded the rapidly rising poor rates, and the need for simple administrative procedures which could be understood by, and imposed on, semi-literate and semi-corrupt local administrators of the Poor Laws like Charles Dickens's Bumble.

These influences were mobilised and brought to bear through pamphleteering, lectures, public debate, an inquiry by a royal commission and parliamentary decision, but many years of patient work and occasional uproar were to follow the Poor Law Amendment Act of 1834 before the outcome of this measure became clear.

The next major innovation in this field was the idea that national minimum standards should be assured for everyone as a right of citizenship through social insurance schemes, adequate education and training, a high level of employment, proper medical care, and so on. The principle was enunciated and vigorously disseminated by persons such as Sidney and Beatrice Webb, and gradually took shape in practice, thanks to further innovations (some of them opposed by the Webbs) which led through the pensions and insurance Acts of 1908, 1911 and 1925 to the Beveridge Report and the reforms of 1948. This time the new principle owed a good deal to private research, official inquiries and skilled advocacy, in which Charles Booth, Seebohm Rowntree, the Webbs, A. L. Bowley and many others engaged; but similar developments took shape in most advanced economies and it was clear that they owed even more to the grinding pressures of urban, industrial society and the political movements which sprang from them. Lloyd George would have put through the crucial legislation of 1911 without any help from people like the Webbs. Indeed, when they came to lobby him over breakfast about their *Minority Report on the Poor Laws*, the party broke up in acrimonious confusion.[9]

A third principle now appears to be emerging which may ultimately supplant the other two, although relics of both the earlier ones will be with us for a long time to come. Poverty, it is argued, should be defined neither as destitution nor as failure to attain a subsistence minimum, but as exclusion from the continually evolving living conditions, opportunities and self-respect available to the mass of the population. Poverty is inequality – the condition of those at the bottom ends of all sorts of dispersed social distributions. Once again the idea was first clearly articulated and disseminated by intellectuals,[10] some of whom have done their utmost to give it practical expression by contributing to discussion within the labour movement and serving in official capacities when invited to do so. But little progress will be made until the idea is carried forward by more pervasive and powerful political pressures, and put into practice through legislative and administrative innovations which are likely to spread over many years.

These examples should not be misinterpreted. I am not drawing distinctions between 'hard' science and social science, or between technological and social policies. I am trying to show how decisions about policy evolve – whether the policies be scientific, technological or social. Innovations in policy may call for new technologies: insurance against unemployment, for example, could not be introduced until a nationwide network of labour exchanges was available to offer people the jobs which were a test of their eligibility for benefit. But a major innovation in policy is not just a better way of attaining familiar ends; it expresses a new way of perceiving society and the rights and duties of its citizens. Even minor innovations have something of this character. They reflect, and contribute to, economic and social change. Their significance and value are open to dispute by those who do not share the perception of society which they express. And the research they ultimately provoke is often more extensive than that from which they are derived.

The impact made by the evolution of our ideas about learning upon policies for secondary education will help to explain what I mean. In 1938, the Spens Committee was dourly determinist: 'Intellectual development during childhood appears to progress as if it were governed by a single, central factor, usually known as "general intelligence", which may be broadly described as innate all-round intellectual ability'.[11] In 1959 the Crowther Committee was cautiously hopeful: 'It may well be that there is a pool of ability that imposes an upper limit on what can be done by education at any given time. But . . . the limit has not been reached . . .'.[12] In 1963, the Newsom Committee was confident: 'Intellectual talent is not a fixed quantity with which we have to work but a variable that can be modified by social policy and educational approaches . . .'.[13] But for the Public Schools Commission in 1970 the essential policy question had changed. *Whatever* the human capacities available, '. . . our whole educational endeavour must be to get more and more children to take their education to a point that enables them to go on learning and adapting throughout their lives'.[14]

Each of these reports drew on research to help in formulating ideas which influenced policy – often profoundly. But the reverse influence was equally strong. The policies which followed from the 1944 Education Act in the aftermath of Spens generated a massive investment in research which was devoted to the prediction of academic attainment and the perfection of selection techniques. Yet, in 1967, the Plowden Committee, which wrote a requiem for the 'eleven-plus' selection procedures introduced after 1944, brushed much of this work aside and pointed to a whole range of new, still uninvestigated problems.[15] Major innovations in technology provide new solutions for old problems. Major innovations in policy reformulate the problems themselves.

Research workers who apply their minds to problems of public policy and government must be aware of economic and social changes and the trends of policy and opinion in their field. They are not obliged to assent to these trends or trim their sails to them: indeed, they need scepticism as badly as commitment. But, whether they intend it or not, they are participants in a continuing debate which deals with ends as well as means; and their findings, if they are worth anything, will contribute to that debate. Their research will seldom be 'mission-orientated' in any simple sense. It may deal with fairly specific, practical problems, but the character, the ends and implications of the mission – for example, who is ultimately to benefit from any changes which result – will often be in question. The categories used by the Illinois studies of technology do not adequately describe their work.

That more lazy-minded dichotomy, 'basic research' and 'applied R and D', is worse still, for it obscures all the main problems to be considered. It may do for research on technology – and, to be fair, that was what it was mainly intended for – but in any discussion of policy-orientated research these terms strew pitfalls in our way. One of them is unwittingly revealed by the afterthought attached to one of the first examples Lord Rothschild uses: '. . . road R & D, sponsored by the Department of the Environment (D.o.E.) on behalf of the motorist (at any rate in part)'.[16] The assumption that the research worker's 'mission' is to help the motorist – or the pedestrian for that matter – would go far to define his problems and the range of acceptable solutions.

Somewhat imprecise though its terms are, the Dainton Committee makes more relevant distinctions:

(a) tactical science – the science and its application and development needed by departments of state and by industry to further their immediate executive or commercial functions. The extent and nature of this activity may vary widely according to the functions served and to the degree that they involve science. At one extreme it may contain a significant element of sophisticated research over a long period; whilst at the other extreme it amounts to little more than a modest intelligence and advisory activity;

(b) strategic science – the broad spread of more general scientific effort which is needed as a foundation for this tactical science. It is no less relevant in terms of practical objectives of the sort we have mentioned, but more wide ranging. For this 'strategic' work to be successful it is necessary to maintain the vigour of the underlying scientific disciplines and to deploy these disciplines with due regard to national goals;

(c) basic science – research and training which have no specific application in view but which are necessary to ensure the advance of scientific knowledge and the maintenance of a corps of able scientists, upon which depends the future ability of the country to use science.[17]

Much policy-orientated research is of the intermediate, strategic kind. But more important than these categories are the links between one kind of work and another. For research contributing to innovations in technology these links are envisaged as a linear process: 'basic' or 'non-mission' research in various fields leads to 'applied' or 'mission-orientated' research on practical problems which produces innovations that can be developed and may be used in many ways. In reality the process is more complex, provoking fresh basic research and new missions as it goes along, but even with these elaborations it remains an essentially linear or transitive affair, starting from the raw materials of theory and data, and leading ultimately to a potentially saleable product – not unlike an industrial process. Indeed, industry does the latter stages of this kind of work pretty well.

But for research which contributes to the formulation of policies and the evaluation and amendment of programmes a different model is needed. For the policies in question – social security or education, for example – people working in four fields must be in active contact with each other. The four fields are: that of *politics* where new policies are approved, major resource allocations made, powers conferred and decisions formally registered; the field of relevant *technologies*, mechanical and social; the field of relevant professional, commercial and administrative *practice* where present policies and programmes are carried out, and new ones are formulated and tried out, and the field of *research* in which – as in the other three – the people interested in social security, education (or whatever it may be) are part of a much larger community concerned with other things. Meanwhile those engaged in all four of these fields participate in the larger universe of voters, taxpayers, clients of the policies in question and members of political movements, which together constitutes public opinion.

Those who are active in each field communicate with those in the others, either directly or through intermediate sections of public opinion. Thus, in response to demands coming mainly from *practitioners* in central and local government, a Planning Advisory Group was appointed to reappraise British town and country planning practice, and its recommendations,[18] published in 1965, were later incorporated by the *politicians* in the Town and Country Planning Act of 1968. This measure introduced new concepts and procedures – 'structure plans', 'action area plans', 'subject plans', and so on – calling for new work and skills in the field of *practice* which coincided with the dissemination of computers, contributed by the *technologists*, and consequential improvements in the gathering and analysis of data. These demands and opportunities prompted new *research* on the analysis of urban and regional development which, drawing on other technologies, furnished *practitioners* with new ideas and analytical methods.

There is no end to the ramifications of the game as the ball is passed back and forth from one field to another. In this case, the academic community contributed little directly to innovations in policy, but responded later with research, some of which is already proving useful to practitioners carrying out the new policies.

The entirely new system of rent regulation introduced in Britain by the Rent Act of 1965 presents a different story. By 1962, it was clear to *practitioners*, particularly in the Ministry of Housing and Local Government, that things were going wrong in the housing market and that the previous legislation in this field needed amendment. *Political* pressures associated with the Rachman scandals (concerning a London landlord, by then already dead) led to the appointment, in the next year, of a committee of inquiry under the chairmanship of Sir Milner Holland. *Research* workers – in particular a group supported by the Joseph Rowntree Memorial Trust – had been studying these problems for some years. A member of this group was appointed to the committee, two others were seconded to the committee's research team, and others contributed evidence to the inquiry. In the committee they had the opportunity of learning from persons in various fields of *practice* – particularly the then president of the Royal Institution of Chartered Surveyors, who contributed the essential ideas which Mr Richard Crossman, the new minister, needed for the Rent Act his party had promised, during the general election of 1964, to introduce. Enacted next year by the *politicians*, this measure led to the creation of a new system of rent officers and appeals committees – new institutions in the field of *practice*, relying on *technologies* of valuation and rent fixing not hitherto used for this purpose. Meanwhile *research* began to reveal some of the defects of the measure.

In this case, research workers contributed a good deal more to the formulation of new policies, and in a small way to their execution. Some of them worked in *ad hoc* groups set up to advise the minister and went on to serve for a while as members of rent assessment committees. But the social system from which innovations in policy evolved resembled that of the previous example in many ways. The relationships between those working in the different fields involved were neither orderly nor linear: they were less like an industrial process than a market place. In this market place, decisions had to be taken when circumstances – particularly political circumstances – permitted or compelled: it was not feasible to wait, as is inevitable in the case of technological innovations, until the necessary research and development work had been completed. Research workers could not present authoritative findings for others to apply; neither could others commission them to find the 'correct' solution to policy problems: they are not that kind of problem. Those in the four fields from which experience had to be brought to bear contributed on equal terms. Each was expert in a few things, ignorant about most things, offered what he could, and generally learnt more than he could teach.

Social Research for Social Policy: The Importance of Individuals and their Networks

Another way of looking at this question is to study the research workers who play a part in the debates I have described. To do so is to dip into the culture – the 'power structure', the social relations, the intellectual traditions – of the country concerned. I have chosen my examples from those who have played a part in formulating ideas about the main social programmes of British government: income maintenance, education, housing, town planning and the personal social services. Other countries would certainly show different patterns. In Britain, other departments of government – concerned with medical care, the management of the economy, defence, or law and order, for example – might be different. Other times were certainly different, and there are signs that things are changing again.

The persons I have chosen to study are an ill-defined but roughly identifiable group: those who have published original research in these fields which has been referred to in serious debates about innovations in policy – for example in the reports of committees of inquiry – and (an overlapping group) those who gained an academic reputation by publication in these fields, hold academic posts, and play an active part in serious policy debates as members of public authorities or committees of inquiry, or as advisers to ministers or shadow ministers, their departments or party committees. I have treated debate as 'serious' if it could readily lead to significant changes in law or practice within the next decade.

My selection does not in any other sense imply an evaluation. It is not an honours list of scholarship or public service, and it is certainly not a 'power elite': more famous and more powerful individuals could readily be found in the universities, in politics and in the civil service. What kind of people are these?

Many (though not all) of them enjoy mastering the gritty detail of social problems and the legal, administrative and professional procedures of the programmes devised to deal with them. They found their way about the worlds of practice and technology before exploring the world of politics. They learnt how means tests really work, who exactly is chosen by educational selection procedures, what really happens to homeless families, or what really goes on in old people's homes; and if they now have less time for the painstaking field work required to produce that kind of evidence they are still in touch with younger colleagues and research students who do it. Research at this level of descriptive detail seldom confers great prestige in the universities, and unless it is very perceptively planned and conducted it produces few policy conclusions of a general kind. But it arms research workers with ammunition which often discredits existing policies, and it ultimately compels the powerful to rethink their assumptions. During the 1950s, when many of these persons entered on their careers, the British social services

had such poor intelligence systems and did so little research that
they were sitting ducks for this kind of ammunition. Henceforth
– it is to be hoped – research workers will have to plan more
intelligently if they are to tell governments things about the
effects of their social programmes which they do not already
know.

Many of these people – often the ones who enjoy the gritty
detail – also enjoy attempting more comprehensive assessments
of society and the directions in which it is heading. Some of the
key figures have formulated these concerns in ways which fired
the interest of others in this brotherhood and ultimately reached
much wider audiences through the heavy-weight journalists and
their readers. Concerns such as Richard Titmuss's about the
impact made by big bureaucracies, public or private, on the life
chances, power and status of ordinary people, and Dr Michael
Young's about the supporting strengths and constricting ties of
the human relationships formed within families and between
neighbours crop up again and again in research and writing on
various fields of social policy.

Many gained their reputations through studies of questions
other than those on which they later became influential. Indeed,
some of them have never done research which offered immediate
'pay-offs' in the form of new policies. Major social problems
seldom have 'solutions' of that kind, and studies of social and
economic history, and the economic and social structure of
urban society[19] – to cite some examples which come to mind –
can seldom be used in that sort of way. But the research educated
them; it enlarged their understanding of society, and gave them
a knowledge of methods and sources, a reputation for technical
competence and personal integrity, and a growing circle of
colleagues, friends and students.

Those who paid for this research were investing, wittingly or
unwittingly, in the creation of this national resource. Usually
the investment was not a heavy one. Much of this research was
done by individuals reading, thinking, digging in the files and
doing their own interviews.

Several of those who later embarked on more costly programmes of research became submerged in half-coded schedules
and computer print-outs, and grew less productive (for a while
at least) as contributors to policy debate. It would be wrong to

assume that massive data-gathering exercises are unproductive for policy-makers, for some of them have been frequently and usefully quoted in debate.[20] But people who have always had to do most of their research virtually single-handed, often in the evenings and at weekends between teaching and other duties, may not be best equipped to handle surveys and computers or to supervise large teams of full-time staff.

Being aligned more often with the left than the right (the Fabian Society is their spiritual centre of gravity, approximately) these social scientists are kept busier by government when the Labour Party is in power. Perhaps for this reason, their more seminal work has often been done under Conservative administrations when public interest in, and funds for, applied research on social problems have fallen to a low ebb. Professor David Glass's *Social Mobility in Britain*,[21] Richard Titmuss's essay on *The Social Division of Welfare*,[22] Michael Young and Peter Willmott's *Family and Kinship in East London*,[23] Jean Floud, A. H. Halsey and J. P. Martin's *Social Class and Educational Opportunity*[24] and Brian Abel-Smith's splendid polemic, 'Whose Welfare State?'[25] – each of them much quoted in policy debates later – were all published during such a period: a remarkable record for a few years that were, on the domestic front, fairly uneventful.

That should remind us that, however involved some of these people may temporarily be in the corridors of power, their strengths are drawn from the academic community to which they belong – as is plain from their references to the ideas of scholars who do not appear on my list such as Professor Michael Oakeshott, Sir Karl Popper, Professor T. H. Marshall, Professor Ralf Dahrendorf and many others less famous.

Most of the social scientists I am discussing work, or have worked, as university teachers of social administration, sociology, statistics or economic and social history: relatively low-status disciplines, until recently at least. They include a few economists, some geographers, and even fewer political scientists, psychologists and lawyers. There would have been more of these if my study had extended to policies for regional development, industrial relations, transport, criminology, electoral reform, and other matters. But scholars from the under-represented disciplines are badly needed in the fields I have examined – and the experience might do their disciplines good, too.

It should be clear by now that I am talking about a number of overlapping and interlocking social groups. Most of the individuals whose work I am discussing know each other personally. Many belong to the Fabian Society. Most probably read *The Guardian*, *The Economist* or *New Society*. Most of them live or work in Greater London. Some institutions have thrown up more than their share of 'influentials' in particular fields. Can it be an accident, for example, that all seven authors of a recent contribution to policy debate studied geography at the same Cambridge college in the late 1950s?[26] Most of the people on my list have at some time or other been students or teachers at the London School of Economics and Political Science (L.S.E.). That shows where the disciplines in which they were trained were strongest 15–30 years ago. (The country-wide explosion in sociology teaching which took place during the 1960s has irrevocably changed the distribution of resources in that discipline. Social administration has followed more recently: in 1966 the L.S.E. had 3 of the 10 professors in this subject; by 1972 it had 3 of 25.) But that is not the whole explanation for the L.S.E. connection. Contrary to popular myths about that tolerant and fairly conservative institution, membership does not determine people's political allegiances; but it does furnish certain common assumptions – such as the idea that it is proper for academics to study the world in which they live and comment publicly on it – and the school's recruitment procedures helped to ensure that wealth and kinship played no part in the selection of its students and staff.

As the disciplines and institutions from which these groups are drawn gain prestige, that open pattern of recruitment may become harder to maintain. Society's elites may begin to compete for entry. But it is unlikely that this country will ever again have an elite so closely linked by kinship as the intellectual families of the nineteenth century – the Macaulays, the Trevelyans, the Arnolds, the Huxleys and the rest – whose history has been traced by Lord Annan.[27]

How are such groups recruited? What selection processes, what patron–client relationships, are at work? All I can say with confidence is that these processes depend heavily on personal, and often accidental, contacts with sponsors who may themselves play little or no part in debates on policy, that they vary from one branch of social policy to another (those concerned with income maintenance seldom overlap with the urban planners, for example, and each have 'risen' by different routes), that the routes to influence have changed, and will change again. The question deserves more serious study.

It would be even more interesting to evaluate the social influence of the loosely related groups I have examined. Some regard them as dangerous radicals; others regard them as lackeys of the establishment, wheeled out from time to time to quieten the nation's conscience, manage the working class and preserve the social order. But that calls for a different inquiry which I shall not attempt here.

Conclusions

What conclusions can we draw from the system briefly glimpsed here – conclusions which would be useful to an administrator who wants to spend the growing volume of funds committed to research in ways which will provide a better understanding of the government's problems, wiser policies, and a more effective assessment of their outcome which may help to amend policies more promptly when things go wrong?

Two warnings must first be given. Since I have derided those who adopt, for policy-orientated studies, principles (for example customer–contractor relationships) derived from technological research, I must stress that those principles are indeed useful in their proper setting and deserve to be more widely applied to problems of technology, mechanical or social. I am only discussing research which may have important implications for policy and is planned for that purpose. Secondly, I have relied on evidence drawn mainly from work on the social policies of central government; not from economic, military or other fields of policy, nor from local government, nor from non-governmental organisations such as firms, universities or churches. (I believe the problems of policy-orientated research in these spheres do not differ fundamentally from those I have chosen to discuss, but I have not demonstrated that.)

My regrettably tentative and imprecise conclusions deal with three closely related questions: the persons who do the research, the social systems in which they work, and the procedures that enable governments to gain their help.

The research workers to look for should of course be the most creative and intelligent we can find. But their motivation is equally important and harder to assess. They must have a policy-orientated cast of mind, or be likely to acquire that in time. They must enjoy thinking in a sustained, rigorous and independent way about the problems of government – which means they take seriously the version of a problem perceived by the government of the moment, but do not confine their own perception of the issues to that version alone. They must want to make the world a better place for people already living in it: the needs of future generations should not be wholly neglected, but neither should they be the main concern. And they must enjoy studying how that could be achieved with the resources poten-tially available for the task – which calls for a capacity to en-visage the alternative uses to which such resources might be put.

Young persons take time to acquire this approach – and very properly too. Responsible scholars recognise that if they are to present conclusions which might ultimately affect many of their fellow citizens they must be more, not less, careful about the quality of their evidence and the logic of their argument than they would be if they intended only to communicate with their academic colleagues. That means we should beware of inex-perienced research workers who want to rush too quickly into prescribing policies, and beware of anyone who seems likely to forget that scholars and scientists have no authority except that which the quality of their evidence, argument and judgement confers upon them. They should not be tempted to become politicians – a reputable but entirely different role. They should remain firmly rooted in the academic world – whether they work in universities or not – where they can keep in touch with their colleagues and students and draw on their help. The research workers who contribute to the development of policies in a particular field are a minority within a much larger com-munity, most of whom have no interest in that field and scant desire to contribute to public affairs of any kind.

Keeping their footing in the academic world and devoting their best efforts to policy-orientated research will generally compel them to reject some of the values of their profession and its most prestigious members. The great figures have always been able – indeed obliged, by their restlessly critical intellects – to operate both in the world of scholarship and in the world of debate on policy. (It would be ridiculous to try to classify as 'pure' or 'applied' the works of men like John Stuart Mill, Huxley, Marx, Keynes or Tawney.) But these were unique. 'Normal science' in a 'mature scientific community' (to use Professor Thomas Kuhn's[28] phrases) does not work like that. It proceeds by applying 'shared paradigms' to problems chosen and defined to be susceptible to solution by the methods derived from these paradigms. For long periods the discipline develops and its practitioners succeed by using these paradigms in more sophisticated and precise ways. The best-established social sciences have similar characteristics. They do not necessarily furnish a setting in which scholars with what I described as a 'policy-orientated cast of mind' will thrive. Therefore we must look for, or create, settings which will support research on policy. It is not an accident that the disciplines which contribute most to this sort of research have often been immature, theoretically speaking, and of low academic status, or that many individual contributors to policy-orientated research have been prepared to disregard conventional measures of academic success, owing to eccentricity, failure (real or fancied), social conscience, private wealth or other reasons.

These conclusions have already turned to the social systems in which research is done. What more can we say about them? At any point in time the disciplines, the institutions, the biases and recruitment procedures which characterise them will reflect past history. In Britain, the dominance of Londoners and the L.S.E. in policy-orientated social research is partly a result of historical patterns which are not always appropriate to present needs. The failure of research workers, until recently, to foresee the problems of Northern Ireland or give much help to those who must cope with them is not surprising: there was little relevant research work going on in the province. The alignment of so many of the best research workers with the Fabian left is due partly to the fact that bodies like the Fabian Society were deliberately created to foster and apply a policy-orientated cast of mind. But it is also, and less relevantly, due partly to the fact that many of the careers in question began during the 1950s, when a Conservative administration was commissioning little research on questions of policy, and those who wanted to do it became naturally associated with the parliamentary opposition, rather than with groups further to the left or right.

We must be continually alert to prevent the recruitment procedures and client–sponsor relations of the past from depriving the public of the help it needs today, and to extend the range of talent which can be brought to bear on policy problems. In Britain, in the fields I have discussed, we need more economists (for lack of their help, the economic repercussions of social programmes and planning policies and the opportunities for attaining policy objectives through intelligent use of fiscal procedures and market mechanisms have not been well enough understood), we need more political scientists and lawyers (some of the conflict which has bedevilled research in fields like race relations might have been more productive if more of the research workers had been trained in the analysis of conflict) and we need centres of strength not only in London but in all regions of the country. It would also be helpful to everyone if Conservative ministers could call on the advice of more scholars sympathetic to their cause who have done good research in the fields I have discussed.

What can government and the public service professions do to move things in these directions? They cannot do much unless there are persons in government doing serious research, and others keeping up with relevant bodies of literature, who know the academic world and how to gain the respect and use the help of people in it. In Britain, central government is making some progress in this direction and Lord Rothschild's proposals for a chief scientist supported by a scientific staff in each ministry will take things further – providing good enough persons from an adequate range of disciplines (including the social sciences) are recruited. But in local government, apart from a handful of distinguished exceptions such as the Greater London Council, this development has scarcely begun. (As a research director repeatedly urged to seek more money from local government, I retort that most local authorities would do better to develop their own research organisations first.)

Government would do well to strengthen and diversify the small but important range of research institutions capable of

helping it forge productive working relationships between the
fields of practice, technology and research. Governmental
research stations, which might work in this way, are seldom used
by academics taking leave from universities in Britain or abroad
to do research; most of them do not sponsor much research in
universities and independent research institutes, or regard it as
their job to build a national array of policy-orientated research
workers interested in their field; and some of them are in any
case reluctant to tackle research with important implications for
policy. The research councils do better, keeping an eye on the
'timeliness' and social purpose of the work they sponsor in the
universities, but their first responsibility is, and should remain,
the advancement of knowledge through good research rather
than the enlightenment of debates about policy. Meanwhile
other bodies such as the Tavistock Institute, the Institute of
Community Studies, the National Children's Bureau, the
Birmingham University Centre for Urban and Regional Studies,
the Centre for Environmental Studies and the Centre for
Studies in Social Policy (to list a few in the order of their founding) have grown up over the years to fill some of the gaps –
though only the Centre for Environmental Studies endeavours,
within its field, to act all these parts. All but one of these bodies
are in the capital. Thus, unless they are deliberately used to
forge links with research workers elsewhere and to allocate funds
to other parts of the country, reliance on this sort of instrument
will encourage the tendency to concentrate resources in and
around London.

When it comes to launching research on problems of policy,
government must consider where the best persons can be found
and the most effective groups built. In Britain that will usually
be in the universities and their associated institutes and centres.
To gain their help – or the help of good scholars anywhere –
government must build a delicate edifice of personal relationships. An official who specifies a problem, makes a tightly
detailed contract with a research worker for its analysis and
sends him off for two or three years to solve it, may be com-
plimented these days by his superiors for good housekeeping.
But if he wants help on problems of policy he is unlikely to have
secured good research workers (good ones of this sort do not wait
around like cabs on the rank to be told their destinations), he

will often be cheated (by those who divert grants to work they find more interesting) and the answer to his question, if it comes, will often be too late to offer much help. In short, he is wasting public money.

But an official who enables a good research worker with a policy-orientated cast of mind to work on problems he formulates for himself (and each agrees to be important) on the basis of a good knowledge of the issues of the day; an official who then keeps in touch with that research worker as his studies develop, and engages him and his colleagues in regular, expert discussions with people in other fields (practical, technological and political) so that their research is attuned to the changing needs of the times, he will secure better workers, get more help from them, and spend public money more wisely.

The main – or even the only – 'output' of research is often assumed to be the computer print-outs, reports and publications delivered at the end of the project. Publication *is* a vital output: without it the research workers' findings cannot be tested by the criticism of their colleagues and rivals. But a large part of any investment in research must be written off to the education of those who do it. Even if research is wholly successful, losing no time in trying out fruitless methods and exploring dead ends – in which case its initial questions are unlikely to be very venturesome – a major study will probably take at least four years to plan, conduct and publish, and often several years more to gain the attention of policy-makers. During that period the policy questions will change: so will the parties in power and the structure of the ministries.

Thus governments must try to hasten and enlarge the education of research workers, and bring their knowledge and skill to bear on questions of policy to which they may be relevant – questions often unforeseen at the time they designed their research projects.

Promoting effective discussion of this sort is a delicate task. It can be done through conferences and seminars, by attaching research workers temporarily or part-time to government, by using them as assessors and advisers to planning inquiries, commissions and committees of inquiry, by seconding civil servants to temporary academic fellowships, and by creating more opportunities for informal discussion between the various worlds involved. Groups of specialist journalists, like the present club of educational correspondents, can play an important part in these networks by providing another means of communication between the experts, practical and academic, and the public at large. A similar club of environmental correspondents has recently been established, but in few other fields have the specialists in communication got together in this way. That, however, is an initiative that others, not governments, must take.

The central theme of this argument can be briefly summarised. In Great Britain, as in other countries, government has good reason to tighten up procedures for commissioning applied research and development work on technological problems. But much of the research we need deals with questions of policy rather than technology, and governments should take steps to promote such work because it will not be effectively or economically done if it is left entirely to institutions with essentially academic functions, such as the universities, the research councils and research foundations. When government has to formulate or evaluate policies and programmes which affect the distributions of income, opportunities and status – when the classic policy issues are at stake – it needs research workers who are prepared to contribute to the multilateral exchanges I have described. These exchanges are more like a market place than an industrial process.

Recruiting a wider range of talent for this market, maintaining rigorous academic standards in it, helping research workers to contribute effectively to policy debate, building and maintaining the social arrangements which enable them to do that, yet keeping these groupings self-critical and open to fresh talent – these are the tasks of anyone who sets out to finance and manage research on policy.

Misunderstandings about the character of that process have done a lot of damage. Potentially helpful research workers have declined to contribute (sometimes with good reason) lest their work be treated as a mere 'input' to policies they have had no part in formulating. Others *have* contributed, on the arrogant assumption that practitioners should gratefully accept 'the findings of research'. Meanwhile practitioners and policy-makers have been correspondingly confused, some being mistakenly deferential and others destructively hostile to research workers. Things go better once it is understood that in policy studies, people from each of these fields should meet on an equal footing. Each has different skills and experience to offer, and each can learn more than he teaches.

3 Government as Clients for Social Science Research*

L. J. Sharpe

Introduction

Public policy has become one of the dominant interests of the social sciences. In the field of political science about which I am most familiar this growth of interest has been very rapid indeed. The number of articles with 'policy' in their title in the *American Political Science Review* (A.P.S.R.), if we omit 'foreign policy' articles, up to 1968 could almost be counted on the fingers of two hands. I have made a rapid scout through the British equivalent of the A.P.S.R., *Political Studies*, and the growth in interest in policy seems to have been even more recent. This upsurge of interest has also been reflected in the appearance of new journals on both sides of the Atlantic, largely or entirely devoted to the study of policy, such as *Policy and Politics, Public Policy, Policy Studies Journal, Policy and Analysis, Policy Sciences* and the *Journal of Social Policy*.

Two factors that could account for this growth in interest seem to stand above the ruck. The first is the growing complexity and intractability of government. Policy-makers, whatever   their

* Reprinted from *Zeitschrift für Soziologie*, **5**, 1, 1976, pp. 70–9, with the permission of the publishers and the author.

previous inclinations, are much more willing than in the past to enlist any aid that might ease their burden. Social scientists have merely responded to this growth in demand for their services. The second dominant factor is a change in the focus of the social sciences, especially perhaps political science, to the output side of government; a new desire to look at society in terms of change and a conscious return to prescription after many arid years searching for a non-existent, value-free haven. One of the effects of this growth in interest in policy has been to kindle an interest in the actual contribution of social sciences to public policy-making. Martin Rein in a perceptive paper has divided the literature on this subject into two camps, the sceptics and the optimists.[1]

The sceptics consider that there is very little scope for social science in the formation of public policy, whereas the optimists believe that there is a potential role for social science and are preoccupied with formulating ideas as to how this role could be made more effective. Broadly speaking, the sceptics' view derives from the pluralist notion that there cannot in practice be 'one right way' of acting in government in a democracy because there can be no public unanimity on policy issues. In an open society there can be no such thing as the public interest, only a series of differing group interests. Social science research therefore follows policy and can never lead it.

The optimist, on the other hand, accepts that in the short run research is determined by prevailing majority views which underpin existing policy, but claims that in the long run research can also itself change such views. Research, in other words, can both follow and determine policy.

I am not sure whether under Rein's definition I am an optimist or a sceptic since I *do* believe that social science can change the prevailing views – paradigms, operating ideologies, ethical systems, consensual frameworks or whatever – but at the same time I am also a pessimist in the sense that I believe that research has only a limited role in public policy-making. In the short term it seems to me it has to follow existing policy. However, I do not think this is because of the pluralist nature of democratic government, but because of its inherent characteristics and because of the predispositions of policy-makers on the one hand, and the nature of social science and the predispositions of social scientists on the other.

In making these assertions I am aware that I have been strongly influenced by the British experience and while it seems likely that some of the factors inhibiting the contribution of social science to policy-making that will be discussed in this chapter are probably common to all representative democracies, it would be imprudent to claim that all of them are. Certainly the relationship between social science and policy-making in Britain seems to be substantially different to that operating in the United States, for example, as I argue below in chapter 15.

Before explaining the inhibiting factors two qualifications must be noted. The first relates to the contribution of social scientists working as permanent civil servants, and permanent research units within government itself. Such in-house contributions by the social sciences to policy-making have an important part to play in modern government, though the fact that it is under the direct control of policy-makers means that it will always be a limited role from a strictly academic viewpoint.

The second qualification relates to economists. For a number of reasons governments are much more receptive to economists than to any other social scientists. Whether at the end of the day their actual contribution is any more significant let alone successful (in the sense that predicted consequences of recommended actions were correct) than its sister disciplines is debatable. The point is that most economists believe that they have got a contribution to make to public policy-making and, above all, policy-makers believe this too. There are a number of reasons for this greater receptivity, the most obvious of which is that economics deals with *the* central policy issue – the allocation of resources. It also enables policy-makers to comprehend society as a whole as a single economy and to relate it to the world economy. The crucial point is that economics confines itself to measureable effects which, among other things, enables it to establish what Shonfield has called a 'causal nexus' between existing policies and a wide range of economic indicators of the consequences of these policies on different aspects of the economy.[2] Policy-makers, in other words, are receptive to economists not only because they believe that what they have to say will help government, but also because economists have a self-contained technique, a demonstrable professional expertise or 'mystery'. It is this mystery, which to the policy-maker comes closest to resembling the expertise he expects to receive from, say, physicians or engineers, that gives the economist the necessary status in the eyes of policy-makers, and it is this automatic status that is of key importance. No other social science apart from statistics, which is a technique rather than a discipline, can match economics in these respects.

At the other extreme, political science is perhaps the least attractive to policy-makers since it appears to have no recognisably coherent technology or explanatory construct to offer apart from a mixed bag of institutional and electoral prescriptions laced with some institutional history and statistical techniques. This is likely to be especially the case where there is a high status permanent civil service with a strong emphasis on intellectual capacity rather than specialist qualifications as in France or Britain. As the guardians of the State machine and the political confidants of ministers they are likely to regard themselves as their own political scientists and will tend to see little point in recruiting outsiders to do the job they regard as pre-eminently their own.

Sociology probably falls somewhere between economics and political science since it has a greater concern with evolving systematic explanatory theory of society than political science so that it has a marginally greater attraction for policy-makers, but much more important, sociology offers expertise on the social reality behind the formal facade of government and especially the actual impact of government policies on society as opposed to that presented through the official, legal and institutional lenses through which government has perforce to view it.

As Peter Berger has put it,

> To ask sociological questions, then, presupposes that one is interested in looking some distance beyond the commonly accepted or officially defined goals of human action.[3]

Given the increasingly egalitarian and humane spirit of government, this sociological perspective ought to be of particular value to policy-makers. However, it has been claimed that sociologists tend to suffer a self-imposed handicap in relation to contributing to public policy-making in the sense that so much of the discipline seems to be not only concerned with the unofficial side of society behind the formal facade but with the 'subterranean'. This predisposition has meant that most sociologists tend to be instinctively hostile to formal, official structures and to government in particular. Ralf Dahrendorf has described the effect of this preoccupation with one aspect of the social order as it affects the participation of sociologists in government in the following terms:

> To define the science of sociology by concern with the un-official and indeed defense of the underdog, means of necessity to define it out of the mainstream of social and political development, a generally benevolent though sometimes maleficent sect of subterranean inquirers, whose frustrations are most likely to lead them to embrace absurd and totally inconsistent beliefs in the possibility of turning the world upside down in order to make the unofficial official, and the subterranean world the place to live for all.[4]

This is a fairly sweeping indictment and it is not my concern to assess its validity, but whatever view is taken of his interpretation, Dahrendorf has undoubtedly put his finger on a crucial factor in determining the success of the relationship between social scientists and policy-makers and that is their respective occupational predispositions. In assessing the validity of the sceptical or optimistic view of the contribution of social science to policy-making we have to extend the discussion to include occupational predispositions and more especially to the inter-play between predispositions and the institutional constraints imposed on each, but particularly those imposed on the policy-makers. Let us first examine the predispositions of the policy-makers.

Predispositions of Policy-makers

The first predisposition of the policy-maker we must note, and one which makes him decidedly less receptive to social science than is usually supposed, is simply that he dislikes too much information. The usual position is that the normal processes of policy-making generate more than enough information without outside academic assistance. More than enough, that is, by the policy-maker's own estimation but not necessarily the estimation of outside observers particularly perhaps social scientists. In the first place the inclination of most policy-makers will be for action (either negative or positive) rather than words. Aggregating information as well as aggregating interests is one of his primary tasks. Government is after all concerned with decisions that usually have to be made within a fairly short time limit and this means that one of its main tasks is closing off as many options as possible by establishing criteria of rejection. Rigorously applied this can mean, if the policy-maker is lucky, that the decision 'selects itself' with the minimum of friction and time wasting and the maximum of plausibility. These are not the conditions under which more information will, or can, be actively sought from outside government, for any new information will almost certainly delay matters. But it may well generate further options as well without providing any new criteria of rejection. Keynes, who had rather more experience of government than perhaps any other British social scientist before or since, pointed out this essential feature of government long ago, yet it is seldom adequately recognised: 'there is nothing a government hates more than to be well informed; for it makes the process of arriving at decisions much more complicated and difficult'.[5]

Of course social science's potential contribution is not confined solely to providing information. It obviously has a demonstrably important part to play in monitoring policy: of assessing how far past policies are fulfilling their objectives. That this is a key contribution that social science can make is emphasised by both Cherns[6] and Rein[7] in what are two of the most persuasive and well-considered discussions of social science and public policy-making. But as Rein points out, even this role may in practice be much more limited than might at first be supposed because research can monitor policy, 'only if government has a policy to implement, that is, if it has established a definite, unambiguous course of action directed to a specific and definable aim'.[8] But, we must ask, is this usually the case? The answer must be 'no', not only because a great deal of policy is inherited from the past and the objectives it seeks to fulfil have been forgotten, but also because a great deal of policy is literally objectiveless in the sense that it either has no objectives that could be defined, or the objectives are so complex or contradictory that no policy-maker is willing to commit himself to any defined set of objectives. This brings us to an important feature of the constraints facing policy-makers, and that is their inevitable reluctance to be pinned down in any situation of political uncertainty. This is because the corollary of policy monitoring is first, that there will follow some judgement of performances, and no government can tell whether the judgement will be favourable or unfavourable. Secondly, and more significantly, so far as major policy is concerned, making your aims explicit gives your opponents a ready-made target to shoot at. In normal circumstances, no politician in the saddle will be willing to agree to that. Even among programmatic parties the maximum ambiguity about precise objectives as can be safely managed without appearing to be irredemiably opportunist is generally the rule. It is only a mild exaggeration to say that unless there are clear advantages to be reaped by stating the real objectives of major policy publicly, or where an incoming government is able to exploit the 'honeymoon' relationship with the electorate, ambiguity about aims is of the essence of democratic government. It is for these reasons, among others, that the programme budgeting fad that seems to have swept over most Western governments from its rather special origins in the U.S. Department of Defence now seems to have either been dropped (implicitly if not always explicitly), or has been shunted into the sidings of homiletic macropolicy techniques of which the corporate management approach that is now being promoted in British local government is a good example.

If there is a role for social scientists as policy monitors, it is likely to be for well-defined and limited middle-range policy and the social scientist involved must be prepared for the possibility that his work will be ignored, or possibly suppressed, if the conclusions can be construed as being damaging to the government.

Even if the policy-makers do seek information from outside government when formulating policy, it is unlikely that academic social scientists will have the information the policy-maker wants. This is because a great deal of academic social science is not about phenomena but about concepts; moreover, that which is not, will not usually be in the form that is useful for policy-making. This is not so much a problem of pure versus applied research, but simply that academic research is general whereas policy is usually highly specific and in addition requires a knowledge of the institutions and processes in which it is to be applied. Cherns has stated the problem as well as anyone. Social science research he claims, 'can only have specific use if it is concerned both as taking a narrow view of the problem it is tackling and has a strategy for its use designed into its methodology. Research of this kind turns out to have low generalisability which does not necessarily mean, but often does, that it is also trivial'.[9]

We have already noted that one of the constraints that the policy-maker has to cope with is the shortage of time and it is a constraint of such importance in relation to the possible contribution of social science to the policy-maker's task that it merits further exploration. In the first place, the policy-maker usually wants to reach decisions as soon as possible for time is one of his scarcest resources, partly because there are usually intense short-term public pressures on him, partly because governments and legislative sessions have fixed time spans, and partly because the legislative process is an insatiable consumer of time. Moreover, the legislative process cannot be by-passed, so if time runs out the most elaborately prepared, most urgent, most worthy proposals remain mere intentions. Even when a longer time scale for policy formulation is deliberately chosen, such as a government-sponsored inquiry, the time available is still likely to be too short for the academic. This is because governments have to be careful who and what research they commission. They will usually require 'peer review' as well as internal vetting of research proposals. Cumbersome financial approval procedures will also have to run their inexorable course, and problems associated with the seasonal character of research personnel recruitment shortens the time available for the actual research still further.

The academic engaged in research for government will also be inclined to resist being rushed precisely because he is now being asked to produce something that may possibly determine events rather than impress his academic peers. And determine events, moreover, in an institutional and policy setting, he may discover after he has begun the research, that is largely unfamiliar to him. This discovery is likely to delay him still further and add to a general sense of unease concerning the pace at which he is required to produce results. Unease, or worse, is likely to occur for the academic in any case since he will become only too aware that what he regards as an end in itself is regarded by the policy-maker as just another factor to be taken into account. Furthermore, it will also become apparent to him that the policy problem he is helping to tackle is merely one problem among many for the policy-maker and once a decision has been made will probably be of no more further concern to him than yesterday's edition is to a newspaper editor. Such attitudes are profoundly disturbing and unsettling to most academics for their time scale is relative posterity whereas the policy-makers' can seldom be longer than next week to next year. Robin Huws Jones makes this point most tellingly in discussing government attitudes to sociological research when he confessed to 'a disloyal spasm of sympathy with the complaint that the sociologists' cry is "Give us the job and we'll spend the next seven years sharpening the tools".'[10] Such considerations have led one American observer who has had a great deal of experience in commissioning outside research for government to conclude, 'the time required for the initiation, conduct and reporting of grant-supported research very nearly guarantees that the results will not be available in time to be useful in policy formulation and implementation'.[11]

The last constraint on policy-makers in relation to the contribution of social science to policy-making is their inability to assess the validity of what the social scientist tells them. In his work for the policy-maker the social scientist will inevitably be involved, one way or another, with facets of human behaviour in relation to government, or the operation of official institutions. Such phenomena, however, form part of the working experience of policy-makers. This working experience is moulded into a series of plausible explanations which in reality may or may not be accurate, but which are jealously guarded by the policy-maker with all the pride and obstinacy that any professional guards the current orthodoxies of his specialism. He is therefore unlikely to discard them easily unless he can be presented with an alternative explanation that is backed by proof, that is, has been validated by controlled experiments. This in the nature of things the social scientist cannot provide. This means that, unlike the respectful attitudes the policy-makers are likely to accord to, say, an accountant or physician, they are likely to greet the advice of social scientists with a mixture of suspicion tinged with incredulity wherever it touches on a policy or political process about which they claim familiarity, whatever the implications of the social scientists' research findings may be.[12]

The social scientist in government will certainly find his advisory role difficult to sustain if his research breaks new ground and his findings refute received opinion; for that is precisely the point where professional policy-makers have to desert him. The risks for the policy-maker, both politician and civil servant, are far too great for them to do anything else.

Predispositions of Social Scientists

We now turn to those predispositions of social scientists and the constraints in which they work that seem likely to be most decisive in determining whether they can make a contribution to public policy-making. We note, first, that the policy-maker's suspicion of the social scientist and his lack of respect for social science tends to be matched by the social scientist's own lack of confidence. This is derived from a number of sources. In the first place, he is only too aware of the precarious edifice of knowledge on which he is perched. He, above all, is aware that his knowledge lacks the validation of, say, the engineer, or even the physician. The social scientist, in other words, tends to share the policy-maker's estimate of himself, . . . 'he has little inner certainty about his work . . . only half believes in it, . . . his data are uncertain, his means of verification lacking'.[13] In the highly charged atmosphere of political decision-making that is so different from the university seminar room, the social scientist is vulnerable, and the policy-maker senses his vulnerability from the degree of necessary indeterminacy in his findings:

> This very indeterminacy then leads to tension between the expert and the policy-maker, since the results of research are rarely decisive. The policy-maker must still perform a difficult act of judgement based on his own views and experience; so he may well question the relevance of a social science that, for

his purposes, is inconclusive and yet raises questions about the limited basis of his own evaluation.[14]

The social scientist, in short, is only too likely to fail the policy-makers when they demand, as they assuredly will, a final, unequivocal conclusion, or recommendation. This brings us to another important characteristic of the academic social scientist, not so much as social scientist but as academic. Outside the lecture room, he doesn't much relish tidy emphatic conclusions of the kind policy-makers tend to favour. Anyone who has participated in an academic decision-making body, however fleeting that participation may have been, is unlikely to need much persuasion that academics are, how shall we say, slow to agreement and even slower to the final decision. Perhaps the social scientist is worse in this respect than academics generally; certainly his whole professional posture and training has been directed against closing off avenues of analysis and in favour of opening them up and revealing their hidden dimensions. And *where he thinks his views may be acted upon,* of careful qualification; of dissembling; of never being pinned down; of not coming to a final conclusion if he can possibly help it.

Another aspect of the social scientist's predispositions that demands brief mention is the fundamental one of ideology or values. All social science research that is likely to be of any use to policy-makers will imply some values.[15] So far as the substantive content of the research is concerned and the conceptual framework in which this content is analysed this much is conceded by most commentators who have considered the role of the social scientist in government. That is to say, it is accepted that the social scientists' contribution cannot be value free but, surprisingly, much less attention has been given to the much more obvious fact that governments are not value free either. The fact that they are not means that the problem facing the social scientist in government is not so much that his own value system colours his research and recommendations, but that these values may be out of tune with those of the government he is advising.

There may also be a value problem arising from the techniques the social scientist employs. The apparently innocent sample survey, for example, which was much beloved by social scientists a few years back, when used as a consumer test of public policy, may be viewed by politicians not merely as a disguised referendum that seeks to outflank them as the legitimate representatives of the electorate, but as a covert attack on democratic government. From the social scientist's point of view what could be more rational and just than to find out 'what people want'? That government may not always be in a position to act upon such knowledge will be conceded by the social scientist, but he is likely to insist that what people want is what democracy is supposed to be about. However, politicians of whatever stripe may regard such notions as an attempt to relegate them to the status of delegates; or that the use of surveys mistakes the complexity of democracy for the demand and supply relationship in economic theory between the individual consumer and the single product firm; or as an attempt to weaken the capacity of democratic government to act on behalf of the majority by making it a prisoner of whatever policy issue that happens to take the fancy of the social scientist.

I am probably overstating the position; my impression is that most advanced industrial democratic governments are much more receptive to systematic policy monitoring research, if only because in a situation where more of the informed public are exposed to social science at the university, there is a need for government policy statements 'to have some rags of legitimation cast about them by quantitative research'.[16] Overemphasis is necessary, however, merely to underline just how fraught with value problems even the techniques social scientists employ can be when applied to public policy-making, let alone their substantive advice or research findings.

The last disposition of social scientists that seems to be relevant to their participation in public policy-making is that the social scientist in government will be a guest. He may not see it quite like that for as a citizen enjoying full political rights he may feel that his participation in policy-making is no more than his due and perhaps even a reflection of an enlightened government. But from the policy-maker's point of view, the social scientist in government is being given a highly privileged position in society that his partners – both politician and bureaucrat – have only attained at some considerable personal cost and in the face of intense competition. They are unlikely, then, to be entirely uncritical hosts. The social scientist will be watched and he will need to be on his very best behaviour. This means that he will be expected to conform to the operating procedures of government in all their formal, ritualised glory in a hierarchical setting that has few parallels in university life.

Yet social scientists, perhaps more so than any other academics, may be the least prepared to be the model guest. From general observation there seems to be a strong tendency for social scientists who are interested in political institutions and public policy, to regard the upper levels of government with suspicion if not mild hostility. We have already noted the self-imposed handicap that it is alleged sociologists face in government because of their preoccupation with the unofficial and subterranean, but this suspicion of government, although possibly linked to sociologists' predilection for the unofficial, is something different. Precisely what its origins are lies outside the ambit of this chapter, but it is of some significance that a dominating feature of much of the academic theory of democratic organisations is derived from the assumption that, whatever the outward forms may be, power is inevitably concentrated at the top. More specifically, that the conventional account of how democratic institutions work is mythical. Whether it is Schumpeter's theory of how the modern democratic state works, Weber's theory of bureaucracy, Michel's iron law of oligarchy, the various elite-mass theories stemming from Mosca, or the elitist account of community power, they all have this characteristic more or less in common. According to Norton Long the tendency to see government always in terms of power concentration and elitism is inherent in the nature of the social sciences:

> Our primitive need to explain thunder with a theology or a demonology results in the hypostatizing of an angelic or demonic hierarchy. The executive committee of the bourgeoisie and the power elite makes the world more comfortable for modern social scientists as the Olympians did for the ancients.[17]

Reared on such an intellectual diet and with such predispositions but imbued with no more than an average enthusiasm for democracy, it is perhaps hardly surprising that our social scientist when first transplanted to government tends to see his new colleagues in a slightly jaundiced light. These are not the most propitious conditions for successful collaboration.

Conclusion

If this cursory run through the respective dispositions of policy-maker and social scientist that are likely to hinder successful collaboration between the two seems to err on the side of pessimism, it must be remembered that, in the United States and Britain at least, it has proved remarkably difficult to uncover many instances where social research has had a clear and direct effect on policy even when it has been specifically commissioned by government. Professor Cherns recounts his own embarrassment when forced by a request to provide evidence of such effects in relation to government-sponsored social science research, and he reminds us that the Heyworth Committee on social studies[18] faced a similar fruitless task, as did no less than five separate investigations in the United States in relation to research sponsored by the Federal Government.[19] As Ida Merriam, Assistant Commissioner of Research for the Social Security Administration of the U.S. Federal Government, has put it:

> There is a growing recognition that much of the federally supported extramural research, particularly in the social sciences, has added little or nothing either to basic knowledge or practical decision-making.[20]

It is true, that there are a number of factors which may obscure the link between research and policy. Professor Cherns points out, for example, how difficult it is to gauge the link because the time span may be too protracted, because we may lack adequate measures of change, and finally, because we often don't know the 'before' conditions accurately enough.[21] He might have added that the effect of social science research on a policy decision may also be obscured because it is purely negative in effect. That is to say, option C was chosen because option

A (initially the most favoured) was ruled out by the findings of the research although the implications of that research (option B) were politically unacceptable.

We must, then, treat the verdict that social science has had very little impact on policy-making with some caution for it seems likely that the reason why its impact has been found to be so low is because the assessments have tended to concentrate on a direct and positive link between research and outcome. It seems much more likely that social research has played, and will continue to play, a much more significant part in policy-making than it is possible to ascertain simply by examining overt linkages. Moreover, its negative role could be crucial in ruling out certain options if not by offering clear guidance as to the final choice in the manner I have sketched out above. Nevertheless, when due allowance is made for these factors, the impact of social science research on policy seems to be remarkably meagre when set against the amount of research directly commissioned by government and we are forced back again to a sceptical rather than an optimistic posture.

Perhaps one consideration that has to be recognised is that government sometimes commissions research not because it ever intends to use it, but, as has already been suggested, because in a more informed age those in power feel they need to legitimate policy-decisions already taken with some independent trappings. This is the 'front' function of research in public policy-making noted by Banfield.[22] It may also commission research merely to head off short-term political pressures by buying time in the hope that such pressures will have subsided by the time the research is completed. Another habit that governments seem to be adopting with increasing frequency in those sectors where the problems are particularly intractable, or where there is too much political uncertainty for explicit statements of policy – land use planning is one example – is to generate greater and greater quantities of information as a substitute for coming to a decision. There is, of course, little social scientists can and need do about such ineradicable short-term habits of government.

There may be a great deal we can do about the long term though. However sceptical we must be about the short-term contribution of social science to government, it is still possible to be reasonably optimistic about its contribution over the longer run. That is to say, social science can make a contribution to changing the dominating ideologies that underpin existing public policy. In short, social science can lead as well as follow policy.

But if it is to do so, social scientists will need to produce better social science. This may sound like a statement of the obvious, but there can be little doubt that, in Britain at least, there is a lot of truth in Hope's bald assertion in chapter 13 below that 'any research worker who comes up with vaguely progressive conclusions is likely to get an uncritical hearing, however rubbishy his work'.[23] If the situation that Hope criticises is to be avoided and social science is to make a contribution to the evolution of new broad-gauge policy – to lead rather than follow the dominant operating modes of public policy – at least two conditions need to exist. First, there must be sufficient diversity of 'consciously defended value systems'[24] to generate an effective debate and maintain its quality. Secondly, there must be social science that consciously takes as its focus the broad-gauge dominating policy consensus, eschews direct entanglements with government and fruitless handwringing about a value-free social science, and makes a frank attempt to combine empirical findings with policy recommendations. This is the social science 'that expresses a new way of perceiving society and the rights and duties of its citizens'[25] and seeks to convert the policy first and by a process of diffusion may get its views translated and transmuted into government policy later. As Donnison suggests in the previous chapter,[26] in Britain, at least, there has been a long tradition going back at least to Bentham and his disciples of this kind of social science, and there is clear evidence that it has had a profound impact on the direction and content of major public policy. Both conditions require the maximum freedom of expression and the maximum opportunity for quiet reflection. But it is doubtful whether the necessary freedom and quiet can be achieved either within government or in independent research organisations. So it may be that the extent to which social science leads rather than follows the policy consensus will depend as much on the number and quality of social science academics who stick to their lasts within the university but who take a rigorously critical interest in public policy, as it does on the number who decamp to government and research organisations.

Part Two

Public Opinion Polls and Social Surveys

Part Two

Public Opinion Polls and Social Surveys

4 Public Opinion and the Polls*

D. E. G. Plowman

The argument of this chapter is first, that public opinion is a complex process that cannot properly be measured by an arbitrary cross-section of opinions; secondly, that pollsters adopt a different definition of public opinion that makes certain value assumptions; and thirdly, that – even on the pollsters' own definition – the measures of opinion on controversial issues offered by the commercial polls in this country cannot readily be validated and are – as practical guides to public opinion – of doubtful value.

The practice of public opinion polling implicitly treats 'public opinion' as the opinions of all members of a defined universe, such as the electorate, as measured by means of standard questions presented to an appropriate sample.[1] It is a sign of the influence of the polls that current discussion of public opinion tends to take this definition for granted. Criticism there certainly is, on both technical and constitutional grounds. But few people challenge the implied definition of public opinion.

Yet the definition seems to be relatively new. No systematic account of the history of the concept of public opinion can be

* Reprinted from the *British Journal of Sociology*, **13**, 1962, pp. 331–49, with the permission of the publishers and the author.

attempted here.[2] The concept has not always been analysed[3] nor the nature of the public giving rise to public opinion been made clear. Nevertheless, the definition seems commonly to have been restricted. During the eighteenth century the term was often used to refer to the power of the rising bourgeoisie in their struggle with the aristocracy, and many nineteenth-century views emphasised the importance of the enlightened middle class. It was more often the critics of public opinion, worried about the dangers of manipulation by the press and other forces, who talked of the 'uneducated masses'.

More recently, the part played by groups, especially pressure or interest groups, has been emphasised.[4] A. F. Bentley, criticising Dicey, wrote 'there is no public opinion . . . not activity [*sic*] reflecting or representing the activity of a group or set of groups'.[5] Pressure groups are often criticised, and it is sometimes argued that the progressive growth of universal adult suffrage has lessened the need for them. Benney, Gray and Pear write that, whereas in the nineteenth century a sharp distinction could be drawn between the small electorate and pressure groups such as the Anti-Corn Law League and the National Reform League, ' "public opinion" and the electorate have now become virtually synonymous', with no longer a 'potentially effective body of public opinion outside the electoral system'.[6] But a contrary view is expressed by Plamenatz:

> Elections . . . decide no more than who shall have power and roughly on what terms . . . The more exacting political demands are made on the citizen's behalf in other ways; they are made by pressure groups which are independent of one another and of the government, and are also sensitive to the needs and hopes of their clients. Their influence depends on the support of the people they speak for, and governments must take notice of them or else risk offending a large body of voters. In a country which has been democratic for a considerable body of time and where there is general literacy, every section of the people is spoken for by some organization or other.[7]

Political scientists and sociologists have given systematic expression to the view that public opinion derives from the activities of restricted numbers of people, typically organised in groups.[8] Blumer defines a public as 'a group of people (*a*) who are confronted by an issue, (*b*) who are divided in their ideas as to how to meet the issue, and (*c*) who engage in discussion over the issue. . . . The public, ordinarily, is made up of interest groups and a more detached and disinterested spectator-like body.'[9] The interest groups tend to set the issues and the disinterested followers act to some extent as arbiters. Interest groups, which are backed by different power and prestige, must act through the available channels in the society, which means that they bring pressure to bear on those capable of making important decisions; and the latter must assess the rival claims, chiefly in terms of their backing or whether they 'count'. Much of the discussion and controversy of public opinion is between these rival factions, which to a great extent both form and express public opinion.[10] Necessarily, different issues have different publics, whose size and membership vary. As Truman writes of the United States, 'a public rarely, if ever, includes the whole of even the adult population', some of whom are unaware of even the most significant events;[11] even the followers are unlikely to form more than a minority of the population for most issues.

To talk about 'public opinion' in the sense of some single body of opinion on a given issue is rather unreal. Blumer points out that it is neither a unanimous opinion nor necessarily the view of the majority, for a minority may have more influence;[12] and indeed there may be no majority.[13] While consensus may be reached on some issues, such as government action to meet natural crises, this may never be so on other issues, notably political ones. Public opinion in the latter case refers to the views of rival interested groups and disinterested spectators and the ways these are taken into account by decision-makers. The common claim by politicians and pressure groups to have 'public opinion' on their side is often unrealistic. The true position may be unknown[14] or opinion remain clearly divided. Often one can talk about 'public opinion' only in the sense that supporters of a defeated view accept the legitimacy of the decision that has gone against them.[15]

According to the foregoing account, public opinion is a complex and changing process. It involves organised groups and unorganised individuals. It involves the processes of representative government, of legislation, administration and justice, the way decisions are taken in these spheres and how opinions are brought before the decision-makers. It raises questions of power, and of whether and how pressure groups might abuse their power; and it raises questions of persuasion and propaganda. One might object to elements in this process, but its existence seems undeniable.

It is clear that such a process cannot be measured or assessed by the systematic sampling conventionally used by public opinion polls. To sample the electorate, or indeed any other aggregate, has two shortcomings. First, it presents an essentially static picture; even the successive sampling used to give trends of opinion will not do justice to the complex interplay of opinions, pressures and decisions in the sort of process under discussion. Secondly, to sample the electorate is to give equal weight to all opinions, even if some are recorded as 'Don't Know' – for random sampling is explicitly designed to give all members of the appropriate universe equal chances of being chosen. But in the sort of process under discussion, all opinions are not of equal weight; in any process of public opinion only a minority of the electorate is taking part and the opinions voiced are often those not of individuals but of organised groups. None of this appears in the typical report of the opinion-polling organisations.

If conventional public opinion polls are not properly measures of public opinion, they do become – to the extent that they are taken seriously – part of the process of public opinion itself. If decision-makers take note of them, they become one of the factors that influence the decision. However, the part played by polls in the process of public opinion has been little studied, possibly because they are regarded as measures of rather than as participants in public opinion; and the evidence of the direct influence of polls – whether on the decision-makers or on opinions or voting intentions as in the so-called band-wagon effect – is both slight and confused and cannot be gone into here. But to the extent that polls form part of the effective process of public opinion, it becomes all the more important to examine their validity; for if this is in doubt, they may come to hinder rather than help the decision-makers' deliberations.

No-one is likely to deny the existence of the process just described. Disagreement will be about whether it should properly be called 'public opinion'.[16] Modern polling works on a model of public opinion based usually on the whole electorate or some similar diffuse aggregate. This equation of public opinion with the electorate seems to be a product both of universal suffrage and of the growth of polling techniques, and its rationale seems to lie in the democratic principle of universal franchise, which treats all opinions as of equal weight. Pollsters may add that it is only the advent of representative sampling that has at last allowed the true nature of public opinion to be assessed.

As a matter of history, it is probably nearer the truth to say that it is the pollsters, rather than the sociologists, who have redefined public opinion. The definitions of public opinion during the past two centuries seem to have referred far more often to the opinions of a limited group of people than to those of the mass. But this does not dispose of the claim for the new definition, the implications of which must be examined with care.

It is unlikely that the appeal to democracy claims that opinions are of equal weight in fact. The evidence to the contrary is too strong. Apart from the Don't Knows, mostly people with only slight knowledge and interest[17] who must be presumed to take little part in public discussion, there are probably rather more who are uninformed on any issue, even if this does not stop them from proffering opinions.[18] Furthermore, the model of society as an undifferentiated mass, formerly prevailing in research into public opinion, voting behaviour and mass communications,[19] has been proving increasingly inadequate, and the recent talk of opinion leaders and the 'two-step flow of communication', probably itself an oversimplification, suggests that even the positive opinions voiced are far from homogeneous.

When pollsters justify their techniques by an appeal to democracy, they seem to be claiming, not that opinions are of equal weight in fact, but that they *ought* to be so in principle. Polls are, in fact, often defended on grounds that are explicitly political. Durant writes: 'It is doubtful whether today a democracy can function either efficiently or fairly without opinion polls',[20] and Julian Woodward writes:

The public opinion survey performs the tremendously important function of an auxiliary ballot box – a ballot box far more flexible than the one found in the polls on infrequent election days. Sooner or later the opinion poll is going to be used by government as a day-to-day public opinion audit. As such it will be a means of holding pressure groups in check and forcing them to put their alleged popular support in evidence. When they do have to do this, and it is already beginning to happen to some extent, the whole pattern of political decision in response to pressure will be modified. . . . The pollsters believe this is a desirable change to be brought about.[21]

Since it is obvious that the views of most people on the complicated details of modern government would be worth little, there is a tendency to claim that the public (as represented in sample polls) is a good judge of ends, of general issues, principles and values. Gallup and Rae wrote in 1940 of their 'feeling of intense admiration for the honesty and common sense' of ordinary people and 'the grasp of broad principle which voters of all types possess'.[22] Elmo Roper wrote in the same year of 'a profound respect for the wisdom of the American people as a whole and with it a firm conviction that if we keep the power in the hands of the people and further develop techniques for making them vocal, we need never fear that this country will ever face the situations now being faced in certain countries of Europe'.[23] The British Gallup Poll has recently written: 'An opinion pollster comes to have a profound respect for the political instincts of the British people.'[24] It is open to doubt whether even values are very meaningful when measured by single polling questions; but it should be noticed that, in defending polls on these grounds, it is the pollsters themselves who are the judges of the wisdom of ordinary people.

The implications of the pollsters' redefinition of public opinion as the opinions of an aggregate such as the electorate seem to be as follows: that these opinions ought to be taken into account by government, on grounds of democracy; that they are of particular value on ends and principles; and that to know them is to have a defence against the machinations of pressure groups. Many people may agree with these views. But they are assumptions, and the first two are value-judgements: modern public opinion polling rests on specific moral and political values. The apparently 'democratic' nature of polling techniques makes the claims at first sight persuasive; but they are far from self-evident.

However, the pollsters' case also depends on the accuracy with which they can measure opinions. It is pointless to praise the value of the opinions of the aggregate unless these opinions can be measured validly, and this the polls claim to do. It will be argued to the contrary (1) that the validity of the polls on controversial issues is hard to establish and (2) that this lack of demonstrable validity undermines the polls' claim to offer government something of value.

Technical studies of opinion polling tend to be concerned with reliability rather than with validity. This is no doubt partly because reliability is in general easier to assess, particularly in the case of opinion-questions, for which it is difficult if not impossible to find criteria of validity. Nevertheless, the problem of validity has in general been glossed over. Although validity is limited by low reliability, it is not guaranteed by high reliability.

Earlier studies suggested sometimes quite considerable unreliability, resulting from factors such as differences in sampling, wording of questions or appearance of interviewers,[25] all of which would limit validity. One must also distinguish the overall validity of a poll from the validity of the individual responses, since the former can conceal what Parry and Crossley call 'dangerous compensating errors'.[26] Even where different interviewers get the same overall distributions from the same or equivalent samples, there may be errors in individual cases that would produce error in the breakdowns of the data.[27] However, it is possible to exaggerate the effects of unreliability. Cantril has argued that, where opinion is firmly crystallised, even deliberate bias of wording may make no difference.[28] In an intensive recent inquiry into interviewer-error, Hyman suggests that there may not be too much bias in general in ordinary field studies. Although there is experimental evidence of various sources of bias, such as in probing, coding or recording of answers due to various expectations of the interviewer, much of the error seems to be either random or a result of specific situations such as certain kinds of question.[29] Much of the error probably cancels

out, at least in the overall totals, and variation between interviewers with interpenetrating samples is in general small and
non-significant, except in the case of certain types of question –
which could be avoided in future surveys. Certainly the polling
organisations are alive to these problems and devote much time
to ensuring reliability by pre-testing of questions, improvement
of sampling methods and selection and training of interviewers.

Even so, high reliability will not necessarily guard against low
validity. Constant errors may run through the standardised
techniques and will not show in differences between interviewers
with equivalent samples. Hyman discusses some kinds of possible
constant error due to the interviewer, arising not so much from
the interviewer's ideology as from his expectations, of kinds that
Hyman calls attitude-structure, role and probability expectations.[30] Such biases may be very pervasive, especially in view of
the homogeneity of interviewers that is so hard to avoid. One of
the disadvantages of overemphasis upon reliability is that in-
validity may be standardised into the techniques used. It is consequently necessary to examine the question of validity with care.
This is especially so as the few studies of validity have indicated
considerable shortcomings, even on questions of fact. An example
is Parry and Crossley's study, where the proportion of correct
responses varied from 98 per cent in a fairly neutral and easily
verifiable instance such as the ownership of a telephone to half or
less on a matter – contributions to the Community Chest – that
was both subject to social pressures and presumed not to be
easily verifiable.[31]

One common line of argument must first be examined. It is
widely assumed that one can generalise from successful forecasting of election results to success in measuring opinions on
other issues. Polls have demonstrated their skill in predicting the
outcome of elections and the record of the British polls is especially good.[32] The polling organisations tend to use this success
as propaganda for their skill in other respects,[33] and Gallup
writes: 'The problem of polling on issues is essentially the same
as the problem of polling on candidates.'[34] Nevertheless, the
generalisation seems invalid, for two reasons.

The first concerns the distinction between overall validity and
the validity of individual responses. Since governments are
elected on aggregate votes, overall validity is sufficient with the

question on voting intention. But individual errors may arise from such sources as mis-reporting of intentions, failure to carry declared intentions out, change of intention during the time lag between the poll and the election or the final behaviour of the Don't Knows. The polls naturally try to keep such errors down, and the evidence of recent British elections suggests that the errors are small and tend to compensate for each other.[35] In the present climate of British elections, with high turn-out and rather few Don't Knows, it is a reasonable prediction that they will go on doing so. But this has not always been so in other elections, and the evidence of Parry and Crossley and others suggests that the validity of voting intention in Britain is higher than with many kinds of question. Above all, one cannot assume in the absence of evidence that most errors will be random and tend to cancel out in questions on opinion, where errors may be greater and where constant errors may operate.

This leads to the second reason why one cannot generalise from voting intention to opinions, a reason so simple that at first it looks like a quibble. To ask how someone will vote is to ask, not for an opinion at all, but for an intention. Intentions are either carried out or not, and the appropriate actions can be readily observed, which makes the assessment of an intention in principle easy to validate. This is not true of opinions.

Consider an election campaign. Although some people never take part and most have made up their minds months or years in advance, a few do change and there is active controversy.[36] This is in many ways a process of public opinion. But it is an unique process. It is suddenly and artificially terminated by the guillotine of polling day.[37] As a result, the campaign is focused not upon opinions but upon the forming and carrying out of intentions, and this is what the polls measure so accurately as a rule. Since the whole electorate counts, a sample poll of the electorate is an entirely appropriate technique. But it is not opinions that are of equal weight, it is votes. The validation of any poll of voting intention is regularly done every election by the Registrar General, who keeps records of actual votes cast in each constituency which can be compared to the polls. But there is no such regular validation for opinions about controversial issues and opinions do not systematically have to be put to the test as voting intentions are. It is not strictly necessary to measure opinions at all in order to forecast votes.[38] To measure intentions and to measure opinions are two entirely different things, and the success of the one does not guarantee the success of the other.

The strongest argument for equating voting intention and issues is put by Gallup thus: 'In the great majority of instances in which the American Institute ... reports the division of sentiment on any issue, the figures can be interpreted as a forecast of the division of opinion which would result if the same question were put to *the entire nation in a nationwide plebiscite or referendum.*'[39] In support he cites three cases where polls successfully predicted referenda on specific issues.[40]

However, it is doubtful whether polls on issues can be treated as hypothetical referenda. In the first place, an actual plebiscite forces people to commit themselves to the specific action of voting, so that it is once again intentions that would be measured by a sample poll. Secondly, the prospect of a plebiscite may affect the answers people would give,[41] so that it is an assumption to treat a routine poll as though it were a referendum. Thirdly, although a government may choose as an act of policy to make use of referenda, it is far from certain whether the opinions so recorded, however concrete they may seem, are in fact meaningful enough to provide guidance.[42] But this raises the question of the nature of opinions, which will be discussed next.

It is easy to show the need for validation of opinion-questions. Consider the case of bias due to differences of social class between the interviewer and the respondent.[43] It is hard to know how to allow for such bias. Cantril and Mosteller suggest matching interviewers to respondents in order to let the bias cancel out.[44] But this assumes that interviewers of different class will bias in known directions and by known amounts. Although Katz found that middle-class interviewers appear to bias working-class respondents in a conservative direction,[45] this might not be true of working-class conservatives. With regard to ideological bias, Stember and Hyman found that interviewers of 'majority' and 'minority' positions did not have opposite effects.[46] But in any case, one can know for sure which technique of matching to adopt only if one has already validated the alternatives.

Opinion-questions differ from factual questions and voting intention through the absence of any agreed criteria of validity. The difficulty stems from the diffuse nature of an opinion. The term is often left undefined. Many definitions amount to something like 'a verbalised stand on some controversial issue', but even this is too narrow, since an opinion can also be indicated, often deliberately, by actions or gestures. Green's distinction between elicited verbal attitudes, spontaneous verbal attitudes and action attitudes[47] applies equally to opinions; the answer to an open-ended question may seem more spontaneous than that to a closed-ended question – although even an open-ended question is eliciting responses. But this is still not a fine enough distinction, since the opinions uttered, whether spontaneous or elicited, may depend on the company. Opinions thought fit for the world at large may not be thought fit for work, friends, the family or even oneself alone; nor need this variation in offered opinions be entirely a matter of conscious censoring, since opinions are rarely consistent and the changes in emphasis or even content may go unnoticed. While men of strong conviction may utter the same opinion at all times, there is no way of knowing *a priori* from a poll finding whether this is so.

It is also often assumed that opinions are full and subtle, needing good rapport and probing to elicit them. But Hyman points out that some opinions are simple and stereotyped, so that probing might distort them by over-elaboration.[48] Many people do not really have opinions at all on many issues, although some of these will still answer questions,[49] perhaps in response to the pressure to have an opinion.[50]

These characteristics of an opinion presumably mean that it is more subject to influence by aspects of the situation such as the wording of the question and the forcing of the answers into pre-coded boxes. The wide variation already mentioned in interventionist sentiment as measured by different questions over five months[51] certainly suggests that it would be impossible to make any sensible estimate of opinion on this topic. Another instance is the study of Crutchfield and Gordon, who presented a Gallup survey question in the standard way and then questioned the respondents further. Only 60 per cent interpreted the question as it was apparently intended; and an original sex-difference in replies to the poll question turned out to be an artifact of

sex-differences in interpretation, not evident among those who
took the intended interpretation.[52] Some of this variation could
perhaps have been eliminated by pre-testing and by specifying
the meaning more clearly in the question – but when opinions
can be so varied and complex, it must be very difficult to
standardise meanings entirely.

Even where interviewer-variation and other sources of bias
do not seem to operate, or where opinion seems, in Cantril's
phrase, to be crystallised, one cannot be sure, in the absence of
validation, that the opinions received are not artifacts of standardised techniques, responses to the situation, or stereotyped
replies for public consumption. We cannot know what the
opinion means to the person, how important it is to him, how
much he knows about the subject or how much he cares, what
qualifications he might make depending upon what contingencies, what other and possibly contradictory opinions he might
hold, how much he would be willing to do about it or whether
he would even notice relevant actions by others. Most of what
gives body to an opinion is missing from the conventional polling
question.

Very little work has been done on the problem of validating
single opinion-questions, although more has been done for
attitude scales and similar measures. Some of the possible
methods of validation will be surveyed briefly.

As illustration, a particular example will be discussed, namely
Dr Mark Abrams' finding that 75 per cent of a sample of 724
people aged 18 and over, interviewed dueing January and
February 1960, said that no more industries should be publicly
owned.[53] This is the sort of issue that polling agencies commonly
take in their assessments of 'public opinion' and the problem is
to see how it can be validated.[54]

The most usual method of validation is to look for independent criteria. In the case of attitude scales, for example, it is
possible to use demographic data such as membership of a social
class or a group or association whose attitudes are generally
known, on the grounds that the average attitude of different
groups should come out in the predicted direction.[55] But this
method is not readily available for single opinion-questions. The
direct validation of voting does not apply, since individual issues
are not distinguishable in the vote. And it is hard to see how the

use of indirect criteria such as those mentioned can help. While it can reasonably be assumed that Conservatives should be more conservative than Labour supporters on a continuous scale, it assumes an unwarranted universality of opinion to say the same for a single question. Indeed, in the case under discussion, Dr Abrams' own data show that there is little relationship between answers to the polling question and support for parties.[56] The same sort of argument can be put forward for other demographic data.

Similar objections apply to the use of behaviour. In the first place, the information is usually hard to get. Secondly, it is hard to know exactly what behaviour will validate an opinion-question. Hyman suggests that this may be possible for fairly specific opinions, but will be difficult for more general sentiments.[57] In the case of nationalisation, not all the electorate spontaneously exhibit actions reflecting opinions on nationalisation. Only minorities take part in the more committed actions such as attending meetings, demonstrations and rallies, writing letters or lobbying; and many people do not appear to undertake even the mildest form of confirmatory action, such as spontaneous discussion at work, in the pub or by the hearth.[58] In any case, people do not always act on their expressed opinions;[59] nor is there any logical reason why expressed opinions and actions should always correspond.[60] (Notwithstanding, it will be argued later that actions indicating opinions occupy a place of special importance in the study of public opinion, even though they do not serve to validate a sample poll of the electorate.)

An alternative criterion is to use judgements of the opinions of selected individuals, the judgements being made by the investigator or in more sophisticated cases by independent experts.[61] Problems here lie in the selection of a typical sample of individuals, for which there is often no adequate basis;[62] in the low reliability often found for judges;[63] and in the fact that, judged against other criteria, the rating of experts may themselves be of low validity.[64] None of these snags is insuperable. But, in addition, this method begs the question of the criteria of an opinion, which would have to be agreed by the judges.

Since independent criteria are so hard to find, it is sometimes possible to do without them. In the case of attitude scales, the use of factor analysis or scale analysis, for example, has theoretical advantages and manages to by-pass the question of validity; but these do not apply to the single questions of much opinion polling. Even with single questions, the replies can sometimes be taken at their face value. An example is the study by Smith and others of attitudes towards Russia, in which the many techniques used, including a standard polling interview as well as other measures of attitudes, were apparently not validated against independent criteria.[65] But, since the aim was to study the part opinions play in personality through the interrelationship of the various devices, independent validation was not really necessary. The fact that one does not properly know whether the devices used actually measured attitudes towards *Russia* does not invalidate the findings. Another example is the common question on self-rated class. Although the replies match up closely neither with such indices of social class as income or occupation nor with position in any local status system[66] and are therefore hard to validate, they are far from valueless, as their use in understanding, say, voting behaviour shows.[67]

Nevertheless, to define an opinion operationally as 'what an opinion-question measures'[68] is logically a curious position, and its availability depends on the uses to which the opinion-question is put. It is difficult to treat a poll finding on nationalisation as a datum in itself, as long as it is put forward as a measure of 'public opinion'. This position cannot be taken at all on the sociological view of public opinion presented initially. It can be taken, logically, on the pollsters' definition of public opinion as the opinions of the electorate, which is tantamount to 'public opinion is what public opinion polls measure'. But it will be argued soon that this position is still unsatisfactory in view of what the purposes of such polls appear to be.

Attempts are made to by-pass validation by arguing on other grounds that the results must be valid. Hyman suggests that one can treat given interviewing techniques (such as probing) as intrinsically liable to produce valid replies.[69] But the evidence that he cites about the somewhat conflicting results of, for example, anonymous questionnaires or the secret ballot technique[70] certainly does not suggest that any technique can be accepted as valid on *a priori* grounds, in the absence of independent validation.

A further line of argument suggests that polls may confirm each other, proving validity by their consistency. This may take the form of independent polls reaching the same results at the same time; of the same results being reached by the same or different polls over a period of time; or by a consistent trend being found over a period of time. Logically, if a measure is repeated over time, it is impossible to distinguish real changes from the effects of unreliability; but it is implausible to conclude the latter if trends are consistent. However, even where trends are consistent, there is still the possibility of constant errors being produced by the various techniques used. Even with voting intention, there appear to be small constant errors.[71] Only if the trend can be 'intercepted' by validation at one point can its general validity be estimated, as happens with voting intention.[72] There is also the problem of the interpretation of the poll, especially when time intervals are great. Abrams contrasts his poll on public ownership with a somewhat similar poll in 1949, arguing that support for nationalisation has dropped markedly in the meantime, chiefly among Labour supporters.[73] But the history of the nationalised industries, the discussions of nationalisation and the recent campaign against it[74] may easily have led to a change in interpretation on the part of the respondents. Other data from the Abrams' survey, to be quoted shortly, suggest that it would be rather dangerous to draw conclusions about public opinion from this apparent change.

The strongest argument seems to arise if independent polls reach the same conclusion at the same time. In the case of nationalisation there is even a special case, the Hurry referendum in 1958–9 of a number of marginal constituencies, in which the results of nearly 2 million questionnaires showed 63.4 per cent favouring no more nationalisation.[75] In view of the technical differences between the two cases,[76] this looks like remarkably close confirmation.

Yet two other questions in Abrams' survey blur the picture considerably. Four (out of six) publicly-owned industries were seen more often as successes than as failures by supporters of all three major parties; and there was a considerable degree of support for government regulation of industry.[77] Certainly the validity of these other two questions can equally be challenged.

But the three questions in conjunction suggest that the opinions offered are not all considered ones.

Unquestionably the poll has, in one sense, been confirmed. Some two-thirds or more of the electorate seem to answer roughly the same question in the same way. Random or haphazard errors have evidently been reduced to relative insignificance. But it is still not clear whether the findings are valid or what they mean. Constant errors and differing interpretations of the question are likely to be reproduced in all technically-adequate polls and masked in the results. Pollsters themselves have contributed to our knowledge of the partly rational, partly non-rational motives and reasons that lie behind an uttered opinion, as well as behind voting. Abrams' data may show merely that people have been brought to the point of expressing not a fairly rational judgement but a non-rational feeling – indicating perhaps wide popular acceptance of an unfavourable stereotype of nationalisation due not only to real deficiencies in the industries concerned but also to loss of confidence amongst Labour politicians and publicists and the intensive propaganda mounted by opponents. We do not know how seriously to take the results. Without this knowledge, confirmation by other polls is virtually another form of reliability.

To sum up so far, one can say that the sophisticated techniques now used and the evidence of reliability, trends and confirmation by other polls suggest that the polls are measuring something consistent. The problem of validation lies in knowing what this is, knowing how much meaning to attach to the replies. No satisfactory answer has come to light. It is not sufficient to concentrate upon reliability. Various techniques are available, such as Gallup's Quintamensional Plan[78] or the use of attitude scales. On *a priori* grounds it might seem reasonable to think that these will reduce error – and they certainly ought to reduce random errors – but they still need not get rid of constant errors, the effects of interpretation and so on. One needs validation to be sure. In the same way, 'filtering' of the Don't Knows in voting intention by assigning them to other categories may improve predictions.[79] But this is known only because elections permit validation of the method of filtering.

It has been argued that public opinion is a complex process that cannot be measured by sampling the electorate; that the

pollsters' definition of public opinion implies certain values –
namely that the opinions of the electorate *ought* to be taken note
of by governments as a defence against pressure groups, especially on general sentiments and values; and that opinions on
controversial issues as measured by polling techniques have no
obvious source of validation. It remains to show why validation
should be so necessary.

First, two qualifications need to be made. One is that no
attack is intended upon sampling as such, but only on the
population usually sampled, the electorate, which from the point
of view of public opinion is an arbitrary population that does not
coincide with the public for any controversial issue. Equally, no
attack is intended upon the polling organisations as such, for
much of their work, on voting intention and no doubt in market
research, is of interest and value. Even their contributions to the
study of political behaviour are undoubtedly of *political* as well
as academic interest. To know that three-quarters of the electorate say they are against further public ownership is of interest to
politicians in planning future action – although the problems of
evaluation still remain. Such a study as Dr Abrams', planned as
an inquiry into Labour's failure in 1959, might be called
'electoral market research'. But, it is argued, it is not a study of
public opinion.

The reason lies in the question of validation. The way in
which a measure is validated, or even whether it need be,
depends upon the purposes of the measure. If, for example,
expressed opinions are to be related to personality, there may be
no need to validate the measures of opinion, which can be
treated as data in themselves. But this is not true of public
opinion polling. Among its diverse uses, such as publicising the
firm or persuading potential customers in business of its expertise[80] or providing the press with entertainment, only one
need seriously concern us, and that is the intention to offer information to the government, the parties, administrators and
others who have to decide on public opinion. This is clearly the
pollsters' intention,[81] and opinion polling seems purposeless
otherwise.

But if this is so, then validation is essential, because decision-
makers need to know the credentials of what is offered them. To
treat the poll results as data in themselves is to beg the question,

however logical this may be on the pollsters' definition of public opinion. For in the conventional poll results there is no way of distinguishing between considered opinions on the one hand and, on the other hand, the various shades of reply resulting from pressures to answer or opinions that are weak or formed through persuasion, propaganda and social pressure, for these may change and so therefore may the opinions, independently of the merits of the case.

To argue that consistent polling results may still not reflect considered opinions but instead, for example, consistent stereotypes of a non-rational kind may seem like a case of the 'rationalist fallacy' that only rationally based opinions are to be respected. But to criticise the argument on these grounds is to miss the point.

Governments need to know the credentials of what is offered to them as 'public opinion'. Despite the theoretical difficulty of validating opinions at all, it seems to the present writer that behaviour, that is acting on opinions, is politically of greater significance than other possible criteria. It is, for example, a reasonable inference that an unknown but probably quite high proportion of those who say they want no more nationalisation (and of course of those who say the opposite) will take no overt action on their views; they will not oppose government action one way or the other; they may not vote explicitly or even partially on the grounds of nationalisation;[82] some may not even notice any government action. It is open to question whether their views should carry any weight. Similarly, in an issue such as noise abatement, the opinions that should carry most weight with decision-makers seem to be those of people intimately concerned, such as those who live near jet aircraft or who make, own, fly or use them. But these are the opinions of the members of the public for the particular issue, in the sociological definition of public opinion set out at the beginning.

In other words, it is being argued that government gets a better guide to public opinion through the current processes of the activities of interest groups and disinterested spectators than it does from opinion polls. The implications of this view need to be stated with care. This argument is not a defence of government by pressure groups as such. The demands of interest groups are often sectarian and not concerned with general welfare; they are rarely representative, even of all their own members; and they may exaggerate their popular support. Governments may often need to resist particular pressure groups, and there is certainly need for investigation of their activities and for discovery of better ways of bringing public opinion to the notice of decision-makers. Notwithstanding, the views of pressure groups are probably sounder guides to government than polls for two reasons: first, although interested opinions are not necessarily rational or well founded, they are likely in general to be based on knowledge and reasoning; secondly, the basis of their claims is often more obvious and easily assessed. The danger of the polls is that they have a specious authority, the authority of 'science' in survey techniques and the authority of 'democracy' in sampling the electorate. Pressure groups lack this authority. It is in principle easy to see that their demands are interested and unrepresentative. Because they claim less, their claims are easier to evaluate.

Some might argue that to oppose opinion polls is undemocratic, through seeming to deny attention to the views of many people. But this would be to misunderstand the argument. Anyone who wishes to take part in the public discussion of any issue can do so by the usual means – joining a party, attending meetings, writing letters, lobbying his M.P. But there seems nothing undemocratic in saying that, if he does not want to take part, such opinions as he has need not carry weight. It seems certainly no more democratic to put forward his alleged opinions and expect them to be taken into account, merely because he happens to have fallen into a sample.

The alternative definition of public opinion offered by the pollsters is in effect an advocacy of constitutional change, in the shape of government by referendum, implying that everyone *ought* to take part in government;[83] and the meaning of what is offered is also very unclear. It can of course be argued that the meaning of the vote is likewise unclear. But this is a matter of constitutional choice. Any government may choose as an act of policy to extend the appeal to the people by way of referenda; and if they did, they might even call in opinion polls to help. But given what we know of the nature of opinions, it is doubtful what the value of this change would be.

5   Survey Data and Social Policy*

Jennifer Platt

There has been a long tradition of using survey data in relation to social policy, though the very term 'survey' now means to sociologists a technique of data collection, that is the systematic and structured questioning, either by interview or by questionnaire, of a relatively large number of respondents, rather than, to quote a 1935 definition, 'a fact-finding study, dealing chiefly with working-class poverty and with the nature and problems of the community'.[1] But some of the older connotations still linger on, especially perhaps outside academic sociology. In 1951 Mark Abrams, in a well-known book, remarked:

> Occasionally surveys originate in an abstract desire for more knowledge about the structure and workings of society; more frequently, however, they are carried out as an indispensable first step in measuring the dimensions of a social problem, ascertaining its causes, and then deciding upon remedial action.[2]

Certainly, whether or not surveys are thought of as inherently connected with a concern for social problems and their remedies, they are very commonly seen as appropriate when decisions or

* Reprinted from the *British Journal of Sociology*, **23**, 1972, pp. 77–92, with the permission of the publishers and the author.

recommendations are to be made on matters of social policy. Royal Commissions and local authorities are regarded as progressive if they initiate them, and students with social consciences are eager to undertake them. Although many textbooks have been written about the techniques of collecting data by the survey method, surprisingly little has been said about the appropriate relationship between survey data and policy recommendations. It seems useful, therefore, to attempt a systematic discussion. (Many classic problems in the broad area of policy recommendation will not, however, be discussed, since they bear no specific relationship to the use of survey data. Thus we shall not attempt, for instance, to say anything about the relative weight to be attached to the interests of the present and future populations affected, the existence of conditions for formal rationality of choice such as the ability to rank preferences transitively, or the problems of measuring costs and benefits.)

For well-grounded policy recommendations to be made, facts, theories and value-judgements[3] are necessary. The making of any policy recommendation implies that there is a desired state of affairs[4] which the policy is designed to promote,[5] and therefore implies value-judgements which have generated a schedule of preferences among alternative states of affairs. The making of any policy recommendation also implies factual knowledge of the current situation which it is designed to perpetuate or change. Finally, theories are needed in order to go beyond existing factual knowledge to predict the consequences of (possible) change. Those who either do not share the value-judgements or do not find the theories convincing, or do not accept that the relevant facts have been correctly appreciated, cannot be expected to support the policy recommendation made; any given recommendation may be criticised at any one of these points, and to be supported must have something to say on each of them.

How, then, can survey data be brought to bear at each point? In order to discuss this, we must first specify in more detail the role played by each of these elements. The process of policy formation can be broken down into three phases: the existing state of affairs, a (desired) future state of affairs, and the mechanisms of change by which the former may become the latter. Empirical data, the 'facts', are relevant to all three phases in the argument. First, they are required in order to describe the existing state of affairs, so that this may be compared with the desired state and, if there are discrepancies, it may be known what requires to be changed. Data are also required for a definition of the desired state of affairs. Value-judgements alone can give an abstract conception of what this would be, but they can give no guide to its practical social feasibility; in an ideal world for instance, communal solidarity might be consistent with tolerance of diversity – but in the actual world it may not be. To predict which patterns of arrangements will have internal sociological consistency one needs theory, which needs data to suggest and to test it. For the same sorts of reason, data are also required for mechanisms of change to be identified and chosen. Thus we have already made the case for the relevance of theories to the two latter phases. They are also, however, required in relation to the description of the existing state of affairs. Having decided that we wish this to be changed, we cannot proceed to select the means of doing so without specifying just what it is that is to be changed; to do this, we must have some idea what causes those aspects of the situation which we find undesirable, since a proposal to remove only symptoms is not likely to be fruitful; a causal account of the situation constitutes a theory. Finally, value-judgements are also relevant at each stage; they are needed to define an existing situation as requiring action or inaction, to choose among alternative mechanisms of change on grounds other than technical efficiency (since means to an end may also be ends in themselves[6]), and to specify the terminal states of affairs which are to be desired.

These abstract statements can be illustrated by a concrete example, for which we will take the much-discussed issue of educational opportunity. (It should be emphasised, however, that this example is only meant to be suggestive; its form is schematic, and the details are not meant as an accurate or fully plausible representation of the real facts. It is intended only to demonstrate how data, theories and values are all needed at each stage if the necessary, though often only implicit, choices are to be made.) Data show that a lower proportion of working-class than of middle-class children get to grammar school; values judge this to be unsatisfactory; theory identifies the cause as discrimination by teachers against children possessing the typical linguistic characteristics of working-class children. Values specify educational equality as the desired state of affairs; available data suggest the theory that this is feasible in principle if class differentials in linguistic characteristics are eliminated, which is conceivable, while the elimination of such discrimination by teachers would be inconsistent with so many other features of our society that it is not practically feasible. The target is then to eliminate the linguistic differentials; theories based on available data suggest a number of different ways in which this might be done. Compulsory removal of all working-class children from their parents at an early stage, which appears likely to be technically the most efficient means, is rejected out of hand on value grounds; from among other possible means to which there is no strong normative objection the value-judgement is made that the cheapest should be chosen.

What use, then, can appropriately be made of survey data? Table 5.1 represents the possible combinations of the aspects that we have distinguished. We shall discuss each of its cells, which are lettered for convenient reference, in turn, although there are not always relevant differences between adjacent cells. Obviously the answer also depends to some extent on the nature of the group studied in the survey, and on the types of questions put to them; appropriate distinctions will be made as we go along. The roles of research sponsor or policy decision-maker and of researcher will not be distinguished, though they are normally differentiated in practice and many significant problems arise from their relationships; the distinction, however, is not relevant to our discussion, which is concerned only with the ways in which policies (whether or not they are actually put into practice) may be formed. When the word 'researcher' appears, therefore, it is to be understood as implying a researcher who not merely conducts research but puts forward policy recommendations based on it.

(A) A survey is clearly an excellent source of data on the existing state of affairs, or at any rate on certain of its aspects, in particular the attitudes, opinions[7] and knowledge of the sample studied. For other aspects, other modes of data collection are often more appropriate. Perhaps the commonest type of survey in practice is of a sample of 'consumers', that is people who are directly involved in the situation of interest but do not have any specialised training or role to play in relation to it. This has obvious advantages as compared, say, to a survey of the general public, most of whom may have no involvement at all in that situation. It also, however, has some less obvious disadvantages. First, the omission of anything like a control group

TABLE 5.1

	Existing state of affairs	Mechanisms of change	Desired state of affairs
Facts	A	B	C
Theories	D	E	F
Value-judgements	G	H	J

may make it impossible to tell whether some of the sample's characteristics (for example extended family organisation) are related to the circumstances of concern (for example dense housing) or to other characteristics (for example having working-class jobs) which, by a process of self-selection, have led them into these circumstances. Secondly, those aspects of a situation on which 'consumers' can give information may not be the only relevant ones, and to know about them alone may be positively misleading. Thus, for instance, in Ann Cartwright's *Human Relations and Hospital Care*[8] one feels the need of data beyond what the patients interviewed could give on the nature of their illnesses and the characteristics of the hospitals that they had been in, though it was indispensable also to know their perceptions of these things. Bruyn has put his finger on one recurring problem when he says:

> . . . Without the perspective which comes from the description of subjective opposites in an institutional setting, a study is bound to serve the interests of social criticism more than the interests of objective analysis.[9]

That is, surveys confined to consumers tend not only to give too narrow a picture of the current state of affairs but also, consequently, to beg the question of which value-judgements should be applied by familiarising the researcher with only one set besides his own. (If, of course, a survey were done of 'producers' or 'experts' only, analogous points could be made, but this has much less often been attempted; the only example that comes immediately to mind is Booth's use of School Board visitors as informants,[10] and that doesn't quite fit the bill.)

(B) As a source of data relevant to mechanisms of change, surveys can be very useful, but here we must distinguish again between two kinds of sample. A survey of those most directly involved in a situation provides information about the conditions which successful means of change must meet by helping to answer questions about the sample's norms, perceptions, attitudes and so on; it does not provide any information about the possible changes themselves, since by definition they haven't yet happened to that sample. For these sorts of data surveys of *other* samples, however, may have a lot to offer, although of course their relevance can only be exploited with the help of theory.

(C) For the same reasons a survey of current 'consumers' can give no help at all in delineating a desired final state of affairs; a survey of some *other* group already in the desired state can serve the function of showing that such a state is possible at least once, though again broader conclusions cannot be drawn from such a finding without the aid of theory.

Other samples may also be less indirectly relevant, in that the practical feasibility of potential mechanisms of change may depend on their reactions to them, and on the social relations between them and the consumers of concern. Thus surveys can provide at least some of the factual data which are needed at each phase of developing a policy recommendation, but the surveys of 'consumers' most commonly undertaken have important limitations in this respect.

(D, E, F) Next we consider the possible contribution of surveys to the formation of policy-relevant theories; there the distinction between the existing state of affairs (D), mechanisms of change (E), and the desired state of affairs (F), does not seem important. Survey data, like any other data, can lend confirmation to theories or refute them, and can spark off new ideas for the theoriser, but they cannot directly provide theories. And, as we have already pointed out, useful theories may come from substantive domains quite different from those of policy concern, although the serendipitous relevance of the superficially irrelevant[11] cannot be relied upon, and the case for 'grounded' theory[12] is an important one.

But to use survey data for this purpose does have some probable, though by no means necessary, consequences. First, there is the likelihood that respondents will put forward their own 'theories' on some of the matters that the sociologist is concerned with, and that he will be tempted by them to elide the distinction between data and conclusions drawn from data, or between the formulation of a theory and its testing. Respondents' theories have special status as *data* (about respondents' theories), but only in the very unusual situation where the sample was one of experts might the fact that *they* held them confer any claim to a special status, different from that of researchers' theories, which might exempt them from the usual procedure of testing.[13] Further, ordinary respondents will typically be aware only of those factors in a situation which their own roles in it have drawn to their attention, and will not have attempted to compare it systematically with any other situations, and so their theories will be based on partial perspectives and inadequate information. For the researcher to accept such theories without further investigation is to abdicate from his function. We may note, however, that respondents' theories should be more usefully suggestive to him when they relate to the current state of affairs, where their experience is directly relevant, than when they relate to mechanisms of change or the desired final state, where there is no reason to expect that they will have any specially relevant knowledge.

Secondly, the nature of survey research is such that the data to be collected have to be specified in advance, except to the extent that open-ended questions may reveal the unexpected. This means that, unless happy accident intervenes, theories can only be tested in any one survey if they have been formulated in advance. Many writers have pointed out that this can be severely limiting; the limitation is particularly important when the theorising refers to possible future states and is designed to be relevant to policy-making. For rational policy-making something near to a full set of the major alternatives needs to be considered, even if many of them are immediately ruled out once stated by their costs or by normative considerations. Anything that prevents such consideration is disadvantageous.[14] The 'causes' of any complex social situation – that is, those circumstances without which it would have been different – are infinite.

If, therefore, one wishes to change it, there are a large number of points which might provide appropriate leverage, though they will of course vary in their effectiveness, practicality and normative acceptability. Theorising that has not recognised a sufficient range of alternatives is likely to be conservative both intellectually and politically in the policy recommendations which it generates, and so may miss the most effective solutions; in particular, it tends to suggest policies which are strategies of cure rather than of prevention.

Thirdly, there are some standard points about the potential weaknesses of survey research which bear on these issues. The first is that there are often reasons for doubting the accuracy of respondents' reports, even when they are given in all good faith; if the researcher does not recognise this, and use such reports with appropriate reservations and checks, his theorising is liable to be beside the point. (This also has implications for our earlier discussion of surveys as sources of data.)

Similarly, the problematic nature of the relationship between attitudes and behaviour must be borne in mind. An expressed attitude is often not directly predictive of the behaviour which might appear to follow from it, which can be affected by social pressures and by the relevance of other attitudes.[15] A rather more important point is that surveys typically, though certainly not necessarily, use unstratified random samples with individuals as their units. This means that the data refer to aggregates rather than to social groups or other meaningful units, and so are likely to suggest social-psychological rather than sociological theories. Thus, for example, cases may appear as individual pathology which can more accurately be seen as responding to social-structural conditions.[16] To the extent that this occurs the resultant theories will not be of so much practical use in producing the desired effects.

(G, H, J) Finally, we come to the contribution that survey data may make to the value-judgements necessary for policy recommendations. (Note that respondents' value-judgements may be elicited by the survey, yet fall under the category of 'facts' in our schema if the researcher treats them only as such.) The distinction between our cells G, H, and J is not very important here; it resolves itself into the question of *whose* value-judgements may be regarded as relevant (present or future populations? the directly only or also the indirectly affected?) and how likely it is that a survey will have covered the appropriate groups? This section will be mainly concerned, therefore, with an issue cutting across both H and J: how far can the researcher legitimately use his respondents' value-judgements as though they were his own?

There are three basic types of relationship between data and recommendation: (1) the survey elicits respondents' opinions, and the researcher transmits a summary of them as his recommendations for action; (2) instead of collecting opinions directly on policy, the survey collects data on attitudes and behaviour regarded as relevant to the policy issue, and the researcher then recommends policies which he thinks likely to be acceptable to the attitudes and to facilitate the behaviour; (3) the survey collects data on attitudes, opinions and behaviour, but the researcher makes policy recommendations which, taking all these into account, appear likely to produce the effects which he for his own reasons regards as desirable. Thus the distinction made here, which we shall maintain is crucial to the logic of the argument, rests on the extent to which the value-judgements used are, or purport to be, those of the respondents.[17]

The type (1) relationship, though somewhat naive, has obvious attractions; its claim to legitimacy rests, at least in part, on the idea that it is uniquely democratic to let recommendations rest on the views of the mass of respondents. This involves, however, the making of a whole range of assumptions, which may well not be intended, and are generally not justified; we proceed to explicate these.

It is only reasonable to base recommendations on respondents' opinions[18] when the following conditions are met:

(*a*) That there are no other significant groups besides those represented in the sample, or its majority, whose opinions differ; if there are such groups, an equally good case can be made out (other things being equal) for acting on *their* opinions. But it may easily be impossible to act on both sets of opinions simultaneously, or at least impossible to do so without incurring costs that neither party wants – in which case action cannot be taken without the introduction of further criteria to compromise or choose between the alternatives.

(*b*) That respondents' opinions are relatively permanent, and not responsive to possible changes in their circumstances.[19] If opinions change rapidly, it may not be practically feasible to change policies often enough to keep in step with them. If the opinions change with circumstances, or the relevant respondents change as old ones die or change their status and new ones replace them, current opinions give no guide to satisfaction with future policies. If, for instance, they usually express dissatisfaction with the weak points of the current state of affairs, they may turn against a policy previously advocated as soon as it has been put into practice. If, on the other hand, they express satisfaction with the current state of affairs, this may only be because they have not experienced and cannot imagine another with which, in practice, they might be equally or better satisfied. Thus it is only if one can be fairly sure that the opinions stated express general and long-run commitments that policy can be expected to succeed in coming into line with them.

(*c*) That respondents' opinions rest on a well-informed consideration of the causes of current problems, the possible alternative ways of dealing with them, and the likely costs and further consequences of adopting each of the different alternatives. If a wrong diagnosis has been made of causes, the solution advocated will not have the desired effect; if the range of possible alternatives has not been considered the best one may not have been chosen; if the costs have not been estimated, they might turn out not to be acceptable; if further consequences have not been thought through, the solutions advocated might have ramifying effects which as a whole would create worse problems than the initial one now solved. That is, the particular opinions might not even be consistent with the respondents' own sets of preferences. The respondents' opinions must also, of course, rest on a correct appreciation of the facts. If average earnings are overestimated, the opinion that they are high enough does not mean much.

(*d*) That it is feasible sociologically, administratively, politically, financially . . . (etc.) to act on the respondents' opinions. If, for instance, they would require a radical diversion of national resources to one narrow sector of the economy, or a sudden and fundamental change in child-rearing practices, the fact that such hypothetical changes would solve a problem does not make suggesting them very helpful to practical policy under normal circumstances, whoever makes the suggestion.

Unless the sample of respondents is a highly unusual one, it is very unlikely that all these conditions will be met (and that the researcher will have adequate evidence that they have been met). Even if the researcher is committed to a democratic belief in the general desirability of satisfying respondents' wishes, other factors besides their opinions must be taken into account if these conditions are not met, and so it will be necessary to do more than just transmit a summary. But the tenability of such a 'democratic' belief may itself in turn be questioned on two grounds, one philosophical and one sociological.

Philosophically, it is logically odd to advocate acting on opinions unless one either shares them oneself or holds some other opinion which leads one to the same conclusion. There are two ways in which this oddness can be avoided: (1) the researcher may just happen himself to share the respondents' opinions,[20] or may have so strong a normative commitment to the desirability of acting on democratic opinion that it outweighs any substantive views he has himself on the particular issue in hand which differ; (2) by happy coincidence, the researcher expects the consequences of acting on the opinions expressed to be different from those anticipated by his respondents, and sees them as desirable, or, less fiendishly, sees them as inherently undesirable but a price worth paying for further consequences indirectly associated with them. In none of these cases, however, can he logically escape from the need to make at least one value-judgement of his own by attempting to rely on those of his respondents. To the extent that he purports to have done so, he is concealing the true structure his argument must have if it is to lead him to a policy conclusion.

Sociologically, there is something odd about treating respondents' opinions as though they were simply given in the situation rather than themselves caused. If one does not do this, other possibilities besides acting on the opinions suggest themselves when opinions on what is desirable do not correspond to the current state of affairs and respondents' satisfaction is desired. One is to try to change the opinions rather than to try to change the state of affairs; whether or not this would be a good policy in a particular case depends on the value-judgements made by the researcher in deciding what to advocate – does he agree with the opinions? how does he evaluate the relative costs of changing the opinions and changing the states of affairs? and so on. Another possibility is to try to change the *causes* of the opinions, as distinct from the reasons for holding them or the states of affairs to which they refer. A survey[21] showed, for instance, that the more comprehensive schools there were in an area the more likely respondents were to say that they favoured them; let us assume that this finding could not plausibly be interpreted as showing simply that those who wanted them in the first place had succeeded in getting them, and that it suggested, instead, that the more people knew about them the more they liked them. The literal-minded 'democratic' response to the initial finding would give a policy of not introducing comprehensive schools into the areas where they did not already exist and so people did not much favour them. The response of trying to change the opinions would lead to a policy of propaganda directed at the minority in each area, attempting to change their views to those of the majority. The response of trying to change the causes of the opinions could produce many policies, but one obvious one would be to introduce comprehensives in the areas which didn't yet have them, on the assumption that opinion there would then come to favour them. (But note that here too the researcher's value-judgements are bound to enter; to bring about approval of the then existing state of affairs it would be technically equally effective to change the opinions of the *majority*, or to abolish comprehensive schools where they already existed.) Thus even if the aim of satisfying respondents' desires is taken as given it may be achieved in several different ways, so that it does not follow from the fact of holding this aim that the only eligible policy is one of acting on their current opinions.

This discussion leads us on to our second possible relationship between survey data and policy recommendation, where the recommendations are only indirectly based on the survey responses.[22] (*Family and Kinship in East London* takes very much this form; housing recommendations are made which are intended to allow scope for extended family and neighbouring patterns to continue, though opinions about housing have not been asked.) This approach assumes that respondents' wishes, whether verbally expressed or only behaviourally implied, should be deferred to, but avoids the 'democratic' assumption that they know how these wishes can best be achieved. Does this approach escape our criticisms?

Conditions (c) and (d) above no longer apply, although of course appropriately modified versions of them still apply to the researcher's own opinions. But conditions (a) and (b) remain relevant if for 'opinions' we substitute 'attitudes and behaviour': the problem of devising one policy to fit more than one set of characteristics remains, though it is much less severe now that some scope is allowed for the policy-maker's initiative. The problem of potential change in the characteristics the policy is to fit is as severe as ever, except perhaps to the extent that reported behaviour may be less volatile than expressed opinions. In another sense this problem becomes worse, for the usual rationale of devising policies to perpetuate existing behaviour patterns assumes that those behaviour patterns are preferred and freely chosen; but this is not necessarily so. It is dangerous to infer that wishes, especially 'real' or unverbalised ones, are expressed in behaviour; both positive social constraints and negative lack of opportunity may prevent their expression.[23] Current behaviour may be taken as showing, by definition, the preferred adaptation to current circumstances, but it cannot directly show what would be the preferred adaptation to other circumstances, or what circumstances would be preferred. At least the asking of opinions does not build in conservatism so directly, although in so far as opinions follow from current circumstances it may do so indirectly. Finally, our further points above still apply, *mutatis mutandis*; a researcher still rationally requires his *own* reasons for advocating policies intended to put his respondents' preferences (however these may have been ascertained) into practice, and thus still has to make value-judgements of his own.

The third and last possible relationship between survey data and policy recommendations is that where the researcher makes policy recommendations which, taking his data into account, appear likely to produce the effects which he for his own reasons regards as desirable. (See below for the special case where his own reasons include a desire to optimise respondents' satisfactions, or 'their own good'.) The researcher openly makes his own value-judgements, and collects data on consumer preferences for his own purposes. Thus discussion of the validity of this approach must revolve around the rationality of the arguments used by the researcher rather than those used by his respondents. In this case condition (*a*) becomes a point about sampling: if the sample studied is not representative, it will not allow adequate predictions to be made. Condition (*b*) becomes a point about interpretation of the data: if the researcher's recommendations are to be effective, he must be able to make reasonable predictions of the ways in which people would behave in the future if each of the alternative possible courses of action were followed, and in order to do this he requires not only information about their current behaviour but a theory. Conditions (*c*) and (*d*) apply again, with the researcher's conclusions substituted for the respondents' opinions; it is probably justified to assume that in this case these conditions are more likely to be met, since the researcher must be more self-conscious about what he is doing and, by the very fact of conducting research, must eventually be relatively well informed about some relevant factors. Finally, our last points no longer apply at all in this case, since the researcher is not attempting to act on other people's opinions rather than his own, nor is he treating these opinions as immutable factors in the situation. (But it is very possible, none the less, that his own opinions may be influenced by acquaintance with the respondents' opinions, or with other aspects of the data).

Our analysis, therefore, leads us to conclude that this third type of relationship between data and recommendations is the most satisfactory one, in that it is the only one that makes explicit the logical structure that must always in fact be present. The argument is logically adequate, unlike that of the other cases, to lead to the conclusions that it produces, and because its stages are explicit its structure can more easily be discussed critically, and its parts may more easily be utilised by other people who do not share all of its appreciations of fact, theories, or value-judgements.

It may be objected, however, that this seems to lead to the advocacy of a situation where social policy is determined by an irresponsible elite of planners guided by nothing but their own preferences. This is not the intention; I advocate only that policies should be developed as rationally as possible, and that claims to 'democratic' legitimation should not be made where the facts do not justify them. The criteria applied to respondents' opinions must also be applied to those of researchers and planners, who are certainly not exempt from the same errors, though they may be trained to try to overcome them. There is no reason why the value-judgements of researchers should have priority over those of anyone else; there is every reason for them to try to make clear what their own are. We mentioned above that the researcher's value-judgements might lead him to want to optimise his subjects' satisfactions, or opportunity to act on their own opinions. In this case the end result might seem very similar to that produced by a type (1) or (2) relationship. In terms of the researcher's motives, it would be; the crucial difference lies in the degree of attention paid to the limitations of the survey method, and so the relevance of various kinds of data, and to the likely effectiveness of the means by which the ends may be attained.

It will be evident, to anyone familiar with the field, that there are many policy-orientated surveys which do not meet our criteria. There are a number of particularly common confusions, which we shall list, though some have already been mentioned in passing.

(1) The confusion between diagnosis and prescription. Respondents' opinions on the current state of affairs are treated as if they were either or both of theories and opinions about possible future states of affairs. This confusion is implicitly made whenever respondents are asked only for their opinions about (and descriptive data on) the current state of affairs, but the survey report ends with recommendations that appear to claim the legitimation of democratic support. They may be excellent recommendations, but they do not have the support of the opinions expressed in the survey. (*Family and Kinship in East London* provides an example of this, in that the recommendations for housing policy made at the end are justified by their correspondence to respondents' wishes, although these do not appear to have been studied.[24]) A researcher who succumbs to this fallacy can be led into excessive radicalism if there is dissatisfaction with the current state of affairs, since he is likely to

recommend solutions whose own implications have not been considered.

(2) The confusion between taking respondents' opinions into account, and acting on them, in devising recommendations. The former is to be advocated, whether or not it is intended to produce a 'democratic' policy, but the latter is not, in rational policy-making, except when the conditions specified earlier are met. It is sentimental to refuse to recognise the typically severe limitations on the value of respondents' opinions; when 'democratic' norms are held the paternalism of thinking in terms of 'their own good' is to be preferred, and whether they are held or not it is necessary to think in terms of costs and consequences.

(3) The confusion of behaviour with opinions. Even if people like their current behaviour patterns, which cannot be taken for granted, it does not follow that they would prefer them, or the underlying attitudes which they appear to the researcher to express, to the alternatives available under different conditions.

(4) The confusion involved in taking the opinions of current 'consumers' alone as sufficient information for 'democratic' policy-making. They may give sufficient indication that something is wrong, but the opinions of others are relevant not only on the current situation but also on the possible costs and consequences of introducing changes. (To follow Young and Willmott's suggestion, for instance, that extended family and neighbour groups should be rehoused *en bloc* rather than as separate nuclear families might be entirely satisfactory to those concerned, but might cause grave dissatisfaction and felt injustice to the people in greater housing need, whose rehousing would consequentially be postponed.) Such information is needed even if 'democracy' is not seen as desirable, since without it all the relevant factors cannot be taken into account.

(5) The confusion of relevance to the problem with substantive similarity to it. This often arises from a lack of interest in theory in general, which leads the researcher to look only at work done in the same substantive area for theoretical ideas that relate to his material, thus missing a lot that could be relevant. The study of the attitudes of American soldiers in the Second World War to being drafted[25] may suggest instructive ways of approaching the explanation of the attitudes and behaviour of patients in British hospitals in the 1960s, for instance. This kind

of oversight can, of course, arise in any kind of research, but it is particularly likely to occur in the policy-orientated since that is by definition concerned with particular concrete situations.

We conclude, therefore, that it is easy to make improper uses of surveys in drawing policy conclusions, and that greater caution needs to be exercised than has commonly been shown. There seem to be three main dangers from such improper uses: unreasonable conservatism in the policy recommendations made, sentimentalism about respondents that produces practical inadequacies in the recommendations made, and the researcher's own value-judgements playing only an implicit (and thus covert) role in the derivation of recommendations.

6 Consumer Opinion and Social Policy*

Ian Shaw

A significant proportion of research in social work shows a strong disposition to take into account the standpoint of the people receiving the social service in question. A focus on the opinion of the client, or, more fashionably, the 'consumer', marks part or the whole of a growing number of studies.[1]

This concern to understand the perspective of the consumer – the person directly involved in the situation of interest, but without any specialised training or role to play in relation to it – as distinct from the 'producer' or the general public, has been produced and moulded by a number of factors. The influence of politically left-wing opinion on social work stands for a favourable interpretation of the value of working-class culture. This has hit social work later than social administration, and has resulted in a distaste for the professionalisation of social work practice, in so far as such professionalism implies an inability on the part of the client to diagnose his own needs, or discriminate among the range of possibilities for meeting them. Furthermore, the interest in 'client power',[2] the growth of consumer groups, and the disillusion with traditional forms of political representation

* Reprinted from the *Journal of Social Policy*, **5**, 1976, pp. 19–32, with the permission of the publishers and the author.

have led to a partial breakdown of the structural isolation[3] of social work clients, and therefore an increased motivation to discover their evaluation of the services offered. This diversification of interest is consistent with the current preoccupation with finding more meaningful indices of social need.

Furthermore, in the realm of casework theorising, the decline of analytic viewpoints and concepts, which encouraged practitioners to discount or explain away any views the client may have, has made it easier for social workers to be alert to rational meaning in the clients' account of his experience. Thus, Goffman points out that the psychiatrist is often under pressure to treat the outpourings of the patient not as directly usable statements of information, but rather as signs of the illness itself, to be discounted as direct information. 'But to treat the statements of the patients as signs, not valid symptom reporting, is of course to deny that the patient is a participant as well as an object in a service relation.'[4]

Finally, developments in research have provided both negative and positive reasons for grounding social work research more firmly on the client's own account of services received. The evaluative and experimental research of the 1960s led into a cul-de-sac. Results depressingly and predictably revealed marginal benefits either from social work in general, or from one variety of social work help as against another variety. One methodological approach that seemed to provide a way out of the *impasse* was that of close exploration and inspection of the meaning of social work to those who participate in it – an approach congenial with the resurgence of interest in qualitative research. British sociology appeared to provide a partial model for such research in the work of the Institute of Community Studies, which, in its programme of study into the relationship between the social services and working-class family life, proceeds on the assumption that the policy-makers and administrators are insufficiently aware of the needs or views of the working-class people who form the bulk of the users of the social services.[5]

Typical studies of this kind are based on fairly small samples of current or recent users of a particular social service. Respondents are interviewed with the aid of a loosely structured schedule, containing a large proportion of open-ended questions, and are asked to describe their experience of the service they received. The research approach is descriptive, with no formal hypotheses, and the account relies heavily on extracts from the interview to illustrate the opinions, attitudes and behaviour of the respondents. Professional and administrative conceptions of the service, as derived from the literature, are sometimes used as a basis for comparison. The study concludes with a number of policy recommendations. These recommendations are typically for improvements or rationalisations in the delivery of existing services, rather than criticisms of an overall deficiency in the extent of the service or suggestions for the implementation of new kinds of services. The studies listed above[6] illustrate the wide range of issues within which recommendations have been made.

Value Commitments

The purpose of this review is to assess the commitment to the consumer and the efforts to formulate policy recommendations, as found in this loosely linked collection of research studies carried out in Britain, and particularly to evaluate the potentiality of social work consumer opinion in formulating social policy. Two main points will be made. First, that it is difficult to know when the opinion of the consumer has been understood properly. Secondly, that even when the views of consumers are known to us, the question of how these views are utilised in the formulation of policy is problematic.[7] 'A whole programme of research'[8] may be needed, but clarification of the precise purpose and utility of such research is an important prerequisite.

Two further points can be made as a preface to the discussion. It needs emphasising that the derivation of prescriptions for action is a central concern in this literature. The studies by Butrym[9] and Goldberg[10] fail to work their data about consumer opinion into the main fabric of the work in ways that are more than incidental and peripheral to the main arguments, but these are exceptional, as a comparison with the work of Bayley, Mayer and Timms, Gill, Triseliotis and Marsden[11] makes clear. For example, Triseliotis starts off his book on adult adoptees in search of their natural parents by saying: 'It was hoped that

answers to certain questions might not only give further understanding of the adoption situation but also point towards desirable areas for legal reform and for practice changes.'[12]

The second remark, by way of introduction, is that the commitment to take into account the standpoint of the consumer of
social policy is a value-judgement, the full consequences of
which cannot be known until the investigation of viewpoints has
taken place. A willingness to tolerate diversity and a belief that
dignity and respect are due to the individual as such are two
values present in the literature. Also, the basic commitment
tends to suggest at least an implicit conflict of interest between
the consumer and the producer.

Discerning Consumer Opinion[13]

Our discussion so far might imply that the role of social work
consumer is a clearly defined one, mutually agreed by all concerned. Recent evidence suggests that this is not so. In their
study of people connected with Southampton Social Services
Department, McKay and her colleagues found that the status of
consumer is not a clear one for the client. Of the clients in their
sample who thought they were still in contact with the social
worker, 10 per cent were registered as 'closed' cases by the
department. In contrast, two-thirds of those who thought they
were 'closed', were registered as 'active'.[14] This helps to explain
why, despite the work done so far, we have limited knowledge of
the user's perspective in the social services, in that it is not easy
for the researcher to maintain a clear and systematic distinction
between the views of the social worker and those of the client.
The views of 'producers' and consumers become confused,
usually at the expense of the consumer.

This partly accounts for the stereotyped response frequently
obtained to questions about levels of satisfaction experienced by
clients, for example by Goldberg and McKay. The failure to
distinguish the views of social worker and client is more obvious
in Butrym's study of patients referred to medical social workers
(M.S.W.s), where the view of social work activity accepted by
the researcher vitiates any use that might have been obtained

from patients' views. For example, she analyses patients' descriptions of social work help in terms of whether it fitted the model of material or emotional help. On finding that only three out of twenty-eight patients can be exclusively classified in one or the other category, she dubiously concludes that the figures 'reflect both the patients' recognition of the psycho-social nature of social work, and the medical social workers' adherence to this reality'.[15]

The recent research by Cohen suggests that the difficulty experienced by users of a social service in finding a language with which to talk about and evaluate services is a further obstacle to discovering the clients' views. He illustrates their lack of vocabulary and familiarity with the services, and the feeling that the actions of social workers were either arbitrary or absurd.[16]

This problem may have been greater for Cohen's sample of retarded mothers than for other groups, but this can scarcely be said of other difficulties experienced by these same women in giving a clear evaluation of the services received. The very idea of evaluating was alien to them – a reluctance to criticise which stemmed in part from the feeling some women had that the service received was a favour rather than a benefit to which they had entitlement. This appears to reflect feelings about the individual presenting the service rather than the adequacy of provision. In Cohen's words, 'If the service is presented by someone regarded as likeable and well meaning the clients may feel disloyal or unfair to him if they criticise the service he represents.'

This particular problem pervades the literature. McKay records the difficulty she experienced in differentiating between consumers' attitudes towards the department, the services received and the individual worker.[17] Bayley found that the appraisal given by the families of mentally handicapped people of the service provided by mental welfare officers depended on the quality of the current relationship with a particular officer.[18] Again, Voelcker, in his study of how the parents of boys appearing in juvenile court understood the procedures, found that parents had a favourable picture of individual probation officers, but little sympathy for probation as a method of treatment.[19]

A further problem arises when the assumptions which lie behind apparently straightforward questions may not be shared by the interviewee. For instance, social work may be viewed by the client as a bartering relationship, entered into for the purpose of gaining specific material ends. The relationship itself may be regarded simply as a means to an end and not part of the end itself. Hence, 'If social work is seen as the "interference" one has to tolerate in order to receive the service, the consumer's evaluation may concern only a part of what the researcher defines as the service. . . . [We] must know what the consumer sees as the boundaries of service.'[20]

Voelcker falls into the same trap of interpreting respondents' comments in the light of assumptions they do not share. He remarks that only two of the parents 'realised the impossibility [*sic*] of keeping to a close schedule' in court hearings. Again, when discussing their views about the methods of disposal used by the magistrates, he concludes that 'many parents have either a wrong or confused interpretation of all types of disposal'.[21] Voelcker apparently has failed to realise that views and activities which seem random to an outsider have order and pattern for a participant.

Finally, pressures of an organisational and professional nature may distort the voice of the client so that it simply echoes back whatever the professionals or the organisations wish to hear. When this happens, attempts to make sense of the client's viewpoint are foredoomed. For example, Butrym tries more than once to explain away disagreements in the responses of patient and social worker. In dividing reasons for referral to the social worker into the two categories of environmental and emotional reasons, a disagreement level of 43 per cent between patients and M.S.W.s is dismissed as not reflecting 'a basic disagreement, but rather a difference in emphasis which hardly seems surprising. . . .' Again, when asking patients 'what sort of training do you think an almoner ought to have?', Butrym is making the assumption, shared by her fellow professionals, that some sort of training is a good thing. This may have been self-evident to her, but it was an assumption clearly not shared by the patients, who had an ideal picture of an M.S.W. which did not include systematic or prolonged training. Small wonder that only a handful of patients could give a clear answer to the question.[22]

Thus, there is a considerable number of reasons which make it difficult to discern the genuine voice of the client.

Utilising Consumer Opinion

We have already remarked that some studies àre concerned only superficially to work consumer opinion into their recommendations. Also, Gill's study is aimed only generally at evaluating consumer opinion of grass roots policy changes. However, the assumption is clearly present in all the literature under review that consumer opinion can be used in the formulation of social policy.

Despite this, the precise ways in which consumer opinion is to be utilised are rarely made explicit. Mayer and Timms recognise limitations in the extent to which client appraisals shape policy decisions without specifying these limitations in more than general terms,[23] but this is a step further than most studies.

Platt's analysis of the research done by the Institute of Community Studies makes fruitful suggestions about restrictions on the use of consumer opinion as a guide to policy.

Limitations on use of consumer opinion
First, there should be no other significant groups of consumers whose viewpoints differ from those in the sample. Other things being equal, if there are such groups an equally good case can be made out for acting on *their* opinions.[24] Unless this point is recognised, minority opinion among consumer groups is likely to exercise a disproportionate influence or be completely overlooked. This condition is more likely to be met when the consumers in question are members of an easily identifiable group. For this reason, Bayley's study convinces one that the particular group of consumers has been adequately sampled. The condition has not been met in the studies by Triseliotis and Mayer and Timms. Triseliotis samples adult adoptees who applied to the Registrar General in Edinburgh, asking to be supplied with information from their original birth entries. He is unable to say whether this group of people were similar in important respects to adoptees who did not make a search, and, in view of the fact that people applying to Register House are only a small proportion of adult adoptees, we have no grounds for thinking that the suggestions they make are typical. The same point applies to Mayer and Timms' sample of past clients of the Family Welfare Association.

In the study by McKay, the researchers obviously feel that the sample of clients ought to be comparable with a wider population. Hence she spends some time comparing the client group with the population of Southampton as a whole. However, the reasons for doing so are not clear – as one would expect, the two groups are different, but what implication this has for using client opinion for administrative changes in the social services department, we are not told.

A second condition that must be met is that consumer opinions should be relatively permanent. If their opinions are responsive to changes in their circumstances, opinions may change, even as a result of policy changes designed to satisfy their opinion. A number of the studies under review do not give satisfactory grounds for thinking that this condition has been met. Indeed, the only study that explicitly recognises the problem is that by McKay, where a follow-up study is planned, to monitor changes in opinion. The difficulty of meeting this condition should not blind us to the fact that opinions collected in circumstances where appraisals of the situation are likely to be fluid[25] are poor indices of general and long-run commitments held by consumers.

Thirdly, consumer opinion must rest upon informed consideration of the possible range of alternatives for dealing with the problem. In McKay's study, it was found that clarity of expectations about what help would be given was related in various ways to the amount of prior knowledge clients possessed about the department. People unclear about what kind of service is available are likely to be still less clear when asked to make suggestions about improvements in the service. This has consequences of considerable significance if the opinions of consumers are to be acted upon, in that resulting proposals are liable to take the existing pattern of life as given, thus producing an inbuilt conservatism. Causes become defined conventionally and the scope of the search for reform is limited.[26] The study by Butrym is particularly weak in this respect. The opinions of patients were ill-informed, and they had no conception of the range of alternative policy and administrative changes, or of the likely consequences of acting on the opinions they were asked to express. In Triseliotis' research, radical proposals are ruled out by the fact that 70 per cent of adoptees wanted the existing system of access to the original birth entry to be continued.[27]

This set of conditions may appear unduly stringent and restrictive. Indeed, in some cases effective rejoinders can be made. For example, speculation by participants in a social setting, about the causes and consequences of aspects of that setting, can partake of the character of a self-fulfilling prophecy. In W. I. Thomas' words, 'if men define situations as real they are real in their consequences'. Policy-makers need to be aware of such effects. In addition, it might be replied that these conditions only apply when the researcher transmits the opinions of respondents without comment. Alternatively, the researcher may collect data on the *attitudes* and *behaviour* of consumers in policy-relevant areas, rather than their *opinion*, and make recommendations which he thinks likely to be acceptable to the respondent. This second rejoinder is often effective, in that it assumes consumers' wishes should be deferred to, but avoids the assumption that consumers know how these wishes can best be achieved. It is no longer necessary to ask that consumers know the range of alternatives in front of them.

The literature under review cannot be rigidly allocated to one of these categories or the other, in that most studies contain recommendations based on a mixture of consumer opinion and attitudes and behaviour. The work by Bayley and Cohen relies largely on attitudes and behaviour, and is stronger as a consequence. Bayley, for instance, delineates in telling detail the experience of mothers caring for their seriously handicapped children at home. He shows the crucial significance of the mother's attitude, and the way in which families manage the 'daily grind' of looking after their children by creating a 'structure for coping'. Occasional visits of emotional support from social workers are inappropriate, when 'structural' help is needed that is regular, reliable and punctual, and directly related to the family's structure for coping with the daily grind and mundane slog of caring for the handicapped. He develops the concept of interweaving the informal helping and caring processes already active in society, with the social services, and radically criticises the inadequacy of seeing voluntary service as supplementary to the official services, rather than the basis upon which all other care is built. His recommendations for a scheme

of residential care in locally based hostels differ from the government White Paper, *Better Services for the Mentally Handicapped*,[28]
which advocates full hospital care for the profoundly handicapped. One of the reasons for this is that by examining the
attitudes and behaviour of the families in his sample, Bayley –
unlike the White Paper – has built the families' perceptions of
what they need into his recommendations.[29]

However, there are two conditions which must still be met.
First, there should be no other significant consumer groups
whose attitudes and behaviour differ. Secondly, their attitudes
and behaviour must be relatively permanent. This second
desideratum may be difficult to achieve in that the researcher
and policy-maker may wish to assume that behaviour and
attitudes have been freely chosen by the consumer. Platt's comment is apposite. 'It is dangerous to infer that wishes, especially
"real" (for example unverbalised) ones, are expressed in behaviour.'[30] While certain consequences may follow from the
consumers' behaviour, these consequences may not represent
their intentions. They may be latent functions of the consumers'
behaviour, neither consciously intended or even perceived by
them.

In our discussion of clients' opinions it has been assumed that
the opinions elicited are about policies yet to be chosen. This is,
in fact, the case in some studies, but often, as in the cases of
Goldberg, Gill and McKay, opinions asked for refer to past or
current policies, rather than to possible future ones. It is decep-
tive to think that recommendations based on such opinions are
accurate representations of what the client would choose.
Opinion about the future cannot automatically be assumed
from opinions about the past or present. Dissatisfaction with
the present does not necessarily indicate preference for future
change and to assume otherwise is to run the risk of undue
radicalism.[31]

Research Methods and Policy

The discussion has so far centred on the logical problems involved in deriving policy recommendations from consumer
opinion. There is also a number of points about the research

methods adopted in the literature under review which bear directly on the utility of subsequent prescriptions for change.

For instance, the studies are typically descriptive, and explanatory material, if it is present at all, is at a very general level. It is out of place here to discuss the development of theorising in this research, beyond making the point that a clear purpose guiding the collection of data is necessary if useful policy decisions are to be forthcoming. The research is at its most interesting and provocative in discussing or speculating about explanations.

This point becomes significant when we examine the analysis of material, and the tendency in some cases to resort to 'ideal type' explanations. When summary statements are made about a whole sample, it tends to imply not merely that a majority, or all of them, share certain characteristics now, but that they are likely to do so in the future. 'To make more differentiated statements indicates the dependence of current characteristics on contingencies, and so is likely to imply superior predictions and explanations as well as more accurate description.'[32]

For example, Triseliotis reports that 70 per cent of his sample wanted the existing Scottish system of access to original birth entries to be retained and improved. This becomes 'almost all of the adoptees' in his discussion, and recommendations are made on the basis of majority opinion in the sample. Again, 80 per cent of the adoptees found the search for their origins helpful in one sense or another, and the 20 per cent 'deviant cases' receive relatively little weight.[33] If individual preferences are used as a basis for social policy, then the possibility of conflicting preferences is raised. General policy will be unable to resolve such conflicts. Gill's study is a further example of explanations being presented as ideal types. Indeed, the only study to deal with this issue in a systematic fashion is that by Mayer and Timms, where the opinions of working-class clients are classified according to whether they were satisfied or dissatisfied with the help, and whether the problems they presented to the agency were predominantly material or interpersonal in character. The use of classificatory devices is clearly essential in this kind of research, although the criteria used by these authors for distinguishing clients on the grounds of satisfaction with service received did not prove highly discriminating, and furthermore, they found it more difficult to obtain good accounts from satisfied clients than from dissatisfied ones. In later discussion of their research, this has led to a concentration of attention on the findings from disenchanted clients.[34]

A second criticism of the research methods used in these studies is the over-reliance on intensive interviewing as a means of tapping the views of client participants. While this is one important way of delineating the distinctive perspectives of all participants in a particular setting, it provides a poor independent measure of what actually happens. If the researcher and policy-maker do not wish to assume that the participants' accounts are the only valid ones, the use of different data-collection methods is indicated, which complement rather than replace interviewing methods. Participant-observation methods, although subject to various kinds of bias, are a fruitful means of obtaining qualitative assessments of settings and actors in those settings, which are partially independent of the actors' own perspectives. The studies under review make no use of participant observation for this particular purpose.[35]

The third point on methodology refers to the sampling methods used. We made the point earlier that there should be no other significant group of clients whose opinions or attitudes and behaviour differ from the sample. Yet this is only a part of the problem, in that samples consisting only of consumers, however representative they may be, inevitably give a partial and at times misleading picture of the current state of affairs. Consequently, they beg the question of which set of values should be applied to policy change, by familiarising the researcher with only one set of values apart from his own. The policy-maker needs to know the opinions of 'producers' and the general public if he is to avoid acting on a too narrow picture of the current situation.[36] And he needs to consider whose value-judgements may be regarded as relevant. Present or future populations? Those directly affected or also those indirectly affected. In the case of Triseliotis' study, for example, the opinion of adopters, natural parents and adoptees who make no search for information about their origins would have been equally relevant to the policy-maker.

Unless an overall perspective is achieved, based on accounts of subjective opposites, research studies are bound to serve the interests of social criticism more than the interests of objective analysis.[37] The implication of this for research methodology is that sampling must be based on a population of *relationships* and not *individuals*. In virtually every case, the work under review is based on samples of individuals, and yet the researchers are generally interested in drawing conclusions about a research population of problems, each of which is perceived by social workers and clients. In such cases the conclusions cannot be upheld from the data. The study of patients referred to medical social workers is a partial exception to this criticism,[38] but the weaknesses in the author's overall research strategy minimise the potential value of the sampling method. Again, McKay's study in Southampton is part of a wider survey of social workers and clients,[39] but social worker–client relationships as such were not sampled. Gill's study of 'Whitegate' is also based solely on consumers, when the opportunity to sample relationships provided by the institutional setting could have resolved some of the problems this sampling technique involves in studies of fieldwork agencies. The weakness is particularly apparent when he comes to discuss staff–inmate relationships in the school.[40] Mayer and Timms base their book almost entirely on a sample of consumers. At points in the book they appear to realise the defects of the method (for example p. 140), and, as they remark, much of the book is about insight-orientated casework procedures. A small sample of caseworkers was made, but this appears as something of an afterthought, and we have no definite knowledge how the information from this sample has been used by the authors. Marsden's work on fatherless families shows a careful regard for problems of interpretation and utilisation of data, and the general failure to obtain information from D.H.S.S. officials, etc., complementary to that from the mothers, was not easily avoidable.[41]

Conclusions

It has been argued that a loosely related body of research has been carried out in social work, in which the focus of attention is on the opinions, attitudes or behaviour of the people who receive particular services. One of the main purposes of this research is the formulation of recommendations for policy change. If such research is to make a useful contribution to the development of social policy, it must come to terms with two problems. First, it is problematic to know when the opinion of consumers has been meaningfully appreciated. Secondly, the utilisation of consumer opinion entails careful research strategy if it is to be fruitfully achieved.

The danger of relying overmuch on consumer opinion is a new one for social work to face. Whereas in the past social workers have tended to regard case accounts given by professionals as records of what really happened, we need to avoid the opposite trap of regarding client accounts in a similar light. For the present, it is probably best for the researcher and policy-maker to bear in mind the four elements of the client's perception of what service is offered, the worker's perception of the service offered, the official description of the service, and the actuality of what service is given.[42]

The positive values of consumer research need little elaboration. They sensitise the public and the welfare professions to the human consequences of social planning, and draw social workers' attention to subcultural differences between them and those they try to help. This implies the need for a better climate of understanding, and therefore the need for better information flow from social service departments about the whole range of services. Consumer surveys are only one of the possible devices for attaining this goal. Direct representation of consumers on local authority committees may serve to convey to the committees the feelings expressed in the studies reviewed here. However, although this possibility has been actively canvassed,[43] such individuals are unlikely to be representative of wider client groups, in the sense of being typical clients, and there remains a difficult link to be forged between the concepts of popular participation and traditional representative democracy.

Having recognised that client and professional opinion are unlikely to be completely consensual, it follows that policies should provide an element of choice, which can only be provided if alternative service patterns are available to individuals. All-or-none solutions, while cheaper to operate, ignore the real diversity of preference among service consumers.

Some difficulties are likely to remain, as, for example, the risk of treating opinion about the present as if it was prescription for the future, and the liability to inbuilt conservatism arising from the fact that clients are unlikely to be acquainted with the range of alternatives open to them.[44] Further, bias is always likely in consumer surveys carried out by consumer groups or social service departments. The research is at its best when it comes to terms with its research method and does not purport to give rigorous measures of the incidence of opinions in the population, and when client opinion is utilised in conjunction with other kinds of research evidence.[45]

Part Three

Action Research

7 Government Against Poverty in School and Community*

A. H. Halsey

President Johnson's declaration in 1964 of 'unconditional war on poverty in America' inaugurated a plethora of legislation, governmental programmes and social science literature. British government and British social science have followed a parallel course. A new generation has rediscovered poverty. But the new partnership of politicians and social scientists is no guarantee that poverty, especially the racial conflict in America now and in Britain in the future for which 'poverty' increasingly serves as a euphemism, will be banished from these rich societies. On the side of government the Democratic and Labour parties have held and lost office, leaving behind no dramatic victories. On the side of the social sciences, conceptual debate remains more distinguished by volume than clarity. And, as Daniel P. Moynihan has pointed out, 'it is the persisting "social fact" of this literature that it not only involves a discussion by individuals who are successful about individuals who are not, but also

* Reprinted from D. Wedderburn (ed.), *Poverty, Inequality and Class Structure*, Cambridge University Press, 1974, pp. 123–39, with the permission of the publishers and the author.

representatives of unusually successful *groups* dissecting unusually unsuccessful ones'.[1]

My task in this chapter is to comment on the British Educational Priority Area and Community Development Project programmes which began, respectively, in 1968 and 1969.[2] But at the outset it is important to underline that it is not revealed truth that poverty (however defined) can be abolished by the methods we are to discuss, under the governments we serve or with ourselves and our colleagues in the social services as instruments. It may be so, and the success of the Education Priority Area and Community Development Project programmes depends upon determination that it is so. Nevertheless it can be argued that no serious changes are possible in the present structure of rewards and opportunities without revolutionary advances in both social scientific theory and the structure of government. It can be more plausibly argued that intellectuals have never conducted a successful social revolution, though they have often played a crucial part in undermining belief in the legitimacy of political orders which are subsequently overthrown. It can more plausibly still be argued that the apparatus of social administration constitutes a large vested interest in the *status quo*. The young and impecunious family caseworker will not easily see herself as the agent of an exploiting class. Nevertheless we cannot ignore the power of the interests of those who run the bureaucracies of welfare – power which expresses itself ideologically if not materially in the shaping of policy and practice. It must be asked how far the established interests of professional social workers carry with them incapacities and ideological barriers to effective work on the abolition of poverty. How effectively can professional social workers communicate with members of the sub-working class? Advances in training methods have undoubtedly been made from this point of view in recent years. Nevertheless, despite the laudable drive towards professionalisation of the social services, it has to be recognised that trained incapacities and vested interests are also involved. Thus experience in the American poverty programmes has shown that in some circumstances trained sub-professionals may be more successful than professionals. For example, Frank Reissman, in describing the 'home-maker' element in the Mobilisation for Youth Programme (which uses sub-professionally trained lower-class mothers to help others with their family problems) offers the following quotation from a middle-class social worker who is comparing the professional with the ancillary worker:

> Indigenous people could teach professional staff a great deal if the latter were willing to learn ... they don't perceive people as problems, or at least disagree with professionals about what constitutes a problem ... Somehow, Mrs Smith was less forbidding to the home-maker than the caseworker, who was frightened of her. She was well-meaning, easily misunderstood, and temperamental. But she wasn't 'paranoid, rejecting, abusive'. Mrs Casey was 'a fine person who cared for her children' and that was the main thing even if she had four illegitimate offspring. To the social worker she was depressed, practically ego-less, 'so self-destructive'.[3]

And later he again quotes the social worker on quality of communication between professionals and their 'clients':

> The lack of felt, in contrast to actual, social distance between home-maker and client is evident in the results from several factors. I sometimes feel like an inhibiting influence when I go along to introduce a home-maker to a client. When I leave, they break out into their own language and vernacular ... empathy rather than sympathy sometimes comes more naturally to the home-maker than the professional social worker.[4]

These problems are by no means exclusively American. Class and status impede relationships, even the relationships of those who are professionally committed to overcoming status barriers.

Other examples relating to the effectiveness of social work in this particular context appear in an unpublished study of some of the problems of immigrants in England[5] which shows that many statutory and professional workers are extremely ignorant of the special difficulties experienced by immigrants and by coloured people who are British-born and some are prejudiced and unsympathetic towards coloured people.

> Mrs Brown was another West Indian whose problems elicited little sympathy from the various social workers who knew her. She was struggling to bring up five children in two rooms on

'the assistance' with the aid of a succession of men-friends. Her health was poor, and whenever she went into hospital the children had to go into care. Then Mrs Brown would continue drawing her social security benefits and children's allowances, finding out too late that she had spent or sent to Barbados money she should never have received in the first place. Now, because the relations she had left them with had died, and they were in orphanages, she wanted to bring her four older children to Britain. This wish no one seemed to regard seriously, and Mrs Brown has so far been unable to get the most basic information about how it could be realised. The health visitor, for example, had promised to 'make enquiries' of a missionary recently returned from the Caribbean, but admitted that she had so far forgotten to do anything about this. The headmaster of the children's school had also once promised to help, but time had passed, and he now supposed her distress must have abated, and he laughed and said, 'Oh, you don't want to worry about her, she's had that problem for two years.' Meanwhile, two of the children have passed their sixteenth birthdays and were no longer eligible to come to Britain as dependants.

The negligent lack of sympathy described here is certainly not typical of all those engaged in social work. Such an example does, however, remind us that we cannot assume the existence of a perfect instrument of official social policy in the existing staff of the social services. There are, in any case, much more formidable obstacles to the welfare society – that is the society in which there is no poverty: and not least among these is the existence of the welfare state itself.

However, what we have to consider is the development of governmentally inspired and financed programmes against poverty which are posited on the assumption that the welfare society may be attained through the legitimate use of the existing political structure. This assumption may, of course, prove historically to have been the most interesting facet of the Educational Priority Area and Community Development Project programmes: as a basis for the abolition of poverty it may turn out to have been nothing more than a shibboleth of liberal society in decline.

Experimental Social Administration

However, within the limits of this political assumption easily the most interesting feature of these programmes is that they postulate a new relation between social science and social policy. They assert the idea that reforms may be seriously conducted through social science experiment. The traditional political mode of reform is to announce a nostrum which is held to be certain in its cure of the social ills to which it is addressed. Here instead there is the promise of a new style in politics and administration – a commitment to inquiry rather than an assumption of omniscience. The idea is that among possible policies about which little is known, a rational plan A seems to be the most viable. The politician commits himself to trying plan A in an experimentally devised situation, but at the same time commits himself to abandoning it if evaluation by the most valid social science techniques show that it does not work and ought therefore to give way to plan B.

The emancipation for administrative civil servants which is implied by this idea can scarcely be exaggerated. It could and should mean for them a quite new relationship with ministers, a substitution of positive for negative responsibility of a kind which they have seldom been challenged to enjoy in the past. It also implies a strengthening of partnership with social scientists in the universities – a development of intellectual exchange from which both may hugely profit.

The role of the social scientists in these projects is crucial. There is no space here to consider the technical problems of evaluating social action. It must suffice to remark that only in a loose sense can these projects be described as experimental and to point summarily to the immense difficulties involved. The laboratory is, by definition, natural and not experimental. There are, for example, political as well as academic determinants of localities chosen for action research. The desired outcomes of action are often imprecisely defined and in any case resistant to clear measurement. The inputs are not completely controlled and the relation between input and output is to that extent indeterminant. We have neither the intellectual tools nor the qualified social scientists demanded by the task. Nevertheless, the challenge is irresistible. It is to become seriously involved in the development of social policy, its definition of ends, its planning and allocation of means and its measurement of results. The task in the case of the Educational Priority Area (E.P.A.) and Community Development Project (C.D.P.) programmes is to produce a theory of poverty and to test it in the very real world of the urban twilight zones.

The Theory of Poverty

What then is a viable explanation of poverty? First, poverty is not adequately conceived in the singular, either in its manifestations or its causes. Multiple and related causes must be recognised, with the implication that a war on poverty is indeed a war and not a single battle. Thus a panel of the Social Science Research Council recently produced a discussion of current research in which six types of poverty are delineated:

(a) crisis poverty;
(b) long-term dependency;
(c) life-cycle poverty;
(d) depressed area poverty;
(e) down-town poverty; and
(f) 'the culture of poverty'.[6]

The complex typology recognised by the expert committee, and the fact that the six types are not clearly distinguishable in practice, must be borne in mind in considering the E.P.A. and C.D.P. projects which address themselves primarily to the fifth type, 'down-town' poverty, and assume the validity of a description of the poor which permits effective intervention using 'communities' or local administrative units as the appropriate arena of battle. On this view the problem is formulated as one where modern urban conditions tend to concentrate social deprivation geographically, especially in the decaying inner ring of conurbations, in such a way as to reduce the quality of environmental service and opportunity. All local institutions, it is argued, are consequently defective – the family, the school, the welfare agencies, the job market and the recreational organisation. Moreover the situation is seen as self-perpetuating; those most capable of doing so move out to take advantage of the opportunities provided elsewhere, be they residents moving to better jobs or better houses or be they school teachers or social workers who live in more salubrious districts and are concerned with this alien territory only in their professional capacities. And the least capable move in, those most in need of and least able to avail themselves of education, housing, jobs and other publicly provided amenities and opportunities (for example immigrants and the downwardly mobile). Thus the inhabitants of the priority or development areas are thought of, correctly or incorrectly, as a sub-working class formed out of selective migration with a distinctive set of economic, social and cultural attributes.

The theory of 'down-town' poverty begins with an elaboration of this description. Its factual base is surprisingly little explored in Britain. In America the description is heavily influenced by concern with the social conditions of negro ghettoes in the northern industrial cities, and the question must therefore be raised as to its applicability to British cities, either generally or more particularly to the districts inhabited by immigrants whose origins and characteristics cannot be exactly equated with those of American negro migrants from the southern cities. It is significant that the label given to this kind of poverty by the S.S.R.C. panel is clearly a transatlantic importation: and though Americans have, in the past few years, begun to produce a description of their version of the sub-working class,[7] to transplant the description without careful inquiry could be disastrous for both analysis and remedy.

On the basis of a review of American social science literature, Rossi and Blum have summarised the characteristics of the poor as follows.

1. *Labour-Force Participation.* Long period of unemployment and/or intermittent employment. Public assistance is frequently a major source of income for extended periods.

2. *Occupational Participation.* When employed, persons hold jobs at the lowest levels of skills, for example, domestic service, unskilled labour, menial service jobs, and farm labour.

3. *Family and Interpersonal Relations.* High rates of marital instability (desertion, divorce, separation), high incidence of

households headed by females, high rates of illegitimacy; unstable and superficial interpersonal relationships character-ised by considerable suspicion of persons outside the imme-diate household.

4. *Community Characteristics.* Residential areas with very poorly developed voluntary associations and low levels of participa-tion in such local voluntary associations as exist.

5. *Relationship to Larger Society.* Little interest in, or knowledge of, the larger society and its events; some degree of alienation from the larger society.

6. *Value Orientations.* A sense of helplessness and low sense of personal efficacy; dogmatism and authoritarianism in politi-cal ideology; fundamentalist religious views, with some strong inclinations towards belief in magical practices. Low 'need achievement' and low levels of aspirations for the self.

As a general description of the poor in any advanced indus-trial society this summary would command the assent of most social scientists. However, the description of down-town poverty which has developed during the 1960s in relation to the Ameri-can poverty programme is more problematical. It is well ex-pressed by H. Gans, who distinguished between a working class and a lower class.

The former is distinguished by relatively stable semi-skilled or skilled blue-collar employment and a way of life that centres on the family circle, or extended family. The lower class is characterised by temporary, unstable employment in un-skilled – and the most menial – blue-collar jobs and by a way of life equally marked by instability. Largely as a result of a man's instability, the lower-class family is often matrifocal or female-based. This is most marked among the negro popula-tion, in which the woman has been the dominant figure since the days of slavery, but it can also be found in other groups suffering from male occupational instability. Although this type of family organisation had some stable and positive features, especially for its female members, the hypothesis has been suggested that it raises boys who lack the self-image, the aspiration, and the motivational structure that would help them to develop the skills necessary to function in the modern job market. Also it may prevent boys from participating in a 'normal' family relationship in adulthood, thus perpetuating the pattern for another generation. These conditions are, of course, exacerbated by racial and class discrimination, low income, slum and overcrowded housing conditions, as well as illness and other deprivations which bring about frequent crises.[8]

The matrifocal family is also described in English studies, for example Madeline Kerr's *Ship Street*, but the essential point here is the juxtaposition of uncertain occupational opportunities with an unstable family structure. In this connection S. M. Miller has drawn the contrast between W. F. Whyte's *Street Corner Society* which described men in an Italian slum in Boston in the late 1930s and Elliott Liebow's *Tally's Corner* (1967) which offers a vivid portrait of a Washington negro ghetto in a blighted section of the inner city in the early 1960s.

Whyte's men were unemployed casualties of the Depression, and members of strongly-knit families. Most of them went on later to employment. On Tally's Corner the men have much less favourable relationships with each other and with their families; their hopes for a different and better future are constantly frustrated. The shift in these two books from the emerging Italian temporarily blocked by an economic depression to the thwarted negro of the affluent society captures the change in the social issues facing American society.[9]

The theory is then, that of a vicious cycle of lack of opportunity and lack of aspiration, so that the 'pathologies' of rejection of the world and the search for gratification in alcohol and drugs, the apathy, drifting and dependence on public aid, are to be seen as adaptations to a life of exclusion from the main stream of society.

It is an open question as to how far British city slums resemble either those of Boston in the 1930s or Washington D.C. in the 1960s, though the signs that coloured immigrants are developing into a 'thwarted social stratum' are clear enough in E. J. B. Rose's *Colour and Citizenship*. But whether or not the theory can be properly applied to the British scene, it corresponds in many respects to the S.S.R.C.'s sixth type – the 'culture of poverty' – and as such has been the subject of a developing debate in America during the 1960s. There is consensus that the poor are different. But the explanation of these differences by those who insist on a situational rather than a cultural theory have profoundly different implications for the strategies of action against poverty.

The culture of poverty approach[10] insists in its simplest form that the poor are different not primarily because of low income but because they have been habituated to poverty and have developed a sub-culture of values adapted to these conditions which they then pass on to their children. It was this definition of the problem which dominated the war on poverty in America and the provisions of the Economic Opportunity Act of 1964 – hence the emphasis on community action and social work rather than on employment policies and the redistribution of income.[11] Recent contributors, however, have returned in one form or another to a situational approach, and this is reflected in the essays put together by Moynihan, by anthropologists like Walter Miller or sociologists like H. Gans or O. D. Duncan. Thus Duncan asserts that 'if there were any chance that the slogan-makers and the policy-builders would heed the implications of social research, the first lesson for them to learn would be that *poverty is not a trait but a condition*'.[12]

Out of this debate something like a constructive synthesis seems to have emerged which makes it clear that the 'poverties' to which urban industrial populations are prone must be understood to have their origins in both situational and cultural characteristics of those minorities which suffer disadvantage and discrimination and to have its cures in both economic and cultural reform, not only at the local or community level but also in the total structure of society.

Community

In attempting to apply the theory of poverty to social action in the context of the E.P.A. and C.D.P. projects, it must be recognised that both the American war on poverty and the transatlantic theorising which we have discussed rely heavily on the idea of community. This word is of ancient usage in sociology. Unfortunately it has so many meanings as to be meaningless.[13] Of course the locality can be a useful natural laboratory for the exploration of sociological hypotheses, as Margaret Stacey recently argued. But she is surely right, too, in concluding that 'it is doubtful whether the concept "community" refers to a useful abstraction'. All attempts to give this concept a precise empirical meaning have failed and certainly in complex societies there is no total social system, that is a social network in which the whole of one's life may be passed, which is also a local territorial unit.

The interest of the concept is fourfold in relation to our present purposes. First, it contains the persistent residue of a romantic protest against the complexity of modern urban society – the idea of a decentralised world in which neighbours could and should corporately satisfy each other's needs and legitimate demands for health, wealth and happiness. There may perhaps even be a special attractiveness in this idea for the administrator of welfare who is simultaneously guilty about his role in the perpetuation of large-scale bureaucracy and at the same time oppressed by the complex technical and human difficulties in the way of pursuing samaritan goals through impersonal means.

The second aspect is more mundane. Americans seem to use the word 'community' out of traditional every-day usage to refer to the small local settlement, typically placed on the frontier of civilisation and remote from the settled centre of government, which has to face the problem of creating and maintaining an ordered social life in the context of commitment to the values of individual freedom and especially freedom from arbitrary central authority. These two aspects together spell paradox for a governmentally managed programme of social action. They seem somehow to call for an administration which is dedicated to get rid of itself; and in this sense the idea is parallel with the Marxist hope that the State will wither away with the creation of a communist society.

The third, and perhaps most interesting, aspect of the contemporary idea of community is its anarchism. I do not mean to refer here to the familiar and traditional suspicion and hostility of local groups to distant government – though this is not to say that either Welsh or Czech nationalism are of no significance.

I have in mind Edward Shils' discussion of student unrest.[14] He points to the significance of affluence for the first generation of its full beneficiaries. It is precisely among the socially selected body of university students that the world's problems can be most plausibly interpreted in terms of social as opposed to economic relations, psychological as opposed to physical un-freedoms, status as opposed to class. Theirs is the first generation to be brought up under the illusion that society is possible without authority. 'In a variety of ways this was the uniquely indulged generation. Parents who were in a state of unprecedented prosperity were persuaded of the merits of hedonism and were capable of giving some reality to its precepts in the raising of children.' For some, therefore, the future holds not 'the danger of death by starvation, but the danger of death by boredom'.

Of course, as Shils points out,

> These views of life, society and the university are not by any means shared by the entire generation of students today in the Western countries. Most of the students in most of the universities still share in the older culture. None the less, the new 'communitarian', 'participatory' culture – which is really the romantic hunger for Gemeinschaft on a more grandiose scale – pervades a substantial minority of the intelligent, sensitive and hyper-active students.

Is it too far-fetched to suggest that this kind of sentiment has also found its way into the new fashions of social work which we are discussing? It is detectable among some of the social work students, including some of the most able. It is one of the elements in the ideology of some of the voluntary community workers in Notting Hill and elsewhere. It may even have some affinity with the vulgarised Freudianism which is sometimes expressed in theories of social casework.

Fourthly, the community is attractive as a framework for social action in that it is a territorial unit in which both political and economic functions are performed. The social services, housing and education, are under the direct control of local government authorities and it would therefore seem to make sense that if something can be done about these political units an appreciable impact on the problem of poverty could be achieved.

But the apparent directness of the community approach may be misleading. As Peter Rossi has argued

> The reasons for social pathology lie in the past and present operations of the total social system of the nation or at least region. The best one can do with social services is to equip a few individuals with enough in the way of skills and knowledge to be able to make their way out of their ghettoes. The opening up of employment opportunities, the achievement of a more equitable distribution of income, and the overcoming of very real barriers of discrimination on a large scale are goals which cannot be pursued successfully within a territory of residence.[15]

It is for this reason, Rossi argues, that the American community action programmes which started out to be mainly the co-ordination and supplementation of existing social services, often ended up in practice as providing the basis for parapolitical and political organisations.

> This is also the reason for the failure of social action programmes directed at changing the quality and quantity of social services delivered to localities. No amount of upgrading of skills or increased quality of education is going to make a dent in a society which does not need the newly skilled workers and derives at least some status benefit from maintaining a depressed group in the society . . . We all gain from poverty: the occupational system has a supply of underpaid workers to do the dirty work of the society; the respectable working class have the joy of a comparatively higher status; and the health, welfare and education industries have clients to fuss over.

Nevertheless despite these limitations we are dealing now on both sides of the Atlantic with an amalgam of rhetoric and reality under the heading of community action programmes. These are defined in the United States under Title II of the *Economic Opportunity Act* of 1964 as

> a programme which mobilises and utilises, in an attack on poverty, public and private resources of any urban or rural or

combined urban and rural geographical area (referred to in
this Title as 'community') . . . to give promise of progress
towards an elimination of poverty through developing employment opportunities, improving human performance,
motivation and productivity and bettering the conditions
under which people live, learn and work.

Similarly the British Home Secretary, in announcing in Parlia-
ment on 16 July 1969 the names of the first three local authorities
(Coventry, Liverpool and Southwark) who had agreed to take
part in the Community Development Project, described it as 'a
neighbourhood-based experiment aimed at finding new ways of
meeting the needs of people living in areas of high social
deprivation: by bringing together the work of all the social
services under the leadership of a special project team and also
by tapping resources of self-help and mutual help which may
exist among the people of the neighbourhood'.

The double objective, with its underlying conflict, should be
noticed in both cases. Resources from central government are
recognised as necessary, but the main emphasis is put on tapping
local and private 'community' resources. There is a drive
towards reducing the burden on the national exchequer as well
as towards the promotion of local autonomy. As a *Guardian*
reporter put it when the British scheme was first announced in
January 1969, 'the problem is not just one of shortage of welfare
funds. People need to be helped to find solutions in their own
way, and to create community services at a neighbourhood
level. Otherwise the fear is that welfare payments are merely
poured down a bottomless pit.'[16] But surely participation and the
growth of consciousness among the organised poor will also
generate demand for more resources from government over and
above whatever new energies for community self-help or re-
generation are produced by the action projects?

Application of the Theory

In social action, research theory is applied in a political context.
Within the framework of the theoretical discussion of poverty
there are large political implications according to whether the

emphasis is put on the structure of opportunities or the raising of levels of motivation. Clearly the E.P.A. and C.D.P. projects are so conceived – in being confined to small geographical areas and endowed with very limited resources – that they have to focus mainly on the second alternative. A basic assumption of the E.P.A. programmes is that the most advantageous point at which to break into the vicious poverty circle is in early childhood, in the primary school or in the pre-school period: and this approach tends to lead to considerable emphasis on work with families, thus raising fundamentally the question of limits to the right of the State, through its agencies to intervene in the relation between parents and children.

But quite apart from this fundamental issue there are three partial interpretations of the general theory which may be distinguished and which have political consequences. On a first view, the cause of poverty is 'cultural deprivation' in the sense of inadequate social parenthood, and the cure consists of improved socialisation with the implication that the main thrust must be towards family casework. In the E.P.A. context this means that the sub-working-class family is held to be the major villain of the piece, failing to provide the early training in literacy, numeracy, and acceptance of work and achievement habits which constitute the normal upbringing of the middle-class child and which prepare the child to take advantage of the opportunities provided in school. An example and an elaboration of this point of view directed towards the more pathological aspect of 'cultural deprivation' would be Sir Alec Clegg and Barbara Megson's *Children in Trouble*, with its description of parental neglect, cruelty and workshyness.

The second interpretation focuses on the other socialising institution – the school. It is the theory that the cause of poverty is educational deprivation. The blame is transferred here to the schoolteacher who fails to provide adequate educational stimulus to the sub-working-class child.

Although they both concentrate on the socialisation process these two interpretations of the theory are often opposed in practice, at least in their emphases. Perhaps it is worth pointing out, given the tremendous stress put by many of the American programmes on the 'community' factors, that evidence for the second type of interpretation is strong. As Gans points out,

Kenneth Clark's studies of negro children in Harlem show that the longer these children stay in school the poorer is their performance and the negro children who begin by being equal with white children in attainment and intelligence when they first enter the primary school, fall further and further behind in the higher grades. Such studies indicate that whatever the effects of the sub-working-class home, additional deprivation is contributed by the school experience itself: and the reasons are not mysterious when class sizes, teacher turnover, age of buildings, etc., are taken into account.

On the other hand these two interpretations have been linked in the British E.P.A. projects which emphasise both pre-schooling and the development of the so-called community school. Pre-schooling is a possible key to unlock community support for improved education: to reverse the process whereby the deprived child is one who has been prepared not for learning but for failure. Here is one of Clegg's infant school head-teachers:

> We have children starting school for whom the words 1, 2, 3, 4, 5 represent a new language, children who are so unawakened to the world around them that the meaning of the colour words, red, blue, etc., is not known. Of the 19 children admitted in September this year there are eight who could not fit red to a red jersey or blue to a blue bead. Looking at a book, having someone read a story from it, or talk to them about it, is a new experience, as is the handling of a pencil or crayon. For some, communication by speech is an art to be acquired in school, toilet training has not been established, and the handling of cutlery needs to be taught. . . .

Playgroups, nursery classes and nursery schools can directly repair these deficiencies; and the effect can multiply. If there is forbearance from the professional teachers and charity from their trade unions, then parents can learn to teach and the primary schools can begin their own task without a crippling handicap of ineducability among their five year olds.

The key to a still larger house is the community school. It is typical that contacts in slum schools between parents and their children's teachers are either non-existent or farcical. At worst the teacher drives through enemy-occupied territory at 9 a.m. to withstand siege until the 4 p.m. withdrawal. At best the occasional 'open evening' attracts the respectable and aspiring Mum, sometimes accompanied by an embarrassed Dad, to a ritual and uncomprehending inspection of the pupils' exhibits while they queue for an inhibited account of Johnny's progress from the class teacher. Odd exceptions here and there suggest that it is possible to overcome this travesty of partnership between parent and teacher. The Plowden Committee found one school in its national survey where 'there is after-school activity on almost every evening during the year when groups of children meet voluntarily for pottery, drama, recorder playing, gardening . . . football, athletics, jumping and agility work. Parents are welcome.' *Genuine* participation could provide the multiplier here. The traditional isolation of school from community reflects the uneasy relation between, on the one hand, the legally protected autonomy of the family and, on the other, the political state committed to the provision of individual opportunity through selective education. Within the traditionally isolated school, chances could be given to the exceptionally able or highly motivated individual, but all too often by subversion of the family (a process as rare as it is inefficient).

The community school holds out the promise of peace and co-operation between teacher and parent. The first dove must be flown by the teacher, especially one who is appropriately trained. The development of courses designed for teachers intending to go to E.P.A. schools and their link to community-orientated curriculum change has been one of the most successful innovations of the E.P.A. projects. But the teacher cannot reconstruct the community unaided. If he is successful at all, the needs of the neighbourhood for health, housing, employment and other services will be found to impinge directly on his teaching tasks. The implication is clear: educational priorities must be integrated into community development, or the E.P.A. must become the C.D.P. The E.P.A. school is impotent except in the context of a comprehensive organisation of social services in the community.

The third interpretation, however, puts the emphasis on the opportunity structure of society and in this sense is opposed to both of the first two interpretations. On this view, high achievement orientation and performance on the part of the sub-working-class child would be irrational until the structure of opportunities for jobs, and indeed all the other elements of citizenship in the affluent society, are provided equally for all, independently of their social, familial and racial origins. There is very little that can be done directly in order to apply this side of the theory within the framework of an E.P.A. action programme. All that can be said is that no amount of success with work on either the cultural poverty of the home or the educational poverty of the school will result in anything but frustration if socialisation cannot be translated into opportunity at the end.

All these three interpretations are at the same time explanations of poor school performance. A parallel can, however, be drawn with independence or dependence on the social services. The view may be taken first, that cultural deprivation leads to both dependency on and incapacity to use the social services intelligently. For example, failure to take up the statutory entitlements may be regarded as a failure on the part of the individuals concerned. A second view, equivalent to the educational deprivation view, regards these services as inadequate for the needs of slum dwellers, for example, the gap between need and supply is interpreted as a failure of comprehension and communication on the part of the welfare bureaucracies. Another example would be that housing services are too narrowly defined, concerning themselves with the letting of council tenancies and not with the search for accommodation, mortgages, etc., in the private as well as the public market. Then the third and radical interpretation would suggest that social services are no more than a palliative while the structure of opportunity, especially opportunities for employment and discrimination against coloured immigrants, continue. This third point of view may be taken to the point of seeing the whole apparatus of both E.P.A. and C.D.P. as a diversion of genuine egalitarian policy into the obscurities of unnecessary research.

The initial aims and objectives of the C.D.P. programme[17] assert the validity, or at least partial validity, of the first (cultural) and second (social services) interpretations of the theory of poverty, but they largely leave aside the implications of the third (structural) approach.

The idea is to involve the people living in the area in community schemes flowing from their own perceptions of need, and translated into action with their participation. It is not assumed that the correct response to a need defined by the project team is for the team to communicate it to the Town Hall, and for the Town Hall to offer a ready-made solution. For example, it is likely that the organisation of pre-school play groups will attract high priority in the plans for many areas. But the most constructive way of developing this kind of activity is held to be one where play groups are requested by the people themselves, and where the Town Hall then provides only such resources as will enable a neighbourhood to run a pre-school group largely by its own efforts, or possibly supported by a voluntary agency.

The underlying general aim of social action is to create a more integrated community, supported by services more integrated in their concepts and practices (even though some of them will remain separately organised). It includes measures to relieve the statutory services by developing voluntary social welfare activity and mutual help amongst the individuals, families and social groups in the neighbourhood, supported by the voluntary agencies providing services within it (some of which are known to be conscious of their lack of relevance to present-day needs, and may be expected to welcome an opportunity to find a new role).

All this assumes the possibility of a degree of consensus about the appropriate standards of living and the proper extent and quality of the public services which may prove unattainable. The ambitions and expectations engendered by an effective C.D.P. programme directed to encouraging people to recognise and define their needs may well give rise to demands which cannot be met locally. The stimulation of deprived communities to improve their situation may lead to demands for more radical changes in social policy aimed at national redistribution of income and opportunities. And it is in this sense – in the awakening of political consciousness and the development of political processes which local institutions cannot contain – that the C.D.P. programme may, albeit unintentionally, be the means of directing public attention to the third or structural approach to poverty. Whether the result would be more redistributive policies or suppression of further experiment must be a matter of conjecture.

Meanwhile it is not to be expected that social action in the experimental areas will mean introducing facilities which are large, expensive or wholly new in conception. The projects cannot, for example, hope to set up new comprehensive schools or to re-house the whole neighbourhood; nor can they hope to invent some panacea which will make good in a few years the effects of long standing social deprivations, some of which extend over several generations. It is not the purpose of the projects to do so. Large-scale remedies are assumed to belong to the steady evolution, as resources and politics permit, of familiar general policies. The C.D.P. programme will depend for its success on the cumulative effect of a large number of individually small but carefully co-ordinated initiatives, few of which will be wholly new. But all will be designed to remedy whatever can be remedied without large-scale redevelopment, and to do so in a way which progressively builds up the capacity of the neighbourhood to express its needs and wishes, of the statutory services to respond with effective understanding of the inter-dependence of all forms of social action, and of both to co-operate with voluntary agencies in establishing networks of communication and co-operative effort. Given this beginning, a substantial multiplier effect might then be expected as deprived people reach the head of the queue for the large-scale remedies.

I have argued that the third or 'structural' interpretation of the theory of poverty is difficult to apply within the framework of the community programmes: if action develops along these lines it will represent an unpremeditated consequence rather than an integral part of the projects. They therefore afford no serious opportunity of experimenting with alternative forms of the hypothesis that the abolition of poverty is possible by large-scale redistribution of national resources.

Conclusion

British administrators and social scientists have embarked, in the wake but also in the light of American experience, on a new programme of evaluated social action against the type of poverty which is characteristic of some of the inner districts of conurbations. Some elements of a theory of poverty are available, though by no means fully explored and heavily reliant on translation across the Atlantic. There is a clear need for better theory based on empirical research. It could be an important product of the E.P.A. and C.D.P. programmes. Meanwhile we are in effect applying theories in the new style of experimental social administration. There are difficulties – political and administrative – in our path, some of which have been discussed. They complicate the search for both more developed theory and effective application. Nevertheless the experiments may well throw new light on approaches to amelioration of poverty and deprivation as manifested particularly in the blighted districts of city redevelopment. They may generate unplanned political movements towards large-scale national reform of the distribution of resources and opportunities in a rich but unequal society.

8 Action Research and Social Policy: some Recent British Experience*

Stephen W. Town

The methodology of action research, whereby the knowledge and research techniques of social science are combined in a practical application to plan and achieve change, has been used in some fields of social science for a considerable number of years. Researchers and consultants interested in the solution of problems in work organisations have made regular use of action research, and have produced a considerable literature on the subject.[1] Systematic attempts to use the interplay of action and research as the basis for promoting planned change designed to deal with social problems appear to be of more recent origin, although since action research is a form of applied research and is often conducted outside the academic world, early attempts to use such an approach may simply have escaped notice through lack of reporting. However, with the exception of the Bristol Social Project in the mid-1950s,[2] there seem to be few examples of such enterprises in Britain prior to the advent of the

* Reprinted from *The Sociological Review*, **21**, 1973, pp. 573–98, with the permission of the publishers and the author.

Educational Priority Area project in 1968[3] and the Community Development Project in 1969.[4]

This chapter discusses the experience of these projects as research enterprises, and points to some of the difficulties involved in conducting action research in the field of social problems. It considers two main problems which face projects of this sort – that of providing findings of general relevance, and that of working in a local situation where there is no single power structure. To demonstrate the significance of these problems, it looks briefly at the conduct of action research in work organisations for comparison.

It is difficult to offer a definition which specifies the criteria of an action research approach without making the definition too wide; this is particularly true at a time when action research appears to be enjoying something of a vogue, with the result that programmes of action which employ a researcher may use the title to claim scientific or academic respectability, while research programmes which contain an element of action may similarly describe their activities to give the appearance of practical relevance. Action research has affinities with social planning, developmental work (such as curriculum development), the social experiment, consultancy, and evaluation research, to name its main research-based affinities; programmes of systematic social action designed to promote change, particularly where based on social science intelligence, are also closely related. Briefly, action research can be described as a process whereby, in a given problem area, research is undertaken to specify the dimensions of the problem in its particular context; on the basis of this evidence a possible solution is formulated, and is translated into action with a view to solving the problem; research is then used to evaluate the effectiveness of the action taken. In this way action research may appear to be a challenging application of social science to the solution of social problems, by combining the knowledge and research techniques of social science both to discover solutions and to provide scientific evidence of their efficacity. Consequently, action research may appear to be an ideal vehicle for the formulation of new social policy, and it seems to be with this goal in mind that both the E.P.A. project and the C.D.P. chose to operate by means of an action research strategy. In each project the generation of new forms of practice which might become accepted social policy appears to have been the central objective.

The E.P.A. project took its terms of reference from the Plowden Report[5] which defined its problem as the poor standard of education found in depressed industrial areas such as the inner city and suggested that '. . . research should be started to discover which of the developments in educational priority areas have the most constructive effects so as to assist us in planning the longer-term programme to follow.'[6] The C.D.P. is similarly concerned with the problems of depressed urban areas, and particularly with the high incidence of multiple social deprivation; action is intended to cover ' . . . the total personal needs of individuals and families, and of the community as a whole.'[7] It is regarded as ' . . . an experimental approach . . . using social science methods of enquiry and evaluation as a built-in support for social action. The research is intended to inform future decision making in social policy.'[8] The projects were thus both concerned with finding solutions to basic social problems manifest in the community at large. Their concern with the formulation of policy necessarily supposes that action research can produce generalised conclusions on the basis of experience, supported by the positive evidence which social science research skills can provide. This approach seems to reflect the model of action research developed in the American Poverty Programme of the 1960s, although one might note that the American experience of action research and evaluated social action appears not to have been very successful.[9]

Writing from a perspective which seems to be more closely associated with action research in work organisations, Cherns offers a rather more restrictive view of the relationship between action research and the formulation of social policy, in that he suggests that the findings of action research represent the solution to a particular problem, within a given context, and are the least open to generalisation of all research procedures.[10] In a subsequent paper he develops a model of different patterns of research which can be regarded as a chain running from the development of an hypothesis in 'pure' research, through the application of this hypothesis to some problem area in applied research, followed by the reformulation of these findings into an operational policy which is given a field test by action research, prior to its general implementation.[11] Action research is then the 'tested realisation of a specific policy option'. In other words, it does not produce the sorts of generalised statements which can be used as the basis for formulating policy; instead it tests out the validity of policy formulated on the basis of prior generalisations.

Both E.P.A. and C.D.P. differ from Cherns's conception of action research considerably. In the first place, neither project was given a specific policy option to test out. Rather the projects were asked to investigate a broad problem area, using only the general guidelines which the Plowden Report for E.P.A. and Home Office circulars for C.D.P. offered.[12] More importantly, however, the nature of the subjects with which the projects were concerned has meant that the solutions which they were required to offer had to have general relevance. For, although the projects operated within specific selected localities, such as the twilight area of a city, the problems with which they were concerned – broadly poverty and social disorganisation – depend not only on specific local conditions, such as the existence of a ghetto, but on the social structure which generates them, and upon the pattern of welfare and social services available to deal with them. Neither social structure nor social services can be changed permanently by efforts in the local context within which an action research project must operate. Consequently an action research project becomes a demonstration of what is possible, by setting up some test situation which shows the value of a new measure implemented as action and validated by research. The findings of the project then become a means of advocacy for this measure as a part of national policy. The E.P.A. project was, for example, concerned with the need for pre-school education and devoted a considerable amount of time to the setting up of pre-school play groups and the testing of pre-school programmes, in an effort to demonstrate the merit of such education. However, unless the value of such action was to be restricted to an improvement of the lot of a few hundred children in a few selected areas, rather than that of deprived children in general, the project had to influence government thinking so as to alter the national policy in favour of the provision of pre-school education over the whole country.[13] Consequently, the project had to present evidence which could be generalised, as the basis for national policy. Such generalisations become the major product of action research.

The scope of action research within work organisations is far more limited than such endeavours and reflects the different conditions under which such projects work and the different requirements which their product is required to meet. However, since action research in industrial settings has a reasonably long pedigree, and a moderately successful history, it is appropriate to look at some of the salient features of such projects, since these provide a model with which E.P.A. projects and C.D.P.s can be compared. The comparison highlights the major problems which have faced these latter projects.

The origins of action research in work organisations in this country are closely associated with the Tavistock Institute. The main starting point in the Institute's involvement in action research seems to be the Glacier Metals Project conducted by Elliot Jaques and his associates,[14] although in reviewing the Institute's work in this field Rapoport[15] notes a number of earlier examples as well as a score of more recent ones. Such projects were generally directed towards changes and improvements in the working of the organisation in question – work group relationships, management structure and management–worker relationships were the typical subjects of concern. Action research was used as a technique appropriate to the Institute's consultancy work – what Sofer terms 'social consultancy'.[16] The consultant used research techniques such as a survey to help identify areas of concern with a view to suggesting and implementing changes; subsequently further research was carried out to assess the effectiveness of the changes made. In some cases the effects of the changes made have been shown by quantitative results – such as a rise in productivity,[17] while in other cases the achievement of a more effective or harmonious management structure has been a satisfactory end in itself. The main objective of such exercises is to be of constructive use to the client (as befits the role of consultant), with the result that attempts to further general theoretical knowledge about what organisations are or how they work, or to derive general hypotheses about the relationship between work and social structure have low priority in many projects. Writing from the perspective of 'straight' industrial sociology, Brown cites the limited extent of theorisation and the unwillingness to take into account other research as his main criticisms of the Tavistock's work.[18] Jaques's book, for example, is little more than an account of the operation and outcome of a particular project, although valuable as such. Similarly, although Sofer offers some interesting general comments on the problems and nature of organisational change, his three case studies are simply presented as illustrative material in a separate section of the book.

In reviewing the Tavistock Institute's involvement in action research, Rapoport notes that a major dilemma which faces those involved in action research results from the divergence of the interests of the academic/scientific community on the one hand and those of the client on the other.[19] The academic orientation stresses generalisation, the elucidation of theory and expansion of knowledge, whereas the client is interested only in the implementation of a specific solution to his particular problem. This dilemma about the objectives of action research can be regarded as a consequence of the role which the Tavistock Institute has adopted in consultancy. Wilson, in the context of the Glacier Metals Project, suggests that the doctor–patient relationship in medical practice, where the practitioner responds to the client's request for assistance and gives primacy to his well-being, is the appropriate model for consultancy.[20] Although such an approach to action research appears to have been valuable in terms of the Tavistock's work, it appears to have a limited application restricted to a specific context. Also the *Human Relations* and psychotherapeutic approach of the Tavistock Institute stresses the importance of satisfactory interpersonal relationships and the adjustment of actors to the context within which they exist. This approach has tended to restrict the degree to which the action researcher considers the goals and structure of the organisation under study, and has received some criticism on these grounds in consequence.[21]

In the approach to action research adopted by the Tavistock Institute, the functions of action and research are merged in the role of consultant. A rather different approach has been developed by researchers in the L.S.E. Industrial Relations and Work Behaviour Unit in their study of the workings of public housing maintenance organisations, which suggests another way in which action research procedures can be used in an industrial setting.[22] Here the emphasis has been on making the findings of applied research more relevant to the organisation under study, by feeding back research findings to the organisation with a view to action; the process of change thus generated then becomes a further topic for the research team to consider. Such an approach aims to make the findings of applied research directly useful to the organisation under study, and helps get away from the dubious 'smash and grab' image of research where researchers study a situation for their own purposes and depart with the vague promise that all will be revealed when the research report is (finally) published. Apart from benefiting the organisation under study, the use of research to generate and then study action seems to be of value to the researcher in that the process allows the researcher to give a practical test of his hypotheses about the workings of organisations and the consequences of different systems of management. This approach to action research differs from that of the Tavistock Institute in that the dominant interest of the Unit appears to be the furtherance of generalised knowledge based on research; the L.S.E. research team *chose* to involve themselves in action research for the sorts of reason already mentioned. It might be added that researchers in the field frequently find themselves invited to advise on the workings of the organisation under study independently of their interests, and that a decision to undertake action research may be a formalisation of such a situation. Unlike a consultant, the action research team at the L.S.E. did not initiate changes themselves but rather served as an advocate for changes; although they were serving the interests of the parties concerned (a public bureaucracy and its clients), the research was independently funded and the researchers were able to choose the extent and manner of their involvement, in the context of their predetermined research interests.

Although the examples discussed so far suggest that action research can be a valuable approach to the study of industrial organisations, there are a number of limitations to its application. Thurley, in his discussion of the work of the L.S.E. Unit, points to the need for there to be a clearly delineated problem area where a high degree of consensus exists amongst all who will be involved in or affected by the project, that there is scope for change. In the case of consultancy work, such a recognition of a problem is presumably implicit in the decision to call in a consultant, although here a consultant is bound to accept a managerial view of the organisation's problems and goals, rather than the radically different interpretation which the workers might offer. The organisational context within which such action research projects are carried out is also important. For unlike projects concerned with 'social problems' (such as income deprivation or deviance) action research in the industrial context takes place within the framework of a single organisation whose attributes include a dominant power structure, a coherent role structure and reasonably clearly articulated goals. An action research project must be accepted, if not invited in, by senior management, and in agreeing the project will accept the dominant goals of the organisation. It is likely also to have at least a limited amount of power to implement systematically whatever changes it sees as necessary. In consequence, the realm of operation of such a project is reasonably clearly defined before it actually enters the field. Although recent thinking in industrial sociology may reject an approach which regards organisations as systems governing the behaviour of their members,[23] this approach does serve as a useful approximation to the actualities with which action research is concerned, since the focus of such work is on either the re-structuring of inter-personal relationships or their harmonisation solely within a given framework.

It should be apparent from this discussion of action research in work organisations, that the process of action research in the field of social problems and policy must differ in a number of important respects which reflect a difference in the scale of the problems with which the different types of project attempt to deal. For, unlike the work organisation, the field of interest in a social action project is not contained within any single organisational structure, nor is the ultimate aim of the project only to produce change in the particular context within which the project operates.

The context within which a social action project works is considerably more diffuse, in the sense that the activities of a project can seldom be confined solely to the province of an existing agency, even though that agency may have defined the problem with which the project has been set up to deal. Thus, although

the E.P.A. projects were concerned with educational deprivation, it was accepted that any attempt to combat such deprivation would necessarily involve work on a child's home background, and hence would go beyond the traditional concern of
the school. In the case of C.D.P., one of the presenting problems
of the target areas was defined as the lack of take-up or receipt of
various existing welfare benefits, which necessarily supposes that
the projects could not work in any existing agency alone. Social
action projects have to work with both the public at large and
with the established agency or agencies with whom that public
has contact. The difficulty which this duality presents is compounded by the fact that social action projects in both Britain
and America have generally been initiated and funded from
outside the project area by either a government or a foundation
interested in the experimental nature of the project's work.
Consequently the framework within which such projects operate
contains a diffuse set of interests and there is no single source of
power whereby a project can ensure that any desired course of
action will be implemented systematically, with the co-operation
of both the public and the existing agencies involved; the matter
becomes the subject of *ad hoc* negotiation.

The experimental purpose of such projects is also reflected in
the typical pattern of project staffing. For the skilled implementation of action requires the expertise of a practitioner, such as an
educationalist or social worker, or a member of some other
relevant profession, while the need to provide reliable information for generalisation requires the skills of social science research. These two requirements are merged in the role of the
consultant in industry, and it is interesting to note that there is
at present no counterpart to this role in education or social
welfare in Britain. Instead, the two requirements are represented
by separate sets of action and research personnel, recruited
specifically for work on that project. Project staff are committed
to the goals of their project, although these goals may be interpreted in different ways in the light of the different professional
orientations which action and research represent. Frequently,
strains within the project are articulated as conflicts between the
protagonists of differing orientations.

The manner in which the E.P.A. projects were set up, and
subsequently operated, illustrates the way in which difficulties

such as those referred to above make themselves felt. The projects' terms of reference were derived from the Plowden Report and were directly concerned with the formulation of policy. The problem with which the projects were concerned was defined as being that of the poor standard of education found in depressed urban areas such as the inner city, and the terms of reference under which the projects operated were described as:

(a) raising the educational performance of children
(b) improving the morale of teachers
(c) increasing the involvement of parents in the children's education
(d) increasing the 'sense of responsibility' for their communities of the people living in them.[24]

Consequently, the projects were required to investigate a wide range of loosely formulated objectives through work carried out in selected local areas. Five such areas were chosen: four of these – in London, Liverpool, Birmingham and the West Riding of Yorkshire – formed part of a loosely integrated exercise managed by Dr A. H. Halsey at Oxford University, while the fifth – Dundee – was an independent but associated enterprise conducted by members of Dundee University and the Dundee College of Education. The sponsors of the projects, who provided the finance and who would receive the final report – the Department of Education and Science (or Scottish Education Department for Dundee) and the Social Science Research Council – had no direct interest in the particular situations in which the action took place. Initiatives attempted by local projects had not only to take into account the local situation and needs which they found, but had also to show replicative value as the basis for discussing a policy with national implications. This duality of purpose might in theory represent no internal conflict within the objectives of the project, since one might expect that perceived local needs would themselves reflect the wider conditions with which a national policy would be concerned. However, the fact that such projects were working at a local level and lacked the power to make anything other than local changes, tended to produce a divergence of interest between the needs of local change and national policy.

Although sympathetic to the aims of the E.P.A. projects located within their areas, the involvement of local authority education departments in the planning and execution of action was limited, if only because of the small scale of the projects (which had an average of only four members of staff) relative to the total concern of the authority. This tended to be a compromising factor in the realisation of project goals, since it meant that there was no authoritative backing for any action which a project might wish to implement. The projects were working largely through or within established organisations, particularly primary schools, and had to negotiate the terms on which they might undertake action with such organisations. Although one might expect such bodies to be sympathetic to the problems of educational and social deprivation, their interpretation of what action could be undertaken to counter such problems might differ. Whereas a project might feel that social education and curricular reform were the areas in which action would be most profitable, a school might feel that its most pressing need was for a more adequate provision of educational equipment, or for the improvement of its premises. For example, in Dundee, at least some teachers rejected the assumptions on which the action project was working, in the belief that the present conduct of education was the most profitable, and consequently rejected the more radical attempts at action initiated by the project.[25] The need for a project to gain the confidence of a school, apart from any claim to elementary justice, meant that a considerable amount of action was then devoted to minor works, such as the provision of resources and the painting of a staff room, or else to lengthy discussions aimed at changing teacher attitudes. Such efforts helped the project to gain the credibility among the teachers which was necessary before more radical action could be undertaken. However, it limited the amount of time that could be devoted to systematic innovation in a form appropriate for rigorous research evaluation.

The need to overcome such resistance proved to be a much greater practical difficulty than appears to have been anticipated in the original conception of the projects, for two main reasons. In the first place, the control which an education authority may exert over its schools differs from the control in an industrial organisation. The professional status which teaching claims, allied to the considerable discretion normally given to a head-teacher in the running of a school, made it necessary to negotiate each piece of action with the head and staff of each school. In addition, as the statement of project objectives suggests, the projects were designed to broaden the conception of education beyond the confines of the school in a way which meant that negotiation with other local authority departments, such as the social services department, had to be undertaken, as well as unattached community work on the ground. Such negotiations tended to distract action workers from involvement in more substantive issues, although one might argue, with justice, that the re-education of teachers and other public servants was an inherent part of the project. More important, however, the fact that individual attempts at action were negotiated on an *ad hoc* basis meant that it became difficult to know in advance what action would actually be carried out (rather than rejected), and hence to plan systematic action and subsequent evaluation.

The E.P.A. projects were designed to last for three years. The need for the project staff to justify this funding, as well as the demands of elementary social justice,[26] made it necessary that some sort of result be achieved within this period of time, despite the difficulties involved in implementing a planned strategy of action research. This resulted in the adoption of a flexible approach whereby a school's intransigence on one front was circumvented by action on another. The fact that the five E.P.A. projects each covered a number of different topics reflects not only the different needs of their particular localities, and the pre-dilections of the particular project teams, but also the differing patterns of resistance which each project met. The difficulty with a flexible approach is that in year one it is not possible to know what will happen in year three, and hence to plan systematic research which could evaluate the action carried out. In his report of the projects Halsey gives a persuasive account of how the requirements of action (making changes) and research (studying the effects of these changes) were in practice bal-anced.[27] The model of action research which he discusses can be represented as a dialectic between action and research, whereby research supplies the rationale for action in terms of social science concepts and understanding, and subsequently evaluates, analyses, and reports the consequences of the action taken. In certain instances research identified a specific problem area, which formed the basis for experimental work carried out on a rigorous basis. However, given the changing nature of the projects' activities, it was possible neither to use research evidence as the basis for planning action nor to evaluate the effects of action in a formal sense by measuring outcome against original intentions.

The way in which action research evolved on the various projects was one which gave primacy to showing achievements by action, rather than results through research, and the conduct of research was subordinated to such ends. It would be misleading to think that such a pattern of action research was intended from the outset of the project. Initially the overall research design which was worked out by the five projects as part of the planned inter-project co-ordination looked far more like an experimental design. Various 'baseline' data were either collected or designated for collection. These data were intended to provide a factual description of a project area not only as a basis for action, but also for subsequent evaluation of action, both in terms of describing the context in which changes took place and in terms of measuring the effectiveness of the programme of action itself. The data included verbal reasoning and reading test results for all children in each E.P.A. school, a survey of teacher attitudes, a survey of parental attitudes, and various other statistics, such as those of attendance rates and pupil and teacher turnover. The task of collecting these data was scheduled for the early months of the projects – in late 1968 and early 1969. It was hoped that it would subsequently be possible to follow up parts of this programme with further testing or surveys towards the end of the projects, in order to demonstrate any gross changes which could be said to have resulted from project action.

This intention of systematically following up the 'pre-test' of the baseline data with a 'post-test' was abandoned early in the life of the projects.[28] The changing objectives of the projects rendered any rigid experimental design inappropriate. The emphasis shifted from a concern with the improvement of measured intelligence by teaching, to a broader conception of improving the environment in which learning takes place. Even though such schemes as improved home–school relationships may promote improvement in test performance – and this may not be their aim – the causal chain by which such a change is effected is long, and it was doubted whether such changes would be demonstrated statistically in less than two years. The fact that experimentation would need rigorous and controlled conditions also militated against such a follow up. Not only did the projects lack the power to impose an experimental situation on the schools, but such a situation would have been out of keeping with the aims of the action research as working in a 'real world' situation. Few of the schemes of action operated in the schools even attempted to make a direct impact on a child's psyche; the majority were rather concerned with improving the home and school environments within which learning takes place, in the belief that this in turn would be reflected in better performance on the part of the children concerned. It would be a sad comment if all the efforts at improving teaching, the school environment and home–school relationships were to show no effect, but it would be unreasonable to suppose that the link between a series of particular provisions, such as the installation of a teachers' auxilliary in each school, fifty extra books in the school library, and an increased awareness of the process of education on the part of parents (as a result of regular coffee mornings), would be demonstrated by a measurable improvement in performance in the short run. When one considers the problem of control in an experiment which would involve a whole school and a whole range of stimuli, introduced for their intrinsic rather than experimental value, the situation becomes quite untenable.

A limited amount of experimental work was carried out in each project on a clearly defined basis, particularly in the assessment of the value of pre-school learning programmes, and in some cases in other programmes of curriculum development. In general, however, the initial research conducted on the projects was not used as a basis for the planning of action, although frequently action was based on the findings of other published research, such as the literature on child development, rather than being based solely on the project director's personal assessment of the situation and its problems. Apart from the need to initiate action as quickly as possible, a serious problem here was the lack of readily available measures which would identify particular problems or cases in a manner which could form a useful basis for action. The consequence of this lack of initial measures was that much of the evaluation of action taken had to rely solely on *post facto* research.

The central difficulty here was that each project's terms of reference were so broad that it was left to the project to define its own operational goals. In some aspects of the projects' work there are adequate concepts which could serve as reference points. Psychology provides an unambiguous, if rather narrow, concept of intelligence together with a series of tests to measure it. However, in other spheres the concepts with which the projects were working and their relationship to the process of education were ambiguous. 'Social education', the community school, and to some extent home–school relationships fall into this category. If one does not know quite how these things relate to education, it is a little difficult to say whether developments in such fields are or are not constructive. Yet, in deference to progressive educational thinking and the type of idealism expressed in the Plowden Report, action in such areas could be justified The conduct of action and the experience based on it then become a process of conceptualisation whereby the project teams reach a fuller understanding of the fields in which they are working. The problem here is that the new practices which emerge from this process lack any independent reference point or statement of goals whereby their efficacy can be evaluated. The idea of the community school, for example, represents one practical attempt to increase the interaction of home, school and environment in a child's education, with the ultimate aim of improving the child's educational performance. However, it was only during the course of the projects that the project staff came to understand what in practice was possible and necessary, in terms of encouraging such involvement, and only at the end of the projects that a full statement of its components was made.[29] Consequently, while the report of the projects advocates the idea and suggests ways in which it can be organised, it does so on the basis of distilled experience reinforced by the findings of other studies, rather than on the basis of any independent assessment of the value of their own work.

Compared with the breadth of the topics which the action covered, relatively little evaluation, in a formal sense, took place; the circumstances under which the outcome of a piece of action could be assessed against a previously defined goal were few.

Instead, the expertise of research was used simply to describe the process of initiating and conducting action – such as the ways in which home–school relationships were improved and how this approach was received by those involved. Such discussion centres not on the outcome of the action (that this resulted in a demonstrable improvement in teaching or learning), but on the process involved in implementing such an arrangement (that parents will not do this, that teachers liked or disliked that). Whether or not such a course of action is desirable or important, given the very general aims of the project, is assessed on independent criteria, which reflect current thinking on the subject. Some of these criteria are drawn from social science theory and research, which, in the example given, emphasises the importance of home–school contact; some are drawn from the values of the researchers, who in the case of E.P.A. projects accepted the ideal of making education more sensitive to the problems of social deprivation.[30] The goals of the action are assumed to be attainable by the action, whose efficacy is not measured or measurable, and the product of the projects becomes a discussion of the feasibility of such action.

The difficulty with this method of discussing and accounting for action (evaluation is not the appropriate term), rests in the premise that it is an adequate basis for advocating the adoption of a policy. Each of the five areas within which E.P.A. projects operated presented a different set of circumstances and the experience gained from them can be regarded as a series of case studies. How far generalisations pertinent to national policy can be made on this basis is open to question. The 'style' of each project depended heavily upon its staff; each project also made a deliberate attempt to meet local needs and conform with local wishes. The success of this approach forms part of the basis for Halsey's advocacy that any policy must be flexible enough to meet local needs.[31] However, the result of this approach is that the research reporting is concerned to a large extent with the interplay of a series of locally generated influences, the particular mix of which cannot be replicated: what is appropriate in one particular situation cannot be transposed to another. The level at which adequate generalisations on the basis of experience could be made would require just the sort of formal evidence about the outcomes of various schemes of action that the projects were unable to produce. Their practical experience remains largely tied to the contexts in which it was gained.

The Community Development Project was initiated in 1969 and has gradually extended its scope to cover twelve separate local projects. Since none of these projects had, at the time of writing, published any major report – a number of projects only started operating in 1972 – it is difficult to analyse their work in the same terms as those used for E.P.A. projects. Early difficulties do however suggest that the context within which the projects are working may present similar problems. The terms of reference of the projects have been left very open, in order to allow different local teams to develop their own approach according to local circumstances. Concern centres on the high incidence of multiple social deprivation such as is found in older urban areas. Although no specific measures for dealing with social need are suggested in the terms of reference, the lines of approach might include: working for a better operation and co-ordination of existing social services and increasing the ability of the community to deal with its own problems both by self-help and by encouraging participation in the decision-making process of the organisations and services which affect them. These objectives have been more precisely defined as:

(1) to improve the quality of individual, family and community life in areas of multiple deprivation, through programmes of social action related to local needs, aspirations and resources

(2) to record and describe the methods adopted in seeking to attain this goal

(3) to test these methods out both by evaluation (a 'research function') and by practical application (an 'action function').[32]

The product of the projects would then be 'a body of material about action, research and evaluation that can be referred to and drawn upon subsequently by researchers, social service professionals, administrators, politicians, information media and the public.'[33] The projects thus have an extremely wide and ambitious brief. Potentially it brings them into contact with every public and social service organisation whose work impinges on the project area as well as the public with whom they deal. Several of the early project teams, after a year or more of work in their areas, have described their strategies as embracing topics as comprehensive as education, employment, health and welfare, transport, the environment and housing.

The project is seen as an action research enterprise conducted within a series of selected local areas (which is in some sense 'the community'). Typically the areas are the twilight districts of large cities although they include a housing estate and a series of former mining villages; population size is generally between ten and eighteen thousand – rather larger than the three to fifteen thousand envisaged in the project's early documents. The envisaged conduct of a project involves separate action and research teams. Research is used to describe the target area, which is defined by the local action and research teams. Action is then planned by the action team in the light of initial research information and on a basis that will allow subsequent evaluation. Action then takes place and is monitored by research, which feeds back the information about the effects of the action to the action team. Subsequently the research team evaluates and reports on the outcome of the action. The initial time-scale of the project is three years, although there is an official commitment to extend funding to five or seven years in the case of promising work. In the event, for reasons discussed below, the conduct of the projects has tended to deviate from this model.

The C.D.P. is financed by the Home Office, through the Community Programmes Department. It was designed to operate twelve different local area projects co-ordinated through the Home Office and its associated consultants. The Home Office is, however, an administrative body and the actual conduct of action and research were contracted out to local authorities and universities or polytechnics respectively. By involving local authorities in the execution of action and universities in the conduct of research within the context of a single project, the Home Office was implicitly acknowledging a duality and ambiguity in the aims of the project. On the one hand, it was felt that local authorities cannot be expected to conduct their own research because (apart from the difficulty of recruiting suitable staff) researchers could not be expected to maintain the necessary detachment from action which would allow impartial evaluation of the project; academic social science researchers, given an applied orientation, could also be better expected to place the experience of a project in the general context of current social policy thinking. On the other hand, it was also felt that an independent agency (such as a university-based project) with no commitment to an area was not the appropriate body to undertake action which would affect the workings of the various existing services in an area, particularly where the effects of action in the provision of facilities might be expected to be permanent. The expectation that action would have substantive consequences for the local population, as well as providing a demonstration of policy, is underlined by the fact that only 75 per cent of funding for project action comes from Home Office grants, whereas 100 per cent of research funding was so provided. Critics of the C.D.P. such as Holman have suggested that this pattern of central government funding and local authority involvement (which requires a sympathetic acceptance of C.D.P. by the local authority which employs the action team and provides 25 per cent of the funding) necessarily restricts the scope of experimentation to topics and approaches to which the local authority is not hostile.[34] To an extent there is validity in this comment, since it is regarded as important that C.D.P. should concern itself primarily with approaches that can subsequently be incorporated into policy, which requires central and local government to be receptive to its ideas. However, action teams, by the innovatory nature of their work, cannot be incorporated into the on-going pattern of local government organisation, and in particular instances have advocated or adopted approaches which have brought them into conflict with local government departments.

The loose partnership of central government, local government and academic institutions in the running of C.D.P. has resulted in an absence of any single source of direction or control. Initially the Home Office provided a central team of experts to assist in the setting up of action projects, while the central research unit which was staffed by Southampton University (although housed in the Home Office) attempted to provide an analogous function for research teams. This central research unit also collaborated with the Home Office central team in formulating the overall project design and selecting the original local project areas. The duties of the two teams formed a close partnership at central level which, it was hoped, would be reflected in the workings of local action and research teams. Certainly, the dual structure is reflected at a local level with the appointment of an action director and staff to a local authority and the appointment of a research director and staff to a university or polytechnic; each team is responsible to its own steering committee. These two teams are expected to work together within the very broad field of interest with which C.D.P. is concerned. Neither team has any general control over the strategy of the other team, although it has become generally accepted that a research team would not undertake field work without the consent of its action team. The teams were expected to reach a common definition of the particular needs and problems in their local area and of the methods which would be used to combat such problems. It was then left for the action team to undertake appropriate action, while the research team would describe the area and its problems, monitor the action taken, and evaluate the impact of the project. Further than this, the roles of the two teams *vis-à-vis* one another were not specified. Nor, at any level, was there in practice any single source of power which could compel action and research teams to act in concert in a specified manner. Thus, although an action team might feel the need for research work which the research team regarded as impossible or unproductive, and a research team might see the pressing need for a course of action on which the action team was reluctant to embark, no machinery existed to deal with these disagreements.

In the face of this uncertainty, action and research personnel have tended to define their roles in a manner which reflects their own personal or professional orientations. While all are committed to the type of social reform with which C.D.P. is concerned, the articulation of such orientations tends to differ. Action teams tend to have backgrounds in client-orientated social services, such as local authority social service departments, or non-statutory organisations such as the Young Volunteer Force Foundation. Both their professional orientation and past experience, as well as their career expectations, place a premium on achieving some sort of worthwhile change (as by setting up a playgroup or citizen's advice centre) in response to immediate and visible needs, rather than working solely as a part of a long-term plan of action, forming a part of an overall action research scheme in which the methods of control, monitoring and evaluation are coherently worked out in advance. In many cases the feasibility of conducting research then takes on a lower priority than the need to initiate action. The orientation of research teams can be contrasted to this approach in that research personnel are usually recruited from academic backgrounds into academic institutions. Although the researchers generally have a similar commitment to social reform, the academic world's approach to this tends to be through publication and the generalisation of particular items of experience. The criteria of theoretical and methodological rigour involved here tend not to be in complete accord with the changing, sometimes *ad hoc* workings of the action project. The situation of researchers is rendered more difficult by the fact that it is easier for an action team to initiate action without the benefit of research than it is for the research team to commence research in the absence of any action.

In the E.P.A. projects the tendency for action and research personnel to manifest differing orientations was countered to a considerable extent by the central co-ordination of the project by Halsey. In his report of the project, Halsey advocates a close relationship between the two orientations as the basis for future success.[35] While the success of this approach is open to question, the separation of action and research in C.D.P., when engaged in an apparently joint enterprise, has led to serious difficulties. Although the Home Office, as funding agency, had the power to exert control over the different branches of the enterprise and ensure their conformity to a single method of operation, it did not exercise any control in practice. The structure of accountability was never clearly defined, and indeed it appears that no written agreements existed between the Home Office and local authorities about the manner in which the projects should be conducted. Although the role of the universities was rather more clearly specified, and some attempts to remind them of their responsibilities were made by the centre, a wide degree of latitude existed here also. Thus, local authorities and universities and their respective teams could hold different views about their roles, responsibilities and functions. They had considerable freedom of manoeuvre and could exploit the lack of clarity to the advantage or disadvantage of the local or national enterprise. This situation tends to reflect the normal pattern of relationships between central government and universities and local authorities; for although local authorities exercise most of their powers by virtue of legislation amplified by central government regulations, they have considerable latitude in the actual conduct of their affairs – the differing patterns of educational provision which exist in various parts of the country are an excellent example of this. Universities similarly are zealous guardians of their own independence. Consequently, local project teams have been able to define their own methods of operation and their own objectives independently of the attempts at both inter- and intra-project co-ordination made by the Home Office and its associated consultants. The fact that no pressure could reasonably be brought on the responsible authorities to ensure that action and research were carried out within a single framework was recognised in a statement by the Minister responsible who announced: 'I am arranging more devolution of responsibility from the centre in order to encourage local initiative.'[36] This announcement came some months after it had become clear that the Home Office was unable to discourage whatever local initiatives took place. It has subsequently been followed by a decline in the size of the central co-ordinating bodies, and a decline in their attempts to organise inter-project co-operation, although in the latter respect a number of different projects have set up their own cross-project working groups on topics of mutual interest.

The research teams have been in a far weaker position than the action teams as a result of this shift in power, since the conduct of research requires the co-operation of the action team. The situation has been rendered particularly problematic by the fact that a number of action teams have interpreted research as a subordinate facility which will allow them to take more informed and effective action, in line with the consultancy approach to action research adopted by the Tavistock Institute. Research teams have, on the other hand, tended to stress their role as observers and analysts of the action and have been reluctant in several cases to become involved in the way suggested by the action team, and in some cases have tended to opt for the more selective involvement as practised in the action research work of the L.S.E. Industrial Sociology Unit. Research teams have been faced with a further problem. Because the action teams are appointed and begin work at the same time as, if not before, the research teams, they are inclined to initiate action at an early stage; research teams have seldom been able to participate in the planning of action in a manner which would ensure adequate subsequent evaluation. The consequence of this asymmetrical relationship between action and research has been the withdrawal of research teams by their parent universities from three of the projects. It has only been with considerable difficulty and after approaches to a number of different institutions that new sponsors for the research were found. Similar problems have been experienced in finding institutions willing to undertake research for the last three of the twelve projects to be set up.

None of the local projects had, at the time this chapter was written (April 1973), been in existence for long enough to allow them to produce substantial reports which might point to the eventual product of the project.[37] However, given the diverse nature of project goals, which makes the E.P.A. project look precision itself by comparison, it seems reasonable to suppose that the extent to which *planned* action can be carried out and evaluated will be limited. The sheer scale of the problems with which C.D.P. has been set up to deal invites two equally unsatisfactory responses. On the one hand, the action team can scratch at the surface of a whole range of immediate and obvious problems without regard either to the difficulties of sustaining such action over a long period of time, or to the need for fitting such problems into some framework which allows evaluation. Alternatively, conscious of the dangers of such an approach, the action team may set out to define its field of operation and the problems of an area systematically, as a prior requirement for action. But a *full* account of the needs, resources and aspirations of individuals, families and community life would be literally endless. Even the middle course of action, in selecting a few obvious problems and attempting to concentrate on these, has its pitfalls when one considers what the conceptual problems are in an experimental solution to juvenile delinquency or infant mortality, attempted at a local level over a three year period. Difficulties of this sort exist independently of the problems of circumventing resistance to change which the E.P.A. projects faced, or of the problems of action research organisations which have faced the C.D.P. up to the present time.

The examples of E.P.A. and C.D.P. suggest some of the difficulties involved in the conduct of action research projects which aim to provide the generalised findings suitable for the formulation of policy. The difficulties involved rest not only upon the problem of planning action which can be subsequently evaluated, but in the position of research as an arm of the project which it attempts to evaluate. Suchman has provided one of the main texts on evaluation.[38] The book is written on the premise that evaluation is technically possible and discusses in detail various strategies appropriate to different situations. It is significant that most of his examples are drawn from the field of health care, where goals are reasonably clearly specified and clear, if crude, measures of success (such as increased rates of rehabilitation or the take-up of services) are available. In the industrial field, management may define the goal of the consultant, and the implied objectives offer unambiguous measures of success in terms of increased productivity or reduced absenteeism. In the field of social policy, goals are often less clear and measures frequently non-existent. Studies which concentrate on quantitative work tend to deal in terms of the measureable at the expense of the (theoretically) significant.[39] Even the E.P.A. projects, which were in part concerned with an attribute for which accepted measures are readily available, found any such meaningful assessment difficult. One university, in accepting a C.D.P. research contract, refused to allow the term evaluation to be mentioned in their terms of reference, on the grounds that the whole concept was problematic. The techniques on which research reporting of a project must depend is one of observation, frequently participant observation. Although observation has a long pedigree in sociological research, its findings have an equally long critique both on the basis of the research reflecting the bias or interest of the researcher, and on the basis of the influence of the research on the subject's response. Halsey suggests that this 'Hawthorne effect' can be used as an aid to furthering the objectives of action;[40] how far the outcome of such action can then be reliably, let alone impartially, assessed is open to question. The greatest vulnerability of research in this sense, however, lies in the very fact that the researcher is involved in the formulation of policy. Policy necessarily requires the articulation of values, if only covertly, and the critic may be forgiven for feeling that the reporting and analysis of a situation by someone committed to it reflects his values.

In these circumstances it might be thought that the proper assessment of the outcome of action should be made by a detached research team which has had no prior involvement in or commitment to a project. Such research, generally conducted on an academic basis, is open to criticism on the grounds of its irrelevance or destructiveness; it fails to meet the needs of or provide answers for those working in the field under study. The detachment which critics deplore is, however, the strength of such research in that it allows the dispassionate assessment of events according to independent and impartial criteria of rigour and validity. But, given that action is to be assessed in this way, it is open to us to question whether there is any virtue in the setting up of a special action project (without benefit of research) in the first place, since applied research could equally well study existing situations, such as the work of a progressive school or of some local community action group.

Compared with the industrial examples I have given, the recent British experience of action research does not appear to be very promising: it faces too many difficulties. However, the industrial experience may not be the most appropriate frame of reference. For the apparent difficulties which the projects face themselves present material of value. An explanation of a failure to achieve a given course of action tends to be more perceptively made than a parallel explanation of success, since one is able to see and to account for the reasons which justify the position of the opponents of that action. While Marris and Rein's account of the American Poverty Programme[41] can be read as an indictment of some of the methods adopted (which itself is useful information), it can also be regarded as an account of the political pressures which face those involved in social reform. The pattern of explanation which Marris and Rein adopt may be the most useful form of reporting which research can give to an action project – although it is to be hoped that its conclusions will not always be so pessimistic. For the study of action situations is the study of situations in which changes are attempted or are being made, and provides the opportunity for observing process. More important, because action frequently involves changes in an individual's role, basic premises which underpin the role and which are predicated by his behaviour are made apparent; such premises may not be evident in routine situations. The interest of research therefore centres not on the consequences of an action itself, but upon why these consequences, rather than others, came about. The systematic collection of such experience would provide a picture of the conditions under which given types of policy cannot be implemented.

The lack of clearly stated goals or concepts has proved a major obstacle for the conduct of any formal evaluation in the field of social action projects, although it is here that the most interesting possibilities for action research may lie. Probably very little of the practical work in which projects such as C.D.P. or E.P.A. have been involved is completely novel, in the sense that the particular approach has never anywhere been attempted before. What is novel is the self-conscious manner in which schemes of action are implemented, as a result of the interplay of theory and practice that the respective orientations of action and research offer. Ideas can be developed and assumptions questioned on the basis of experience. What results would be the formulation of hypotheses and theories as a result of experience, rather than the testing out of such theories; in this way the process is akin to what Glaser and Strauss term the discovery of grounded theory.[42] From the point of view of policy formulation this could lead to a clearer understanding of alternative goals, a means of redefining concepts such as educational deprivation and of reformulating possible policy measures such as community education.

The sort of conceptualisation and context description which action research in the field of social reform can offer is clearly at a prior stage to 'the tested realisation of a specific policy option'; it has evolved as a substitute for a more formal method of action research. It may continue to evolve as a new, different and valuable type of applied social science methodology. Nevertheless the price paid for it is considerable, both in terms of the finance required to sustain action and research,[43] and the neuroses which its ambiguities develop in the action and research personnel.

9 Action Research: Experimental Social Administration ?*

George A. N. Smith

In braver, brighter days before the white heat of technology had finally cooled, and C.D.P. was as yet but a glint in some under-secretary's eye, grew up the idea of 'experimental social administration'. The aim of linking social science and government closely in policy development had long been established; but setting up small-scale experimental projects where action and research combine to promote and test new policy was very much a product of the 1960s – with their hard-to-recapture optimism over the power and effectiveness of government action against poverty.

Much has been made of the American origins of these·ideas, particularly the 'War on Poverty'. But this is to overlook the form they took in Britain: one that led several Americans to deny paternity.[1] There, at least in educational programmes, the dominant model of research involvement in action, was either the campus-based experimental school with its one-way glass

* Reprinted from R. Lees and G. Smith (editors), *Action-Research in Community Development*, Routledge and Kegan Paul, 1975, pp. 188–99, with the permission of the publishers and the author.

screens and closed-circuit T.V., or the evaluation of programmes already in full operation – for example the series of national studies on Head Start. The idea of selecting a handful of pilot areas, introducing action and research teams directly sponsored by central government to test out future national policy, though it finds echoes in some of the early American programmes, fits far more naturally into the apparently more centralised structure of British administration.

The Plowden Report on primary education confidently reflects this approach. 'Research', it stated, 'should be started to discover which of the developments in educational priority areas have the most constructive effects so as to assist in planning the longer term programmes to follow.' And the E.P.A. action-research programme was to be 'a preparation for later advance'. If only it could all have been that simple.

Though not the first in the field, C.D.P. was the archetype. In origin it preceded the E.P.A. programme, which was conceived, produced and written up before C.D.P. was fully operational. E.P.A. was closer to a university-based research project, being funded and organised through a university department on a fixed research grant. It had no formal or regular relationship either with the relevant central government department or the local authority where each project was based. In contrast C.D.P. involves central government directly through the central team at the Home Office, which was originally backed by a central steering group with interdepartmental representation. Action staff are formally employees of the local authority; universities and polytechnics are responsible for the research teams. It is hardly surprising that much of the history of C.D.P. has been an attempt to get this cumbersome structure to work. Yet in its original form – with the local action team bringing in the 'local community' to complete the picture – C.D.P. clearly embodied what were seen as the necessary elements in 'experimental social administration': a grand alliance of central government, local authority, specially appointed innovators, the local population, research and evaluation.

This cathedral-like structure owes much to the views of C.D.P.'s 'founding fathers', particularly to Morrell. But it cannot be written off entirely as an idiosyncracy; for it incorporates many of the central assumptions about policy development held by both researchers and administrators. As Halsey notes in chapter 7, 'the challenge' to social scientists and administrators of field testing innovation 'is irresistible'. And the approach has had many imitators since, though each has naturally tried to simplify the original model, learning from C.D.P.'s often bitter experience.[2]

Action-research is now well established, with most central government departments involved in at least one experimental scheme, and more on the way. A significant proportion of people engaged in social policy research is involved in this type of project, with some forty researchers in C.D.P. alone, and perhaps as many again on other schemes. But whether they become a permanent mechanism for policy development must in part depend on restatement and revision of the original idea of field testing new policy, which so far has been handed down from project to project without fundamental re-examination.

The idea of 'experimental social administration' was attractively laid out in the early C.D.P. literature. It promised a new relationship between social science and social policy – one where reform 'may be seriously conducted through social science experiment'. Rational social science inquiry would feed in to a more rational social policy; politicians and administrators alike would be free of the need to promote or defend untested programmes; the commitment would be to experiment and inquiry. But there were snags: 'the language of "social problems" may all too often disguise an underlying conflict of political and social interests', and the view that these problems could in fact be solved by reform 'may turn out to have been nothing more than a shibboleth of liberal society in decline'.[3] But these warnings were treated as the inevitable academic small print and relegated to a mental footnote as C.D.P. was developed.

The all-inclusive and rational model of C.D.P. that emerged, where research was first to contribute to the identification of an area's problems, then participate in developing suitable programmes, and finally evaluate their success or failure, left little room for the idea that the social scientist must remain as 'a critic of the social order', or the possibility that 'the theory of poverty to which the social scientist is led through his service to a governmentally financed experiment may call for political action unacceptable to his political masters'.[4] There was no obvious bridge between the administrators' view of research as a technical process, and the social scientists' concern to retain a critical and independent stance.

In practice the experience of C.D.P. has been very different from the 'coolly' rational, tightly articulated experiment of the original literature. What went wrong? One response is to point to the cumbersome organisation, the rapid turnover of staff at the centre, the lack of continuity and the steady erosion of C.D.P.'s importance nationally, particularly when similar programmes were wheeled out by other departments. Yesterday's programmes quickly lose their glamour. Another response, sometimes favoured by researchers as they struggled to apply a textbook research design, was to blame the type of person appointed to direct local action – charismatic figures not content to work through more conventional solutions or apply a programme consistently. If only action men could have been more like researchers, able to try out a programme dispassionately. Echoes of this argument run through Jonathan Bradshaw's account of the Batley welfare rights experiment.[5]

No doubt these problems contribute to the difficulty. But as Town points out in the previous chapter there has been an excessive tendency to concentrate on the internal problems of action-research, on the inevitable tensions between its components, and see these as the major cause of the problem. Clearly the key reason, pinpointed by Marjorie Mayo and John Bennington,[6] is that the issues in which C.D.P. was drawn involved conflicts of interest, particularly when projects began to move away from the original social and community work brief. Here there were no solutions without costs for one group or other, and naturally resistance to what could be seen as a partisan approach. The original assumption had too easily been that the interests of different groups could in the final analysis be reconciled and technical solutions found, though they would need high diplomatic skills to be successfully implemented.

An analysis which recognises basic conflicts of interest is now commonplace within C.D.P. It has led at least at a theoretical level to the rejection of the original model of field-tested innovation, though this has not yet been replaced by any clear alternative approach. In practice, projects continue to follow a mixed strategy, adopting some elements of the original package, while rejecting others. What is now needed is a more detailed examination of the assumptions which underpin the idea of 'experimental social administration' to see whether some part can in fact be salvaged, or whether it must be finally abandoned as a misplaced attempt to introduce a more rational form of policy development to a world where decisions are solely the product of competing interest groups.

The assumptions underlying 'experimental social administration' can be grouped under three headings – assumptions about action, about research, and about the proper audience for any findings. But they are not independent. Combined they provide an apparently logical sequence where the appropriate audience is the obvious final step – a model of tested innovation too easily accepted and uncritically applied in very different situations.

Action

The traditional mode of reform, it was argued, was 'to announce a nostrum which is held to be certain in its cure'.[7] In contrast, experimental social administration would bring in objective standards of proof to test these claims. But old ideas die hard. And a basic assumption has been that social experiment would reveal which in reality were the 'nostra'. Research would supply the necessary imprimatur. This might be called 'the crock of gold' assumption – the belief that somewhere, if only we could find it, was the 'solution' – a uniquely successful scheme of action. Of course, none would admit, if pressed, that there are such panaceas; but the way we set about the search implies that we expect to find them. Four related points support this argument.

First, action-research is almost always linked with those nebulous, but attractive areas of social policy, where imagination quickly outruns our ability to translate ideas into practice – 'community education' 'the community school' 'community development' as an answer to social problems in the inner city, or the technicians' favourite, a 'total approach' to urban management for the same end. The promise is of dramatic change: the assumption that experimental action and the 'superior vision' of research will somehow identify the magic ingredient.

Secondly, there is a heavy emphasis on 'programmes' – a belief that successful action can be discrete and self-contained. As a result there is pressure to minimise the importance of the social context for a programme's effects; one form is the attempt to develop 'teacher proof' materials and kits in education: another when evaluation grosses up the results from different areas to produce an overall verdict – win or lose. 'Not so much a programme, more a way of life' rightly became a catchphrase on the E.P.A. projects.

Thirdly, there is the tough minded response of research to this promise of dramatic change: one that places the onus of proof on the programme, and reinforces the success/failure mentality, with no middle ground – a properly sceptical stance to exaggerated claims, but it implies that there must somewhere be a programme with dramatic effects. We cannot set standards of success so high that none will pass. If in fact single programmes have at best no better than marginal effects, the wholesale use of tough minded evaluation would be disastrous. It will sap confidence in reform, and encourage a drift to apparently more radical but vague and untested ideas. The American poverty programme is full of examples – the Westinghouse study of Head Start and its aftermath being a classic case. As an evaluation strategy it would contrast with a more charitable approach which would screen a range of programmes to pinpoint the more successful.[8]

Finally, search for 'the crock of gold' restricts evaluation to one or possibly two outcomes, conveniently ignoring what may be important side effects. Rory Williams, in a discussion on the Community Hospitals' evaluation, suggests that this is because 'the classic method of disciplining the element of value has been to choose one effect, or set of effects, and concentrate on what produces it'.[9] This is the way to establish causal links; but in the evaluation of practical schemes, the risk is of selecting outcomes that reflect the interests of particular groups, especially those who have commissioned the research. As Williams points out, medical evaluation has naturally concentrated on the primary effects on the patient, and the economic costs of treatment, but not for example on the social costs to the patient's family. This restricted focus encourages the belief that the purpose of evaluation is to identify the next step 'on the approach to perfection', rather than set out the costs and benefits for different groups involved in any change. Here evaluation would be expressed 'as a trade-off between consequences.'

This latter way of looking at evaluation has important implications; for it immediately lifts evaluation from a technical accounting exercise to a far more sociological activity. And it begins to build a bridge between the social scientist's role as technician and as social critic. By mapping in the unforeseen costs and benefits of change, and putting forward the perceptions of otherwise unrepresented groups, the evaluator is in some small way adopting a more critical and independent stance; one where he is beginning to present 'conflicting definitions of reality'.[10] Far from providing cut and dried answers, evaluation here must in most cases serve to heighten the problems of choice: there are no 'solutions' – unless it is decided to ignore the costs for one group or other.

C.D.P.'s organisation with its original centre-periphery arrangement – local projects feeding their findings to a central team – reinforced the belief that there would be a series of clear policy messages piloted in action and tested by research. And C.D.P.'s all-embracing structure promoted the view that conflicts of interest could be reconciled by the right approach. Both sustained the assumption that uniquely successful 'programmes' would be uncovered. This, in turn, led on to two further sets of assumptions.

The first concerns the question of 'access' – the assumption that action teams would be able to implement their plans, and research be free to evaluate them. Nobody, of course, assumed that C.D.P. would run without snags, but as Marjorie Mayo has shown,[11] the tendency was to play down potential problems, partly to win over hesitant local authorities and partly to maintain central support. The result was that far too little attention was paid to the problems of implementation. In the original formulation where team leaders were to work with staff seconded from other departments, the possibility that this might have effectively crippled any action was not considered, though the checks and balances were finely conceived.

Though an experiment, C.D.P. is not free of the normal statutory constraints, and therefore cannot introduce changes which would elsewhere require legislation. Projects are formally part of a local authority, and may be barred from intervening in areas outside the scope of their parent body. Projects have increasingly come up against these checks, as the range of action has expanded. Yet the problem here is at least open and clearcut, even if there is no solution. Perhaps more important are the more subtle pressures and constraints which prevent, deflect, or slow down any action. Against these, a local project's resources are puny – one reason why a common early element is the need for projects to build a support base among local people, elected representatives or sympathetic officials.

Again the original concern to draw out findings for a central purpose turned attention away from the problems of mounting even pilot action. And though mentioned as a function of research, it was clearly secondary to evaluating the results of the action. The dilemma for research is whether to watch the race, setting up elaborate machinery to record exactly who wins – or whether to study and inevitably be drawn into the jostling and argument at the start, the wheeling and dealing to see whether there is a race at all. These preliminaries may form the main activity in a short-life project like C.D.P. The key question is whether the scheme has been set up according to plan. If it is, the effects are often self-evident.

The second set of assumptions centre on the problems of interconnection between one piece of action and another at the local level. Again the logic of the original model was that single findings could be drawn out for more general application – an approach conveniently close to standard practice, where a single idea once accepted is universally applied. Yet this ignores interaction at the local level between social context and any new programme, or in C.D.P., between one programme and another. One scheme may be successful only because it operates alongside another; and conversely the project's links with one group in the area inevitably affect its chances of working with others.

Perhaps more importantly this single focus ignores what in C.D.P. is loosely termed a project's 'strategy' – a recognition that the project is not merely a vehicle to test out an assortment of ideas – some attempt is made to relate one piece of action to another. A strong message of much action-research has been the need for local diagnosis and analysis before action on a wider scale. Ironically, instead of presenting hard generalisable results, and itself withering away, the experimental project argues in effect for an extension of the action-research process. In part this may be the well-known phenomenon where educators see more education as the answer and social workers, social work. Yet at another level it represents an alternative model of policy development, where instead of a single programme applied across the board, there is an attempt to concentrate developments in a single area, to lay down a matrix of related programmes.

Action, then, scarcely resembles the cool intervention of experimental social administration. C.D.P.s operate in a turbulent area where they must trim before superior forces. The sudden effects of new national policies, housing finance or rate revaluation, local clearance or redevelopment, or of industrial change and closure, far outweigh the small resources and power of C.D.P. It is a major activity merely to analyse and comprehend these changes at the local level, harder still to mount effective counteraction.

Research

Closely linked to action, research experiences many of the same problems; and there is a growing literature on the tensions in action-research.[12] Like action, it was too easily assumed that research would have free access to observe and measure what happened: as if research was a process with no thickness, its measures truly non-reactive, the researcher a silent shadow of the action, able at a glance to take it all in and pronounce a verdict.

Even in research on its own, this is less and less the position, as more groups become suspicious and organised enough to bargain over the conditions for research. For a long time this has been the case with professional groups; now it is spreading as research concentrates on particular minorities, immigrants or the poor.[13] Perhaps this is one reason why the researcher so readily accepts that the problems are 'out there', and heads off to set up a survey of the general population, rather than bargain his way into local authority or other bureaucracy; at least with the general population he cannot be 'closed out' completely.

With action-research, activity is concentrated in a small area, and the effects of research on future action cannot be ignored.

Research is inevitably drawn into the complex process of bargaining that surrounds the development of almost any programme. Access cannot be guaranteed, however independent of the action the research team might wish to appear.

A further assumption found in the original model, and taken up by field-workers in a different form, is the belief in the 'superior vision' of research: that it could without difficulty discern success or failure, or that it had techniques to identify problems and priorities rapidly at the local level. Yet the conventional weapons of research are cumbersome; heavy field-pieces dragged slowly into position, and aimed with difficulty, hardly suitable for the swift moving, rapidly changing targets of an action programme. There would be danger, too, if in the drive away from the ground level, research was expected to play the face-to-face role 'on the door-knocker' – of drawing out an area's problems and priorities; this could too easily become a simple head count, with little attention to strength of feeling, or the views of key individuals who mould local opinion.

In the uncertain situation of C.D.P., the pressure is on research to provide certainty, by identifying the central problems and picking out the answers. But researchers have hardly learnt to operate under these conditions, and cannot fill this role adequately. The risk is that by failing to deliver the complete solution, the role of research in action will be demoted. This would ignore the contribution research can make, in offering alternative definitions of the situation, exploring the social context of the action programme, monitoring its progress from a slightly less involved standpoint and making selective formal studies and evaluations. Much of this can only be done in close dialogue with the action team – and is not an independent technical process.

Audience

Given the central structure of C.D.P. the audience was naturally at the centre – and the original central steering group, comprising central and local government representatives was the mechanism. Its role was to consider 'recommendations to central government/local government/voluntary organisations regarding the organisation of the social services in the light of the project's success, and make reports accordingly to the appropriate ministers.' Marjorie Mayo has traced the rise and fall of this apparatus;[14] in practice it was never really put to the test, as it was set up before local projects were in operation, and fell into disuse before they were well established, partly perhaps because there was no steady stream of 'findings' to be digested and sent off to the relevant authority. And many of the early recommendations, instead of being demands for innovation on a wider scale – more information centres, more community workers – where there might have been less resistance, dealt with existing policy that had negative consequences for project areas. The steering group was for projects a route to other government departments when local contacts had failed. And as many of the issues raised touched central points in other departments' programmes where there was little chance of *ad hoc* change being made, the mechanism was largely ineffective.

The 'up, across and down' method[15] of lodging results depended on the other assumptions about action and research being met; that projects would come forward with well tested and clearcut programmes, technical solutions which would be immediately acceptable. The assumption too was that this central forum would translate any such findings into policy recommendations for all levels of the system, in many ways a reversal of existing practice where statutory authority frequently takes over and formalises the initiatives of voluntary groups. C.D.P. itself represented central government intervention into an area where there was already rapidly expanding voluntary activity. The model of central dissemination of results, too, ignores the distribution of power in the system, at a minimal level the power to block developments. Again the assumption was that the findings would be self-evident and uncontroversial, and therefore there could be no reason for opposition.

But the experience of C.D.P. has been very different. As projects expanded their work beyond the original social service brief, they became involved in areas where conflicts of interest were open and acknowledged; they began increasingly to resemble other pressure groups in the same line of business, though with the ability to assemble data effectively, and argue their case from strong local experience. For such pressure groups the internal 'up, across and down' approach represents only one possible audience, and not necessarily the most effective, as C.D.P.'s national importance was eroded.

One small example, almost a field test of the effectiveness of the two different approaches, illustrates the change. In Birmingham, a large proportion of the project population is from Pakistan and was affected by the 'Pakistan Act' under which they must register as British citizens or become aliens. Naturally with language difficulties, complex forms and documentation, the procedure of registration caused difficulty. The project carefully assembled evidence on the problem, particularly the difficulty of getting reliable advice on how to complete forms. With additional evidence on the regional and local distribution of Pakistanis, this was presented 'up and across' to the relevant departments (within the Home Office) to argue for the very limited objective of decentralising some part of the information services – all of which was based in Croydon. After some pressure for a response, a meeting was held between the project team, other groups concerned with immigrant problems and officials from the department. Again the case was presented as a rational argument for change in response initially to a clear local problem along the lines of the original C.D.P. model. But it was immediately clear that the department for its own internal reasons was not prepared to accept the change: and there presumably the matter might have rested. However, the project at the same time had brought the problem to the attention of one of the local M.P.s, Roy Jenkins, who wrote to the then Home Secretary, receiving back a lengthy letter, promising to keep the matter under review. Discussions were then proceeding between the C.D.P. teams and officials. A few weeks later came the General Election of February 1974. Roy Jenkins became Home Secretary; the decentralised information service began a pilot operation in Birmingham a few weeks later.

Again the picture derived from the original C.D.P. model with its central forum of 'cool' rationality where policy questions would be ultimately decided, breaks down on closer examination. No such forum exists. Even other parts of the same department have their own interests and reasons for not responding to a rational case. But note that this is not an argument in favour of abandoning rational evidence altogether, that the sole determinants are power and interest. Clearly the simple idea that experimental action plus research would be adequate to produce change is unfounded, but the presentation of evidence is a powerful way of engaging otherwise reluctant groups in argument, an entry ticket to the forum but not a trump card.

. On this analysis, local projects have broken away from the original tight relationship with the centre as the main audience. Other routes may be more effective, if the issue is contentious. And there is no particular reason to go via a central mechanism where the audience is other local groups. Indeed 'horizontal diffusion' to groups at the same level may be a more effective way of spreading ideas about community development, than to have them imposed through the 'up, across and down' method.

In the face of this change, the conventional research practice of compiling a massive final report looks increasingly out of place. First there is the growing number of possible audiences, including a greater accountability to the local project area, a group largely ignored in most research projects, yet one on whom the resulting publicity falls most heavily. And second there is the question of timing. Important policy changes will not wait for final reports, and there has to be more continuous sifting and presentation of evidence.

Policy development rarely proceeds in predictable straight lines. The particular coincidence of political forces, definitions of the problem, research interest and resources present at the birth of a project, is unlikely to be found at its conclusion – or if it is, this must be more luck than design. In part the continual revision of objectives in C.D.P. is an attempt to keep pace with the changing definitions of deprivation and inequality, but it has yet to develop a mechanism for the necessary second stage where its experience can be regularly fed into policy debate.

Experimental Social Administration?

Experimental social administration has taken a battering; many of its original assumptions have been shot away. Can anything be salvaged? Or must researchers either return to academic aloofness, shunning the disorganisation, the muckiness of practical reform as a possible context for research, or turn instead to partisan support of particular action? Clearly the original model was too simple to cope with the problem of conflicting interests, where there was no universal solution, but different possibilities each with its costs and benefits for different groups. Here there is no technical way of finding the most effective solution. It depends on standpoint and definition of the problem. Most effective for whom?

But nevertheless programmes will be evaluated, 'in the absence of formal, objective studies . . . by the most arbitrary, anecdotal, partisan and subjective means'.[16] In America

> Congressional committees will hold hearings and parade before them a stream of witnesses who will testify on the one hand how marvelous the program is and how many needy mothers and children are being helped by it, and on the other, how mismanaged and frivolous the program is and what a shameful waste of the tax-payers' money.[17]

And in Britain, presumably the same process – though the means are less public.

Yet if we look again at the experience of C.D.P. there is an alternative role for research and evaluation trying to emerge; one that opens up possibilities by presenting the range of effects from any change and bringing forward the attitudes of otherwise unrepresented groups. This would contrast with an evaluation designed merely to pin a success or failure label on a single programme. Set against the grand claims for field-tested social policy, this may seem small return for the blood and sweat spent on action-research, but it could lead to more rational and more complex decision-making, by making available more information on the costs and benefits of any change – though there is of course no guarantee that this information will be used.

C.D.P. has progressed from social and community work, where there is some consensus about objectives and programmes, to issues such as housing, planning and job opportunities where there are obvious conflicts of interest. Clearly the same model of tested innovation is unlikely to apply in both situations. Where there is agreement about objectives, but the means are in dispute, then something close to the original model may be feasible. Some of the operations in the E.P.A. project were of this kind, for example the testing of a reading kit, an acceptable answer to an acknowledged problem – though even here there are questions of side effects – on other parts of the curriculum, or on school organisation, that a simple study of improvement in reading quotients might miss. And these could have important implications for any wider implementation of the kit.

There is a second form of evaluation where programmes are under development – sometimes called 'formative evaluation', a stage before full field-testing, where there is continuous feedback of effects, so that improvements in design can be made. Frequently the first and second forms are run together, and an inadequately developed programme is put to the test. It has been argued that C.D.P. is in this state, expected to present precise conclusions, before ideas have been fully developed in practice. But this is to ignore the turbulent conditions under which C.D.P.s operate; the project is subject to the full range of pressures that apply to any programme; there is no laboratory where schemes can be developed before being tested in the real world. The idea of a 'formative' stage may be more applicable to areas such as medicine or education with their easily identifiable, captive population of 'subjects', children or patients.

Much 'action-research', however, clearly falls into an entirely different category of 'experimental social administration', if it can still claim that apparently 'scientific' title. The goals are extraordinarily vague, as John Greve pointed out for C.D.P. – nothing less than the reassertion of basic democratic ideals, and the area of operation, 'community development', 'community education' or 'a total approach' to urban management, surrounded by a rhetoric of promise that could not conceivably be met. Yet pilot action and research in these areas, however frustrating for participants, is one way of placing the debate on a surer footing, exposing the rhetoric and indicating where promise may lie. Such an exploration must be unsatisfactory to those who expect precisely tested outcomes, or to researchers anxious for a stable situation to set up their evaluation. The dilemma is that almost by definition areas of social life where there is the leisure and stability to test out options in a systematic way, will tend to be those of specialist rather than general importance. Where the choice of policy is crucial, there major interests are in conflict; any testing of options must inevitably be a messy business.

Part Four

Social Indicators

10 Social Indicators: Systems, Methods and Problems*

Sir Claus Moser

Introduction

Interest in social indicators has become so widespread that some recent writers have (understandably enough) referred to a 'social indicators movement'. The stimulus has come from many directions. In the policy world, increasing interest has become evident in quantitative assessments of social conditions, changes and problems – to assess what is happening, to pave the way for policy decisions and to monitor the effects of policies. At programme or project level, activities connected with programme planning and budgeting systems and with programme evaluation have provided further stimulus. As a result, there is a search for indicators of many kinds, with functions which are descriptive, predictive or prescriptive. Some think of social indicators as being very numerous, others as a small set of aggregative measures.

To this policy interest in the subject has been added that of statisticians themselves. With the elaboration of the economic accounts largely achieved, and with considerable advances in

* Reprinted with permission from *The Review of Income and Wealth*, **19**, 1973, pp. 133–41.

many aspects of macro and microeconomic statistics behind them, statisticians in government would anyhow have turned more attention to social statistics; as it happens, substantive and policy pressures have led in the same direction. As a result, in addition to trying to improve individual social statistical series, they have begun to tackle two more far-reaching objectives: the construction of integrated frameworks of social and demographic statistics (social accounts), and the establishment of social indicators.

Academic social scientists have also become increasingly interested in this subject, often with the aim of going beyond mere indicator-construction and towards the analysis of social change and the elaboration of explanatory or predictive models.

Most of the activity in fact comes from the United States, both in academic and official circles. Latterly, other countries have also begun to make progress, and one can now discern activity in most European countries. Links between official work, usually aimed at improving information systems for decision-making, and academic research of a more fundamental kind, however, remain poor. Work is also being sponsored at international level, notably within the United Nations family of organisations and O.E.C.D. There are some risks of duplication here, and in an area where there is so much to be done care must be taken to make the most rational use of resources.

Our work within the U.K. Government Statistical Service is new and we cannot as yet report empirical findings or produce specific indicators. The aim of this chapter is to summarise progress on our attempts to sort out the various concepts of social indicators, to relate these to other aspects of social statistics information systems, and to set out the next steps of our work. The chapter is written from the standpoint of one particular government statistical office, and from the starting position that, though social indicators can be valuable and enlightening, they are not in themselves a panacea for decision-making.

The Uses of Indicators

For the policy-maker, whether in government, local government or elsewhere, social indicators at their best would give a pointed summary of the *state* of society in given fields, of *social changes* relevant to them, of outstanding *social problems* of the day and emerging social problems of the future, and of the *effects of social policies and programmes* (thus linking with P.P.B.S. and programme evaluation activities). The information conveyed by the indicators, if well structured, can help in the formulation of policies and, in so far as they relate to manipulable variables, directly aid a policy-maker's actions. But it is best to think of indicators as contributing to his background enlightenment, and influencing his choice of goals and strategies, rather than aiding decisions directly. Indicators are particularly helpful for medium- and long-term planning. At a subsidiary level, social indicators can measure the extent to which goals and strategies are achieved and can be of significant use for management.

On the question of coverage, it is clear that all the fields of social policy – housing, health, crime, education, population, social security, employment etc. – are obvious candidates for inclusion, and the choice made for research or for a Government's information programme can up to a point be pragmatic and indeed opportunistic. The same perhaps holds of the 'sub-fields' (for example, mental health, higher education) chosen for attention. What is important, however, is that, whatever the choice of fields and sub-fields, the structure of indicators should not be confined to these boundaries; indeed the forming of relationships and models spanning several fields (for example, linking housing and health, education and juvenile delinquency, etc.) is one of the main challenges in the social indicators field. The question becomes even more complex when one turns to problem areas rather than fields of social policy. Examples are poverty, social mobility, equality and social participation.

The range of indicators can be coterminous with all that relates to the quality of life, and might also well cover subjective aspects like satisfaction, motivation, and so forth; this lends importance to attempts to look at indicators also from the point of view of the 'consumer', that is, in terms of the aspects of education, housing, social services, etc., that matter most to the people at the receiving end. This is not only important in itself, but also conceivably as a basis for 'weights' in composite indices.

What is a Social Indicator?

There is no agreed definition of social indicators. In fact, the literature shows considerable difference of opinion and some confusion. To some writers, they are virtually equivalent to 'good social statistics', as long as they are time series and permit suitable disaggregation. This usage is not necessarily wrong, but it is not helpful. Nor is it useful simply to equate social indicators with important or 'key' series. A restricted usage must be based on a more precise concept.

In this context, a number of delineations of social indicators are worth discussing.

(1) It is often argued that a major distinguishing feature of social indicators is that they should be *normative,* in the sense that a move in a particular direction could be said to be 'good' or 'bad'. Here it is necessary to distinguish between the indicator as a statistic and the context of its use. It is the latter which confers upon the indicator any normative character it may have and to be normative may thus be a frequent but not a necessary characteristic. It is easy to conceive of indicators on which there is no general consensus as to which direction of movement is 'good' – but which are generally agreed to form an important element of the information required for 'enlightenment'. Other indicators may have opposite normative characteristics in different circumstances, for example, the birth rate is likely to have very different implications for, say, Australia and India. Moreover policy changes can reverse interpretations.

(2) A different kind of criterion is that social indicators should relate to *outputs* rather than inputs of social programmes, for example, to improvements in health rather than to expenditure on health services, to the raising of educational levels rather than to attendance at school. In short, indicators should relate to ends rather than means. There are two conceptual difficulties with this. One is that there are often aims which are 'intermediate' ends: thus school attendance is in one sense an end, in another a means to the end of better education. In the same way statistics demonstrating the redistribution of income in one sense measure the outcome of taxation and social security policies, but in another sense redistribution of income is a means towards

achieving more equity in the standard of living, which it may or may not achieve. The other problem is the difficulty of measuring outputs. Often, for better or worse, input measures have to be used as proxies for output measures.

(3) In some writings, it is held that social indicators should necessarily be *combinations* of series, that is, index numbers in the conventional sense. This is an undesirable restriction of the term. Apart from anything else, the technical objections to such indices – most basically the problem of weighting – are substantial. All the inadequacies of concepts, measurement, interpretation are compounded, and in our approach, work on index number combinations is envisaged for later stages.

(4) It is commonly assumed that social indicators should be *comprehensive* or aggregative measures, that they should relate to broad concepts like educational level or juvenile delinquency rather than specific aspects of them like numbers of young people achieving particular qualifications or committing particular crimes. This is sometimes associated with the argument for composite indices, but the two do not necessarily go together. Rather is it a concept of the indicator being representative of, or summarising, a broader concept than itself, and in this sense it is indeed central to the whole idea.

(5) This brings one to the criterion that – for preference – a series (or combination of series) should be termed a social indicator only if it belongs to a *structure* or *system* of series: or, to put the point differently, if it can be explicitly and quantifiably related to things/concepts/series other than itself. In short, if it is genuinely 'indicative' of something. This implies that indicators should be part of some kind of model whether explanatory or predictive, in the sense that economic indicators relate to economic theories and fit into models. Comprehensiveness, discussed in (4), is an aspect of this, in that the indicator is chosen to represent, or be a summary of, a wider concept, and thus in principle requires quantifiable relationships between the two. In short, this requirement is that the series, to rank as an indicator, should have a place within some sociological or social policy model. In our approach to work on social indicators, this last criterion carries special weight, with special concentration on output measures, and on individuals and families rather than institutions.

The Role of Theory

Social indicators and social accounts are often compared to economic indicators and the economic accounts. The analogy should not be pressed too far, if only because (a) the unifying thread of a monetary measure is not helpful with the former as it is with the latter (which it dominates) and (b) the economic measurements are backed substantially by theory concerning the structure of the economy (which helps the economic accounts) and the relationships within the economic cycle (which helps the economic indicators). In short, economic indicators readily fit into models.

However, this should not discourage us. In the development of the economic accounts and indicators, pragmatic empiricism and theoretical developments in fact went side by side, re-inforcing each other. It would be untrue to say that their con-struction was completely based on economic theory. Theories were developed, but simultaneously, and in parallel, series were selected for improved measurement, relationships between them and others were investigated and formalised, models were gradually built up, theories were improved in turn, and so forth.

So it should be with the social accounts and social indicators. There are no sociological theories about society in general on which a structure of indicators can at present be based, nor is this a major drawback. There is, however, a number of 'middle-range' theories relating to specific fields or sectors – for example, to occupational mobility, education, migration, mental health, etc., and more of these are needed so that quantitative relation-ships and models can gradually be built up. These theories should give us insight into social change and perhaps eventually into the manipulation of policy instruments for the improvement of social conditions. They should also enable us to make predic-tions by relating inputs of money, manpower, etc., to outputs in terms of, for example, improved education or improved health. What we currently lack is understanding of how the inputs are converted within a complex society and system of institutions into outputs. Although social accounting of the type developed by Stone can pinpoint changes in output in the cases where these can be measured, it does not in itself demonstrate the mechanism of change; it is a systematisation of the data, not a model or theory of interrelationships. But social statisticians need not wait for theories before improving their measurements. The inductive approach, from measurement to theory-building, can and should go on alongside.

Future Tasks

In looking at future work, it is clear that social indicators cannot be considered in isolation from the whole complex of social statistics, and that it is important to distinguish between the different parts and functions of an information system.

Without going into details of the nature of information systems, certain points are clear. One is that a government's information system is meant, and should be designed, as much for enlightenment as for decision-making. Social indicators should not be thought of as solely, or even primarily, geared to decision-making; their message especially before theory develops will often be too ambiguous for that. Another relevant point is that an information system has to operate at many levels, not only in that it has to serve people responsible for different degrees of detail, but also in that it has to relate to broad goals, strategies for achieving them, and specific projects within those strategies. It also has to relate to differing time spans from urgent short-term issues to long-term planning. And it has to serve both in the preparation of policies and in the monitoring of their effects. Indicators can in principle be required for all these purposes.

In this context, the tasks ahead can be summarised under a number of heads.

Improvement of the infrastructure
It goes without saying that a prerequisite of all the other developments is a good 'infrastructure' of basic social statistics. By and large, social statistics are less developed than economic statistics. Pressure to improve economic statistics came from a number of directions, above all from the needs of modern governments to steer and tune their economies and forecast future changes. This led to the development of comprehensive models and integrated systems of statistics which are now well advanced.

Having achieved this level of understanding and measurement of the economic situation thoughts have turned to the need to measure the quality of life produced by the state of economic health or ill-health which has been discerned. So recently there have been increasing pressures to improve the statistical basis for social policy, to forecast social changes and to monitor the results of policies. With this impetus, there have been considerable improvements in individual series across the whole social policy field, and continuing efforts are being made to improve the scope, frequency, speed and comprehensiveness of social statistics. Yet much remains to be done, especially in improving regular statistics on social resources (in money and manpower terms), on the utilisation of resources (for example, take-up of social services) and, above all, on unmet social needs. Quantitative studies of social change, and of the impact of social policies, are still often hampered by poor data.

As regards sources, this calls for improvements in administrative data, and in the range, regularity and frequency of censuses and surveys. Continuous surveys, and replicated studies, are of particular value. But there are some signs of 'survey-saturation', so that care needs to be taken in launching into surveys. Also, the considerable fears concerning interference with privacy need to be borne in mind in developing social statistics.

The improvement in comprehensiveness, detail, frequency and general quality of all social statistics is clearly of great importance. But in practice, one cannot do everything at once, so that priorities have to be established, and the identification of priorities can well be governed by the fields where social indicators are most in demand.

Development of output measures
The most essential element in the work on social indicators is the development of genuine output measures or greatly improved proxies for output. This means the identification of primary, secondary and subsequent objectives for broad policy areas, for more specific strategies and for specific programmes. The relevance of this for programme planning, budgeting, and for programme evaluation, is obvious, and the new elements in the machinery of government in Britain which select and review specific policies are closely concerned with these developments.

But output measures must also be evolved for broader bases than are involved in the programme context.

The difficulties of developing output measures are well known, and it is all too easy (as is conventionally done in the national accounts) to use input (that is, cost) measures instead. To get over this is a major challenge regarding social indicators. It is essential to move gradually, and continuously, towards assessing the benefits of, for example, educational policies, housing programmes, health service changes, and so forth. Some of these effects will be measured in the national accounts, in so far as, for example, higher education or better health increases production. But these contributions cannot at present be disentangled, and this is an obvious area for research. In addition, there are 'consumption' effects of education, health and other social programmes which would not in principle be reflected in the national accounts, but which should be tackled in the work on social indicators.

Social accounts
Recently attempts have been made to develop a system of social and demographic statistics by linking them into a single set of accounts. It is the natural aim of statisticians to seek linkages and attempt to impose standard classifications and definitions on related data. Most progress has been made so far in the work by Richard Stone, which began with matrix tabulations of the flows of people through the educational system. This work has been extended to other 'life sequences' (for example, health), elaborated to permit various sub-classifications and conceptually evolved to facilitate the estimation of probabilities of a person in one given 'state' or circumstance moving to another. Whatever the policy uses of this system of accounts, there is no questioning its value for illuminating what is happening in, say, an educational system; and there is no doubt that it is a good framework for the improvement of statistics.

Other kinds of system are under discussion. One possibility is to set up 'social service accounts', linking tables on the expenditure on given social services, the manpower involved in them, their utilisation, and – hardest of all – on their ultimate effects. All such efforts can be illuminating and, at the best, helpful for the systematisation and improvement of statistics. This is, of course, a long-term task of even greater complexity than the structuring of the national accounts both conceptually and in terms of measurement. It is a task in which government statisticians and academic researchers have to share. As with social statistics generally, social indicators can be useful as a 'way into' the construction of the social accounts, identifying which sub-accounts should have priority.

Selection and presentation

The multitude of series involved in the 'infrastructure' of social statistics, or in social accounts, is enormous. For public consumption, and indeed for policy-makers, selected packages have to be prepared. Such a one is the C.S.O.'s new publication *Social Trends* in which a number of significant statistical series relating to social policies and conditions are brought together annually. There is no pretence that these form an integrated system of tables along social accounting lines, but the confrontation of tables on different aspects of social life helps to produce a more rounded picture of the social scene than emerges from conventional statistical compilations. No sophisticated criteria are used to make the selection. Value-judgements are made based on assessment of the importance of particular issues and problems at a given time, and of the relevance of particular series to enlightenment of them. As a way to producing better understanding of social changes, this kind of venture deserves high priority. It also stimulates discussion of data gaps and is a necessary background to the development of social indicators.

Development of relationships and models

It follows from what has been said in our approach to social indicators, that the greatest challenge lies in the development of theories and models linking together different series in the statistical system. At the most ambitious level, this would call for general theories of social change; but much progress can be made – indeed must be made – via 'middle-range' theories and models relating to specific fields and problems. Relationships can be of different kinds. Most obviously they can be between inputs, resources, utilisation and outputs of particular programmes; but they can also link together outputs of different but overlapping policies.

The essence of the former type of relationships can be illustrated as follows, taking juvenile delinquency as an example. The first issue is to decide on suitable *output* measures. Various indices of juvenile crime might be considered, derived from recorded crime figures, court appearances, convictions, sentences, etc. The problems are well known, and at best such recorded crime indices are a proxy for total juvenile crime; apart from anything else their usefulness as output measures is affected by variations in recording efforts and efficiency, changes in sentencing policy, and by the problems of the 'dark' figures of unrecorded crimes. All this is to say that in developing output measures for programmes and policies concerned with juvenile crime, it is desirable to go beyond obvious measures derived from official crime statistics; and criminologists are of course much concerned with this.

Whatever the choice of output measures, the system of related indicators should cover four types of series. First, there are *inputs*, such as police, probation schemes, approved schools and so forth, measured in money and manpower. Second, there are *other influences*, such as housing, social amenities, education and health, which may bear on juvenile delinquency.

Third, there are *basic factors* relating to the juveniles themselves, such as their age, sex and background, which may affect their disposition towards crime. These three sets of factors combine with a fourth, the *institutional framework* (that is, utilisation of prisons, approved schools, etc.), which helps to translate given inputs into ultimate consequences or outputs. All these kinds of variables would need to be involved in a model relating to juvenile delinquency. And what is important is that they include factors on the input side which the responsible authorities can 'manipulate' explicitly with these specific outputs in mind (for example, the responsible Ministry can decide the resources that go into crime prevention and detection) as well as factors which, though still manipulable by the authorities, would have other aims as their *primary* objectives (for example, housing or educational policies); as well as variables which are in no sense manipulable. The same is true analogously of economic models.

To develop the various relationships involved in such models needs hypotheses, their empirical elaboration and testing, the formulation of better and more sophisticated hypotheses. It is not the kind of thing a government's statistical office can, or should, do by itself; it requires a collaborative operation between government and academic researchers.

Concluding Remarks

As we have seen, the term 'social indicators' is used in many different senses. This is perhaps unfortunate and can often be confusing. In our work, we shall increasingly try to restrict the term to time series which relate to individuals or households, that are measures of output, and fit into an explicit structure of series, that is, into a set of relationships. As such they will find their place alongside the general context of the improvement of social statistics and the development of social accounts. All these activities will complement one another. The improvement of social statistics, including their better presentation, is clearly a matter for the Government Statistical Service. So is a fair part of the work on social accounts. But when it comes to the development of social indicators in the sense of models and sets of relationships, a joint effort with academic researchers is necessary. We hope to encourage this, starting with two or three quite specific policy-problem areas. We also hope that, from the very outset, this work can have an international flavour, with two or three countries contributing to the work on given policy areas.

11 Social Indicators, Urban Deprivation and Positive Discrimination*

John Edwards

Intellectual initiatives in the realms of social policy are rarely, if ever, spawned within government departments. After nearly a decade of debate within universities and research establishments about the nature and causes of, and the solutions to the problem of urban deprivation, a unit was established in 1974 within the Home Office to 'co-ordinate inter-departmental effort on urban deprivation and other linked urban problems'.

Its heralding was received with enthusiasm in some quarters, heavily tinted by cynicism from others, but it is entirely welcome that after a decent lapse of time, the debate has been drawn closer to the institutions of policy formulation and execution. It would be even more welcome if the deliberations of this unit could be shared – publicly – through the medium of learned, not so learned and professional journals, with all those both within and outside government service who from years of experience have much that is useful to contribute. Silence will

* Reprinted from the *Journal of Social Policy*, **4**, 1975, pp. 275–87, with the permission of the publishers and the author.

engender more cynicism, a shared and open discussion cannot be other than wholly beneficial.

It is safest to begin with technical rather than policy issues. One technical problem to which the new unit is no doubt applying itself is the nature, use and efficacy of social indicators of urban deprivation. Any programmes for the alleviation of urban deprivation must – in the short term – necessarily be programmes of positive discrimination, involving the allocation of additional resources on a partial basis. And positive discrimination programmes must necessarily make use of social indicators to identify where and to whom the additional resources should be allocated. (It must be mentioned in passing that long-term *solutions* cannot be achieved with positive discrimination programmes alone – nothing short of a fresh look at the way we allocate housing resources, education provision and income rewards will be sufficient – but it will be a long time before that nettle is grasped.)

The social indicators necessary for the identification of potential recipients of the benefits of positive discrimination programmes are essentially simple, low-level, technical measurements. Within the family of social indicators, they are the lesser brethren, as becomes clear from a perusal of definitions and typologies of social indicators in general. Elaine Carlisle has defined a social indicator as '. . . the operational definition of any one of the concepts central to the generation of an information system descriptive of the social system';[1] and Bernard Cazes has maintained that, 'The construction of a social indicator means replacing a concept deemed strategic from the scientific or practical point of view with one or more measurements, thereby giving that concept an operational definition.'[2] Such definitions refer to those levels of measurement concerned with the 'state of the nation' type of exercise, or the monitoring of the goal achievement performance of major social programmes, and indeed, most of the literature on (if not the practice of) social indicators, has been about this type of indicator. Again, Elaine Carlisle identifies four types of social indicator, classified according to usage:

> *informative indicators*, the purpose of which is mainly to describe parts of the social system (such as housing, education, health, welfare) to monitor changes taking place in those parts;[3]

predictive indicators, which form an integral part of a theoretical construction which enables theoretical extrapolations to be made from past and present measurements;

problem-orientated indicators, which are measures of social problem areas, designed to point the way to potential policy or programme solutions;

programme evaluation indicators, or operationalised programme goals – bench-marks against which the progress of particular programmes can be measured.

Quite clearly then in theory, social indicators are made manifest in several forms of varying complexity. In practice, however, in this country at least, we have hardly begun to scale these evaluative heights. Apart from the annual volumes of *Social Trends* since 1970, we in Britain have hardly developed or made use of predictive, problem-orientated or programme evaluation indicators. No doubt our reticence to make use of the latter two types stems, in part, from our preference for policies to alter situations rather than programmes to 'solve' problems. If one is adequately to describe the use of social indicators in this country, it is necessary to introduce a fifth type of indicator – the type which has found most use in this country, and the type with which this chapter is concerned. This fifth type might be called *decision-making indicators*, or low-level instruments which facilitate the making of necessary decisions. In concrete terms such an indicator is usually a variable, descriptive of certain demograhpic, environmental, pathological or service provision characteristics, frequently aggregated on a geographical basis, which can be used alone or in conjunction with other variables, to identify areas or aggregations of population with particular characteristics deemed relevant for the implementation of a social programme or potential programme. Thus, if a particular programme requires the distribution of additional resources on a selective basis (for example, extra provision to educationally deprived areas), then some measures must be found which will identify and locate these areas, and such measures will often take the form of census data, school records, and so on.

Such indicators are a far cry from measures of the 'state of the nation', or social accounting, but, for better or worse, they represent where the greatest use has been made of indicators in this country. They are none the less important despite their low-level character. They are essential for the proper implementation of positive discrimination programmes, and they are subject to the many pitfalls and problems which beset the use of more sophisticated indicators. Perhaps because they are so often seen only as technical instruments, the many strictures laid down about the use of indicators in general – such as the necessity for clear concept formulation, logical concept operationalisation and the dangers of inherent value bias – seem to be ignored in their application. It is with these and other social implications of the use of low-level social indicators that this chapter is concerned.

The Uses of Social Indicators

In Britain, the use of social indicators for the identification of priority areas has had only a brief history, but the past few years or so have seen a sudden mushrooming. Social indicator work has either been tied to specific programmes such as Education Priority Areas, General Improvement Areas, the Urban Programme and the Housing Action Area programme, or to the more general 'social malaise' or 'stress area' approach. Though the studies peculiar to particular towns and unrelated directly to positive discrimination programmes far outnumber those tied to and developed for such programmes, it is likely that the use of social indicators in the implementation of social programmes within the urban deprivation field will grow considerably in future years. This being the case, there are some timely lessons to be learnt from the body of work which has accumulated so far.

Though the intention here is not to elaborate on the statistical problems involved in the use of social indicators, some discussion of the broader technical issues involved – especially in the use of small-area data – is relevant to a debate about the social implications of social indicators.

Programmes such as the Community Development Projects, the Urban Programme, the Education Priority Area programme, and current studies such as those on the Cycle of Deprivation (in the Department of Health and Social Security) and the three inner city studies forming part of the 'total approach' in the Department of the Environment, all point to a growing interest in and concentration upon areas of multiple deprivation and areal concentrations of people in a situation of deprivation, rather than specifically defined and non-area-concentrated benefit recipients (such as, for example, the recipients of Family Income Supplement). This clearly perceptible shift will generate the need for more area-based indicators of deprivation and it is upon these that attention will be focused.

The main essentials of area-based indicators for social programmes are that they should be applicable over the country as a whole (since most programmes will be nationally applicable); they should be comparable over the country as a whole (that is, should not be based on different definitions in different areas); they should be easily and, if possible, cheaply available; they should be simple, up to date, and ideally should be based on as small an area as possible. Urban deprivation (in its conventional wisdom sense) may be – and often is – manifested in small pockets, often only a matter of a few streets or blocks, and for this reason alone data based on local authorities or even wards are quite inadequate. The only data source which fulfils even most of these requirements are the enumeration district data in the ward library statistics of the census, and it is from this source that the most profitable indicators will be drawn. The enumeration district data are not without their faults however. At the moment we have decennial 100 per cent censuses (but with some data analysed only on a 10 per cent basis), and mid-decade 10 per cent censuses. Fresh data should therefore be available (assuming that the mid-decade census is continued) every five years, but since it can take up to two and a half years from census-day for the small area data to be made available, the situation can arise where data some seven years old have to be used. This is far from ideal, but it is unlikely that major shifts in the relative status of urban areas will occur over such a time period, and where they do – for example as a result of slum clearance, gentrification, and so on – the local authority should be aware of this, and should be able to make the necessary emendations. A second drawback arises with the 10 per cent enumeration district data, which can be liable to bias and sampling errors.[4] This is a more intractable problem but not one serious enough to destroy the validity or usefulness of the data. It is unlikely that either bias or sampling errors inherent in 10 per cent data are sufficiently great to affect the overall relative position of small areas on a national basis. Neither is the field of urban deprivation one in which statistical exactitude is either necessary or very meaningful – as is argued more fully below.

Possible alternative sources of small area indicators of urban deprivation are limited, and none adequately meets the requirements set out above. There is a number of studies of social pathology – or 'social malaise' studies[5] – which have supplemented the use of census data with information on the incidence of crime, unemployment, school truancy, delinquency, mortality and morbidity, and a selection of indices based on the provision of services for the 'disadvantaged' such as free school meals, social service provision, meals on wheels and the like. All these data suffer from one or another of several serious disadvantages as far as their use in social programmes is concerned. Much of the data is not available at the small area level – or if it is, the areas are not co-terminous with enumeration districts; much involves laborious collection, collation and analysis; none is collected and collated in the same way and based on the same definitions over the country as a whole, and much of it reflects the levels and types of provision made by local authorities, rather than situations of deprivation or even 'social need'.

Much of the debate on area indicators of deprivation and the calculation of composite indices has been concerned with issues of statistical sophistication and exactitude. Some fairly complex computations such as factor analyses, canonical analyses, principal components analyses and cluster analyses have been applied to the data in an attempt to produce composite indices, and the validity of 10 per cent census data for the construction of such indices has been brought into question. As far as the *practical application* of social indicators in the implementation of social programmes is concerned, much of this debate is not only unproductive but positively misleading. It ignores the situation to which the data refer and the uses to which they will be put. First, urban deprivation has never been adequately defined, it is at best an ambiguous term and in all probability its nature and manifestations are constantly shifting. The application of precise and detailed statistical techniques to such an ambiguous area is about as meaningful as using a micrometer to measure a marshmallow. Secondly, urban deprivation is a description of the human condition – often a miserable condition – and politicians, administrators and social scientists have no moral qualifications which enable them to measure fine degrees of misery. Any attempt at accuracy in the 'arithmetic of woe' is spurious. Finally, and more practically, the designation and application of social indicators must always be seen firmly within the context of the use to which they will be put. They are but a crude exercise to identify some areas – and some concentrations of population – for which a claim can be made that they are amongst the most deprived and therefore deserving of additional benefits. The selection of the areas or populations to which these benefits will be given will be made not solely – or even mainly – on the basis of what the social indicators say. The social indicators will be but one of a number of inputs to the decision-taking process. They will be weighed against convenience, political expediency and such notions as 'balance' and 'fairness'.

For all these reasons, it is sufficient that social indicators of urban deprivation should be simple, and free from the most obvious biases. Such simple techniques as the standardisation of variable scores, and the application of basic cluster techniques,[6] are of sufficient accuracy and prevent the most blatant biases.

One further aspect of the use of area-aggregated data will be mentioned but briefly here. Data relating to characteristics of the population of an area (as opposed to the physical structure of the area or its dwellings) can be subject to easy misinterpretation. Only to a very limited extent can certain characteristics of an area's population be accounted for by attributes of the area itself (the high incidence of bronchial infections in an area close to a factory emitting airborne irritants is a case in point). To the extent that the population of an area exhibits on average a greater incidence of a characteristic (low income, black skin, unemployment), it is likely that they have brought that characteristic to the area, and the fact that they are concentrated there is a result of the ecological processes of social spacing in the city as effected largely through the operations of the housing markets. Area social indicators therefore do not necessarily – or even usually – indicate deprivation *in* an area, but rather the results of the operation of urban markets on people who are less qualified to compete in those markets.

Social Indicators and Value Consensus

The prevailing approach to the use of social indicators in this country – as evidenced in a number of 'malaise' studies – has been almost entirely empirical. To put it less charitably, it has been a hotch-potch approach in which any variable deemed by the researcher to be even vaguely relevant to 'social stress', 'disadvantage', 'social need', 'social pathology' or 'social malaise' has been thrown into the statistical melting pot and those which emerged glued together by high correlation coefficients have been used as composite indices of urban deprivation. There are two serious consequences of this approach. First, it has diverted attention away from the need to define clearly (even arbitrarily) what is meant by deprivation – with the subsequent result that some sloppy and misleading concepts have entered the conventional wisdom. Secondly, by assuming a consensus of opinion as to what constitutes deprivation it has delayed the recognition of the fact that social indicators and the social programmes of which they may be a part are neither objective nor value free, but rather are (or should be) the subject of value-assumptions and value-conflict. By concentrating on technical and statistical problems, a gloss of objectivity and value-freedom has been laid upon an issue which is both conflictive and potentially politically divisive. The first of these consequences is considered in the next section; the second is taken up here.

In considering the value-implications of social indicators, it is not possible to separate the indicators from the positive discrimination programmes of which they are a part. There are three levels at which value-judgements must enter the designation and implementation of positive discrimination programmes.

First, there is the designation of the problem itself. That a particular part of the social system becomes designated as a 'problem' requiring some form of political initiative is not the result of national consensus – it is frequently a political decision precipitated by the interests of those who are most vocal or influential, or by the political expediency of needing to be seen to be concerned about an issue that has achieved topicality. Pressures of the former kind can frequently lead to programmes with high goal-achievement performance; those of the latter kind rarely do. Two designated 'problem areas' which have emerged over the past decade have been 'the immigration problem' and 'the problem of the inner cities'. They are referred to (mainly by politicians) as 'problems which the nation faces', cleverly suggesting that 'the nation' is of one mind and in consensus in designating them as a problem. In fact of course most immigrants and many inner-city dwellers would strongly deny that they constituted a problem, and for the property speculator, the inner city is no problem at all – it is his field, 'ripe for the picking'.

Secondly, once the problem area has been designated, it must be defined, or at least described. This again is an area of value conflict. Having decided that there is an 'inner-city problem' or a problem of 'urban deprivation', the constituent parts must be identified and defined. It could be argued that the fact that urban deprivation has not been defined in such a way as to make explicit the sort of policy required for its solution (as opposed to its alleviation) is itself the result of value-conflict. So long as urban deprivation can be assumed to consist of substandard housing, overcrowding, inadequate schools and inadequate people, then policies and programmes can be implemented which both appear to be relevant to the problem and which are politically feasible. Were alternative definitions of deprivation to be considered (such as basic inequalities in the means by which housing, jobs and education are allocated), then the inadequacy of present programmes and the political non-viability of the necessary solutions might be made evident.

Thirdly, and at a more basic level, the choice of social indicators by which to identify the recipients of the benefits of social programmes itself involves value-judgements.[7] The hotch-potch approach to social indicators mentioned above, by default, makes a number of value assumptions about the nature of the problem the indicators are delineating. Thus, by including such measures as crime statistics, juvenile delinquency, referrals to social services departments and the like, an assumption is made or at least implied that urban deprivation has something to do with personal handicap, inadequacy or villainy. It could be argued (and is, in the next section), that such characteristics in fact have little to do with urban deprivation.

It should not be a cause for concern that all these issues are subject to value-judgements and conflict. Social structure and process is not based on consensus, rather conflict is of the essence. Neither is this to argue against the formulation of positive discrimination programmes; but it should be recognised that the formulation of any such programmes is in effect a statement of value and as such open to attack, not only on technical matters but on more fundamental social and political grounds.

Social Indicators and Social Theory

Reference has been made at several points above to the need for a definition of the phenomenon to which social indicators refer. If there is one common feature of all social indicators it is that they are *operationalised concepts* – the manifestation in quantifiable form of·some notion which in itself may not be quantifiable. In short, social indicators must be indicators of *something*. Obvious as this may be, it appears to have escaped most of those who have worked in the small-area social indicator field in this country. It would appear to be an inescapable logic that, if one requires indicators of urban deprivation, the first task is to define clearly what one means by this concept. (This is not to say that the development of social indicators must await the substantive and exhaustive working through of a definition of deprivation, for, as indicated above, this is not something on which consensus will ever be achieved – and nor should it be. Rather, it is a matter of stating clearly any value-judgements implied, 'nailing ones colours to the mast' and producing a definition. If it doesn't hold water, there will be no shortage of colleagues to point this out – but the onus will be on them to produce something better.) Having produced a definition (and preferably a backing theory), the way is then clear to derive suitable indicators or operational-ised measures of that concept. This process of derivation will be much constrained by the availability of suitable data (as suggested above, the only suitable source is the census enumera-tion district data) and the measures which it is practicable to use will fall far short of any idealised, derived indicators.

None the less, if the indicators dictated by practicality – however inadequate – can be defended by and be seen to be derived from a definition, they are at least open to a more thorough interpretation, they will have meaning in terms of a theory, and their shortcomings as measures of the phenomenon in question will be made more obvious.

This is a process which has clearly not been gone through in most British social indicator studies. Rather, a multitude of available variables has been thrown together, composite indices produced from variables with high intercorrelations, and areas selected on the basis of high scores on these composites. The end result has been to define (assume) deprivation in terms of the indicators used to identify its areal concentration. With varying degrees of statistical sophistication this 'cart-before-the-horse' exercise has been repeated in Liverpool, Southwark, Waltham Forest, the Greater London Council, Newcastle upon Tyne[8] and in exercises by the Milner Holland Committee, the Inner London Education Authority and the Greater London Development Plan.[9]

The overall results of this failure to tackle theory has been as suggested above, confusion of ideas about what urban deprivation really is. More serious than this, however, is the fact that the failure to derive definitions of deprivation, and the inclusion of an array of ill-assorted variables, may have been positively retrogressive. First, a number of the studies listed above have made use of data relating to the provision of local authority services. Not only are these measures not of deprivation – or even of need – but of present levels of provision, departmental efficiency and departmental priorities, but they serve to reinforce a belief in the efficacy of present means of provision when in fact what may be needed is a radical rethinking of the ways and means by which needs are met.

Secondly, and more important still, many studies have included in their assortment of variables measures of social pathology – crime indices, truancy, delinquency, mortality, and so on – and these have served only as red herrings to divert attention away from the true nature of urban deprivation. In short, they have focused upon social pathology and personal handicap (mental, physical and emotional) when in fact these have little to do with urban deprivation. To be sure, those with such handicaps are seriously disadvantaged in the competitive process of urban life, but, if urban deprivation means anything, it means the disqualification that is brought about by social structure and process, not by personal handicap. In short, the solutions are not to be found in social work or psychology, but in the political arena where major priorities in the fields of housing, education and income distribution are decided.

Urban deprivation is the structural inability to compete effectively in those markets which most affect people's life chances – the employment, education and housing markets. Each of these markets represents a situation of competition and conflict where a few win handsomely, most manage adequately and some fail miserably. Unlike most competitions, however, not everyone starts with equal chances, some are set for success and others doomed to failure almost before they are born.

The three markets are closely interlinked, such that disadvantage in one will often determine disadvantage in the others. If a child's parents are poor and live in an inner city area of decay, the chances are that he will go to a poor school; his education will be deficient and the opportunities for advancement through examination success will be low or absent. He will progress to a secondary modern school and will likely emerge at the earliest opportunity to take up a job which offers low pay, low security and no future. His social position and lack of money will effectively disqualify him from competing effectively in the housing market, and in areas of acute housing shortage he may well end up once more in an inner city area – if he ever left.

This represents a necessarily sketchy – and wholly inadequate – outline of some of the processes which constitute urban deprivation. Much elaboration of the interlinkages and the means by which the highly valued resources of housing, education and employment are allocated is possible, but this is not the appropriate place for this. Hopefully, however, sufficient has been said to give an indication of a theoretical structure behind the definition, and to give point to the assertion that deprivation is deeply rooted in social processes. The implications for social policy solutions flow from this assertion but they need not be elaborated here.

The fact remains that 'solutions' couched in terms of positive discrimination programmes will be with us for some time and the immediate task may be to make these more responsive to the true nature of the problem. The implications for the derivation of social indicators with which to implement these programmes are therefore as follows. Given the constraints of data availability and the necessity to identify areas or pockets of urban deprivation, what are required are measures of the locational concentration of people in a situation of disadvantage in the housing, education and employment markets. Such measures as are available from census data are inadequate – but they are the best we have.

One final point on the use of area-based data should be reiterated. This is that area-based data about population characteristics give representation to the end result of the processes operating in the housing markets and must be interpreted by means of, and through, these processes. People are not only or even mainly deprived because of the area they live in, but rather, they live where they do because they suffer disqualifications in housing, employment and education. This chapter has attempted to outline some of the social consequences of the use of social indicators. If, as seems likely, the use of social indicators will increase along with the proliferation of positive discrimination programmes, an awareness of the unintended consequences of their use becomes that much more important.

12   The Politics of Social Indicators*

Jack Brand

Social indicators are very big business these days. Lots of political scientists and sociologists are working on them. Lots of other people are currently re-wording their research applications so that the magic phrase can turn the stone heart of some Foundation into dollars. I believe that the idea of an 'indicator' is a good one. My note of caution is entered because I believe that over-statement is liable to wreck the credibility of this approach. I am going to discuss two aspects of 'social indicators' which are little regarded; first there is the question of their relation to policy goals. Without a clear idea of this I believe that one cannot use indicators. Secondly there are some points about the uses of social indicators by a political organisation for goals which may have nothing to do with the domain of the indicator.

Social indicators is a phrase which can be used legitimately in at least three ways. First it can refer generally to a set of statistics organised in such a way that information is provided for policy-

* Reprinted from the *British Journal of Sociology*, **26**, 1975, pp. 78–90 with the permission of the publishers and the author.

makers. Thus it would be very difficult to know how to develop a housing policy if there was no information about the existing stock or about the numbers of families living, let us say, in what were considered to be overcrowded conditions. Of course, one has then to develop some composite measure of housing need which may put together a number of the 'lower order' measures. The second use of the term concentrates on one particular aspect of the situation with which the policy-maker is concerned; namely the operation, the success or failure of his own policy. This use of 'social indicators' asks specifically for some measure of how far the policy in question is meeting its stated objectives. Given, for the sake of argument, that the aim of the comprehensive school policy, was to prevent able children from being victims of an error in the predictive power of the eleven plus exam, what evidence is there that there is still a reservoir of untapped ability which is left to drain away in classrooms for what is supposed to be the 'non-academic'? Given that the aim of the National Health Service Act was to improve the general level of health in Britain, what is the evidence of success? These apparently simple questions are, of course, extremely difficult to operationalise. Finally, by using social indicators we can look at the total 'impact' of a policy and not just at the intended consequences. This is important since the side effects of a regulation or piece of legislation can be more important than the other considerations. Thus, it is arguable that post-war housing estates may have given people a roof over their heads, but one must also remember that the speed with which they were put up and the lack of social, shopping and recreational facilities meant that they developed as areas of high social and mental strain. A tourist plan may bring many visitors to a remote and beautiful area but the indigenous culture will disappear and questions of aesthetic or other environmental pollution may be raised. This use of 'social indicators' comes very early in the discussion. It is present throughout the volume edited by Raymond Bauer[1] and the foreword itself describes the book as being about 'the impact of the Space Program on American Society' and the need to anticipate the consequences of (rapid technological) change.[2] In what follows my comments apply equally to these uses. Where one particular use is of special importance I shall indicate it.

Policy Goals and Indicators

First I want to make a simple point. Every use of the term 'social indicators' implies the acceptance of certain goals by the policy-maker. Without these goals it is quite clear that the second use – monitoring the performance of a programme – would not exist. Let us consider this. When a policy is being formulated or administered one can collect all kinds of data which could be relevant. Inevitably, a selection is made. I would argue that this selection is based on the acceptance of certain goals. It would be of no interest to find out the degree of overcrowding in a slum if one had no idea about the values of living in decently spacious accommodation. There would be no point even in counting how many houses were available if one did not want to calculate a short fall with the intention of providing for it. If one considered people in slums as if they were animals, one's only consideration might be the preservation of law and order. The same considerations apply to the study of impacts. It sometimes appears that such a study is something of a fishing expedition. On the contrary, any given policies, or indeed any action at all, has many many consequences. In studying the impacts, we do not look for every consequence, but only at those which have some implication for the value system we consider to be relevant. Goals again are involved.

In all of these meanings, then, there is implicit the idea of social goals. My first argument is that very often, when we speak about these indicators, the goals are not explicit. I want to argue further, that, without being explicit on this, social indicators can be made a useful tool.

One type of situation in which goals are not specified occurs when there is genuine doubt about them or where the research worker simply has not bothered to become clear about them in his own mind. This can easily result in the squirrel syndrome where enormous quantities of data are collected; vast schemes are launched for archiving and retrieval systems and all kinds of highly qualified programmers are hired; and that is all. The problem is, that the data are useless: except for continuing the research grant, of course. There may be many reasons why they are useless but very often the main one is that no one ever paused to ask what use the data were. Use is at least partially defined in terms of the social goals which are set and one function of such goals is that they focus one's attention on the sorts of information which is relevant to these values. We are all familiar with the idea of an information overload and the difficulties of taking decisions under these circumstances. The policy-maker who has his priorities clear can often sift out precisely what he needs from the endless possibilities of the information that he could have. The value-free statistical squirrel will have collected a lot of data but the odds are strong that they will not exactly be what are needed when someone comes along with a specific policy problem.

In some cases it may appear that a goal *has* been set because the aim of 'social health' is proclaimed. Thus the desired condition for society appears to be as uncontroversial as the preferred state of the human body. It only takes a moment to realise that, in the first place, the idea of physical health itself is not straightforward. Another moment will lead to the realisation that the analogy cannot be transferred to society. Especially in social indicator work in the United States it has been assumed that there is consensus on social goals (that is, what constitutes social health). This assumption by some writers is certainly not shared by all Americans. In fact, it is a little difficult to see how university people in a country with such active minority groups could conceivably make this assumption. The concept of 'social health' is an unconvincing attempt to assume this consensus. Such an assumption will only confuse the situation.

Very closely linked to the 'social health' idea is that of rationality. It is argued that technology today is opening up new fields. Its implications and side effects are such that we need constant information (social indicators) to monitor them and, if we have this information, all will be well. Rational decision will be made on the basis of full information. We seem to be asked to believe that, if all the facts were known, there could only be one decision in conclusion. That this is not true is, of course, a common-place. The reason again has to do with goals. Even if we could get a common set of facts, people could rationally use them in very different ways. Consider, for example a set of information about the levels of deprivation in a slum. The implications to be drawn are almost endless. One conclusion might be that we should rehouse the people, provide massive support in terms of services such as social work and education, and see that there was employment for all who could use it. At the other extreme one might decide that this sump of social misfits and criminals should be separated as much as possible from the rest of the town, that it should be subject to intensive police action and patrolling and perhaps that it should be progressively demolished so that its inhabitants would be forced to find accommodation elsewhere away from the corrupting atmosphere. Clearly these sorts of conclusions could be drawn from the same sort of data and thus illustrate quite different social goals. In between these extremes there are all kinds of variations. The versions of urban renewal and the policy for rehousing in the United Kingdom and United States show very clear differences in social goals. However, the point can be taken a little further. Rationality does not restrict the conclusions to be drawn if one is able to agree what evidence is relevant. This is, of course, linked to the point made before that the specific social goals which are accepted specify also what evidence is relevant. This makes it even less likely that there can be unique rational approval for social policies if only all the facts were known. The whole trick lies in the way in which the problem is defined by the policy-maker and by the research worker.

In an extremely thoughtful paper 'On Being Useful'[3] Nathan Caplan and Stephen D. Nelson explore this question of the specification of the problem. They point to the tendency in American social research for a 'person blame' explanation of behaviour to be used rather than a 'system blame' approach. This former way of defining the problem involves locating the problem in the individuals in the situation which is being studied rather than in the system.

> If matrifocal family structure is argued to be the basis for deviancy, non-achievement and high unemployment among blacks, the opportunity structure, discriminatory hiring practices and other system defects would appear less blameworthy as the causes of poverty among blacks.[4]

Clearly 'system blame' approaches are used in the United States, otherwise such programmes as Headstart and the Model Cities would never get off the ground. It is still possible to ask

whether they are more than symbolic actions. The point is, however, that 'person blame' approaches are often used as a kind of
fall back when the research worker finds that his 'system'
approach is not working or when he considers that it is unwise
to challenge the system. There is a suggestion of this sort of
problem in a recent account of a statistical exercise to identify
Educational Priority Areas in London.[5] The aim was to build an
index of Educational Deprivation which would take up points
made in the Plowden Report.[6] When considering the items for
inclusion in the index the authors report that it was decided not
to include such features as pupil–teacher ratios, age of school
building, provision of amenities, etc. They go on: 'After discussion it was decided not to use these criteria the main argument
being that the Plowden concept was not about existing provision
in the schools but about the educational and social handicaps
faced by the children.'[7]

It is a little difficult to think of a better candidate as an indicator of social handicap than a high pupil–teacher ratio. There
may be evidence to show that there is no such relationship but it
is not adduced by the authors. It might seem that such a 'system
blame' category might be rather threatening to the Education
Authorities. This point could be made even more forcibly about
the age of the school building and the nature of the amenities
and services. It is, perhaps, not surprising that the authors go on
to report: 'when the component analysis was carried out, it was
not possible to extract principal components accounting for a
large part of the total variance'.[8]

Given the fact that they had missed out some variables which
should at least have been looked at, it is surprising that they
explained as much of the variance as they did.

There is another way in which a 'quasi-goal' may appear
to be 'quasi-set'. Recently, many American studies of social
indicators have turned from 'objective' data such as pupil–
teacher ratios or number of people per room in houses and
have concentrated on 'satisfaction' data.[9] It is argued that:
'The quality of life must be in the eye of the beholder and it is
only through examination of the experience of life as our people
perceive it that we will understand the human meaning of the
great social and institutional changes which characterise our
time'.[10]

This is all very true and the authors here made important contributions to the debate. However, I believe that this approach also has very serious drawbacks. It is certainly important that policy-makers should know whether residents are satisfied in education or housing and which aspects call for the most criticism and what decisions appear to have been inappropriate. Policies are eventually for people and a statistic that tells one that the density per room has been dramatically lowered may not reflect the very real dissatisfaction with, for example, living in high flats: the inconvenience, the loneliness, the inaccessibility to shops, buses and so on. All this is the useful side of the 'satisfaction' approach. The useless side comes in when we assume that the *summum bonum* of public policies is public satisfaction. It may be, but then a decision has to be taken along these lines, because in fact, there are other possible aims in policy-making. Of course, this is an argument that goes back to John Stuart Mill and beyond but it is worth pointing out here, that, for example, what is considered as justice to a minority group in Britain may be in conflict with the aim of majority satisfaction. It is very possible that the Ugandan Asian policy which would satisfy the majority of the British people would not be one which took into account the claims of these immigrants. One might ask what possible aim one could want other than a satisfied, happy society. The answer is quite easy. It is possible to want a just society or a creative society and both of these goals can conflict with satisfaction. Satisfaction, upon examination, does not even seem to be necessarily related to social health, whatever that is. If one had taken a poll of German society in 1938 one would probably have come up with higher levels of satisfaction than was the case in 1932, but what does that mean?

Let me make two final points about satisfaction measures as indicators. First they can be used by governments to duck their responsibility for decision-making. One cannot run a city or a country by public opinion poll as we are continually told by our leaders. On the other hand, some of them have a good try at this when they cannot think of anything else to do. The British Labour Party's policy with regard to the E.E.C. is a classic example. The second point is that satisfaction data can also be used to manipulate the public. There are certain sorts of situations, where one can be sure that respondents will answer a question by saying that they are satisfied with a service. The attitudes of people to the National Health Service in Great Britain are an example of this.[11] Furthermore, a clever politician can ask the questions in such a way that he gets the answer he wants and this applies especially to data on satisfaction. Here is a situation which can clearly lead to majestic inaction.

In any of the circumstances above it is impossible to construct a useful indicator because one does not have a well-defined criterion or goal to direct one's attention to relevant data or to evaluate the information once it is collected. The very first requirement for constructing and using indices is that we should have these guidelines.

There are other circumstances where goals are set in a way which is not wholly useful.

The most important point here is, of course, that most policies try to achieve several goals. It then becomes difficult to know which of them to choose in constructing the index. This is clear from looking at any report, say of a Royal Commission, from a White Paper or from the Preamble to an Act. A few examples will make the point. In section 7 of the 1944 Education Act there is a statement of the stages and purposes of education in England and Wales.

The statutory system of public education shall be organized in three progressive stages to be known as primary education, secondary education and further education and it shall be the duty of the local education authority for every area, so far as their powers extend, to contribute towards the spiritual, moral, mental and physical development of the community by securing that sufficient education throughout these stages shall be available to meet the needs of the population of their area.

Of course, this statement is intentionally vague because local education authorities had to be left free to interpret the Act as it seemed appropriate to their circumstances. On the other hand, if one wants to construct indicators of the performance of the Act, for example (the second meaning of social indicator), this section is not really a help. Even if one were to specify clearly the operationalisation of the words 'spiritual, moral, mental and physical' one has still to settle a question of priorities. It is true that later sections of the Act and administrative memoranda and regulations go on to specify what is the meaning of the Act in more detail. It is worth noticing that such specifications do not have to do with the purposes of the Act itself. For example, the 1944 Education Act goes on to speak about the duty of the local authority to secure adequate buildings, to provide for religious education of various sorts, to make arrangements for the governing and management of the schools and for the provision of ancillary services such as milk and meals. However, it would be rather more difficult, either from the Act or from subsequent measures to derive an index of what was the provision of 'good education'.

The same point comes out when one looks at the reports of Royal Commissions or White Papers where the aims of the government are often spelled out more clearly. In the first paragraph of the Redcliffe Maud Report, for example, we read that 'The pattern and character of local government must be such as to enable it to do four things: to perform efficiently a wide range of profoundly important tasks concerned with safety, health and well being, both material and cultural; to attract and hold the interests of the citizens; to develop enough inherent strength to deal with national authorities in a valid partnership; and to adapt itself without disruption to the present unprecedented process of change in the way people live, work, move, shop and enjoy themselves'.[12] As a matter of fact in this case, as in the previously quoted case of education, it is possible to construct social indicators but it is difficult to get ones which are accepted by everyone. Moreover, governments are interested in several goals at once and rarely say which order of precedence should be observed. Often the substantive goals are left vague although the administrative paraphernalia are specified in great detail.

Both of these points have to do with governments or organisations and their operation but there is a more general point about indicators. Many goals are multi-faceted. It is extremely unlikely in many cases that a single indicator will catch everything that is meant by a concept of an aim. Although it is very important that we should be clear about goals in the construction of indicators we should also be conscious of the fact that it may be impossible to catch every meaning with one type of approach.

There is a final point about goals which the index constructor should beware. Notoriously, all organisations including governments make statements of aims for effect rather than with the intention of carrying them out. The problem is often that it is not clear which aims are proclaimed only for effect and of course, the proclaimer of the aim is not going to admit that he has no real interest in operationalising this aim. One example will make the point clear. In the course of the debate on local government reform, both the Conservatives and the Labour Party claimed that one aim of the reform should be to increase democratic participation. If one looks at the reform proposals it is difficult to believe that the larger units will attract more public interest. On the contrary such evidence as exists – for example from Scandinavia and from the reforms of metropolitan governments in the United States – shows with only a couple of exceptions, that public participation levels have gone down after the enlargement of the area.[13] One is tempted to believe that the real reason why the government and the commissioners expressed this goal was that they felt it to be a necessary genuflection towards the values of local government and the idea of a lively conscious community. One should, therefore, consider carefully the status of one's goals (for effect or for action) before deciding to measure them.

Before we leave the question of goals it is good to take a sideways glance at the economic indicators which are used. It is instructive to summarise how they are used since much of the work on social indicators was developed because people felt that non-economic consequences had been ignored.[14] The whole debate on social indicators is in the context of the discussion on social accounting.

There are economic indicators of many different things: of the business cycle, of growth, of the labour market and so forth. In an interesting article[15] Drakatos discusses those relevant to the business cycle. 'The leading indicators may seem to be a curious selection, certainly one would not be able to give the theoretical reasons why these indicators rather than others should give the best advance signals.' In other words, when this author was writing there was no relationship between which variable appeared to precede the condition that was interesting (booms or slumps) and any explanation of why this should be so.

In the past few years the situation has changed. Now there is quite a lot of economic theory linking the indicators to the phenomena they are trying to predict or explain. This theory building has, indeed, led to change in the sorts of statistics which were collected. In the old days forecasters had to work on data which were largely collected as a by-product of the administrative process. Often it was inappropriate. With the development of the models, economic statisticians have been able to specify exactly what they required. As early as 1954, Carter and Roy[16] pointed out the importance of a model if one is to use statistics. It follows that people who develop social indicators should be working towards the building of models which will integrate the data they are using. As a first step it is certainly all right to look for indicators with predictive validity: but as a long-term aim we should be looking for construct validity. At the moment there is a tendency simply to collect statistics which are interesting or which will add to the might of the data archive. Surely the approach should be rather to set one's potential indicators into models of some aspect of the social system. I emphasise 'some aspect' because I do not really think we can construct a model of 'society' whereas we could do this job for the housing market, for the educational system or perhaps for the development of democratic participation.

One final comment about the analogy between social and economic indicators. The latter have the great advantage of having a cash and, therefore, a countable value. Social life is often not so easy to measure. In *The Logic of Social Enquiry* Scott Greer describes how measurement can become a cargo cult of the social sciences.[17] Just as the Papuans build their mock aeroplanes and landing strips and hope that the cargo will be attracted, social scientists mock up some figures for basically unmeasured phenomena and expect the millennium. Unhappily, they get as much scientific cargo as their co-religionists get in the way of real goodies. Greer's message for us is twofold. If you are going to measure you must pay a great deal more attention to the validity of your instruments. Secondly, it is completely illogical to believe that unquantifiable information is of less importance than that which can (just) be quantified. In studies of the impact of policies or the quality of life we ignore that at our peril.

The Uses of Social Indicators

We turn from considering goals specifically to looking at the ways in which governments might use indicators. This is really a continuation of the former topic because it involves a consideration of the effect of government goals on the uses of information.

One important contribution to this discussion has been Dr Biderman's account of indicators as 'vindicators'.[18] Alternatively, this might be described as the 'fig leaf strategy of government'. The procedure is simple and well known. When you are threatened by some unpleasant development, do a statistical appraisal of the situation. Unless you are extremely unlucky you will be able to get some figures which will justify you in doing what you were going to do anyway – often nothing. Even better, get someone in a university or research agency to do the study for you. You have a fair chance of knowing what he is going to say anyway so you can hand pick your chap and when he finally presents his report (usually two years late anyway, which is all to the good) it vindicates you. There is a further point. Even if the figures don't come out the way you would have preferred, by having 'done research' you have shown a concern with the subject. You can rely on quite a few people assuming that research is a prelude to action and then forgetting about the whole thing. You can forget it too.

A second point, perhaps obvious, is that certain sorts of social indicators are embarrassing and even threatening to some people in government. A clear example of this sort of thing is regularly given in relation to the City of Glasgow. There are a great number of social problems that at least some of the responsible officials have tried to do something about. However, when some data are released by some other body which indicates just how bad the situation is, the ranks close. It is also possible that the social indicators may be directly threatening not just to one's pride but one's position or livelihood. One use of social indicators, for example, was to monitor the performance of government. Suppose it becomes clear that the agency in question is not doing too well; it is unlikely that they will be enthusiastic about the formulation and publication of that information.

These are rather elementary points about the uses of social indicators or indeed of any information. There are a couple of more sophisticated points about the ways in which governments work which have a relevance here.

First of all we should remember the work of Dahl, Lindblom and Braybrook on decision-making. In several books[19] they discuss the strategy of disjointed incrementalism. They argue that American administrators work in a particular way which involves responding to problems rather than setting up plans which reform whole areas. Moreover, they respond only when it is inconvenient to do anything else. Braybrook describes the process as being incremental, serial, reconstructive and disjointed. Policy-making is incremental because it considers only those policy choices which are a little different from the policy already pursued. Bureaucrats and politicians are very unlikely to make a radical change of course even on the basis of a great deal of evidence because their capital and psychological investment in the *status quo* is too great. Furthermore, it is not humanly possible for people to review all the possibilities that might be open. Policy making is disjointed in that there is rarely an attempt to see a policy in 'global' terms. No-one sets a hierarchy of objectives but rather problems, difficulties and embarrassments are dealt with as they come along. Most governments are far too busy for the Olympian view.

A great deal of what Wildavsky says about Planned Programme Budgeting applies to the uses of social indicators. P.P.B. like social indicators is represented as a 'rational' way of deciding policy. It is a technique of budgeting which focuses on the 'output categories' like governmental goals, objectives and products of programmes instead of inputs like personnel, equipment and maintenance as in a traditional budget. Wildavsky points out that the proposed procedure would put a great strain on a budget-maker. Many of his points arise directly from the Braybrook, Dahl, Lindblom approach. He shows, for example, that the budget-maker would no longer be able to use experience of previous budgets as a guide and this would involve a great deal more work. They would no longer be able to fragment the problems to be solved and again this would cause considerable strain. He also draws our attention to more important factors namely that in the course of budgeting there is more to the aims of the decision-maker than the objectives of a programme. He has to live with other policy-makers and thus one of his aims will be to keep his friends happy. In the course of discussion he is likely to redefine his aims many times. This may not be a bad thing but part of a developing understanding of what the subject is about. All these points can be made of the uses of social indicators.

This suggests a rather limited role for social indicators. If these authors are giving an accurate picture of the ways in which bureaucracies work, it would certainly mean that whole policies would be kept under scrutiny so that they could be altered if any imbalances appeared. Rather one would expect governments to act when someone with sufficient political clout felt that something had to be done. And that brings us back to goals. Lest it should be thought that these remedies apply only to U.S. government there are independent witnesses from Britain too. Many of those who worked as economic advisors both before and after the Labour victory of 1964 comment on this. Alec Cairncross, for example, quotes one civil servant as remarking 'No one bothered to decide important matters – what always received prior attention was what was urgent'.[20]

Those with experience of the situation after 1964 are rather more acid in their comments. Dudley Seers says, for example, of the methods of the British Civil Service:

> One feature of this aristocratic way of conducting business is the practice of taking account of the views of all officials of a necessary seniority, including those belonging to other departments. Rarely is any attempt made to get to the fundamental sources of disagreement. These are papered over in compromises when briefs are drafted or committee papers prepared. . . . There is a great reluctance to study closely the fact of the future. Officials tend to settle for the policies that involve as little difficulty as possible for the ministry in the short run.[21]

The second point is that one almost certain result of developing social indicators will be a move towards centralisation. This is in line with the developments in government anyway but it is certainly true that once one starts to collect data the probabilities are raised that it will be used to centralise decision-making. Again a value is involved. The collection of statistics by anybody means that an attempt is being made to control the situation. This much we have agreed earlier in the chapter. It follows that the development of social indicators will inevitably lead to centralisation of decision-making. The government developed economic indicators when it required a centralised control over the activities of business. In exactly the same way social indicators will clearly lead to greater government control over the activities of local government, for example, in social work, the provision of houses, road building and so forth. Many central government spokesmen have emphasised that the data they collect will be disaggregated and in this form they will certainly be useful for local government.[22] There is no doubt, however, that the monitoring of local government performance will lead to more control over what is happening locally. If this were not the case there would really be no point in constructing the indices. There is, of course, a philosophical question about whether one wants high quality with centralisation or a high degree of independence with less centralisation. I do not want to involve myself in this argument just now, but I would like to point out the consequences of certain procedures. I should also like to point out that, contrary to the assumption of many government and quasi-government statements there is no evidence of a relation between centralisation and quality of performance.

There is a final point, which I would like to make. Any goal is temporary, therefore setting the goals by large bureaucratic machines, like central government, could so easily lead to ossification. It is not necessarily the case that a high standard of performance ensured by the central government at one time will result in a drive for an up-dating of these standards or a change in priorities when conditions are altered. In times of rapid social change we need to build into our data collection systems some flexibility in the same way as flexibility should be built into other parts of the machine.

Conclusion

Let me summarise the points which I have made in this chapter and make one or two suggestions for the future.

I have been rather critical of the effort to develop social indicators and especially of some work by American social scientists. This does not mean that I dismiss social indicators as useful tools. On the contrary I believe they are a very necessary stage in the development of social science models. I also believe that they are necessary for making social science socially useful. To achieve these aims some consideration must be given to the points that I have made above. First of all, it is absolutely essential that we should be clear about our goals when we are constructing these indicators. In practice this will mean that we have to be clear of our goals at the beginning of the exercise because as research goes on, these goals will change. For the social scientist it must always be our concern to be conscious of these policy aims and implications. In the work which has been done on indicators the aims which are implied are usually extremely fuzzy. The second point is that indicators only become fully useful if they are part of a model of some system. This was the way in which economic indicators grew up, and we should certainly set our mind to this now. Once again I do not see theory being worked out which would provide models to make the indicators meaningful.

I believe the implications of these two points are that social indicator sets should be developed as part of a small exercise with clearly defined goals within a limited geographical area in which these ideas can be decided. There is little point in trying to develop indicators on a national basis before we have tried them out in a more clearly defined situation. Part of the definition of the situation must be a field of study in which there are unambiguous goals.

13 Indicators of the State of Society*

Keith Hope

This chapter describes as simply as possible some uses to which social indicators may be put in the conduct of social policy analysis. After a brief glance at the history of social statistics it goes on to examine in a general way the properties of a good social indicator, and ends with some observations on the institutional conditions under which good social indicators, and useful social policy research, are likely to flourish.

One of the first difficulties we face in a discussion of social statistics is the ambiguity of the word 'statistics'. The word itself comes from the same root as 'state' and originally it meant the practical study of the state, in a very broad sense of that word. Naturally, one approach to the study of the state is to compute its population, to record the numbers of its citizens engaged in various forms of economic undertaking, and to estimate its national wealth. All these are numerical enterprises and so statistics came to be identified with the collection of quantitative facts about a state – the sort of facts that appear in *Trends in British Society since 1900*[1] or in the *Annual Abstract of Statistics*.

* Original material © 1978 Keith Hope, based on a paper delivered to the British Association for the Advancement of Science meeting at Leicester, September 1972.

But then questions arose about how to interpret the numbers so painstakingly collected, how to draw inferences from them, how to precipitate from them a small array of significant indices, how to make comparisons, whether between countries or between the conditions of the same country at different points in time, and how to use such comparisons to test hypotheses about the determinants and consequences of social change. The mathematicians then got to work and produced the very complex analytical techniques which now go by the name of statistics. It is possible to see this second shift in the meaning of the word 'statistics' taking place in the pages of the *Journal of the Royal Statistical Society* over the past century or so.

The change in the meaning of statistics from numerical facts to techniques of analysis and estimation left statistics in its original sense in the doldrums. Little progress was made except in the sphere of economics, where the success of national income accounting led to an extension of numerical recording to other aspects of economic life. The backwardness of non-economic statistics was revealed when the United States National Aeronautics and Space Administration, familiar to us as NASA, asked the American Academy of Arts and Science to study the direct and indirect effects of the American space programme on American society. Immediately the research workers came face to face with the two basic problems of measuring induced social change which are, first, the problem of measuring the state of society at two or more points in time, and second, the problem of distinguishing changes which are the effect of the programme which is being studied from underlying trends which are going on independently. It was evident that a necessary condition of the solution of these problems was the provision of sets of social yardsticks against which various aspects of society could be measured and against which changes could be plotted with some reasonable degree of objectivity. These proposed measuring instruments were christened 'social indicators', and so it was that the social indicators movement, which had existed under other names for at least two centuries, was given new impetus by the American space programme.

The re-birth of the social indicators movement as a piece of practical politics is forcing sociologists to face up to problems of technique and measurement which, with some honourable exceptions, they had formerly slighted or neglected. These problems, which call for the construction of schedules, inventories, assessment procedures and tests of many different kinds, are considered less interesting and of lower stature than broader questions of sociological theory and analysis, though as a matter of fact nothing is better calculated to force the sociologist to define, rectify, analyse and tighten up his concepts than an attempt to construct means of measuring them. Sociologists, however, have in the past proved themselves rather more apt at denigrating the measuring instruments of their rivals, the psychologists, than at producing procedures of their own.

Because the modern social indicators movement was born in the United States, it has certain characteristic strengths and weaknesses, and it is in the hope that we can profit from the one and avoid the other that I want to outline them briefly here. So far as the strengths of the American movement are concerned, these follow from the long tradition of sample survey in the United States. Being a large and heterogeneous country with strong anti-government and anti-centralist values one might have supposed that the United States would have lagged behind Europe in the collection of statistics. But in fact the American constitution, which was a product of the Enlightenment, contains in its first article a provision that a census shall be conducted every ten years, and the early presidents saw to it that this duty was not neglected. The combination of this constitutional provision and the character of the country ensured that statistics of all sorts were regularly collected, but on a sample rather than a universal basis. This is the way, for example, that American unemployment figures are arrived at, in contrast to our system of unemployment registration returns. Both types of procedure have their merits, but the characteristic virtue of the sample survey method is that, because it involves a relatively small number of people, it is possible to use more highly skilled enumerators and interviewers, and to collect more information from each person or household studied. Thus it comes about, for example, that the best indicator of the quality of housing is the Appraisal Method introduced by the American Public Health Association. It is clear that, in the development of social indicators in this country we should take over as much as we can of such instruments as the Americans have laboriously constructed and tested. We are, however, only too familiar with instances in which the worst rather than the best features of foreign customs and practices are imported. I would like, therefore, to issue a warning against three kinds of misconceptions which formerly characterised some American thinking about social and psychological measurement, but which have been largely abandoned because of their obvious limitations.

The first misconception is the former American tendency to operationism or ascriptive validity, that is the tendency to make such assertions as that 'intelligence is what intelligence tests measure'.[2] Closely bound up with this kind of operational definition of theoretical concepts is the tendency to ascribe virtue to a measuring technique in consequence of the beauty, complexity, familiarity or novelty of the procedures which went into its manufacture. How often do we read nowadays in the newspapers that the computer has come up with certain predictions? – as if the mere fact that the calculations were carried out by programmers using a computer rather than by clerks doing mental arithmetic gives the whole exercise superior scientific status. This kind of validation by technology is not only irrational, it is also anti-empirical since it locks the research worker or the administrator into a world of abstractions whose relations with the real world which he is seeking to study or change are unknown. (It is also anti-theoretical since nothing clarifies theoretical concepts so much as the attempt to produce *and validate* measures of them.) So the first possible defect of the social indicators movement against which we should be on our guard is the tendency to operationism and ascriptive validity.

But there is a broader, more ideological aspect of the American scene which stands out with particular clarity when it is viewed from a European standpoint, and that is the power and pervasiveness of the call for consensus. The urge to achieve universal agreement is, of course, perfectly understandable in a society which drew its people from such a diversity of origins and which must constantly seek to minimise differences that might become a source of dispute and instability. Nevertheless we must be on our guard when we find writers on social indicators who come close to saying that, if only the spectrum of social facts could be laid out before the parties to a dispute by the refractive power of prismatic indicators then all argument would be at an end, and social policy, or at least the desirable aims of social policy, would be agreed by all right-thinking Americans. That is a view which is not likely to be shared by those of us who are accustomed to the ideological divisions of European politics. We know that, in the last resort, our own social preferences come down, in Tawney's words, to saying 'One cannot argue with the choice of a soul; and, if men like that kind of dog, then that is the kind of dog they like'. It should be noted that among American sociologists the assumption of consensus is now giving way to empirical investigation of the extent of cultural diversity and associated differences in people's values.[3]

The drive to consensus manifests itself in the social indicators movement when it is implied that a social indicator which is based on people's perceptions or conceptions of the social facts – for example, their views on the relative damage to society done by different crimes – should be based on consensus. I want to suggest on the contrary that some social indicators of the future will be based as much on dissensus as on consensus. The absence of consensus may take several forms; if we are considering the social grading of occupations, for example,[4] people may simply not be sure how they want to grade occupations, or they may have rather imperfect knowledge of particular occupations, from which it follows that there will be a partial failure of consensus in the estimates of the social ranking of jobs made by different individuals. This is not a significant form of absence of consensus since it does not imply that people are disagreeing in the application of a measuring instrument, but only that they are not using it very skilfully and in a rather poor light. Real dissensus or disagreement occurs when people who have been enlightened on the facts of the case continue to differ on the relative ranking of occupations, and this dispute can take either of two forms: the psychological and the sociological. That is, a man's judgements may be rooted in the peculiarities of his talents and character or they may derive from his class situation, his membership of a particular social group, or his upbringing in a particular moral milieu. In spite of their name, social indicators seek to cover both psychological and sociological dimensions of consciousness. This is inevitable since, until we have actually constructed our indicators we cannot investigate their typical determinants, and in any case we cannot confine welfare to one or other of the two categories. It is quite possible that tolerance of noise, for example, is psychologically rather than socially determined. To produce adequate indicators for the problem of noise it will be necessary to identify psychological types who react differently to different kinds of noise and to study both the distribution of overall reactivity to noise and the reactions of the types to the various kinds of noise. Similarly, in the social sphere, if different classes of persons have different assessments of the utility of, say, different leisure facilities, then it will be essential, if we are to be in a position to assess trends in the *relative* satisfactoriness of social provision, to measure the different types of facility separately. Too great an emphasis on obtaining generally agreed measures may cause us to neglect aspects, particularly distributional aspects, of society which may be of the greatest relevance to the broader aspects of consent, namely consent to the legitimacy of the current state of the social contract. Dissensus, so far from inhibiting the development of social indicators, could be an important pointer to the sort of indicators that should be developed.

Although the intellectual and social case for the measurement of dissensus is very strong, it must be recognised that it is pitted against forces of a different order. As Richard Rose has said 'when a politician is seeking to strike a bargain between groups with conflicting values, he would actively encourage the dissemination of more ambiguous information concerning the terms of settlement'.[5] In the case of a social indicator, ambiguity is simply achieved by a process of averaging, thus washing out the specific contributions to the average of its elements or components, in particular eliminating those components which are of differential salience to different groups in society. The effect is a tyranny of the average and a denial of the interests of the particular. In this case the particular may be a small minority in society or it may be everyone, since everyone may deviate significantly from the average in some direction or other.

One common way of blurring the meaning of a social indicator is to reduce it to money terms before reporting it. For example, an index of the housing stock may be reported in terms of the costs which would be necessary to bring houses up to a certain standard. Such figures can be hopelessly misleading because they are subjectively estimated, they vary with local costs and with differences in local relative costs, they ignore non-monetary aspects of the environment such as pollution by smell and, in a period of inflation and uneven technical progress, they do not fulfil the basic criterion of being comparable over time. It is a general principle that, whenever a weighting system, such as a set of money costs, is applied to an array of discretely-assessed facts such as the points awarded to various aspects of a house, then. the component features should be analysed and reported, and the effects of using different weighting systems should be studied.

Now we come to a third respect in which we can learn from a misconception of American social policy research, one which is, I think, still in vogue in the United States. We have already touched on a former tendency to treat the facts as conditioning policy without any admixture of moral evaluation. Linked with this is a tendency to regard social policy as mostly a matter of effecting changes which are marginal in amount and temporary in duration. The typical American word for an unsatisfactory social state is 'problem', something, that is, which can be solved and thereby disposed of; and the typical word for ameliorative social action is 'program', something, that is, which has a pre-ordained beginning, middle and end. Thus it is that social scientists in the United States frequently talk as if it were possible to jump to the goal of the 'Great Society' without first passing through a period of building a Welfare State. There is a distinct tendency to see public social provision as emergency breakdown and repair rather than as a service and maintenance contract. When we compare the short-term, problem-orientated ideology of the proponents of the 'Great Society', with the long-term philosophy of the Welfare State, it is possible to see that the sorts of indicators appropriate to the two cases might differ in significant ways (though of course there would be much overlap). The Great Society puts its emphasis on achievement, and a typical educational indicator would be the measured reading age of children. The Welfare State places its emphasis on the cherishing of dispositional qualities and reserves of health, skill and character. A typical educational indicator would be a measure of the span of concentration of children.

It is a matter of common observation that, in public administration, the most important characteristic of a piece of social technology is not its elegance, validity or fitness, but simply its existence at the moment in time when administrators wake up to their need for it. Since social indicators will undoubtedly come in time to perform some of the functions of an examination by which the performance of politicians is judged, and since one of the functions of an examination is to define the curriculum, it is clearly important to ensure that, when social indicators are required, those which fall to hand shall be relevant to the needs and aims of a Welfare State.

It is of course possible to argue that there is less need for social indicators in Britain than in the United States. Our political processes are highly centralised and unusually sensitive to currents of opinion. Furthermore our executive is comparatively unimpeded by constitutional, parliamentary and legal trammels. It is an obvious fact that the extent of pollution of our atmosphere and environment began to decline several years before North America became worried by its apparently greater problems. Social indicators may be needed merely as amplifiers in a society which conducts its business as a dialogue between stentorian lobbies and a deaf Congress.

When, at the end of the Second World War, it was proposed that a survey should be made of the housing stock of Britain, the proposal was turned down for the very adequate reason that the task of repairing damaged houses and building new ones was so obvious and of such magnitude that nice questions about the state of the existing stock were premature. It is marginal adjustments that call for precision instruments; when the direction of travel is obvious to all and the end of the road is not yet in sight, detailed attention to map and compass is simply a distraction from the journey. Any attempt to institute complex procedures of research into the 'effective' distribution of resources may simply cover up a failure either of moral perspective or of political will.

The standpoint of this chapter may be stated succinctly as follows. Social indicators are not essential but they may be useful. If they are not so constructed that they are useful then they will be positively harmful. We have in fact committed ourselves to using indicators and therefore we have no option but to see to it that the indicators we use are satisfactory.

Since we have already elected to undertake a considerable amount of social policy research we are obliged to do it competently, because in so far as we do it incompetently we create an intellectual haze which parts the administrator from his natural wits and blinds the citizen with 'science'. Social indicators may be considered to be a desirable counterbalance to the spread of 'expertise' of all sorts in local and national government and welfare services. They could become a useful adjunct of welfare consumerism and a technical prop to participatory democracy. If, however, the professionals (in this case the sociologists and students of social administration) wrap them in the same intellectual evasions as the planners, or the social workers, or the health service administrators have brought to their spheres of activity, then the only consequence will be that the citizen has yet one more source of mystification to contend with.

It will certainly be averred against me that the greatest mystification of all is created by statisticians and quantifiers who do arcane things with computers. My contention is that although these technicalities are unavoidable, when they are over and done with their logic must be able to stand the test of common rationality. I foresee more danger from intellectual confusion than from technical complexity, for the latter will yield to sustained critical examination whereas the former is unfathomable and can only discourage probing and investigation. A social indicator should be sufficiently perspicuous in its structure and logic to yield up its meaning in response to the probing of a research chemist or a technician who is undertaking an investigation on behalf of his citizen's action committee, party, or pressure group.

Before embarking on a statement of the principles which ought to inform the construction of good social indicators, it is necessary to make some remarks about their interpretation, since we shall all have to learn how to manipulate these new symbolic counters of political debate, if we are not to be manipulated by them. These remarks are occasioned by reports which appeared in the newspapers some time ago stating that a proposal by the Schools Council to alter the marking system for General Certificate of Education Advanced levels had been rejected. The proposal was that marking should be done on a twenty-point scale, in place of the existing much coarser scale, and that a child's certificate should carry not only his assigned mark but also a message to the effect that his true mark could lie anywhere within two points above and two points below his assigned mark. These desirable reforms would have had the effect, first, of mitigating the impression that children's performances fall into discrete categories on a discontinuous scale, and second, of removing the spurious impression of infallibility which is conveyed by a single unqualified mark. To say that the true mark may lie anywhere within a range of four points is simply a way of saying that this is the range of disagreement which has been found to occur when different examiners mark the same paper.

An informed approach to social indicators, like an informed approach to examination marks, requires us to acknowledge that all statistics contain errors, and to accept graciously the offer of the statistician to tell us what the order of magnitude of the errors is. It is not in our own interests to refuse to be told about the admitted inaccuracy of the figures, rather we should be on the lookout to detect unadmitted biases and inaccuracies.

Now I turn to a consideration of the distinguishing features of a useful social indicator. In the past it has been customary to use as social measures characteristics of aggregates such as wards of a city or regions of a country. This is a very natural starting point for research workers because social administrators collect, assemble and report their data in this way. From its very beginnings sociology has tried to argue its propositions on the basis of such aggregated data. Indeed, one of the greatest disappointments suffered by sociology students when they turn from classical sociology to modern empirical work is the sense of let-down which they get as the clear-cut contrast of the classical theorists – clear cut because they relate to typical characteristics of aggregates, with little or no reference to the extent of diversity within the aggregates – blur and melt into the fuzzy and qualified generalisations of latter-day fieldwork. The analysis of data averaged and summarised over areas or institutions is technically known as ecological analysis, and it is becoming more and more common as indices of average teacher input, or mean patient bed-days, or crimes per head of population are fed into computers.

The initial attraction of the data to the research worker is irresistible – I have done several such analyses myself – but the

conclusions that typically emerge are either uninformative or
unsupported by the evidence. Typical of an ecological argument
which goes beyond the evidence adduced is a paragraph in the
Plowden Report *Children and their Primary Schools* in which we
read

> A relationship has been found between the number of children
> in a family and the age of onset of puberty; few children in
> the family is associated with early puberty and many children
> with late puberty. The difference in physical development is
> at least partly nutritional in origin. The National Food
> Surveys have shown that families with many children spend
> appreciably less on food per head than families with few
> children.[6]

However much our common sense may assent to the truth of the
conclusion of this argument, a little reflection will convince us
that the evidence adduced does not actually constitute a valid
argument, since the National Food Survey might have shown
an entirely opposite result without disproving the conclusion.

Basic fallacies of this type are committed with distressing
frequency by workers with ecological data. In essence the
fallacy involves taking two true propositions, the first to the
effect that people in category X tend to have more of characteristic A, and the second to the effect that people in category X
tend to have more of characteristic B, and deducing from them
the conclusion that one and the same people in X tend to have
both A and B. The fallacy is patent and has been pointed out
many times, but it is perpetrated in study after study, with and
without the help of computers. If, however, we go through the
literature of ecological analyses expunging this fallacy we are
left with very few conclusions of substantive interest. It must be
inferred therefore that the social indicators movement of the
future, if it is to get beyond the simple enumeration of discrete,
unrelated indices (a development which is quite essential if our
statistics are to reflect the many-sided situations of different
social groups in our society) must break free of the ecological
approach and concentrate on the collection of information at
the individual rather than the aggregate level.[7]

Although the ecological fallacy has always been fallacious, it
has not always been as misleading as it is now. This is because in

the past social problems of various kinds did in fact have a fairly high degree of geographical concentration, and the life-situation of the bulk of the population in defined areas was, so far as we can see in retrospect, homogeneous and predictable.[8] It is arguable that nowadays there is an increasing diversity of economic, social and psychological circumstances behind the front doors and picture-windows of our apparently homogeneous housing estates. The fitful tide of affluence has been very selective in its encroachment, picking out a couple of houses here, and passing by a flat there, and we may suspect that the activities of the social network operate to exacerbate the inequalities of the market situation, since one of the strongest deterrents to the uptake of selective welfare benefits is the knowledge that more affluent neighbours 'will talk'. Similarly, neurosis and disability, redundancy and accident, strife and separation do not strike by the street or the parish (except in so far as local authority housing managers try to corral problem families on certain estates).[9] If there is one change that quantitative thinking can be expected to bring about in our intellectual life it is a shaking-up of our stereotyped ideas about 'the working-class school' or 'the middle-class area'. Sociologists' ideas about the extent of uniformity within collectivities such as schools or social classes, and about the extent of correlation between different social conditions, will gradually become modified and accommodated to the multifarious diversity of contemporary society. But this development will take time. An intellectual revolution of this kind is ordinarily accomplished, not by developments in the conceptual apparatus of the mass of practising sociologists, but by the supplanting of one generation of workers by another. It is just such intergenerational processes of accelerating intellectual and cultural development that help to constitute the increasing diversity which we observe in society at large.

An analogy from the development of neurophysiology may illustrate the implication of this alleged social diversity for techniques of inquiry. In the days when physiologists thought that the brain might be a relatively undifferentiated soup of grey matter, they studied its working by inserting large and clumsy electrodes which tapped the functioning of whole groups of cells. Now that we know that some individual brain cells perform highly particular functions it is necessary to study them by the use of micro-electrodes that can monitor the operation of single cells, but it was only the introduction of the micro-electrode which enabled us to discern the particular functioning of cells. If the social indicators movement[10] devotes its energies and resources to studying as many of the social, economic and environmental characteristics of individual households as possible, and if it applies to the data refined methods of analysis which enable us to obtain a composite picture of the varying life-situations of social collectivities large and small, then we shall almost certainly find that our society is a good deal more complex than our sociologists have suspected and our administrative arrangements have provided for.

There is, however, one type of collectivity which has become more, rather than less, important as it has diversified internally, and that is the family economic unit. The alleged fact that the family is more fragile than it used to be does not in any way detract from its importance as a unit of analysis. (Indeed, consideration of the various kinds of family disruption which were so frequent in the nineteenth century – from death in childbearing to early induction of children into domestic service – leads one to doubt the facile assumption that instability is greater now than formerly). Empirical investigators have as yet taken little note of the ramifying effects of the not uncommon practice of both spouses working at roughly the same occupational level. Some sociologists of education used to claim that the abolition of the direct grant would withdraw an element of state subsidy from privately-financed pupils and would reduce their number. But my prediction is that independent day schools for boys will flourish as never before because more of their places will be paid for out of the joint earnings of professional parents. However, girls will again suffer relative to their brothers because the parental income will not always suffice to educate all the children in a family. Again, it will become important to look at a spouse's income as a source of independence (for both partners) analogous to inherited capital, and at a spouse's occupational status as potentially disruptive of the status hierarchy of an organisation.

One of the sources of the social indicators movement is the 'human capital' approach to welfare. This had its roots in the observations of economists on the difficulties which developing countries face in the use of physical capital. Economists, noting the rapid recovery of Germany after the Second World War, and contrasting it with the painful growth of Third-World countries where comparable equipment was being used much less efficiently, came to the conclusion that the telling difference was the presence in Germany of an educated and industrially socialised workforce. And so, it was argued, education, instead of being treated as an item of consumption in our national accounts, should be treated as an item of investment, and our stock of education and training should be regarded as human capital matching the physical capital to which it was applied. One of the declared aims of the social indicators movement is the measurement of non-physical human resources such as the health, education and qualifications of the populace.

Immediately we are faced with a puzzling question. What sort of capital are people like? Are they like lathes or buildings or rolling-stock or patented processes or what? As a simple-minded suggestion I propose that they are like Harry Ferguson's tractors, or like those machines which are said by their manufacturers to perform every laborious task in the garden or small-holding with an array of attachments. To spell out the analogy: an educated person is, usually, more or less well-fitted to undertake a number of tasks, but he is not likely to be using all his capabilities in any one job. The various aspects of his education may reinforce one another or they may interfere with one another in the performance of a job. As he exercises some skills others may grow rusty and out of date. An addition of one year of education, or one more qualification, to his existing stock may improve his efficiency – or it may induce him to desert economic activity in favour of contemplation – becoming a monk or an academic. In the case of women, education may be a differentia distinguishing a frustrated housewife from a contented one. Because a person is a carrier or embodiment of education rather than a mere owner of it there are costs of reciprocal interference between different skills, there are suboptimalities as well as additivities in his exercise of them, and there are costs of maintenance and of switchover as he moves from one job to another.

If there is any truth in these analogies then it follows once again that the effective educational level of a population cannot be adequately measured by aggregated indicators. Two societies with very similar numbers of 'A' level certificates may be in very different educational states because in one a small number of persons has several certificates each, while in the other certificates are more evenly spread. The situation can become very complicated when all kinds of qualification are taken into account. Two societies with different distributions of qualifications may in fact represent the same country at two points in time and it follows that, if we are to say anything more informative than that 'there is more education about nowadays', we must find means of assessing the educational preparedness of individuals, resolutely turning our backs on the appealing and simple, but virtually useless, task of totting up certificates.

A further principle which may be advanced as a defining characteristic of a rational social indicator movement is attention to the distinction between the state or stock of a particular social good and the use to which that good is put. We have already alluded to the case of the educated housewife. The distinction between capacity and use will become more and more important with the passage of time. There have always been wealthy persons who used more than their fair share of resources but we are now in a state of society where a *significant proportion* of an *enlarged population* is looking for ways of spending its *more-than-proportional share* of an *enlarged national income*. Naturally, in this situation, maintenance of a truly distinctive life-style by any social stratum calls for the exercise of more and more ingenuity in choice of expenditures, ingenuity which is doomed to frustration since less wealthy strata, because they already engage in transferrable sumptuary expenditure, can switch their spending patterns without waiting until they have caught up in the economic race.

Some of the effects of this state of affairs, such as the marketing of a limited issue of effigies of Tutankhamen in basalt, are of only marginal concern to the social indicators movement. But examples of under-utilisation such as the occupancy of family houses by elderly widows, and the purchase of a second house for various purposes, must undoubtedly be taken into account.

We must always bear in mind that a social indicator is basically about people, and if it offers us a measure of some physical characteristic, such as noise or golf courses or buses or houses, which is thought to be relevant to the welfare of people, then it is essential to the rationale of the exercise that some means should be included of assessing the actual bearing of the environmental characteristic on people. This does not mean that we should naively attempt to take people's happiness into account in our calculations, since that would introduce all sorts of tangles and produce some odd results. But it does mean that, in order to perform its functions of alleviating hardship, lightening disability, easing constraints, and mitigating the evils of mobility and affluence, the State must monitor both the provision which exists and the ways in which that provision is actually applied.

Once again our principle points explicitly to the need to study individuals and households, rather than aggregated data thrown up as a by-product of administration. To mention an obvious example: we might pride ourselves on a great expansion of education for leisure only to find, when adequate indicators become available, that the people with the most leisure are those who are least likely to have acquired skills for its use.

In sum, then, we have three principles that combine to define an adequate set of social indicators as a wide-ranging combination of measures applied to households and to individuals in those households. The first principle states that, as areas become less homogeneous social problems become more particular in their incidence. The second is that in so far as indicators are measures of human resources they must take into account the peculiar features of resources that are embodied in human beings. And the third is that indicators of capacity or stock must be related to indicators of use or availability.

Whenever a bureaucracy is set up we know that, whatever its ostensible purposes, it will seek to bend those aims to the convenience of its internal organisation, and the more vague and diffuse its aims the more readily will they be made to serve the 'needs' of the bureaucratic organisation. Furthermore, we are all aware that the expression of official standards in quantitative form frequently has the effect of defining them as maxima. It is unlikely that the social indicators movement, and the social research which will stem from it, will be exempt from these twin bureaucratic dangers. The social indicators movement, though humanitarian in its ostensible aims, could readily be wrested to undesirable ends. As a weapon in the armoury of social control it could simply be used to blind the populace with science. A sound social indicators movement would have gladdened the heart and strengthened the arm of many of the great reformers of the past 150 years or so. What I fear is not that such a movement will develop but that an intellectually-frustrating and socially opaque imitation will emerge from an unholy alliance of administrators and social researchers in which the former pay the latter to obscure as many issues as possible in a fog of seemingly relevant but logically unrelated numbers.

My reason for saying this is that the situation in this country lacks a basic ingredient for the development of good social policy research, and that is the ingredient of technically informed criticism. British sociology lacks that plurality of openly competing institutions which, in Popper's terms, ensures that work of integrity is done even by scientists who lack integrity. When a physicist published an observation of a new sub-atomic phenomenon recently it was reported that forty papers disputing, confirming, or explaining the phenomenon had been published within six weeks of the original announcement. Reading Watson's account of the discovery of *The Double Helix*[11] one becomes aware that each laboratory director is on the lookout for ideas and talent which will keep his team in the pages of the international journals. British sociologists, it seems to me, have opted out of the international journals in the quantitative, analytical field (which are, in effect, the American journals) to such a degree that one wonders whether they have any part to play in the development of indicators.

The logic of devolving the work on sociologists is clear. Sociology claims to be an empirical social science. It must therefore employ devices to measure key social variables. Why not, therefore, adapt and extend those devices for application in social policy research? The difficulty about this argument is that a serious question-mark hangs over the suggestion that sociology in Britain is, or even claims to be, an empirical social science. When it is compared with the American discipline with the same name one is forced to ask whether it should not perhaps be described as observational, interpretive journalism, rather than social science.

The contrast between the British and American sociological disciplines is of course in part attributable to their differing origins, the one in German historical studies (from which economics, in contrast, made an early escape when it fell under the influence of the Austrian analytical school), and the other in native investigations of a country so vast and heterogeneous that the concept of variance could not for long be neglected.[12] A further difference is in the nature of the societies studied: American investigations of social mobility ask whether their traditionally open society is becoming more rigid, whereas British investigations ask whether a rigid society is becoming more open, and it is possible that this difference in starting point reflects a real difference between the two societies.

What is relevant to our present concerns is, however, not the origins of the contrast but the differences in the nature of institutions that perpetuate it. Although there is evidence that Americans are not really so opposed to 'welfare' as they once were[13] (but it should be noted that the word 'welfare' in the United States conjures up an image of cash benefits or stamps, whereas in Britain it is primarily associated with services) they are still not very sure about its legitimacy. The United States is a society which is not heartily convinced of the need for social welfare and social planning. There is a greater diversity of consciously defended value-systems within the sociology profession than there is in Britain, and as a consequence of this diversity the intellectual debate is keener. In this country any research worker who comes up with vaguely progressive conclusions is likely to get an uncritical hearing, however rubbishy his work. The latter-day versions of discussions which used to fill the pages of *The Edinburgh Review* are now to be found in *The Public Interest*, for which there is no modern British equivalent.

It might have been hoped that publication of the Black Papers on education would have represented the opening shots in an intellectual war whose effect might have been to eliminate the laxity among social researchers, but in fact the contest has not yet developed beyond a skirmish.[14] It is not at all clear that either side in that debate would have any real interest in objective, independent data on educational standards, however defined. Certainly, neither side has set about collecting any. Nevertheless, while the ideologies of left and right hurl their symbolic shafts at one another there is an alternative ideology which for want of a better name can be called consumerist or populist. This holds that if children and their parents think that education standards matter then they do matter, and it is up to the sociologists to earn their salaries by undertaking competent research into them. Similarly, if educational policy hinges, as the debate would appear to suggest, on the question of how far differences in cognitive ability are due to genetic factors, then sociologists must begin to collect data relevant to the question (so far all the 'work' that has been done in this area by British sociologists has consisted of throwing brickbats at the research of others).

Sociologists, by and large, claim that they are practising a theoretical discipline in which empirical evidence is the arbiter of theory and opinion. One naturally expects, therefore, in surveying the hundreds of sociologists now at work in Britain, to find a significant proportion of them busily engaged in prosecuting longitudinal inquiries, panel studies, twin studies, controlled trials, double-blind experiments, rating studies, instrumentation exercises and calibration studies, and reporting the results in journals. In fact they are doing virtually none of these things. With few exceptions they are lecturing, writing books about books, engaging in journalism, and talking about the thesis they never quite finished or the bit of participant observation that they may do one day. For many of them their one essay in empirical inquiry is the occasional questionnaire survey, usually of one particular locality, factory or social collectivity. In consequence, as one would expect, their empirical work is lacking in expertise. In particular, they are incompetent to undertake investigations which require knowledge of quantitative techniques.

The wits, and the techniques, of our social researchers need sharpening, and no amount of teaching in the context of an anti-quantitative culture will suffice. What is required is the consciousness that the aims, design, execution, analytic acumen and lucidity of presentation of one's work will be subjected to rigorous scrutiny by competent and suspicious critics who may speak from a different social experience and a different political persuasion. In the United States there is a number of journals, circulating widely among a sizable college-educated public and feeding material into the mass media, in which leading sociologists as a matter of routine evaluate the academic competence and social implications of each other's work. The vehicles for such a debate are not nearly so well developed in Britain. Since public, critical, academic pluralism does not exist it must be invented. The balance of research and criticism should be righted by incorporating a formal assessment process in any research which is set up to answer questions that have general administrative and political implications, and that of course includes work on the development of social indicators. Such an assessment would be undertaken by competent empirical researchers who were not themselves involved in the work they were assessing, and the authors of the work would have the right of formal reply, so that the document which was laid before the administrators and the public would contain the original work, an appraisal of it, and a comment on the appraisal.

In many cases the assessment would be of considerable value in itself, since one of its functions would be to interpret the results of the research to the policy-makers.[15] But the main virtue of the proposal lies in the probable effect of the prospect of critical review on the research worker himself, particularly on the stringency of his thinking at the design stage, which is where much research begins its decline into disaster (and which often, if the truth were told, has only a sketchy and ambiguous existence).

One of the difficulties of participation in government by members of the public is the ignorance that we all feel when we face the experts – because we do not fully understand their jargon or the initials by which they refer to departments and projects, and because we cannot follow their tables and maps and diagrams. There are two ways of preventing the human eye from seeing colours, one is to keep it in the dark and the other is to bombard it with the whole spectrum of colours which sum to make white light. Similarly it is possible to overwhelm the public with information by serving it up in indigestible quantities. One of the important functions of a sound set of social indicators is to provide a limited number of salient figures which summarise and illuminate large quantities of background data. One hopes that the time will come when a watchful public will impose a demand for clarity and relevance on social research, for what is at stake is not merely the resources which go into the research but the degree of self-determination in our society. A general sense of defeat before a rising tide of esoteric but apparently germane documents cannot be good for participatory democracy.

If we seek a model and a warning which will give us some idea of the possible course of development of social research as a profession then we shall probably find it in the planning profession. The characteristics of planners, their large-handed sacrifice of the present to a glorious future, their belief that they have privileged access to higher values, their swift changes of fashion, and the chaos caused by the sudden demise of their projects in mid-career as political control moves from one party to another, all these are present to some degree among social researchers. There have been stirrings, notably in the London motorway inquiry, of a move to call the planning profession to account by forcing it to make explicit its values and assumptions and to publish feasible alternatives to its recommendations.[16]

The relative absence of informed criticism in British social science is partly a consequence of technical backwardness (a backwardness which would be easier to explain if it were not that we have a strong statistical tradition and the leading literature is all published in English). But it is also not unrelated to the strongly centralised nature of cultural and political life. If it were not for government backing, most social research, including the social indicators movement, would dry up. But the dependence is two way, in that to an increasing degree government policy statements are expected to have some rags of legitimation cast about them by quantitative research. The worrying thing is that more and more research is commissioned – because policy documents must make some reference to research – but much of the work repeats the mistakes of the past, and the overall quality remains disappointing and well below the standard of the best American work. The distinguishing features of research as legitimation are not that its inferences are just, or even that its conclusions are correct, but first, that its conclusions are not incompatible with administrators' preconceived ideas, and second, that it is in tune with the current academic orthodoxy and unlikely therefore to promote controversy, since controversy, whatever its ultimate outcome, totally nullifies the legitimating function.

My impression is that social research commissioned by government departments is of particularly poor quality. Implementation of the Rothschild report *A Framework for Government Research and Development*[17] might produce speciously relevant work, but much of it would, on the present showing, be quite disreputable. A government department tends to promote research on services rather than problems, and this often means that alternative ways of dealing with a problem are not compared because they come under different departments. A department may, of course, have competent advisors, but it does not have the institutional structure for ensuring that advice is properly processed and applied. The advantage of a research council over a department as an initiator of research is that it has institutions which are specifically designed to maintain contacts, keep a panel of advisors up to date, obtain counterbalancing opinions, tap a range of disciplines, and compare local with international standards. Government departments are very liable to 'capture' by particular intellectual cliques. Furthermore, and the importance of this point can scarcely be exaggerated, there is no way of knowing how long a department will take to process a research application. The applicant is in the position of a suppliant begging alms and waiting on his patron's pleasure, whereas a council has explicit rules on the timing of applications and the duration of processing them. There is very little possibility of keeping a coherent research team in being when the source of money is a department whose decisions are often taken, or delayed, on a highly personal basis. Government-sponsored social research is a field in which patronage and Gresham's law march hand in hand.

The task of a department should not be the commissioning of research (it should channel this through the relatively impersonal and more technically competent procedures of a research council). Rather should it be a conscious attempt to spell out the decisions which policy-makers are likely to be facing over the next few years. The major problem which is raised by this conception of a civil servant's contribution to research is not the difficulty of forecasting future options, but the difficulty of persuading a department that entertaining a possibility is not equivalent to committing oneself to a policy.

This discussion of the social indicators movement began by pointing out that its ethos is closely allied to that of American social policy generally, which is a policy of marginal adjustments in response to perceived specific problems, rather than a policy of maintenance and service to keep the wheels of the whole social structure turning. I cannot conceive any set of social indicators which, if they had been in existence in 1940, would have had the effect of generating the White Paper on the National Health Service which was produced in that year as part of the bargain by which the support of the representatives of the lower orders was secured for the war effort. The concept of a National Health Service was essentially ideologically determined, its realisation was a redistributional bargain between classes, and the details of its administrative structure were a series of inspired compromises between the ideals of its conception and the interests and prejudices of those who would have to make it work. The fact that it has served the bulk of the nation so well for so long, and that we are still in the process of realising some of its basic provisions, cannot be attributed to social indicators or quantitative social research because these scarcely existed in 1940. Sir Karl Popper has gone so far as to suggest that his amiable character, the piecemeal social engineer, 'will avoid undertaking reforms of a complexity and scope which make it impossible for him to disentangle causes and effects, and to know what he is really doing'. This injunction was intended to rule out revolution but, taken seriously, it would also rule out most of our existing reforms.

In the paper from which I have already quoted, Richard Rose points out that, whereas in Washington administrators tend to act like politicians, at Westminster, such is the prestige of administration that a politician on becoming a minister typically recasts his self-image to that of an administrator. It is, therefore, possible to imagine that social indicators, when they become available, will to a not unimportant degree replace ideologies as the symbolic counters of politicians and, because the sorts of games that can be played with them are so limited, the administrative conceptions of politicians will be constrained by the poverty of their symbols. It may of course be argued that the broad brush which created the Health Service is no longer required and that social indicators are well suited to the sort of small changes of course which will be required in the future. However, that argument carries with it obvious dangers. Telescopes and theodolites are designed to improve the range and accuracy of unaided human perception, but instruments of this kind typically restrict vision to a minute fraction of the perceptual field. This does not matter because their users employ them, not as mere improvers of vision, but as adjuncts to a process of intellectual exploration which is carried on in the armchair and on the calculating machine as well as in the field. Social indicators, as aids to the administrative perception of society, could prove to be severely limiting in their effects. However partial it may be there is nothing quite like personal social experience to make one discriminating in the interpretation of social statistics. Even today many of our policy-makers have little relevant personal experience which could give them insight into the stories which social indicators have to tell. For example, in a radio interview in September 1974 Sir Keith Joseph spoke of how elated he had been when, as housing minister, he had signed orders to pull down hundreds of old dwellings and replace them by high-rise flats, and how correspondingly betrayed he had felt when he was later told that by this action he had been destroying communities and fomenting neurosis. At the time of the broadcast he was engaged in a debate in which he featured as a protagonist of unemployment.

Social indicators, even well-constructed social indicators, are not good in themselves. Their value is dependent on the institutional framework within which they are used. The best guarantee I can suggest for ensuring that they are not misused is that they should be competently constructed according to public and comprehensible, even if technical, criteria. If they are, then it will be in principle possible for journalists and members of the public to bring their experience to bear in assessing the information which the indicators contain. It is imperative that, by one means or another, social indicators be kept in the public political arena.

Part Five

Conclusion

14   A Question of Numbers ?*

David Eversley

The question of the right use of mathematical, and particularly statistical methods, in the social sciences has produced a huge literature. I am not qualified to discuss this, nor I think has it any great bearing on the central theme of this chapter. Reference to the pioneers of the use of numerical methods in the social sciences will occur only in order to illustrate particular problems, not in order to join the great debates on survey methods, on the use of models, and other topics which fill the pages of our learned journals. Nor do I wish to take issue with what Sorokin calls quantophrenia[1] or the cult of numerology or what might be called the deficiencies of *homo mensor*. I am less concerned with the question whether one can deduce from particular observations a set of generally valid laws, or whether such laws are in fact appropriate to social science, than with the question whether useful practical inferences may be drawn, and whether 'objectivity' is enough to achieve changes in policy and opinion. The formulation of laws is usually desired in order to use existing data for forecasting the future: this again is a problem with which we cannot deal here, while recognising that any attempted policy application involves some belief in the ability to forecast

* The text of a Runnymede Trust Lecture given in London on 22 March 1972, reprinted with the permission of the author.

results of certain courses of action, and to influence opinion by quasi-scientific demonstration.

The main question is: how useful is statistical evidence, however good, as an instrument for social policy-making and opinion forming? In this process there are various stages, such as problem identification, testing of policy options, and implementation. But the central problem is this: how does the use of numerical methods relate to other means of persuading people that a problem exists, or does not exist, that a particular solution should be adopted, or not adopted, that a causal chain exists, or does not exist? I have come to this problem in a number of ways, and though the fields in which I have worked are rather dissimilar in other respects, the matter of the relationship between quantitative and non-quantitative ways of reasoning is common to them. There is, strictly speaking, a third fundamental method of arguing about causalities and policies. This is by using pure logic, or deductive reasoning. Quite often, social scientists discuss such matters as social structure neither in terms of observation in the quantitative sense, nor in terms of statistical evidence, but in terms of a model which subsumes all the variables they consider important. It does not matter whether they quote facts of one kind or another (statistical or not) in support of the rightness of their logical deductions: the essence of the model is that it has its own inner, compelling logic.

Let us take examples from three fields in which I have worked to illustrate some of the difficulties involved. As an economic historian, brought up in the school of Tawney and Ashton, I was taught to research into facts, and to array these facts into a coherent story. From such researches one then produced, by inductive logic, causal explanations: about the origins of the Industrial Revolution, or the causes of the Great Depression. Although there have been early examples of economic historians using statistics in support of their theories (notably Sombart and Weber), the great tradition of the subject was almost entirely descriptive, with texts inter-larded here and there, in the manner of Sir John Clapham, with carefully chosen statistics. In other words, historians knew what they did because they were readers of documents, and because they had intuition, and they appealed to whatever numbers were available to help them convince their readers. Over time, these statistics became more plentiful, as new sources were discovered, and with historians like Elizabeth Schumpeter, T. S. Ashton and Phyllis Deane, the numerical basis gained strength. But one always had to remember that the statistics which were available were often fortuitous survivals: trade accounts, the ledgers of a single firm, a tax return. Refutation of theories therefore often took the form of taking another set of statistics, perhaps equally fortuitous in origin, and proving the opposite view.

One must also remember that contemporary statistics were quite often collected to serve purposes rather different from those for which they were used by later historians: for instance, to prove the necessity, or otherwise, for a population restraint policy, to evade duties on foreign trade[2] or to prove the success, or otherwise, of a government's social policies or methods for promoting trade and industry.

I tried to work with somewhat more neutral methods of presenting statistics in relation to some chosen subjects; first the effects of the Great Depression of the 1870s on investment,[3] and later, in the field of population, using parish registers to try to explain the growth of population in the eighteenth century.[4] These were modest beginnings, twenty years ago, and there has now grown up, in Cambridge, a great industry of historical demography, computer based and strictly avoiding any explanation of what happened to population in history until many hundreds of thousands of facts, births, deaths and marriages, could be made into a single watertight logical system. Our own study in this field has progressed from a study of ten parishes in Worcestershire, for which all calculations were still done on a manually operated machine, to an investigation of 10 000 Quaker families from the seventeenth to the nineteenth century, now beginning to show results which are turned out by a computer in Newcastle, on a programme written by the Cambridge Group. The interesting point is that my partner in this study is an American historian of theories and ideas, Richard Vann, whose aim it is to throw some light on the origins of Quaker social and political attitudes with the help of the same statistical facts which I am trying to use to determine the onset of family planning and the period in English urban history when sanitation began to reduce infant mortality.[5] Numerical methods have penetrated into some entirely new fields of study.[6]

From economic history and historical demography it is only a short step into current population studies, and here numbers are the essence of a discipline, which began as political arithmetic, in the days of John Graunt and William Petty, from whom there is a straight succession to David Glass, the most important living exponent of the method of demographic study based strictly on ascertainable facts, and owing little to hypothetical speculations.[7] Malthus and his disciples, and latter-day imitators, belong to the other school of population students: those who conceive a grand design, and then use numbers only as evidence that they are right.[8]

Policy and the Numbers Game

It was only in the field of race relations, however, that I was properly brought face to face with the relationship between policy and the numbers game.[9] This is not the place to rehearse the sordid history of the attempt to scare the country into the belief that it was about to be overrun by great hordes of alien invaders who would, within measurable time, become the majority of inhabitants not only of some of our great cities, but also a sizable, and threatening minority elsewhere.[10] Whereas Malthus had merely confined himself to the assertion that mankind had a tendency to multiply too fast for its own good, and believed that there was a good chance of averting catastrophe if people would only act prudently and morally, our contemporary prophets of doom foretold civil strife, the breakdown of our culture, our way of life, in the absence of draconic measures to redress the balance. It has been the main task of the Institute of Race Relations to combat prejudice, to set the record straight, to investigate methods of dealing with the problem, such as it is.

The particular task which we performed for the Institute was to try to provide answers to the allegation that even though the unrestricted immigration of coloured Commonwealth citizens had been stopped in 1962, the provision that those already here might bring over their dependants meant that the growth of the non-white population of Britain would continue at a very high rate because, it was alleged, each of the males already in the United Kingdom had at least one wife, and a large number of children, so that not only would the absolute number of first generation immigrants increase but the foundation would be laid, given the high fertility of these people, for a progressive increase of the ratio of the coloured population. Using imaginary figures for the numbers of dependants still to come, and the birth statistics of one or two selected Caribbean and Asian countries, it was possible to produce a picture designed to cause grave anxieties, if not downright hostility, in the white population. Estimates varied, but it was thought possible that by the end of the century there would be five, seven or even ten million coloured people here, forming, according to one's assumption about the reproductive habits of the white population, and its propensity to emigrate in the face of rapidly deteriorating conditions in England, anything up to 15 or even 20 per cent of the whole population, quite apart from the emergence of the predominantly black cities.[11] Now the answer to this sort of scare can be given in various ways:

(1) Liberal and humane intellectuals may dismiss the whole matter as being of no consequence: it is not worth spending any time on refuting prognostications which, whether true or false, do not affect any issue of significance: believing all men to be equal, we do not care about the colour of their skin or the shape of their noses.

(2) We can try to prove that the prognostications are false, and perhaps, that a mistake was made by suppressing part of the truth, or by quoting statistics out of context, and so on.

(3) To assert that though the subject is not one of importance to right-thinking men, and although the statistics used in the argument are false, it is not worth refuting the assertions since the whole debate is merely a minor symptom of a deep-rooted disease in a basically sick and doomed society, so that both argument from first principles and attempts at empirical refutation are bound to fail. What has been striking in the recent debates about both matters of race relations and other subjects, for instance the environmental controversies, is the absence from the field of debate of some of our greatest social investigators who take this detached attitude towards these emotional issues.

The work we eventually undertook[12] was of the empirical kind: we investigated the known facts about the sex, age and marital composition of the existing immigrant population, derived from data relating both to those already in this country and those in their home countries, and deduced from these the likely number of wives and children under sixteen who might still arrive here, if they all chose to come, within the next few years.

We calculated maximum values for each category, and in the event, the arrivals in the three years following the publication of our monograph, proved to be a little less than these maxima, so that one could say that the work we did was reasonably satisfactory as demographic forecasts go.

But two observations must be made. First of all, it is quite impossible to detect any lessening of the fears about the future racial composition of this country as a result of this and similar efforts, let alone the other manifestations of racial prejudice (for example, about the fertility of immigrants, their morals and manners). Secondly, if we were right, this may to a large extent have been accidental, since the statistics on which we based our work may have been much less reliable than we thought, since the methods of extrapolation used were criticised at the time by experts in the field as being unwarranted, and since some of our assumptions (for example, about the reflux of immigrants to their own countries, and the degree to which their reproductive habits were affected by separation and in the long run by assimilation in the new environment), may have been wrong.[13]

Statistics and the Planner

From 1969 to 1972 I was a planner, not primarily concerned with land use, but with social and economic objectives of planning in the widest sense, allocating not only land but other scarce resources to a common objective – the welfare of people in London.

At the Greater London Council, statistics are produced, put on computers, printed out, evaluated and inserted into policy documents at a truly astonishing rate. 'Number-crunching' is a specialist activity, and there are a large number of people engaged in it. Many years ago, when I first became interested in this subject and perhaps under the influence of Barbara Wootton, I fancied that all that was needed to produce sound policies were accurate facts, preferably long series of statistics which could be averaged, extrapolated and generally manipulated with the help of the techniques then becoming popular.[14] Thus, in relation to the overspill problem in the West Midlands, as it was then called, we thought that the obvious solution, that is two new towns, could be made generally acceptable by proving from population and housing statistics that no other method was possible, and we published a small monograph which said this with the help of rather a large number of tables.[15] The West Midlands got their new towns, but I do not believe it was due to our monograph. My impression is that the planning of this organised regional re-structuring was a political response to pressures which were becoming uncomfortable – on the Green Belt, on the housing authorities, on the social services.

Then came what is widely regarded as a landmark in the history of the use of statistics in the business of devising strategies. The Robbins report on higher education[16] surely became the acceptable basis of long-term planning mainly because of the elegant persuasiveness of its text tables and statistical appendices, produced by Claus Moser, now head of·the Central Statistical Office. Sir Claus Moser has been an important agent in promoting the possibility, nationally, of examining existing policies and future options in the light of a much larger array of facts than was previously available.[17]

But to return to planning. The later 1960s saw an important growth in the application of numerical methods to land use and transportation problems. A fashion grew up for models, systems, and networks, largely originating in the United States, and the British empirical approach demanded that data be collected to be fitted into the hypotheses which the models provided. At first, only transportation problems were surveyed to obtain data, but gradually the process extended to all forms of economic activity and social structure. This is not the place to examine these methods in any detail. They do not in any case form the only type of statistical approach to planning. Almost any policy which was desired, defended, or attacked, could be seen in terms of statistical proofs – or lack of them. Whereas, in 1940, the Barlow Commission[18] could still report in largely qualitative terms and produce a long-term regional policy which is still with us, the 1960s saw a new generation of investigations which stood or fell by their statistical contents. Perhaps one should cite here the various regional and national economic studies, the Hunt Report on the Intermediate Areas,[19] and Reddaway's Report on the effects of Selective Employment Tax.[20] They are all good examples of how figures can be used to convince the reader of the validity of both assertions and denials. Thus, from exactly the same set of statistics, Sir Joseph Hunt recommended that Merseyside should be de-scheduled as a development area, and Professor A. J. Brown concluded that it should not.[21]

At the Greater London Council I began to realise just how much could be done if one seriously set about collecting and processing data. Under Bernard Benjamin, the Research and Intelligence Unit had become a major factory, as well as a warehouse, of facts relating to London. When a large part of his former unit was handed over to Strategy Branch it was with the intention of mobilising this great wealth more quickly in the interests of policy-making. Of the many hundreds of volumes or shorter papers handed to the Panel which inquired into the Greater London Development Plan from 1970 to 1972, the majority either consist of statistical tables, or at any rate are based on key presentations of statistical material. In other words, it seems to be accepted that if it can be put down to percentages, quartiles, disaggregated by sectors, compared with the region, interpolated, extrapolated, have a curve fitted, or show an R bar square value of over 0.9, it must be evidence.

Now despite this mass of material, and the undoubted expertise of those who compiled it, what stands out the most is the fact that, internally, the expert officers of the G.L.C. differed a great deal as to the significance of their own figures. Thus to take only a single issue, something which for short we call 'social polarisation', a term in itself devoid of much meaning but generally taken to connote a situation where a particular area, such as London, is tending to produce, not a smooth and continuous distribution of income or social status groups around a mean, but a tendency for middle income and status families to move out, or not to migrate inwards, so that, in the end, there are relatively greater concentrations of the better-off at one end of the scale, and a very much larger number of worse-off people at the other end. Now we all had the same set of statistics in front of us, and we split into three groups: those who believed, like Bernard Benjamin, that it was all nonsense, a rather larger agnostic group in the middle, and a small group at the other end who could see signs that it was already happening, enough at any rate to advocate a prophylactic set of policies.[22]

This is a situation one recognises as occurring constantly in other fields of the social sciences. It is familiar in the debates on the causes of population growth in eighteenth-century Britain (and for that matter, Western Europe in general). It is normal in attempts to interpret criminal statistics, facts about mental illness, and the effects of certain educational policies.

What therefore interests us are the larger questions underlying the whole strategy of social research, the importance of quantitatively based judgements and, indeed, much further than that, the possibility of objectivity. To this subject Gunnar Myrdal devoted an important lecture in 1967.[23]

Myrdal is the more important as an exponent of the possibilities of objectivity because in his most famous own work, *An American Dilemma: The Negro Problem and Modern Democracy*[24] as well as his later writings, he has consistently exposed the impossibility of keeping beliefs and the values that are based on these beliefs out of social science investigations, and stressed that the important thing is to *declare* these subjective influences, not to attempt to pretend that they do not exist. He does not deny that more factual information can help to dispel prejudices, especially against racial minorities, but it requires a high standard of general education to expose the prejudiced observer as an ignoramus. But, of course, he realises that factual research specifically directed towards the dispersal of popular and institutional prejudices is in itself not value free. Following his call, much research has been done on the methods that are useful in changing public and individual opinions: we will not follow him into these fields. Although this chapter is concerned with the use of statistical methods, it will be obvious to the reader that the author, like most of his generation, can only approach the problem as a whole with the warnings which Myrdal gave, in his mind. Such a personal avowal, Myrdal would claim, is in itself a necessary pre-condition for informing the reader of one's own bias. The lecture referred to, in fact, like this chapter, begins with a 'personal note', that is an account of how Myrdal came to hold the opinions he did.[25]

Numbers and the Human Sciences

It is necessary to say something both about the significance of numbers in themselves as well as the possibility of using them to produce the detached or objective approach.

That our remote ancestors attached great importance to numbers is a commonplace. Apart from the somewhat misguided attempts to find mystical mathematical formulae in connection with the Great Pyramids of Egypt, there is evidence that astronomy, and closely related to it, speculation about the future, was the first science which linked mankind to quantitative observation. It is commonplace, too, that the fourth book of the Pentateuch is not only called Numbers but actually begins with an injunction to take a census. And of course but for a well-administered attempt to take another census, Bethlehem would scarcely figure in our culture as it does.

Both the anxieties about the size of the population and the magical properties that numbers themselves possess, have survived the ages, though one would not say that the almost mystical faith shown in statistical tables by some of our contemporary pundits owes anything to the practice of astrology, or that the office of the Registrar General is motivated by the same considerations as King Herod.

What is more important is the derivation, from the first beginnings of accurate observation by the earliest astronomers, surveyors and physicians, both in the West and in the East, of our great scientific traditions. The theories and controversies in the field of natural science, however, have been of a different order from those which were concerned with what we now call the human sciences, though the division into natural and moral philosophy is of relatively recent origin.

From Archimedes through Galileo and Newton to Einstein, the physical sciences developed in one way, the human sciences in another. With a few notable exceptions such as Galileo and Tycho Brahe, proponents of new scientific theories have not aroused persecution or popular emotions. To be proved wrong, for instance, as were so many medical experts by Koch and Pasteur, was no great disgrace. Deliberate faking was frowned upon, though such episodes are more of interest to specialists than to the public at large. The Piltdown Man or Lysenko give rise to cynical comment, but such cases do not excite the passions of outsiders. Whether the universe is in a steady state, or exploding, is not of great interest to politicians.

The human sciences are a different case altogether and it is worth investigating a little further why this should be so. First, one must perceive their essential humanness. Piaget,[26] in an essay explaining the backwardness of the subject by its recent origins, at the same time gives very good reasons why most people prefer to perceive reality intuitively, if they can see it at all, rather than experimentally. Even experiments where they can be performed at all, are generally the result either of a need to verify hypotheses already deduced from general principles, or intuitively conceived from often unconscious observation.[27] This then is one root cause of the difficulty: that in the social sciences, to a large extent, we deal with matters which are the subject of universal experience and observation, and on which we have views whether we are the man on top of the Clapham Omnibus, or Gunnar Myrdal. If we are well educated, what we have read will of course form part of our total apparatus of perception, and if we are self-conscious humanists and liberals, we shall also instinctively try to guard ourselves against unwarranted interferences, and base our experiments on a careful elimination of the possibility of building on prior prejudices, though, as Myrdal shows, the attempt usually fails.

The social scientists have for a long time been engaged in the search for the controlled experiments. They have been obsessed by a peculiar form of envy for the physical scientist and the familiar pre-conditions for his type of experiment with inanimate matter: the possibility of precise measurement, the testing of almost any hypothesis in laboratories, the ability to verify a theory by the fulfilment of a prediction. More particularly, the natural scientist can construct his experiment with a limited number of variables, in finite space, and within a limited time-span in which all other factors may be held constant, or subject only to controlled and observed variations.

These conditions are not normally attainable in the fields discussed here. It may be said that there is nothing new in this: that in fact every elementary manual of social research says so. But perhaps it is still worth pointing out just how far the lack of similarity between physical and social research can go. For instance, it is true, when discussing inter-group relations, that the 'environment' is part of the investigation. But this may be simply a matter of background, of setting the scene. Basically such research is concerned with the effect people have on each other, not on their interaction with their environment. But space, and its properties, can become the essence of the enquiry. G. Cherry, looking at a poor part of Newcastle upon Tyne,[28] observed that there was a relationship between overcrowding and a large collection of social ills: poverty, delinquency, ill-health, educational under-achievement. His first conclusion was that overcrowding was the cause of this social pathology. But, of course, it was the other way round: people who were poor, sick, or inadequate found the cheapest and nastiest shelter available in the city and then crammed themselves into such housing up to and beyond its capacity, to reduce per capita cost, and because there is too little of such housing. Cherry might have observed that throughout the country even fit local authority housing has much more overcrowding than owner-occupied housing. Or again take another well-known urban situation: neuroses associated with new towns, suburban estates, or high-rise buildings. It is often assumed that the act of putting families in such new dwellings causes breakdowns of individuals and families. Those of us who have our own reservations about certain types of development usually cite particular investigations (for example those of Fanning[29] on neuroses in high-rise married quarters in B.A.O.R. settlements as evidence); others prefer Willmott and Young[30] on the iniquities of Harold Hill, and Americans have a whole string of researches into the New Town Blues going back to Harold Orlans's[31] study of Stevenage. Norman Dennis's onslaught on the city fathers of Sunderland[32] is the latest in this long line of attacks on the planning system. Now most of these studies offend in one way or another against what would be considered elementary rules by a natural scientist. They are in themselves unobjectionable by the canons of social science, but because of certain limitations they are capable of being misused by those who read them. For instance, Willmott and Young did NOT say that it was wrong to clear urban slums, and to build modern houses on the edge of the country. The wise-after-the-event pundits who have now found out that children reared in the L.C.C.'s showpiece estate at Roehampton have found outlet for their energies in persecuting homosexuals on Wimbledon Common have not actually said that public housing should never be built in a desirable visual environment. All these investigations in fact are about a number of connected features and activities: first, there is the physical framework: slums, modern estates, open spaces, industrial tracts, transport systems, noise, pollution, dirt, fresh air, balconies, lifts, safety grilles, backyards. Then there is the system of social and economic relationships: kinship patterns, mothers-in-law, child-rearing practices, women going out to work, the place of pub, bingo hall, football stadium or chapel in the pattern of life. Then there is the nature of the individuals and the families involved: wives of serving soldiers are not in the same kind of universe as Bethnal Green furniture workers' families, or Sunderland shipyard craftsmen. The skill-group which formed the *avant-garde* of Stevenage settlers is very different from the Shotts miners who could not be moved to Fifeshire, in one of the classical sociological planning investigations of the post-war years.[33] Coloured immigrants, Sparkbrook Irish, or the newly rich ex-urbanites of North Worcestershire, to name some of the groups which occur in some recent monographs,[34] are unlikely to interact with each other, their neighbours, or their environment, in a similar way.

Lastly, there is the time factor, always the '*n*th' dimension of any environmental or population situation. Radioactive substances have half-lives, historians from Gibbon to Toynbee have believed in the rise, decline and fall of nations. But we forget that the environment matures, populations undergo structural changes over time. Middlesborough was a raw, frontier settlement in the middle of the nineteenth century, without laws or morals by some contemporary accounts, peopled by a conglomerate of immigrants forced into slavery by alien capitalists. Less than a hundred years later, the first sociological study of post-war Middlesborough,[35] intended to prepare for its rebuilding, shows the intricate relationships of a closely knit, even inward-looking community, which the planner would disturb at his peril. Dagenham, as raw and formless an estate as could have been devised in the 1920s for the under-housed of inner London, could, by the 1960s, exhibit as rich a pattern of relationships, and offer as much evidence of corporate consciousness, as many of the new foundations which the industrial revolution spawned in the north and the Midlands.[36]

It is interesting to note how often investigations which were deliberately styled 'experiments' lacked the true pre-conditions for controlled experimentation in the scientific sense, and were later on criticised for their faulty methodology, thus destroying the conclusions. One famous instance is the Hawthorn Experiment,[37] conducted in the United States, a long time ago now, to observe workers' reactions to environmental conditions as opposed to mere monetary incentives. The upshot was, or so the authors believed, that it could be proved that friendliness on the part of the supervisors, good lighting, and similar improvements in general conditions, could achieve great increases in output at much lower costs to management than extra payment. In the past few years, criticisms of these findings have increased enormously, first, on the basis previously mentioned, that even the figures given do not bear out the conclusions, and second, that the 'experiment' measures too few variables and did not hold enough of the general situational factors constant. In other words, like was not compared with like.

Similarly, the Fanning Experiment, already cited,[38] a piece of research conducted in Germany which measures the incidence of nervous and physical disorders amongst two groups of service families, some in low-rise family housing, some in blocks of flats, illustrates the limitations of such methods. Since allocation of housing was not apparently based on rank, pay, or other circumstances, it could be assumed that it was fairly random division of a population of essentially homogeneous character. He did in fact find that there was a higher incidence of pathological phenomena among people in the blocks of flats, by a significant margin. Most other studies were not comparative, and for the good and simple reason that the people who live in high-rise blocks of flats are not the same as those who are allocated local authority low-rise dwellings, or rather, that it will be a very difficult task to produce well-matched samples from both populations.

The point of these two investigations is that they both concern topics on which most of mankind feel more passionately than they do about the state of the Universe or the theory of relativity. In one case, the experiment basically turned on the question whether employers could get more out of their workers without paying extra wages, and in the other, we are dealing with deep-rooted fears and phobias which are engendered by the choice, faced by so many people today, of whether to stay in a slum or be re-housed 100 feet off the ground. Experiments therefore, even if they can be conducted on a truly scientific basis, are both the outcome of strong feelings, and the results, whichever way they go, are of significance for the lives of ordinary men and women.

Clearly this is not the place to expand further on the question of methodology of the social sciences in general, on the use of questionnaires, samples, survey methods in general. These matters have been explained by those much better qualified to do so.[39]

In a great many fields with which we are now concerned in London like the connection between home environment and educational attainment, the effects of rising real incomes on the propensity to become more mobile, or the effects of redevelopment as opposed to rehabilitation, similar difficulties arise. Two possible remedies may be suggested. We will deal first with the normal response of the social scientist: a call for yet better methods, more statistics, more surveys. The other possibility, to be discussed later, concerns the recognition that certain subjects which arouse deep emotions, or arise first because some people have deep feelings about some matters, are not, perhaps, as amenable to scientific methods as is sometimes thought.

The Limits of Technical Improvement

There are now available great refinements for methods of sampling and design of questionnaires. The arts of field surveys and census taking have made great strides. New statistical techniques have been developed to give more precise answers about interrelationships – that is, in correlation and regression methods. A few years ago it became possible to use computers for multiple regressions. What this means, is that if we have a situation where we have a dependent variable (say the number of children born to mothers who married between 20 and 24 years of age) and a number of independent variables,[40] such as occupation of father, educational status of mother, type of dwelling, religion, nationality and so on, and where we have a large number of 'cases', or, as they are commonly called, observations (usually relating to area totals since we are heavily dependent on the anonymous group statistics provided by the census), it should be possible to work out an equation that tells us how important a role in achieving the value of the dependent variable is played by the independent factors.

Without a computer, such an equation, even for 50 observations and 6 variables, would take an army of calculating machine operators an incalculable amount of time: with a computer (and now there are library programs available for such operations), it is literally a matter of a few hours at most even for programs with 15 variables and hundreds of observations. We can tell the computer to carry out the regression step-wise, that is to eliminate progressively the less important independent variables so that we are left, in the end, with only, say, four factors which between them 'explain' 85 per cent of the variations (the R bar square value).

I used the word 'explain'. But, in fact, as many have found to their cost, the equation finally explains nothing, not at any rate causally. We know from the equation that – let us say – the most important factor in attaining certain levels of education is the social class of the father; but whilst we can say for certain that there is an association between this factor and the dependent variable, we cannot say that the one caused the other. Clearly, in this case, it is not a reversible situation. But what is truly an (independent) variable we cannot easily discover in many situations. When we were looking, a few years ago, at the factors determining married women's activity rates, we found that of all the possible 'independent' factors the most important was the percentage of women in the labour force thirty years before the current census, or, in plain English, whether the current generation's mothers had worked or not. This was far more important than social class, distribution of husband's occupation, the number of children, and so on.[41]

On reflection, the situation was not so simple. When we looked in detail at the areas where this phenomenon manifested itself most strikingly, we found it in the textile areas of Lancashire where today many of the traditional towns no longer have a predominance of employment in the textile industries. Instead we found that employers in industries which make the best use of married women's labour, including part-timers, naturally sought locations in the areas where there was spare labour and often disused mills which could be had cheaply. So much for our 'independent' variable. In other words, demand affected supply, and vice versa: they were interdependent.[42]

A similar situation arose in another investigation in which multiple regression methods were used. The subject was that of 'household fission', that is the propensity of larger households to dissolve into smaller ones. This is a severe problem in Britain today, and one of the main reasons why we never catch up on our housing needs. So we tried to measure this phenomenon both in Britain and in other countries, using household size as our dependent variable and as independent variables, socio-economic group, occupational structure, age structure, fertility, educational attainments and so on. But there were, behind these averages, rather important variations in our individual observations.[43] We finally found that the most important factor was the availability of dwellings at prices people could pay – something the regression analysis did not show, because we did not have the data to add another independent variable. All we can safely predict is that if we go on building houses in London at the rate of 30 000 or more per annum, households will get smaller and smaller, on average. What we cannot guarantee, or even regard as likely, is that the dwellings thus created will go to those most in housing need. We could end up with even larger differences than there are now between the household size of relatively affluent owner occupiers, in new houses, or old age pensioners, on the one hand, with low occupancy ratios and much under-occupation and, on the other hand, overcrowding and sharing of obsolescent dwellings by the poor, large families, and those whom discrimination or regulations keep out of the better accommodation.[44]

So what we are really saying is that the application of yet better methods which have proved efficacious in the natural sciences often does not even give us unambiguous answers when applied to human situations, let alone dispel prejudice or convictions derived from highly subjective intuitions. Of course natural science too has its indeterminates, its as yet unexplained phenomena, but basically action (that is, policy), like building bridges or administering antibiotics, depends on precisely measured and explicable interrelationships. But in the social sciences the sort of optimism displayed for instance by Barbara Wootton twenty years ago,[45] about the possibilities opened by quantitative methods, has not, in my view, been justified.[46] As an aid to clearer thinking they are often useful, or as a means of positively disproving hypotheses, but beyond this point we can rarely go.

One gets the impression that the increasing sophistication of statistical methods cannot resolve the basic one-sidedness of all quasi-experimental analysis in the social sciences. I say 'quasi', because of the origin, already mentioned, of the prior hypotheses in personal observation, but also because of our inability to conceive of all variables in any total situation, and our natural propensity not to measure those influences which defy reduction to ordinal numbers. When people ask about the probability of achieving a slowing down in the rate of growth of the world's population, one is tempted to reply: what are the chances of the Pope declaring himself in favour of birth control; what are the chances of discovering a male oral contraceptive which lasts for a year, and so on.

In a famous investigation conducted between 1943 and 1958, known as the Indianapolis Study and published under the title 'Social and Psychological Factors affecting Fertility',[47] Kyser and Whelpton studied 23 hypotheses explaining reproductive behaviour. The study was confined to fecund, white, protestant, native women to reduce the incidence of a few well-known factors producing fertility differentials. In the end they found that fertility was related more to broad socio-economic characteristics than to psychological factors. But of course here we had a relatively homogeneous group in one town, and thus the findings, published in five volumes, are not surprising. It does not exclude the possibility at all that the attempt to reduce fertility in South-east Asia will in the end depend on culturally conditioned attitudes. The first territories where birth control has really caught on are mainly peopled by Chinese.[48] We will not attempt to state even qualitatively the characteristics of these Chinese which determine attitudes which lead in turn to the adoption of family planning – even if I thought it was so simple and that there were not some other, intervening environmental, climatological or nutritional variables which we have not measured.

When Numbers are not Enough

We now turn to another side of this problem. We said earlier that differences of opinion in the field òf physical (and for that matter molecular and biological sciences nowadays) do not arouse such passions as do some of the debates in the human sciences. Even here a very large number of subjects are confined to the academic common rooms. Only a small band of professional economists can become excited about Phillips curves and Talcott Parsons causes raised eyebrows only among specialists in sociology. But there are other debates of our own time, and earlier ages, which spill over into the public arena, in which the researcher finds himself in the middle of political and ideological debates, and where the heat and passion of the discussion, often conducted in some of the more popular newspapers and radio and television, ensures that virtually nobody can claim complete neutrality. In practice, it is not surprising to find that these subjects very often relate to the most elemental feelings we have: about birth, life and death, about food and shelter, about danger in, and to, our environment, about the distribution of incomes and wealth. Foremost among these subjects is population, both in the quantitative and the qualitative sense: one need only mention Malthus, Darwin and Galton in this connection. Among the nineteenth-century authors, next to Malthus and Darwin, only Marx attained equal popular fame, and he long after his death. Malthusianism, Darwinism and Marxism–Leninism are still the great formative influences on the debates about population growth, the origins of inequality and the distribution of incomes.

I regard the field of race or community relations, in many senses, as a special case of the perpetual obsession mankind has shown with its problems of life and death, and its living standards. Like John Rex,[49] I would reject both the extremes of functionalism and of the idea of limitless conflict between classes, and I would follow him in seeing prejudice not as a personality disorder but as a function of a particular social and economic system. But while competition for housing, fears of undercutting in the labour market, and prejudices concerning the habits of immigrants in general are adequately explained in Rex and Moore's framework, there is a special group of factors related to the alleged super-fertility of the immigrants, the fear of competition for the attentions of women and of 'racial deterioration' through mixed marriages, which further distinguish this particular field of social investigation from some others. Experiment and the formation of working hypotheses seem to me to present particular difficulties in this case.

Let us extend this to another current debate, that on the environment and world population. The Doomsday Syndrome, now perhaps on its way to being put into perspective by writers like John Maddox,[50] manages to combine most of the characteristics of the debates which have become familiar: the fear of the world being overrun by people, especially non-whites, the possibility of famine, the danger of poisoned air and water. To this is added, in Britain, a particular fear, perhaps not so prevalent elsewhere, that population growth means the loss of valuable agricultural and recreational land. We need not enlarge on the many historical, social and psychological factors which probably underlie the general panic, but some common factors stand out: the habit of blaming other people's reproductive habits for all the world's ills, the attempt to face problems of distributive justice by alleging that cessation of population and economic growth will save the world, the class bias of most conservationist movements, and so on.[51]

To show the problem, we need only recall such assertions as: 'All large cities will be inhabited mostly by blacks by the end of the century', or 'West Indians have six children apiece', or 'Land needed for housing Britain's extra population by 1991 will seriously reduce the output of British agriculture and make us completely dependent on imported food', or 'There will be a world famine by 1975', or 'More people are dying from violence, road deaths, and chemical poisoning than ever before', 'Standing room only by 2050', or 'World full in 60 years' and 'Immigration and pollution are making us into a stunted and deformed race'.

I should like to record two conversations with my friend Harry, relating to his perception of colour and beauty, by way of more homely illustrations of the general case.

We are north of the Park, in darkest Paddington, and the street of tall, grey, crumbling houses looks particularly unattractive on this full day, though the weather is very warm, and the refuse from the overflowing dustbins smells offensively. Children play between the wrecked motor cars. There are people in the street – sitting on the flights of steps leading to the front door, standing in small groups outside the shops, talking to each other out of open windows. 'Look at all the blacks', says Harry, 'the whole street is taken over by the blacks'.

Surveys of similar streets in Sparkbrook[52] in Birmingham, and in parts of Notting Hill, [53] rarely found more than a third of the whole population of such a street inhabited by those born in the New Commonwealth, or their offspring – about 40 per cent was the maximum. So why does Harry think the whole street is black?

First, having been brought up in a white-faced environment, he notices a black face as something unusual, a whole group of black faces as a notable phenomenon. The sight of such people would completely blot out any whites who may have been around. It may of course be true that the people he saw were predominantly black. It was warm, and since they mostly live in overcrowded conditions, they would naturally tend to congregate out-of-doors, or on their doorsteps, or at their windows – they have no gardens to speak of, and there are no parks to which they can go. However, it may be that they have a greater propensity than whites to form neighbourly groups in the open. If they follow a fairly general pattern of employment among the unskilled immigrants, many of them may have been either unemployed, or on shift work, and therefore more likely to be seen in their neighbourhood in broad daylight.[54] They may have been more colourfully dressed, laughed more or talked more loudly. In other words, they were noticeable, and no amount of statistics would convince Harry that the whole street was not taken over by the blacks.

Here is the record of another remark which my friend made, and the conclusions one might draw from it:

On a fine Spring day, Harry and I were waiting by the traffic lights in Kensington Road to cross over into the park. When the lights changed in our favour, a large red sports car came to a rapid but silent standstill in front of us. In the driving seat was a blonde wearing dark glasses. My friend Harry said, 'Isn't she a smasher!', and since I know him to be a connoisseur both of cars and of girls, I asked him which he meant, the Lamborghini, or its driver. 'The girl, of course', he said, 'Lamborghinis are overrated'.

As we strolled through the park, I reflected on the reasons why Harry should have thought the girl was exceptionally attractive. Let me begin by listing some of the possible reasons for his observation.

First, absolute objectivity. Suppose there is such a thing as an internationally agreed norm of feminine pulchritude. Suppose this is known to Harry and he can apply rapid checks while crossing the road, and the girl rates A1.

Secondly, conditional objectivity: reasons why on the whole it is more likely that a girl driving an expensive sports car should be more beautiful than the rest of womankind, so that one starts from the hypothesis that she is not, at any rate, ugly:

(1) If her father is wealthy, he had a better chance of marrying a beautiful woman, so that the girl may have inherited good looks.

(2) If she is married, her chances of landing a rich husband who can give her a Lamborghini are better if she is good-looking.

(3) If she is not married and has no rich father, it is still possible that her chances of buying or borrowing an expensive car are increased by good looks which enable her to earn various kinds of lucrative living and make the right sort of contacts for her.

Thirdly, factors which make objectivity difficult to attain. Supposing the girl is, in fact, rather plain. However, she has for years been well fed, acquired natural tan on frequent holidays, has afforded the best dentists, and spends a great deal of money on cosmetics, hairdressers and, of course, clothes. Given all these aids, any observation of what the girl is really like becomes a matter of stripping from her all the trappings of care and affluence, which is of course not possible short of a clinical process of anatomical dissection, quite apart from the dark glasses.

We are now moving rapidly towards the more subjective elements of Harry's observations. These may be initially summed up as a set of environmental conditions: given the facts that it was a fine Spring day, that we were standing in a part of London associated with wealth and ostentatious good living, given all we know about Lamborghinis and the sort of people who own or drive them. In other words, we should almost have to find a good reason why such a girl should not be attractive.

We now bring into the open all the subconscious pressures to which the observer is exposed. Advertisers, for instance, have played on our minds ever since we can remember a tune in which red sports cars, pretty girls, and fine Spring days all have their place, whether they happen to be publicising holidays, cosmetics, cars, cigarettes or even precision grinding services.

It is interesting to note (and this is a subjective impression as far as Britain is concerned, though the matter has been extensively studied in the United States) that by the early 1970s *black* women (and to some extent, men) were figuring in similar advertisements (though not for expensive cars). Admittedly, they were fairly light-skinned, straight-haired, and small-nosed (and in all probability the models were not of pure African stock). We have learned, in this country, not through statistical demonstrations, and not only in order to appeal to a black clientele, that 'black is beautiful', or at least that it can be beautiful. There is in fact evidence that prejudice against black-skinned people is neither old nor deep-seated – as Mortara pointed out long ago, the Virgin Mary worshipped in Brazil was usually black, and examples are fairly numerous in Europe. In other words, there are no absolutes – only conditioned, temporary and spatially limited attitudes – and this makes their measurement so very difficult.

The feelings of whole communities are influenced by tradition, experience and propaganda. Individuals differ according to the depth of the impression made on them by environmental pressures, or received wisdom. Even the most educated cannot free themselves from the atavistic attitudes of what some call loosely the 'Judaeo–Grecian Tradition'.

Now all this is commonplace. Our whole system and thought is cliche-ridden, traditionally forced into associations of things and attributes. Dawns have been rosy-fingered since Homer, and women fickle since Virgil. Mills have been dark satanic from the days of Blake, and the poor have had their faces ground since the prophet Isaiah. The country is good, and cities are bad. Virtue resides in the tilling of the soil. To sow and to reap, to help a ewe lamb, to muck a byre, to prune a tree, these are, in themselves, good things to do. Even acts which by themselves are of doubtful aesthetic value, like gelding a horse, branding an ox, shooting a pheasant, or killing a pig, assume the halo of their rustic setting. In contrast, cities are the abodes of the wicked, and all that is done in cities is conducive to wrong-doings.[55] Babylon was the Mother of Harlots, not to speak of Sodom and Gomorrah. From Virgil through Shakespeare to Wordsworth, the poets have praised the soil: farmers blest beyond all blessings, far from the clash of arms; pearls have hung in cowslips' ears, and splendour has been in the grass. But black people are mostly, and perhaps increasingly, found in the foulest parts of our cities.

Thus we are deeply steeped in prejudice. An acre of sour meadow supporting a flea-ridden sheep is a sign of national strength: to put houses for 20 homeless families on the same acre is desecration of the environment. A till of tradesmen on their fat ponies churning up the kale field in pursuit of a never-seen fox is sport, but a line of cars parked along a grass verge, complete with transistor radios and picnicking families, is encroachment. In population mythology, the country (and that means the peasant women as well as the rabbits) is fertile, the city is barren, thanks to infection, prostitution, bad food and bad air. This has given the country the edge over the town for most of recorded history, and only recently have the urban reproductive failures assumed an aura of sanctity. Miners were poor, hard working and had large families: bankers were rich, idle and had problems about heirs.

Now when one quotes, in rebuttal, even such simple statistics as the census, the actual land use changes since 1945, or F.A.O. records of food production, one is met with complete unwillingness to listen. If one tries to counter with more sophisticated answers, incorporating age-specific fertility rates, the sad story of demographic predictions in the past, or Norman Borlaug and the Green Revolution,[56] active hostility is aroused. Usually someone quotes Disraeli on 'Lies, damn lies and statistics', the more erudite refer to a little book by Darrell Huff called *How to Lie with Statistics*[57] or, very occasionally, Stephen Leacock's 'Boarding House Geometry', but the net effect is the same. Malthus was believed (or rather people believed what they thought he said), William Godwin was not. (He was wrong too.) Galton and Pearson's *Studies in National Deterioration*[58] found widespread acceptance in the early years of this century, visions of the perfectibility of mankind went unheeded. Oswald Spengler had a wider readership than Nansen or Norman Angell, and we have the prophet Arnold Toynbee in our own time.

The Proper Use of Statistics - and of Political Judgement

The Doomsday Syndrome, like the Malthusian Spectre, and the vision of racial deterioration, belong to a growing category of subjects where knowledge of numbers is not enough. Two questions arise: what is the proper use of statistics in this situation, and how does one deal with the growth of hysteria and prejudice where it occurs? One may expect other forms of population fears to emerge again, for example it is probably only a matter of time before someone starts noticing the rather persistent falls in fertility in the United States and the United Kingdom in the past eight years and begins to worry about the 'dying out of the race' – again of course linked with the belief that this phenomenon is confined to the white parts of the two nations.[59]

As to the first question, I have lost none of my belief in the efficacy of statistical methods as such. The body of facts now collected in this country is becoming more adequate for the analysis of our social and economic problems. But increasingly, the justification of this effort (apart from the obvious one that scientific knowledge is worth obtaining for its own sake) must be the encouragement, stimulation and direction these facts give to those who are professionally engaged in the making and administration of policy in its widest sense. There is a widespread tendency to regard Whitehall, let alone Town and County Halls, as centres of reactionary attempts to undo what progress has been made in this country in the space of a generation towards more enlightened policies in the field of social services, education, housing, community relations, criminology, the drive against pollution, and similar fields. Some deny that there has been any progress, for example in the field of income distribution, and they may be right. But my impression is, both as far as national and local administration are concerned, that the deeds of government do not match the wilder promises to set the clock back. If this is so, it is probably because in their quiet way public servants who can read and interpret statistics properly, are able to dissuade their political masters, of whatever complexion, from committing acts of folly.

It is of course a continuous struggle, and sometimes a tactical retreat must be conceded before the next step forward is taken. Legislation is passed, or orders are made, that appear to some of us rather foolish. Facts are collected and processed, the folly is exposed, legislation is amended, orders are rescinded, acts not enforced. I do not think that this is a speculation of wild optimism. It is a history of social reform in this country since Bentham. I refuse to believe that our more scientific age is more prone to fly in the face of facts than the Royal Commissions which took evidence from Edwin Chadwick and Michael Sadler. As Myrdal is wont to say: 'Facts kick'.[60]

But to communicate the truth as we see it and subject to all the possible errors of collection and interpretation mentioned, to a wider public, that is a different matter. The simple slogan shouter will always be heard more easily than the man who has found that the ratio of the semi-inter-quartile range to the median of income distributions in Greater London has risen by 4 per cent since 1965. I have myself had to develop, in my years at the G.L.C., new techniques of over-simplification of what I believe is the truth when being given 5 minutes to present to my political masters matters which I might not be able to put over in three lectures to my students. This in itself is dangerous, but I would say that if more of those who play the numbers game learned to simplify their findings when the occasion requires, something might be gained.

But, and this brings me to my second question, will even a great advance in the technique of presenting quantitative information be effective in combating hysteria and prejudice?[61] Not only do these manifestations, as so many studies have shown, have their root causes in history, in economic inequality, and in bitter experience of violence, death and unemployment, but they are not all confined, as we have learned to our cost, to the ignorant and vulgar populace. Science, and social science, is not blameless. Hitler and Mussolini had their scientific lackeys, as had Stalin. In our own days we have enough examples of the learned behaving in rather extraordinary ways. I do not for one moment doubt the good faith of Professor Eysenck[62] and Jensen, but they may be wrong, and in any case they are unwise in the present situation to proclaim their doctrine, even if it is true.

The role of quantitative methods in the social sciences is clearly growing. The collection and manipulation of statistics has become an indispensable, and indeed, central part of policy-making. But it is no substitute at all for political morality, or judgement. Edwin Chadwick did not hesitate to use rather spurious statistics about the cost to the nation of a working man who dies from typhoid to cajole the Parliaments of his time into sanitary reform.[63] But what basically moved the nineteenth-century legislators and political philosophers to action was their own morality – whether evangelical, as in the case of the Clapham Sect, or humanist, as in the case of Brougham and Mill. The mixture of Methodism and Marx, as Morgan Phillips used to call it, was the foundation of modern British socialism. The will to reform, to cure abuses, to pacify strife-torn communities, to bring some relief to world poverty, this stems from convictions other than those rooted in numerical proofs. Statistics are a tool, an aid to the initiated. As purveyors of usable tools, the social scientists have a role to play, even those who do not use statistics, but formal logical models; or those now increasingly rare, like Ferdynand Zweig[64] and Oscar Lewis who rely on their intuition to know what is important in the structure they observe.[65] What we must all learn, those who are concerned about the state of the world, is to communicate, as educators, or even as agitators against those who we feel threaten our civilisation, whether they do so by their actions or inaction or just thoughtlessness. The study therefore of social psychology, of communications theory, of history and of political science is at least as important as the study of statistics or formal sociology. But we can go further than this. We have seen that those fields where feelings of prejudice and hatred run deep are characterised by the experience, whether in the past or in the lifetime of the present generations, of danger, death, disease, and famine. Here we can come back to John Rex,[66] and his analysis of the urban situation in Birmingham. First, let us deal with the total situation of the city, its housing and employment problems, the inadequacies of its social services and its educational system (or that of London or any other city for that matter). Let us remove the basic causes of anxiety. It is useless looking at race problems or anti-semitism or the population scare outside this context. True, they are special cases: but precisely because they do touch so much on the life experience of individuals. In many cases, we have hundreds of years of bitter memories to overcome.

In other words, no amount of science will overcome the fundamental handicap of the policy-maker in these fields that are central to the urban social planner's concern. He must realise that priority must be given to remedying those conditions which give rise to prejudice and friction. The manifestations need not be so spectacular as riots and bomb outrages: protests come in many forms, and so does silent suffering.

A Plea for Value-judgements

If all this sounds like a plea for value-judgements, the charge is not altogether rebutted. We need only look back six or seven years to the proceedings of the Roskill Commission on the Third London Airport.[67] Social science found Cublington, value-judgements and unquantified philosophies about the environment added to intuitions about regional planning found Foulness. This is characteristic of the Open Society – it is its enemies that would deliver us to the mercies of the model-makers, the survey analysts, and the linear programmers.

It may even be that on occasion we have to go back even further from the modern social-statistical approach to the older but no less valuable non-quantifying techniques of the social anthropologist like Oscar Lewis. We might also consider that famous compromise of the movement which has become famous as Mass Observation. In his introduction to *Britain Re-visited*,

Tom Harrison, recounting the early days of his technique, cited Richard Fitter: 'It was no accident that several of the early mass-observers were birdwatchers. There was a great similarity between the new methods that Mass Observation was pioneering in social anthropology, and those with which Max Nicholson and others were revolutionising field ornithology.'[68]

What causes one disquiet is that both training and research in so many fields should have lost their way in the deadly pursuit of the unattainable. It is a far cry from the days when Tawney or Hoskins adjured their economic-history students to put on their boots when searching for historical truth. The computer and the abstractions of the Land Use Game, or other simulation methods, are now becoming substitutes for powers of observation and the application of common sense. The result is that we are less able than ever to understand the nature of the world around us. It is not only that in this bizarre situation merely traditional values (which of course are of the utmost importance in the study both of the environment and population) tend to be ignored, as not being quantifiable, but that in the attempt to rid the situation under scrutiny of all subjective elements, of the accidental or merely transient characteristic, the observer not only divests himself of prejudice, but robs the situation, and those who figure in it, of some of their most important attributes. The search for purity is in fact a quest for scientific sterility. The answers obtained from the use of refined models may in some abstract sense be truth, but they are neither real nor useful and they are probably not even true if by that we mean that they must have some use in helping us to understand a current situation or make some future provision.

One does not wish to limit the freedom of social scientists to investigate what they feel is interesting. But as one so often has to write on applications for grants from the Social Science Research Council: 'I do not dispute the value of this method in itself, but if it is meant to throw light on the problem the applicant says he wishes to illuminate, I can only say that it cannot possibly do so.'

At night, a German proverb runs, all cats are grey. If we want to investigate the colour problem in Britain, we should pick a street which my friend Harry says has been taken over by the blacks. If one wants to know what motorways will do to

London, we can examine the effects of Westway on Acklam Road even though we know that none of these roads will be built so near to any dwellings which will stay up for more than a year or two, and even though we know that the noise for people who live in Cromwell Road is far worse.[69] If we have to site an airport, we will put it out of earshot of any English village, even though we know that every day half a million Londoners endure worse suffering than would ever fall to the people of Buckinghamshire. If we have to introduce the peasants of Asia to the virtues of birth control, we will rely more on an evangelical crusade mounted by their own leaders in the cause of saving a country, than on social attitude measurements devised at Ann Arbor. In 1967 a manual was published (entitled *Variables for Comparative Fertility Studies*)[70] intended for field surveys largely in the less-developed countries. This contains suggested questionnaires with 5 questions in the household list, over 100 questions in what is quaintly termed the 'core list' and a further 100 questions in the 'expanded list'. A high proportion of these are attitude questions, or questions which might be termed self-analysis, of which the following may serve as examples:

'How many children would respondent want if money, housing and things like that were no problems at all?'

'If respondent wants fewer or more children than she expects to have, what is the reason for the discrepancy?'[71]

In practice, the antithesis between the totally quantitative or formal logic approach, and the older, historical, often intuitive and qualitative approach, is not often found to be so important. The process of formulating policies nearly always begins with the recognition of a problem, the desire to explain an existing phenomenon or the wish to predict future situations. This recognition is rarely scientific: it may be political, sentimental and highly personal. In the debate which follows about what action should be taken, quantities are found to be necessary to support argument. Scientific investigation is mandatory. At this point, the models, the systems, the networks and the equations come into their own. Soon the original problem may have been temporarily lost sight of. Sometimes the flight into pure theory then assumes a life of its own (as it has done, for instance, in the fields of spatial analysis and stable population theory). Meanwhile, the original problem remains: rapid population growth, poverty, migration pressures, congestion, homelessness, regional unemployment. Partly aided by the theoretical research and partly confused by it, partly illuminated by statistical tests and partly thrown into a disarray of apparently contradictory and self-defeating series of figures the policy-maker, the doctor or the planner, become impatient, then finally selective, perhaps take refuge in intuition and prejudice – and makes a decision which is not wrong just because it fails to accord with one particular piece of scientific reasoning.

We end where we began. The truth of a particular observation is not always demonstrable by reference to value-neutral tests, even if there are such things. We are not therefore absolved from trying to devise such tests: but we are not forced to abdicate the right to make decisions apparently not in accordance with these tests. That is because in their nature attempts to reduce the phenomena of human existence in its total environment to a single manageable network capable of being quantified and responding to numerical and logical manipulation, must be doomed. We may therefore await the outcome of this scientific activity which we call social research, but we need not agree in advance that we will abide by it. As our skills increase in the technical field, so they must also grow in that quality which one can only call judgement. It is the deplorable lack of this particular quality, not the imperfections of our research technology that is most often felt today, in the real world.

The social scientist, as he has become more numerate, has also become more arrogant, more remote, and less able and willing to communicate. When he learns that quantitative methods are mostly a means to an end, not an end in themselves, he may perform a more useful role in society.

15 The Social Scientist and Policy-making in Britain and America: a Comparison*

L. J. Sharpe

A striking characteristic of the literature on social research and social policy is the extent to which it either is American, or is strongly influenced by American experience. For example, of the twenty-six citations by Professor Cherns in 1968 only four are British, although the article is apparently discussing the British situation.[1] Why does this matter? Before answering this question there are two important exceptions that must be noted. The first concerns the discussion of the role of economics in public policy-making. For a number of reasons economics has a greater potential contribution to make to public policy-making than the other social sciences. The most obvious of these is that it deals with the central policy issue – the allocation of resources. It also deals in measurable effects which among other things enable it to establish what Shonfield has called a 'causal nexus'[2] between

* Reprinted from *Policy and Politics*, **4**, 1975, pp. 10–18, with the permission of the publishers and the author.

existing policies and a wide range of economic indicators of the consequences of these policies on different aspects of the economy.[3]

The second aspect of the literature on the potential contribution of social science to government that must be absolved from the charge of overoptimism relates to trained social scientists working as permanent civil servants, or to permanent research units within government itself. Although there are still relatively few of the former they have grown rapidly in numbers and examples of the latter include the Home Office Research Unit, the Research and Development Group of the D.o.E., the Civil Service Pay Research Unit, the research programme of the Civil Service College and the Central Policy Review Staff. That this type of in-house social science aid to policy-making has an important part to play in modern government cannot be gainsaid although it will always be a limited one. The present chapter is concerned, however, principally with discussion of university-based social science research and the temporary secondment of individual academic social scientists to government.

To return to the question posed a moment ago, why does it matter if the literature on the need for social scientists in government is largely American-inspired? At a fairly high level of generality it probably doesn't matter much because there are obvious points of broad similarity between the two countries, and judging by the 1966 O.E.C.D. report on this subject, with other Western democracies as well.[4] But if we want a reasonable modicum of accuracy and more especially if we wish to discuss the real possibilities for social science in government in this country in the future, it has to be recognised that American society is decidedly more sympathetic and receptive to the social sciences than is British society.

It is difficult to pin down this kind of broad difference between the two countries with any precision, but no British social scientist who has ever visited the United States can have failed to be aware that he was in a milieu that took his calling seriously. The nearest analogy is perhaps that of an English chef visiting Paris. This is not the place for a detailed discussion as to why this should be so, but one reason is that the social sciences as a whole have a higher status as academic disciplines in the United

States than they do in Britain and they have been firmly established as such for a longer period.[5] The higher status of social science and social scientists in America may also be derived from the fact that American culture is more predisposed than most to believe in the beneficial effects of rational inquiry as an aid to decision-making of any kind. It is after all the home of scientific management and there seems to be a much wider acceptance of the utility of harnessing the latest technique to do service in the decision-making process – to reducing the process to a technology – that is somehow profoundly alien to British political practice. What is perhaps more relevant, this tendency is linked to the wider American democratic tradition. Don K. Price has made the point that the effect of the scientific spirit of the Founding Fathers was to destroy 'the traditional theory of hereditary sovereignty and to substitute the idea that the people had the right, by rational and empirical processes to build their governmental institutions to suit themselves'.[6] That this tradition was very much alive at least up to the late 1940s is revealed in Lasswell's discussion of the role of the social sciences, or as he prefers to call them 'policy sciences', in public policy-making:

> It is probable that the policy-science orientation in the United States will be directed toward providing the knowledge needed to improve the practice of democracy. In a word, the special emphasis is upon policy-sciences of democracy, in which the ultimate goal is the realization of human dignity in theory and in fact.[7]

The notion of a policy science is still very much alive in the United States.

Such an exalted place for social science has no parallel in the British political tradition. On the contrary, it is profoundly suspicious of the university world altogether and social science in particular. It gives much greater weight to knowledge as accumulated experience – *he who does knows* – and in its extreme form sees practical experience as the only legitimate source of knowledge. As G. H. Hardy has it:

> Statesmen despise publicists, painters despise art critics, and physiologists, physicists, or mathematicians have usually

similar feelings; there is no scorn more profound, or on the whole more justifiable, than that of men who make for men who explain. Exposition, criticism, appreciation is work for second-rate minds.[8]

This elevation of practice over commentary, exposition and theory is also reflected among other things in the extent to which so many of the professions in Britain, not least those which play a large part in government, still conduct their education and training outside the ambit of the universities. The epitome of the government's response to a policy problem in the United States is to select the professor with the highest reputation in the field, give him a generous research budget and put him on a contract. The epitome in Britain is to set up a committee of inquiry made up largely of distinguished practitioners in the chosen policy field with a token academic who may or may not be invited by his colleagues to organise research. There has undoubtedly been a strengthening of the social science input to the activities of committees of inquiry and royal commissions in recent years. Some royal commissions have actually designated a social scientist as research director who has undertaken or commissioned extensive research.[9] Similarly on other commissions and committees, the social scientist member has undertaken such a role unofficially.[10] However, it remains to be seen how far these developments reflect a permanent change in attitudes and even if they do there will be some way to go before Britain approaches practice in the United States where university social science departments are by British standards much better adapted to, and often heavily dependent on, government for their maintenance.[11] The long debate about whether or not the social sciences are, or ought to be, the 'policy sciences',[12] C. Wright Mills's attack on 'abstracted empiricism',[13] and Merton's concern lest academic social scientists be reduced to the role of 'bureaucratic technicians',[14] all have their origins in the fact ·that a large slice of American academic social science is sustained by research sponsored by government or other extra-mural agencies. Moreover, the long-standing tradition of American social science 'which emphasises empirical focus, reliable technique and precise data'[15] has made it much more amenable to such ties.

The exploration of causes must admittedly always be a bit speculative, but what cannot be denied are the palpable indications of the much greater importance attached to academic social science as an aid to policy-making by government in the United States as compared with Britain. This may be graphically illustrated by the much greater amount of money spent on it by the Federal Government. In 1970 it allocated £145 million for social science research when the comparable figure for the United Kingdom was £5 million[16] and in 1971 the U.S. figure increased to nearly £200 million.[17] It must be remembered that this staggering figure leaves out of account the very much greater funds that flow to university social science departments from private foundations in America as compared with their British counterparts and the funds that come from state and local government.

Another dramatic reflection of the very different attitudes of the governments of the two countries to the role of social scientists in government is the extraordinary extent, by British standards, to which university social scientists have been brought directly into the Federal Government over the past decade and a half. Professor Kissinger, who as Secretary of State for Foreign Affairs had one of the most important posts in the Executive, was only the most celebrated example of a long line of very distinguished academic social scientists who have been brought in to fill some of the most important offices of the Federal Government since 1960. Others include Professors Rostow, Roche, Bundy, Gullion, Schelling, Yarmolinsky, Schlesinger, Galbraith and Moynihan. A handful of academics have been appointed to relatively minor ministerial posts in Britain in recent years, the Lords Bowden, Balogh, Kaldor and Crowther-Hunt, for example, and one – Sir Claus Moser – was appointed to a senior civil service post as Director of the Central Statistical Office. During the period 1964–6 the first Wilson government also brought in a number of academic social scientists – the now-famous 'Whitehall Irregulars' – but they were mostly economists and the example has not been followed by any government since. Taken altogether, these changes hardly compare with the American attitude towards academic social scientists in government which has been summarised by Moynihan thus:

... there is no place on earth where the professor reigns, or has done up until very recently as in the United States. For the past 30 years in our society the intellectuals – the pro- fessors – have influenced almost without precedent in history. The economists primarily (I am leaving aside the whole phenomena of the physical sciences), but increasingly also the softer social scientists, the sociologists, the political scientists and the psychologists.[18]

Another major difference between the political-cum- administrative traditions of the two countries that suggests caution in assuming that the American experience is very relevant to British conditions occurs on the 'user' side of the policy-making partnership – the politicians and the civil servants. Let us look at the politicians first. The greater recep- tivity of American government to social science may not only reflect higher public esteem, but also the much greater extent to which politicians employ 'aides' and research assistants of all kinds. The American politician does not expect to do his own speech-writing, letter-writing, fact-gathering, background read- ing and, some would add, thinking. He employs a team of aides to do all or most of these things for him. The American politician, like so many of his countrymen, is the proud and unselfconscious beneficiary of the age of organisation and in many respects he has to be because, unlike his British counterpart, he has to take a direct hand in policy-making almost from the day he arrives in Congress. And this applies whether or not his party has captured the Executive and/or the Legislature. Furthermore, many Con- gressmen rely heavily upon university contacts in their home districts and states for policy-consultation. Professor Robert Peabody estimates that upwards of two hundred Congressmen regularly hold informal brains trusts at their home state univer- sity.[19] Thus the whole ethos and style of American politics is strongly impregnated with the tradition of drawing upon the outsider as a vital element in policy-making.

In Britain, in contrast, most M.P.s, even those with Cabinet aspirations, seldom employ anything more than a secretary and possibly a personal assistant. The latter, until the advent of the Rowntree Trust scheme which finances research assistants for Opposition front benchers, usually performed their tasks out of personal admiration rather than monetary reward. British politicians, once they decide to make politics a vocation, develop – have to develop – a very strong sense of self-sufficiency which seldom leaves them until they attain office when they can then look to the civil service for all the policy-making aid they want. And they are likely to have a great deal more respect for these civil servants than they ever had for academics. Even if they don't, ingrained habits of intellectual self-sufficiency allied to the broader national traits already discussed combine to leave a very restricted place for social scientists except in clearly defined and often largely technical activities. One of the effects of this system is that there must be a cadre of high intellectual quality in the leadership group of the major parties to an extent that is unknown in the United States. In the case of the Labour party, this cadre tends in fact to include a high proportion of ex-social science and history academics, or academics *manqués*. In 1964, which was something of an *annus mirabilis* of this phenomenon, the Cabinet of the first Wilson government contained no less than six ex-social science dons including, of course, the Prime Minister himself.

In short, it is only a mild exaggeration to say that British politicians who reach ministerial rank (and therefore a right to take a hand in policy), in so far as they perceive that social science is of any assistance in policy-making, tend to regard themselves as their own social scientists. If ministers do bring in social scientists, as, for example, a few of them did during the 1964–70 Labour governments, they tend to do so on a personal basis; that is to say they bring in academics they know, whom they can trust, and whose particular point of view they share.

Let us now turn to the other half of the policy-making partnership, the higher civil servants. Here again there are some important differences between the two countries. In the first place, the British civil service is permanent, enjoys security of tenure, has high academic standards of competitive entry, promotion by merit in a strongly hierarchical career structure, has an exceptionally strict code of political neutrality and recruits virtually the whole of its higher echelons from its own ranks. At the level where new policy is made it is also dominated by generalists rather than technical specialists who share a strong sense of corporate identity.

Although the American federal civil service now shares to some degree all these characteristics except the dominance of generalists and a sense of corporate identity at the top, it has none of them to quite the same extent as the British civil service.[20] Yet it is likely that it is the combined effect of these characteristics that make it very much less receptive to the assistance of social scientists, or indeed of any outsider, for they all combine to give the British civil service at its upper reaches a relatively high status, a sense of omniscience and intellectual security to an extent that is not possible at the equivalent level in the American federal civil service. The British higher civil service, like its 'masters', has in a word a much stronger sense of self-sufficiency.

This difference is reinforced by the fact that, unlike their American counterparts, they are not subject to the effects of the separation-of-powers doctrine which requires them to explain their proposals to Congressional Committees in public. Nor do their proposals have to face the critical scrutiny of the professional staffs (often again recruited from the universities) of the Congressional Committees. As Gene Lyons has put it:

> The need for knowledge and analysis in making government decisions on complex issues is increased by the process of checks and balances inherent in the operations of the American political system. Not only is the government accountable to the general public, but the separation of powers within the government requires the President and Congress account to each other.[21]

There may be a further consideration that makes American government more dependent on the assistance of academic social scientists. This is derived from the fact that the United States is unique among Western democracies in lacking a permanently organised social democratic party that is able to compete on approximately level terms with the other major parties and whose broad egalitarian aims have the effect of promoting the interests of the poorest section of the population. This absence of a working-class movement means that the style of American politics is ideologically much more homogeneous than most in the sense that it lacks the conventional Left versus Right conflict that is common to the party systems of other

advanced industrial societies. It tends to see the broad conditions of American society as, if not ideal, at least as good as it is
possible to achieve without endangering individual liberty. This
is a tradition that views government as largely a question of
transient problem-solving and assumes that however difficult or
obdurate the problem it can always be tackled by greater
temporary inputs of money and expertise by government without any need to attempt any fundamental shift in the existing
distribution of economic and social resources in society. Keith
Hope puts his finger on this aspect of the American political
tradition with enviable precision in chapter 13 above:

> The typical American word for an unsatisfactory social state
> is 'problem', something, that is, which can be solved and
> thereby disposed of; and the typical word for ameliorative
> social action is 'program', something, that is, which has a
> pre-ordained beginning, middle and end. Thus it is that
> social scientists in the United States frequently talk as if it
> were possible to jump to the goal of the 'Great Society' with-
> out first passing through a period of building a Welfare State.
> There is a distinct tendency to see public social provision as
> emergency breakdown and repair rather than a service and
> maintenance contract.[22]

This characteristic of American politics means that the
Federal Government has to conduct periodic bursts of activity,
'carried out on a stretcher',[23] in order to maintain some sort of
parity of welfare with comparable countries in relation to the
poor. It also creates the paradox that the one country among the
advanced industrial democracies which is least inclined to
favour government intervention is in practice periodically very
dependent upon such intervention. Instead of being a product of
a continuous doctrinal battle within the political system about
the speed and direction of the secular trend to greater equality
within society (which is very roughly what seems to happen in
other Western democracies), social amelioration has often to
come from on high, from the Executive branch in large doses
dressed up as emergency measures to combat a temporary
national crisis.[24]

Such was a lot of the New Deal legislation, the social legislation of the Second World War period, and the 'War on Poverty' initiated by Presidents Kennedy and Johnson. But such sudden demands on government cannot be achieved by the existing agencies of the Federal Government and since the problem is seen as being largely non-ideological the national predisposition to see social science as a saviour comes into its own. During the heyday of the 'War on Poverty' for the decade ending in 1968, federal funds available to the social sciences increased no less than sevenfold.[25] Henry Riecken has summarised the general attitude at these periods when discussing the conclusions of a number of reports on the need for more social science in government made in 1968:

Overall the tone of these reports is consistent – a heavy emphasis on the desirability, need, and prospect of bringing social sciences into closer conjunction with the practical affairs of society. This is perhaps a response to the current awareness, widespread and uneasily acute, that all is far from well in American society, and the expectation that rational methods, grounded in scientific work, can help to steer the country through its troubles.[26]

Not only are federal agencies unable to cope, there are also insufficient civil servants imbued with the necessary sense of hope and drama, or equipped with the necessary knowledge of the conditions and arcane habits of the recipients of the proposed new enactments that will 'make America over'. Ambitious social science professors with a liberal bent may be seen as ideal candidates in many respects for filling the breach in such exciting times. Thus the notion of making good the deficiencies of government by expanding research is also matched by the notion of improving the quality of administrators by importing social scientists into government. So, when Rexford Tugwell, after Franklin D. Roosevelt's first election, announced that the academics who like himself were *en route* to Washington would 'speak truth to power' he was articulating what now amounts to a traditional link between social science and American government that has few parallels in other countries. Among American political scientists who specialise in American political institutions a sojourn in Washington seems to be regarded as an essential feature of their careers.

Now it may be that for a number of reasons, not least the way in which social scientists participated knowingly and unknowingly in some of the less savoury aspects of American foreign policy, this tradition is on the decline.[27] There has also been profound revulsion by a large section of the American social science academic community during the later, if not the earlier, stages of the Vietnam War against any form of co-operation with the Federal Government. In some cases revulsion has been so intense that returning professors have been denied their former university posts by their colleagues.

However, it seems unlikely that the present distaste for co-operation with government will last if only because the partnership, as I have suggested, is so fundamental to the needs of both partners. In any case if the tradition is on the wane this does not materially alter the contention that the American experience up to now is inappropriate for British conditions.

Further Reading

Social policy research is a very large field. A comprehensive bibliography would run to many thousand items. The following *short* and *highly selective* list of suggestions for further reading is intended to provide a way into the field by means of which the reader may explore further. Many of the works cited themselves contain further bibliographies. Particularly useful material is marked with an asterisk.* The selection reflects particularly the themes of the present volume; its predominantly British orientation; and the interests and biases of the editor.

The History of Empirical Social Research in Britain

General sources
*P. ABRAMS, *The Origins of British Sociology 1834–1914*, Chicago, University of Chicago Press, 1968.
*N. GLAZER, 'The rise of social research in Europe', in D. Lerner (ed.), *The Human Meaning of the Social Sciences*, New York, Meridian, 1959, pp. 43–72.
*P. LAZARSFELD, 'Notes on the history of quantification in sociology', in H. Woolf (ed.), *Quantification*, Indianapolis, Bobbs Merrill, 1965, pp. 147–203.
*A. OBERSCHALL (ed.), *The Establishment of Empirical Sociology*, New York, Harper & Row, 1972.

The nineteenth century to 1870
*N. ANNAN, *The Curious Strength of Positivism in English Social Thought*, Hobhouse Memorial Lecture, Oxford University Press, 1959.
N. ANNAN, 'The intellectual aristocracy', in J. H. Plumb (ed.), *Studies in Social History*, London, Longmans, 1955, pp. 243–87.
M. J. CULLEN, *The Statistical Movement in Early Victorian Britain*, Hassocks, Sussex, Harvester Press, 1975.

*D. V. GLASS, *Numbering the People*, Farnborough, Saxon House, 1973.

W. FARR, *Vital Statistics: a Memorial Volume*, edited with an introduction by M. Susser and A. Adelstein, Metuchen, N.Jersey, The Scarecrow Press, 1975.

*O. R. MACGREGOR, 'Social research and social policy in the nineteenth century', *Br. J. Sociol.*, **8**, 1957, pp. 146–57.

E. P. THOMPSON and E. YEO (eds.), *The Unknown Mayhew*, Harmondsworth, Penguin, 1973.

1870–1914

*A. BRIGGS, *A Study of the Work of Seebohm Rowntree*, London, Longmans, 1961.

S. CAINE, *History of the Foundation of the London School of Economics*, London, L.S.E., 1963.

A. FRIED and R. ELMAN (eds.), *Charles Booth's London*, Harmondsworth, Penguin, 1971.

R. J. HALLIDAY, 'The sociological movement, the Sociological Society and the genesis of academic sociology in Britain', *Sociol. Rev.*, **16**, 1968, pp. 377–98.

*E. P. HENNOCK, 'Poverty and social theory in England: the experience of the 1880s', *Social History*, **1**, 1976, pp. 67–91.

P. KEATING (ed.), *Into Unknown England 1866–1913: Selections from the Social Explorers*, London, Fontana, 1976.

P. KITCHEN, *A Most Unsettling Person: an Introduction to the Life and Ideas of Patrick Geddes*, London, Gollancz, 1975.

B. NORMAN-BUTLER, *Victorian Aspirations: the Life and Labour of Charles and Mary Booth*, London, Allen & Unwin, 1972.

*H. PFAUTZ (ed.), *Charles Booth on the City*, Chicago, University of Chicago Press, 1967.

*T. S. SIMEY and M. B. SIMEY, *Charles Booth: Social Scientist*, Oxford, Oxford University Press, 1960.

*B. WEBB, *My Apprenticeship*, Harmondsworth, Penguin, 1938.

S. WEBB and B. WEBB, *Methods of Social Study* (reprint) Cambridge, Cambridge University Press, 1976.

1914 onwards.

The literature of this period is much less substantial and more fragmentary. See also footnotes to chapter 1.

P. ANDERSON, 'Components of the National Culture', *New Left Review*, **50**, 1968, pp. 3–57.

*A. CHERNS and N. PERRY, 'The development and structure of social science research in Britain', in E. Crawford and N. Perry (eds), *Demands for Social Knowledge*, London, Sage, 1976, pp. 61–89.

D. V. GLASS and R. GLASS, 'The Social Survey', in *Chambers Encyclopaedia*.

A. H. HALSEY (ed.), *Traditions of Social Policy*, Oxford, Blackwell, 1976.

T. HARRISON, *Britain Revisited*, London, Gollancz, 1961 (about Mass Observation).

C. MADGE, 'The Birth of Mass Observation', *Times Literary Supplement*, 5 November 1976, p. 1395.

MASS OBSERVATION, *The Pub and the People* (reprint), Welwyn, Seven Dials Press, 1970.

*C. MOSER and G. KALTON, *Survey Methods in Social Investigation*, London, Heinemann, 1971, chapter 1.

L. MOSS, 'Sample surveys and the administrative process', *Int. soc. Sci. Bull.*, **5**, 1953, pp. 482–94.

W. A. ROBSON (ed.), *Man and the Social Sciences*, London, Allen & Unwin, 1972.

F. TEER and J. D. SPENCE, *Political Opinion Polls*, London, Hutchinson, 1973, chapter 1.

F. A. VON HAYEK, 'The London School of Economics: 1895–1945', *Economica* (new series), **13**, February 1946, pp. 1–31.

A. F. WELLS, *The Local Social Survey in England and Wales*, London, Allen & Unwin, 1935.

General Discussions of Social Policy and Social Research

Britain

*M. ABRAMS, *Social Surveys and Social Action*, London, Heinemann, 1951.

M. ABRAMS, 'Social surveys, social theory and social policy', *S.S.R.C. Newsletter*, **24**, 1974, pp. 11–14.

A. CHERNS, 'Uses of the Social Sciences', *Hum. Relat.*, **21**, 1968.

A. CHERNS, 'Social Science Research and its Diffusion', *Hum. Relat.*, **22**, 1969, pp. 210–18.

*A. CHERNS et al., *Social Science and Government*, London, Tavistock, 1972 (includes annotated bibliography).

*E. CRAWFORD and N. PERRY (eds), *Demands for Social Knowledge*, London, Sage, 1976.

J. B. CULLINGWORTH, 'The politics of research', in his *Problems of Urban Society 3*, London, Allen & Unwin, 1973.

D. V. GLASS, 'The application of social research', *Br. J. Sociol.*, **1**, 1950, pp. 17–30.

P. HALMOS (ed.), *The Sociology of Sociology*, Keele, Sociological Review/University of Keele, 1970.

*A. H. HALSEY, 'Social scientists and governments', *Times Literary Supplement*, 5 March 1970.

F. F. RIDLEY, 'Policymaking science', *Polit. Stud.*, **18**, 1970, pp. 242–5.

*L. J. SHARPE, 'Social scientists and policy making', *Policy & Politics*, **4** (4), 1975, pp. 3–34.

T. S. SIMEY, *Social Science and Social Purpose*, London, Constable, 1968.

L. SKLAIR, *Organised Knowledge*, London, McGibbon & Kee, 1973.

United States and elsewhere
The following is merely a sample of the large and continuously growing literature, particularly concentrated in the United States.

N. CAPLAN, 'Social research and national policy: what gets used, by whom, for what purpose and with what effects?', *Int. soc. Sci. J.*, **28**, 1976, pp. 187–94.

*N. CAPLAN and S. D. NELSON, 'On being useful', *Am. Psychol.*, **28**, 1973, pp. 199–211.

Y. DROR, *Public Policy-Making Re-examined*, San Francisco, Chandler, 1968.

Y. DROR, *Design for Policy Sciences*, New York, Elsevier, 1971.

A. ETZIONI, *The Active Society*, New York, Free Press, 1968.

W. B. FAIRLEY and F. MOSTELLER (eds), *Statistics and Public Policy*, Reading, Mass., Addison Wesley, 1977.

H. FREEMAN and C. SHERWOOD, *Social Research and Social Policy*, Englewood Cliffs, Prentice Hall, 1970.

I. R. HOOS, *Systems Analysis and Public Policy: a Critique*, California, University of California Press, 1972.

I. L. HOROWITZ (ed.), *The Use and Abuse of Social Science: Behavioural Science and Policy-Making*, New Brunswick, N. Jersey, Transaction Books, 1975.

*I. L. HOROWITZ and J. E. KATZ, *Social Science and Public Policy in the United States*, New York, Praeger, 1975.

M. JANOWITZ, 'Sociological Models and Social Policy', New York, General Learning Corporation, 1971.

D. LERNER and H. LASSWELL (eds), *The Policy Sciences*, Stanford, California, Stanford University Press, 1951.

*C. LINDBLOM, *The Policy-Making Process*, Englewood Cliffs, Prentice Hall, 1968.

W. B. LITTRELL and G. SJOBERG (eds), *Current Issues in Social Policy*, London, Sage, 1976.

*G. LYONS, *The Uneasy Partnership*, New York, Russell Sage, 1969.

*D. MACCRAE JR, *The Social Function of Social Science*, Yale University Press, 1976.

R. K. MERTON, *The Sociology of Science*, Chicago, University of Chicago Press, 1973, especially chapter 4.

S. M. MILLER, 'Policy and science', *J. soc. Policy*, **3**, 1974, pp. 53–8.

S. S. NAGEL (ed.), *Policy Studies and the Social Sciences*, Lexington, D.C. Heath, 1975.

H. ORLANS, *Contracting for Knowledge*, San Francisco, Jossey Bass, 1973.

A. RANNEY (ed.), *Political Science and Public Policy*, Chicago, Markham, 1968.

*M. REIN, *Social Science and Public Policy*, Harmondsworth, Penguin, 1977.

A. RIVLIN, *Systematic Thinking for Social Action*, Washington D.C., Brookings Institution, 1971.

P. ROSSI and W. WILLIAMS, *Evaluating Social Programs: Theory, Practice and Politics*, New York, Seminar Press, 1972.

*C. H. WEISS, *Using Social Research for Public Policy-Making*, Farnborough, Teakfield, 1978.

The Governmental Context of Social Policy Research in Britain

Government reports
Report of the Committee on the Provision for Social and Economic Research (Chairman Sir John Clapham), Cmd. 6868, London, H.M.S.O., 1946.

Report of the Committee on Social Studies (Chairman Lord Heyworth), Cmnd. 2660, London, H.M.S.O., 1965.

Higher Education (report of committee under chairmanship of Lord Robbins), Cmnd. 2154, London, H.M.S.O., 1963.

Report of the Committee on the Civil Service (Chairman Sir John Fulton), plus 5 volumes of evidence, Cmnd. 3638, London, H.M.S.O., 1968.

A Framework for Government Research and Development, Cmnd. 4814, London, H.M.S.O., 1971 (includes both Lord Rothschild, 'The organisation and management of government R. & D.' (Rothschild Report) and 'The future of the research council system' (Dainton Report)).

Framework for Government Research and Development (White Paper), Cmnd. 5046, London, H.M.S.O., 1972.

Social Science Research Council, Annual Report, annually since 1966, London, H.M.S.O.

See also:
O.E.C.D., *Social Sciences and the Policies of Governments*, Paris, O.E.C.D., 1966.

The role of research in British Royal Commissions
*R. Chapman (ed.), *The Role of Commissions in Policy-Making*, London, Allen & Unwin, 1973.
   T. J. Cartwright, *Royal Commissions and Departmental Committees in Britain*, London, Hodder, 1975.
   D. Donnison, 'Committees and committeemen', *New Society*, 18 April 1968, pp. 558–61.
*A. Shonfield, 'In the course of investigation', *New Society*, 24 July 1969, pp. 243–4.
For an illuminating comparison with the United States, see:
*M. Komarovsky (ed.), *Sociology and Public Policy: the case of the Presidential Commissions*, New York, Elsevier, 1975.

Research in central government
There is no satisfactory unified account of the place of social research in British central government. The reader is referred to chapter 1, footnotes 5, 9, 10, 58, 69, 74, 83, 84, 93, and 96.

A comparison: the growth of government-supported medical research in Britain
   H. Himsworth, *The Development and Organisation of Scientific Knowledge*, London, Heinemann, 1970.
   A. L. Thompson, *Half a Century of Medical Research: Vol. 1, Origins and Policy of the Medical Research Council*, London, H.M.S.O. for the M.R.C., 1974.

The Organisation and Institutionalisation of Social Research, with Reference to Britain

*B. Benjamin, 'Research strategies in social service departments of local authorities in Great Britain', *J. soc. Policy*, **2**, 1973, pp. 13–26.
   G. Benveniste, *The Politics of Expertise*, London, Croom Helm, 1973.
   M. Bulmer, 'Social survey research and postgraduate training in sociological method', *Sociology*, **6**, 1972, pp. 267–74.
*E. Crawford and N. Perry (eds), *Demands for Social Knowledge: the Role of Research Organisations*, London, Sage, 1976.
   H. Friis, 'Division of work between research in universities, independent institutes and government departments', *Social Sciences Information*, **5**, 1966, pp. 45–51.
*L. Klein, *A Social Scientist in Industry*, London, Gower Press, 1976.
   P. F. Lazarsfeld and J. G. Reitz, *An Introduction to Applied Sociology*, New York, Elsevier, 1975, chapter 7.
   A. J. Meltsner, *Policy Analysts in the Bureaucracy*, University of California Press, 1976.

*R. O'TOOLE (ed.), *The Organisation, Management and Tactics of Social Research*, Cambridge, Mass., Shenkman, 1971.

J. PLATT, *Realities of Social Research: an Empirical Study of British Sociologists*, University of Sussex Press, 1976.

*P. ROSSI, 'Researchers, scholars and policy-makers: the politics of large-scale research', *Daedalus*, **93**, 1964, pp. 1142–61.

H. SELVIN, 'Training for social research: the recent American experience', in J. Gould (ed.), *Penguin Survey of the Social Sciences 1965*, Harmondsworth, Penguin, 1965, pp. 73–95.

M. SHIPMAN (ed.), *The Organisation and Impact of Social Research*, London, Routledge, 1975.

*Social Science Information. Issue devoted to research in universities, independent institutes, and government departments, vol. 6, No. 4, 1967, with contributions by A. Cherns, P. Converse, R. Dahrendorf, J. Galtung, R. Likert, P. Rossi, T. Segerstedt, A. Touraine, A. T. M. Wilson, H. Friis.

M. STACEY, 'Sociology and the Civil Service', *S.S.R.C. Newsletter*, **13**, 1971, pp. 8–11.

E. TRIST, 'The organisation and financing of research' in UNESCO, *Main Trends of Research in the Social Sciences and Humanities: 1 Social Sciences*, The Hague, Monton, 1970, pp. 693–811 (includes 200-item bibliography).

A. WESTOBY et al., *Social Scientists at Work*, S.R.H.E., University of Surrey, Guildford, 1976.

B. WHITTAKER, *The Foundations: an Anatomy of Philanthropy and Society*, London, Eyre Methuen, 1974.

H. WILENSKY, *Organisational Intelligence*, New York, Basic Books, 1967.

Public Opinion Polls and Survey Research

The footnotes to chapters 4, 5 and 6 provide guidance on further reading. Specifically on Britain, two general works consider different aspects. The former contains a bibliography.

*F. TEER and J. D. SPENCE, *Political Opinion Polls*, London, Hutchinson, 1973.

*J. PLATT, *Social Research in Bethnal Green*, London, Macmillan, 1971.

Interviewer-respondent interaction is discussed in:
M. BENNEY and E. C. HUGHES, 'Of sociology and the interview', *Am. J. Sociol.*, **62**, 1956, pp. 137–42, reprinted in M. Bulmer (ed.), *Sociological Research Methods*, London, Macmillan, 1977, pp. 233–42.

*H. Hyman, *Interviewing in Social Research*, Chicago, University of Chicago Press, 1954.

*R. Kahn and C. F. Cannell, *The Dynamics of Interviewing*, New York, Wiley, 1957.

S. Payne, *The Art of Asking Questions*, Princeton, New Jersey, Princeton University Press, 1951.

S. Sudman and N. Bradburn, *Response Effects in Surveys*, Chicago, Aldine, 1974.

Problems of the validity of survey research data are discussed by:

*H. Blumer, 'Public opinion and public opinion polling', *Am. sociol. Rev.*, **13**, 1948, pp. 542–54.

I. Deutscher, 'Public and private opinions', in S. Nagi and R. Corwin, *The Social Contexts of Research*, New York, Wiley, 1972, pp. 323–49.

*I. Deutscher, *What We Say/What We Do*, Brighton, Scott Foresman, 1973.

D. L. Phillips, *Knowledge from What?*, Chicago, Rand McNally, 1971.

A bibliographical guide to some of the journal literature is:

W. Belson and B. A. Thompson, *Bibliography on Methods of Social and Business Research*, London, L.S.E./Crosby Lockwood, 1973.

Action Research

The British E.P.A. and C.D.P. Projects

Children and their Primary Schools (The Plowden Report), London, H.M.S.O., 1967.

*A. H. Halsey and others, *Educational Priority* (4 volumes), London, H.M.S.O., 1972.

R. Lees, *Research Strategies for Social Welfare*, London, Routledge, 1975.

*R. Lees and G. Smith (eds), *Action-Research in Community Development*, London, Routledge, 1975.

R. Lees, G. Smith and P. Topping, 'Participation and the Home Office C.D.P.', in C. Crouch (ed.), *British Political Sociology Yearbook 3*, London, Croom Helm, 1977, pp. 237–72.

E. Midwinter, *Priority Education*, Harmondsworth, Penguin, 1972.

G. Smith and P. Topping, 'Action research: perspectives and strategies', in J. Haworth (ed.), *Leisure and Involvement*, London, 1978.

American sources

P. CLARK, *Action Research and Organisational Change*, New York, Harper, 1972.

*P. MARRIS and M. REIN, *Dilemmas of Social Reform*, Harmondsworth, Penguin, 1974, chapter 8.

D. P. MOYNIHAN, *Maximum Feasible Misunderstanding*, New York, Free Press, 1962.

H. W. RIECKEN and R. F. BORUCH, *Social Experimentation: a Method for Planning and Evaluating Social Intervention*, New York, Academic Press, 1974.

*E. SUCHMAN, *Evaluative Research*, New York, Russell Sage Foundation, 1967.

T. TRIPODI, *The Uses and Abuses of Research in Social Work*, New York, Columbia University Press, 1974.

C. H. WEISS, *Evaluation Research*, Englewood Cliffs, Prentice Hall, 1972.

*C. H. WEISS (ed.), *Evaluating Action Programs*, Boston, Allyn & Bacon, 1972 (contains 22-page bibliography).

L. A. ZURCHER and C. M. BONJEAN (eds), *Planned Social Intervention*, San Francisco, Chandler, 1970.

Social Indicators

*M. ABRAMS, 'Subjective social indicators', *Social Trends*, **4**, 1973, pp. 35–50.

R. A. BAUER, *Social Indicators*, Cambridge, Mass., M.I.T. Press, 1967.

J. I. DE NEUFVILLE, *Social Indicators and Public Policy*, New York, Elsevier, 1975.

*O. D. DUNCAN, *Toward Social Reporting: Next Steps*, New York, Russell Sage Foundation, 1969.

*A. ETZIONI and E. W. LEHMAN, 'Some dangers in valid social measurement', *Ann. Am. Acad. polit. and soc. Sci.*, September 1967, pp. 1–15.

B. GROSS, *The State of the Nation: Social Systems Accounting*, London, Tavistock, 1966.

J. HALL, 'Subjective measures of quality of life in Britain', *Social Trends*, **7**, 1976, pp. 47–60.

P. M. HAUSER, 'Social indicators', in his *Social Statistics in Use*, New York, Russell Sage, 1975.

P. L. KNOX, 'Social indicators and the concept of level of living', *Sociol. Rev.*, **22**, 1974, pp. 249–57.

K. C. LAND, 'Theories, models and indicators of social change', *Int. soc. Sci. J.*, **27**, 1975, pp. 7–37.

K. C. Land and S. Spilerman (eds), *Social Indicator Models*, New York, Russell Sage, 1974.

D. L. Little, 'Social indicators and social policy: some unanswered questions', *Futures*, February 1975, pp. 41–51.

B. C. Liu, *Quality of Life Indicators in U.S. Metropolitan Areas*, New York, Praeger, 1976.

*C. Moser, 'Measuring the quality of life', *New Society*, 10 December 1970.

*O.E.C.D. *Measuring Social Well-Being*, Paris, O.E.C.D., 1976.

E. Sheldon and W. Moore (eds), *Indicators of Social Change: Concepts and Measurements*, New York, Russell Sage Foundation, 1968.

*A. Shonfield and S. Shaw (eds), *Social Indicators and Public Policy*, London, Heinemann for S.S.R.C., 1972.

Toward a Social Report (principal author, M. Olson), Washington D.C., U.S. Government Printing Office, 1969; reprinted Institute of Social Research, University of Michigan, 1970.

Toward a System of Social and Demographic Statistics, United Nations Department of Economic and Social Affairs, Statistical Office, Studies in Methods F18, Geneva, 1975.

*L. D. Wilcox *et al.*, *Social Indicators and Societal Monitoring: an annotated bibliography*, Amsterdam, Elsevier, 1972. (Very comprehensive bibliography of this subject up to 1972).

W. Zapf, 'Systems of social indicators: current approaches and problems', *Int. Soc. Sci. J.*, **27**, 1975, pp. 479–98.

Examples of Social Policy Research

British examples
The following are a few instances of fields in addition to those mentioned in chapter 1, footnote 48, where applied research has made some impact.

Education
*H. Glennerster and E. Hoyle, 'Educational research and educational policy', *J. Soc. Policy*, **1**, 1972, pp. 193–212.

Industry
C. Sofer, *Organisations in Theory and Practice*, London, Heinemann, 1972.

R. K. Brown, 'Research and consultancy in industrial enterprises: the Tavistock studies', *Sociology*, **1**, 1967, pp. 33–60.

Planning
D. DONNISON and D. E. C. EVERSLEY, *London – Urban Patterns, Problems and Policies*, London, Heinemann, 1973.

Social Services
B. DAVIES, *Social Needs and Resources in Local Services*, London, Michael Joseph, 1968.

Social Work
*M. DAVIES, 'The current status of social work research', *Br. J. soc. Work*, **4**, 1974, pp. 281–303.

American examples
From the very large American literature, the following are examples of important policy issues informed by (often controversial) social research:

Education
*F. MOSTELLER and D. P. MOYNIHAN (eds), *On Equality of Educational Opportunity*, New York, Random House, 1972.
C. JENCKS *et al.*, *Inequality*, Harmondsworth, Penguin, 1973.

Industry
*L. BARITZ, *Servants of Power: a History of Social Science in American Industry*, Middletown, Conn., Wesleyan University Press, 1960.

Poverty
D. P. MOYNIHAN (ed.), *On Understanding Poverty*, New York, Basic Books, 1969.
J. L. SUNDQUIST (ed.), *On Fighting Poverty*, New York, Basic Books, 1969.
I. MERRIAM, 'Social security research: the relation of research and policy planning in a government agency', *J. soc. Policy*, **1**, 1972, pp. 289–303.

Race and family structure
*L. RAINWATER and W. YANCEY, *The Moynihan Report and the Politics of Controversy*, Cambridge, Mass., M.I.T. Press, 1967.
A. BILLINGSLEY, *Black Families in White America*, Englewood Cliffs, Prentice Hall, 1968.

The academic consolidation of policy research: the example of applied sociology in the United States
* *The American Sociologist*, **6**, 1971. Special issue on 'Social research and public policy'.

J. D. Colfax and J. L. Roach, *Radical Sociology*, New York, Basic Books, 1971.

N. J. Demerath iii *et al.*, *Social Policy and Sociology*, New York, Academic Press, 1975.

A. Gouldner and S. M. Miller (eds), *Applied Sociology*, New York, Free Press, 1965.

*P. F. Lazarsfeld *et al.*, *The Uses of Sociology*, New York, Basic Books, 1968.

*G. T. Marx (ed.), *Muckraking Sociology*, New Brunswick, New Jersey, Transaction Books, 1972.

R. K. Merton, 'Notes on problem-finding in sociology', in *Sociology Today*, New York, Basic Books, 1959.

Value-relevance, Politics and Ethics in Social Research

Values, objectivity
L. Bramson, *The Political Context of Sociology*, Princeton, New Jersey, Princeton University Press, 1961.

R. Dahrendorf, *Essays in the Theory of Society*, London, Routledge, 1968, chapters 1 and 10.

R. Lynd, *Knowledge for What?*, Princeton, New Jersey, Princeton University Press, 1939.

K. Mannheim, *Ideology and Utopia*, London, Routledge, 1960 (first published, 1936).

*G. Myrdal, *Value in Social Theory*, London, Routledge, 1958.

G. Myrdal, *Objectivity in Social Research*, London, Duckworth, 1970.

*M. Rein, *Social Science and Public Policy*, Harmondsworth, Penguin, 1977.

J. Rex, *Key Problems in Sociological Theory*, London, Routledge, 1961.

*G. Riley (ed.), *Values, Objectivity and the Social Sciences*, Reading, Mass., Addison-Wesley, 1974 (contains bibliography).

T. S. Simey, *Social Science and Social Purpose*, London, Constable, 1968.

P. Starr, 'The edge of social science', *Harvard educ. Rev.*, **44**, 1974, pp. 393–415.

*Max Weber, *The Methodology of the Social Sciences*, Glencoe, Free Press, 1949.

The politics and ethics of research
J. A. Barnes, *Who Should Know What? Social Science, Privacy and Politics*, Harmondsworth, Penguin, 1978.

R. L. Beals, *The Politics of Social Research*, Chicago, Aldine, 1969.

*S. J. Deitchman, *The Best-Laid Schemes: a Tale of Social Research and Bureaucracy*, Cambridge, Mass., M.I.T. Press, 1976.

*I. L. HOROWITZ (ed.), *The Rise and Fall of Project Camelot*, Cambridge, Mass., M.I.T. Press, 1967.

I. L. HOROWITZ (ed.), *The Use and Abuse of Social Science*, New Brunswick, New Jersey, Transaction Books, 1975.

L. RAINWATER and D. J. PITTMAN, 'Ethical problems in studying a politically sensitive and deviant community', *Social Problems*, **14**, 1967, pp. 357–66.

*L. RAINWATER and W. J. YANCEY (eds), *The Moynihan Report and the Politics of Controversy*, Cambridge, Mass., M.I.T. Press, 1967.

*G. SJOBERG (ed.), *Politics, Ethics and Social Research*, London, Routledge, 1970.

Social Problems, **21** (1), 1973, special issue on 'Social control of social research'.

M. USEEM and G. T. MARX, 'Ethical dilemmas and political considerations in social research', in R. B. Smith (ed.), *Social Science Methods*, New York, Free Press, 1970.

D. WARREN, 'Some observations from post-riot Detroit: the role of the social researcher in contemporary racial conflict', *Phylon*, **34**, 1973, pp. 171–86.

Privacy: the Citizen in the Face of Social Research

American Statistical Association Conference on Surveys of Human Populations, 'Report', *Am. Statistn.*, **28**, 1974, pp. 30–4.

O. AUKRUST and S. NORDBOTTEN, 'Files of individual data and their potentialities for social research', *Rev. Income Wealth*, **19**, 1973, pp. 189–201.

*J. A. BARNES, *Who Should Know What? Social Science, Privacy and Politics*, Harmondsworth, Penguin, 1978.

*BRITISH ASSOCIATION FOR THE ADVANCEMENT OF SCIENCE, *Does Research Threaten Privacy or Does Privacy Threaten Research?*, London, 1971.

R. W. CONANT and M. A. LEVIN (eds), *Problems of Research on Community Violence*, New York, Praeger, 1969.

C. C. GOTLEIB and A. BORODIN, *Social Issues in Computing*, New York, Academic Press, 1973.

F. W. HONDIUS, *Emerging Data Protection in Europe*, Amsterdam, North-Holland, 1975.

E. JOSEPHSON, 'Resistance to community surveys', *Social Problems*, **18**, 1970, pp. 117–29.

Journal of the Market Research Society, **18** (3), 1976, issue on survey response rates.

D. MADGWICK and T. SMYTHE, *The Invasion of Privacy*, London, Pitman, 1974.

J. MARTIN and A. R. D. NORMAN, _The Computerised Society_, Harmondsworth, Penguin, 1973.

A. R. MILLER, _The Assault on Privacy: Computers, Data Banks and Dossiers_, Michigan, University of Michigan Press, 1971.

*W. PETERSEN, 'Forbidden knowledge', in S. Nagi and R. Corwin (eds), _The Social Contexts of Research_, New York, Wiley, 1972, pp. 289–321.

Privacy and Computers, Ottawa, Information Canada, 1972.

Records, Computers and the Rights of Citizens, Washington D.C., U.S. Government Printing Office, 1973.

Report of the Committee on Privacy, Cmnd. 5012, London, H.M.S.O., 1972.

A. M. RIVLIN and P. M. TIMPANE (eds), _Ethical and Legal Issues of Social Experimentation_, Oxford, Blackwell, 1977.

*J. RULE, _Private Lives and Public Surveillance_, London, Allen Lane, 1973.

Security of the Census of Population, Cmnd. 5365, London, H.M.S.O., 1973.

*E. SHILS, 'Privacy and power', in _Center and Periphery_, Chicago, University of Chicago Press, 1975, pp. 317–44.

P. SIEGHART, _Privacy and Computers_, London, Latimer, 1976.

*SOCIAL AND COMMUNITY PLANNING RESEARCH, _Survey Research and Privacy: report of a working party_, London, S.C.P.R., 1974.

*M. WARNER and M. STONE, _The Data-Bank Society: Computers, Organisation and Social Freedom_, London, Allen & Unwin, 1970.

A. F. WESTIN and M. A. BAKER, _Data Banks in a Free Society: Computers, Record-keeping and Privacy_, New York, Quadrangle, 1972.

Notes and References

Chapter 1

1. Cf. P. Abrams, *The Origins of British Sociology 1834–1914*, University of Chicago Press, 1968, and S. Cole, 'Continuity and institutionalisation in science: a case study in failure' in A. Oberschall (ed.), *The Establishment of Empirical Sociology*, New York, Harper, 1972.

2. Cf. D. V. Glass, *Numbering the People*, Farnborough, Saxon House, 1973.

3. Cf. S. Caine, *A History of the Foundation of the London School of Economics and Political Science*, London, Bell, 1963.

4. D. E. G. Plowman, 'The Main Fields of Social Administration Research', paper for S.S.R.C. Bristol Conference, 1970, mimeo, p.7.

5. A. Cherns and N. Perry, 'The Development and Structure of Social Science Research in Britain', in E. Crawford and N. Perry (eds), *Demands for Social Knowledge: the Role of Research Organisations*, London, Sage, 1976, pp. 61–89.

6. *Report of the Committee on the Provision for Social and Economic Research* (Chairman Sir John Clapham), Cmd. 6868, London, H.M.S.O., 1946.

7. *Higher Education: Report of the Committee appointed by the Prime Minister under the Chairmanship of Lord Robbins, 1961–63*, Cmnd. 2154, London, H.M.S.O., 1963.

8. *Report of the Committee on Social Studies* (Chairman Lord Heyworth), Cmnd. 2660, London, H.M.S.O., 1965.

9. M. Nissel, 'Government Social Statistics', *Stasticial News*, **25,** 1974, pp. 1–6.

10. *Social Trends*, published annually by H.M.S.O. since 1970.

11. B. S. Rowntree, *Poverty: a Study of Town Life*, London, Longmans, 1902; B. S. Rowntree, *Poverty and Progress: a Second Social Survey of York*, London, Longmans, 1941; B. S. Rowntree and G. Lavers, *Poverty and the Welfare State*, London, Longmans, 1951.

12. 'The Future of the Research Council System' (hereafter Dainton Report), in *A Framework for Government Research and Development*, Cmnd. 4814, London, H.M.S.O., 1971, p. 3.

13. *Report of the Committee on Social Studies*, op. cit., 1966, p. 2.

14. There are alternatives. A. Cherns, in *Social Science and Government*, London, Tavistock, 1972, proposes a distinction between pure basic research, basic objective research, operational research and action research. M. Davies, in 'The Current Status of Social Work Research', *Br. J. soc. Work*, **4**, 1974, pp. 281–303, distinguishes administrative, exploratory and theoretical research, each of which may be descriptive or evaluative.

15. J. A. Heady, 'Application of Research Results', paper given to the Society for Social Medicine, September 1976, mimeo, p. 3.

16. Lord Rothschild, 'The organisation and management of government R & D', (hereafter Rothschild Report), in *A Framework for Government Research and Development*, Cmnd. 4184, London, H.M.S.O., 1971.

17. Dainton Report, op. cit., p. 5.

18. Rothschild Report, op. cit., p. 3.

19. Cf. Donnison, chapter 2.

20. Cherns, op. cit., p. 30.

21. A. Shonfield, 'Research and public policy: lessons from economics', in A. B. Cherns *et al.* (eds), *Social Science and Government*, London, Tavistock, 1972, p. 68.

22. Ibid., p. 71.

23. J. M. Keynes, *The General Theory of Employment, Interest and Money*, London, Macmillan, 1936.

24. H. Glennerster and E. Hoyle, 'Educational research and educational policy', *J. soc. Policy*, **1**, 1972, p. 196.

25. N. Annan, *The Curious Strength of Positivism in English Social Thought*, Hobhouse Memorial Lecture, Oxford University Press, 1959. For a contrasting view see P. Anderson, 'Components of the national culture', *New Left Review*, **50**, 1968, pp. 3–57.

26. P. Abrams, op. cit., p. 150.

27. Ibid., p. 111.

28. Ibid., p. 150.

29. Ibid., pp. 85–8.

30. Ibid., pp. 88, 140.

31. Ibid., p. 140.

32. Ibid., p. 149.

33. C. Moser and G. Kalton, *Survey Methods in Social Investigation*, London, Heinemann, 1971, p. 486.

34. Cf. S. Stouffer, *Social Research to Test Ideas*, New York, Free Press, 1962; M. Rosenberg, *The Logic of Survey Analysis*, New York,

Basic Books, 1968. For a brief introduction see M. Bulmer (ed.), *Sociological Research Methods*, London, Macmillan, 1977, Part Two.

35. M. Abrams, *Social Surveys and Social Action*, London, Heinemann, 1951, p. 2.

36. Ibid., pp. 124, 125.

37. D. V. Glass, 'The application of social research', *Br. J. Sociol.*, **1**, 1950, pp. 28, 18.

38. A. Shonfield, 'In the course of investigation', *New Society*, 24 July 1969, p. 123, discussing the Duncan Committee on Overseas Representation, of which he was a member. On the role of research in British commissions and committees, see R. Chapman (ed.), *The Role of Commissions in Policy-Making*, London, Allen & Unwin, 1973, and D. Donnison, 'Committees and Committeemen', *New Society*, No. 290, 18 April 1968, pp. 558–61. For a comparison with the markedly different American scene, see M. Komarovsky (ed.), *Sociology and Public Policy: the Case of the Presidential Commissions*, New York, Elsevier, 1975, discussing the role of research in commissions investigating population, violence, obscenity and law enforcement.

39. Cf. *Children and their Primary Schools*, Central Advisory Council for Education, London, H.M.S.O., 1967, Vols 1 and 2; M. Kogan, 'The Plowden Committee', in R. Chapman (ed.), *The Role of Commissions in Policy-Making*, London, Allen & Unwin, 1973; H. Acland, *Social Determinants of Educational Achievement*, unpublished D.Phil. thesis, Oxford University, 1973; H. Glennerster, 'The Plowden Research', *Jl. R. statist. Soc.*, Series *A*, **132**, 1969; with J. S. Coleman *et al.*, *Inequality of Educational Opportunity*, Washington D.C., U.S. Government Printing Office, 1966; F. Mosteller and D. P. Moynihan (eds), *On Equality of Educational Opportunity*, New York, Random House, 1972; C. Jencks *et al.*, *Inequality*, London, Penguin, 1973.

40. G. Myrdal, *An American Dilemma*, New York, Harper, 1944; E. J. B. Rose *et al.*, *Colour and Citizenship*, Oxford University Press, 1969.

41. R. Pinker, *Social Theory and Social Policy*, London, Heinemann, 1973, p. 12.

42. J. Rex, *Key Problems in Sociological Theory*, London, Routledge, 1961, p. vii.

43. P. Abrams, op. cit., p. 153.

44. T. S. Simey, *Social Science and Social Purpose*, London, Constable, 1968, pp. 20, 193.

45. A. Shonfield, op. cit., p. 79.

46. Central Statistical Office, *Social Trends*, No. 6, 1975, London, H.M.S.O., p. 9.

47. A. MacIntyre, 'Is a comparative science of politics possible?', in P. Laslett, W. Runciman and Q. Skinner (eds), *Philosophy, Politics and Society – Fourth Series*, Oxford, Blackwell, 1972, p. 8.

48. Compare S. R. Parker, C. G. Thomas, N. D. Ellis and W. E. J. McCarthy, *Effects of the Redundancy Payments Act 1971* (London, H.M.S.O., 1971), with R. Martin and R. Fryer, *Redundancy and Paternalist Capitalism*, London, Allen & Unwin, 1973, especially chapter 1 and appendix 2, 'Redundancy and Public Policy'. On poverty and income maintenance see especially P. Townsend (ed.), *The Concept of Poverty*, London, Heinemann, 1970. On transmitted deprivation see M. Rutter and N. Madge, *Cycles of Disadvantage*, London, Heinemann, 1976.

49. For a review of their contribution see: Max Weber, *The Methodology of the Social Sciences*, Glencoe, Free Press, 1949; K. Mannheim, *Ideology and Utopia*, London, Routledge, 1960; G. Myrdal, *Value in Social Theory*, London, Routledge, 1958; R. Dahrendorf, *Essays in the Theory of Society*, London, Routledge, 1968, chapters 1 and 10; J. Rex, op. cit.; and for a useful collection of papers G. Riley (ed.), *Values, Objectivity and the Social Sciences*, Reading, Mass., Addison-Wesley, 1974.

50. G. Myrdal, *The Political Element in the Development of Economic Theory*, London, Routledge, 1953.

51. J. H. Goldthorpe, review of Simey, *Social Science and Social Purpose*, in *Br. J. Sociol.*, **20**, 1969, p. 229.

52. Cf. S. Cohen, 'Criminology and the sociology of deviance in Britain', in P. Rock and M. McIntosh (eds), *Deviance and Social Control*, London, Tavistock, 1974, pp. 1–40.

53. S. Cohen and L. Taylor, *Psychological Survival*, Harmondsworth, Penguin, 1971, especially the appendix; S. Cohen and L. Taylor, 'Prison research: a cautionary tale', *New Society*, No. 634, 30 January 1975, pp. 253–5. For a more general review of problems of access in social research, see R. Habenstein (ed.), *Pathways to Data*, Aldine, Chicago, 1970.

54. H. C. Kelman, 'The relevance of social research to social issues: promises and pitfalls', in P. Halmos (ed.), *The Sociology of Sociology*, Keele, Sociological Review Monograph No. 16, 1970, p. 86.

55. Cf. L. Rainwater and D. Pittman (eds), *The Moynihan Report and the Politics of Controversy*, Cambridge, Mass., M.I.T. Press, 1967.

56. Cf., for example, the issues of the journals *Social Policy*, **6**, No. 4, January/February 1976, and *Society*, **14**, No. 4, May/June 1977, especially articles by J. S. Coleman, R. Farley and R. C. Rist.

57. 'Policy research and the role of the academic sociologist: is there a role?' by T. Acton and R. Redpath, paper given at British Sociological Association conference, Easter 1977, mimeo.

58. A. H. Halsey, 'Social Scientists and Governments', *Times Literary Supplement*, 5 March 1970, p. 251.

59. M. Janowitz, 'Sociological Models and Social Policy', New York, General Learning Corporation pamphlet, 1971; also in M. Janowitz, *Political Conflict*, Chicago, Quadrangle, 1970.

60. M. Rein, *Social Science and Public Policy*, Harmondsworth, Penguin, 1976, pp. 28, 29, 30.

61. Ibid., p. 259.

62. Cf. D. V. Glass, *Numbering the People*.

63. Cf. M. Susser and A. Adelstein (eds), *Vital Statistics: a Memorial Volume of Selections from the Reports and Writings of William Farr*, Metuchen, New Jersey, The Scarecrow Press, 1975, especially pp. iii–xiv.

64. P. Abrams, op. cit.

65. S. Cole, op. cit.

66. Ibid., p. 109.

67. Ibid., p. 113.

68. A. Westoby *et al.*, *Social Scientists at Work*, S.R.H.E., University of Surrey, 1976, p. 1.

69. C. S. Smith, 'The employment of sociologists in research occupations in Britain in 1973', *Sociology*, **9**, 1975, p. 310.

70. Department of Education, *Statistics of Education*, Vol. 6, Universities, for 1975 and earlier years to 1965, London, H.M.S.O.

71. A. Cherns and N. Perry, op. cit., p. 65.

72. Cf. M. G. Kendall, 'Measurement in the study of society', in W. Robson (ed.), *Man and the Social Sciences*, London, Allen & Unwin, 1972, pp. 131–48.

73. F. Teer and J. D. Spence, *Political Opinion Polls*, London, Hutchinson, 1973, p. 19.

74. On the government social survey, see: C. Moser and G. Kalton, op. cit., pp. 13–15; L. Moss, 'Sample surveys and the administrative process', *Int. soc. Sci. Bull.*, **5**, 1953, pp. 482–94; L. Moss, 'The governmental social survey: an aid to policy formation', O.P.C.S. Papers G59, 1959, mimeo; L. Moss, 'Survey research and government', O.P.C.S. Paper G67, 1968; L. Moss, 'Social research and government', paper given to the Market Research Society, 1971, mimeo; P. Redfern, 'Office of Population Censuses and Surveys', *Population Trends*, **4**, 1976, pp. 21–3.

75. See Moser and Kalton, op. cit., pp. 15–17; the introductory chapter by Downham, Shankleman and Treasure in F. Edwards (ed.), *Readings in Market Research*, London, British Market Research Bureau, 1956; and the *Journal of the Market Research Society*.

76. Cf. F. Teer and J. D. Spence, op. cit.

77. Cf. M. Abrams, 'Subjective social indicators', *Social Trends*, No. 4, 1973, pp. 35–50; J. Hall, 'Subjective measures of quality of life in Britain, 1971–75', *Social Trends*, No. 7, 1976, pp. 47–60.

78. Cf. D. Donnison, 'Pressure group for the facts', *New Society*, No. 376, 11 December 1969, pp. 935–7.

79. See Social and Community Planning Research, *A Review of the First Five Years 1969–74*, London, S.C.P.R., 1975.

80. Cf. D. Smith, *The Facts of Racial Disadvantage*, London, Political and Economic Planning, 1976; and C. Airey *et al.*, *Technical Report on a Survey of Racial Minorities*, London, S.C.P.R., 1976. *Survey Research and Privacy: Report of a Working Party*, London, S.C.P.R., 1973.

81. P. Rossi, 'Researchers, scholars and policy-makers: the politics of large-scale research', *Daedalus*, **93**, 1964, p. 1155, note 1.

82. H. Selvin, 'Training for social research: the recent American experience', in J. Gould (ed.), *Penguin Survey of the Social Sciences 1965*, London, Penguin, 1965, pp. 73–95.

83. Sir Claus Moser, 'Staffing in the Government Statistical Service', *Jl R. statist. Soc. Series A*, **136**, 1973, pp. 75–88; J. C. Pite, 'The deployment of staff in the Government Statistical Service', *Statistical News*, **30**, 1975, pp. 12–16.

84. Central Policy Review Staff, *A Joint Framework for Social Policies*, London, H.M.S.O., 1975.

85. Central Policy Review Staff, *Population and the Social Services*, London, H.M.S.O., 1977.

86. O.E.C.D., *Measuring Social Well-Being: a Progress Report on the Development of Social Indicators*, (O.E.C.D. Social Indicator Development Programme No. 3), Paris, O.E.C.D., 1976.

87. Donnison, chapter 2, p. 57.

88. Ibid., p. 55.

89. C. S. Smith, art. cit., p. 312.

90. C. Cunningham, 'Research Funding in the United States', *S.S.R.C. Newsletter*, Special, September 1971, p. 19.

91. A. Cherns and N. Perry, op. cit., p. 75.

92. Cunningham, op. cit.

93. N. Perry, 'Research Settings in the Social Sciences', in E. Crawford and N. Perry (eds), op. cit., pp. 137–89.

94. C.P.R.S., *A Joint Framework for Social Policy*, London, H.M.S.O., 1975, p. 1.

95. R. Clark, *Tizard*, London, Methuen, 1965, Chapter 15.

96. Rothschild Report, op. cit.; Department of Health and Social Security, *Annual Report on Departmental Research and Development*, London, H.M.S.O., 1977; M. Rutter and N. Madge, *Cycles of Disadvantage*, op. cit.

97. J. B. Cullingworth, 'The Politics of Research', in *Problems of an Urban Society, Vol. 3, Planning for Change*, London, Allen & Unwin, 1973, p. 188.

98. N. Perry, art. cit., p. 186.

99. P. Rossi, art. cit., pp. 1149–50.

100. J. B. Cullingworth, op. cit., p. 187, quoting C. Wright Mills.

101. R. Crossman, *The Diaries of a Cabinet Minister: Vol. 1: Minister of Housing, 1964–66*, London, H. Hamilton and J. Cape, 1975, p. 24.

102. L. J. Sharpe, 'Social Scientists and Policy Making', *Policy and Politics*, **4**, No. 4, 1975, p. 28.

103. N. Annan, 'The Intellectual Aristocracy', in J. H. Plumb (ed.), *Studies in Social History*, London, Longmans, 1955, pp. 243–87.

104. Sharpe, op. cit., p. 28.

105. Sharpe, op. cit., p. 28.

Chapter 2

1. *Science, Growth and Society: A New Perspective*, Paris, O.E.C.D., 1971, pp. 102, 104.

2. T. Hägerstrand, *Innovation Diffusion as a Spatial Process*, Chicago, University of Chicago Press, 1967.

3. *Technology in Retrospect and Critical Events in Science*, Chicago, Illinois Institute of Technology Research Institute, 1968.

4. Ibid., p. 12.

5. Ibid., p. 17.

6. 'The Organisation and Management of Government R & D', *A Framework for Government Research and Development*, Cmnd. 4814, London, H.M.S.O., 1971.

7. *Report from the Commissioners for Inquiry into the Administration and Practical Operation of the Poor Laws*, 1834.

8. Under the Public Assistance Order, 1930.

9. 'The Chancellor [Lloyd George] was unable to get a word in, and was evidently partly amused and partly annoyed. Sidney became so excited that he quite spoilt his breakfast'. W. J. Braithwaite, *Lloyd George's Ambulance Waggon*, London, Methuen, 1957, p. 116.

10. Professors Richard Titmuss, Brian Abel-Smith, Peter Townsend and Dorothy Wedderburn and Mr Tony Lynes have done most to develop this line of thought in Britain. Many would date its origin from Professor Titmuss' seminal paper on 'The social division of welfare', reprinted in *Essays on the Welfare State*, London, Allen & Unwin, 1958.

11. *Secondary Education with Special Reference to Grammar Schools and Technical High Schools* (the Spens Report), London, H.M.S.O., 1938, p. 185.

12. *15 to 18*, London, H.M.S.O., 1959, p. 206.

13. *Half Our Future*, London, H.M.S.O., 1959, p. 6.

14. *Second Report of the Public Schools Commission*, London, H.M.S.O., 1970, p. 109.

15. *Children and their Primary Schools*, Central Advisory Council for Education (England), London, H.M.S.O., 1967, paragraph 1165.

16. 'The Organisation and Management of Government R and D', *A Framework for Government Research and Development*, Cmnd. 4814, London, H.M.S.O., 1971, pp. 3–4.

17. 'The Future of the Research Council System', ibid., p. 3.

18. *The Future of Development Plans*, Planning Advisory Group, London, H.M.S.O., 1965.

19. Examples of such early works are: D. E. C. Eversley, *Social Theories of Fertility and the Matthensian Debate*, Oxford, Clarendon Press, 1959; Ruth Glass, *The Social Background of a Plan: a study of Middlesborough*, London, Routledge, 1948; Peter Hall, *The Industries of London since 1861*, London, Hutchinson, 1962; John Vaizey, *The Costs of Education*, London, Allen & Unwin, 1958.

20. The continuing flow of reports from the two longitudinal studies of cohorts of children born in 1946 and 1958, by Dr J. W. B. Douglas, Dr Ronald Davie and their respective colleagues are excellent British examples.

21. London, Routledge, 1954.

22. London, Rathbone Memorial Lecture, Liverpool University Press, 1956.

23. London, Routledge, 1957.

24. London, Heinemann, 1957.

25. In N. MacKenzie (ed.), *Conviction*, London, McGibbon & Kee, 1958.

26. *Spatial Policy Problems of the British Economy*, by Michael Chisholm and Gerald Manners (eds), David Keeble, Peter Haggett, Peter Hall, Raymond Pahl and Kenneth Warren, Cambridge, Cambridge University Press, 1971.

27. Noel Annan, 'The Intellectual Aristocracy', in J. H. Plumb (ed.), *Studies in Social History*, London, Longmans Green, 1955.

28. Thomas S. Kuhn, *The Structure of Scientific Revolutions*, 2nd enlarged edition, Chicago, University of Chicago Press, 1970.

Chapter 3

1. M. Rein, *Social Science and Public Policy*, Harmondsworth, Penguin, 1976, chapter 3, 'Values, social science and social policy' (first published, 1973).

2. A. Shonfield, 'Research and public policy', in A. B. Cherns *et al.* (eds), *Social Science and Government*, London, Tavistock, 1972, pp. 67–80.

3. P. Berger, *Invitation to Sociology*, Harmondsworth, Penguin, 1963, p. 41.

4. R. Dahrendorf, 'Social institutions, economic forces and the future of sociology', unpublished opening address to the British Sociological Association Annual Conference at the University of Kent, 1975, p. 7.

5. Quoted in R. M. Titmuss, *Poverty and Population*, London, Macmillan, 1938, p. 5ff.

6. A. B. Cherns *et al.*, *Social Science and Government*, London, Tavistock, 1972.

7. M. Rein, op. cit.

8. Ibid., especially pp. 127–30.

9. A. B. Cherns, 'Social sciences and policy', in P. Halmos (ed.), *The Sociology of Sociology*, University of Keele, Sociological Review Monograph No. 16, 1970, p. 55.

10. R. Huws Jones in *The Almoner*, **12**, No. 2, p. 61, quoted by A. Sinfield, 'Which way for social work?' in P. Townsend *et al.* (eds), *The Fifth Social Service* (London, Fabian Society, 1970), p. 28.

11. J. D. Cowhig, 'Federal grant supported research and "relevance": some reservations', *Am. Sociol.*, **6**, 1972, supplementary issue on sociological research and public policy, p. 67.

12. R. K. Merton, *et al.* (eds), *Sociology Today*, New York, Basic Books, 1959, p. xv, note 5, for a brilliant description of such attitudes. Merton is describing general lay attitudes to sociology but they also apply with equal force to most policy-makers' attitudes to social scientists.

13. W. Lippmann, *Public Opinion*, New York, Free Press, 1965, p. 7.

14. G. Lyons, *The Uneasy Partnership*, New York, Russell Sage Foundation, 1968, p. 10.

15. For a discussion of this problem in relation to policy-making see chapter 2, 'The fact-value dilemma' (first published 1974), in M. Rein, op. cit.

16. K. Hope, chapter 13 of this volume, p. 264.

17. N. E. Long, 'The local community as an ecology of games', in L. A. Coser (ed.), *Political Sociology*, New York, Harper, 1967, p. 148.

18. *Report of the Committee on Social Studies* (Chairman Lord Heyworth), London, H.M.S.O., 1965, chapter 7, 'The use of research'.

19. A. B. Cherns *et al.*, op. cit.

20. Quoted in Rein, op. cit., p. 97.

21. A. B. Cherns *et al.*, op. cit., p. xxvii.

22. E. C. Banfield, *Political Influence*, New York, Free Press, 1965, p. 283 ff.

23. K. Hope, chapter 13 of this volume, p. 261.
24. Ibid, p. 261.
25. D. Donnison, chapter 2 of this volume, p. 49.
26. Ibid, pp. 48ff.

Chapter 4

1. Gallup quotes the following 'working definition of public opinion' from Bryce: 'aggregate of the views men hold regarding matters that affect or interest the country'. G. Gallup, *A Guide to Public Opinion Polls*, 2nd edn, 1948, p. 84. No reference to Bryce given.

2. See Paul A. Palmer, 'The concept of public opinion in political theory' in *Essays in History and Political Theory in Honour of Charles Howard McIlwain*, 1936, pp. 230–57, upon which the following account draws.

3. See, for example, criticisms of Bryce by David B. Truman, *The Governmental Process*, 1955, p. 216.

4. For example, Truman, op. cit.

5. Palmer, op. cit., p. 252.

6. M. Benney, A. P. Gray and R. H. Pear, *How People Vote*, 1956, pp. 13–15.

7. J. Plamenatz, 'Electoral Studies and Democratic Theory. I. A British View', *Polit. Stud.*, **6**, 1958, p. 9.

8. See, for example, H. Blumer, 'Collective Behavior', Part 4 of A. McC. Lee, *New Outline of the Principles of Sociology*, 1946, pp. 185–93; 'Public opinion and public opinion polling', *Am. Sociol. Rev.*, **13**, 1948, 542–49; Truman, op. cit.

9. Blumer, 1946, op. cit.

10. Blumer, 1948, op. cit.

11. Truman, op. cit., p. 219.

12. 1946, op. cit.

13. Truman, op. cit., p. 220.

14. This is why the offers of the pollsters are tempting. Gallup claims to have shown very slight popular support for a U.S. campaign for large old-age pensions, which was claiming widespread backing. (See V. O. Key, Jr, *Politics, Parties and Pressure Groups*, 3rd edn., 1953, pp. 676–7.) But, as will be argued later, this sort of finding is almost as difficult to interpret as the pressure campaign it was used to discredit.

15. For a discussion of legitimacy, see A. Lawrence Lowell, *Public Opinion and Popular Government*, 1913, pp. 9 ff.

16. See, for example, T. M. Newcomb in *Am. Sociol. Rev.*, **13**, 1948, 549–52.

17. For example, P. F. Lazarsfeld *et al.*, *The People's Choice*, 1948.

18. H. H. Hyman and P. F. Sheatsley, 'The current status of American public opinion', *National Council for Social Studies Yearbook,* **21**, 1950, 11–34, p. 16.

19. For public opinion, see Blumer, 1948, op. cit.; D. Riesman and N. Glazer, 'The Meaning of Opinion', *Pub. Opin. Q.*, **12**, 1948–9, 633–48. For voting behaviour, see Lazarsfeld *et al.*, op. cit.; B. Berelson *et al.*, *Voting*, 1954; R. S. Milne and H. C. Mackenzie, *Straight Fight*, 1954 and *Marginal Seat*, 1958. For mass communications, see H. Blumer, 'Suggestions for the study of mass-media effects', and K. and G. E. Lang, 'The mass-media and voting', in E. Burdick and A. J. Brodbeck (eds), *American Voting Behavior*, 1959. See also more general criticisms of the mass model, such as D. Katz and P. F. Lazarsfeld, *Personal Influence*, 1955, or E. Mayo, *The Social Problems of an Industrial Civilization*, 1949.

20. 'Public Opinion Polls have been Very Unfairly Pasted', Social Surveys (Gallup Poll) Ltd., 1959. Lindsay Rogers criticises Dr Gallup for similar claims, although Albig thinks the criticisms overdone. See L. Rogers, *The Pollsters*, 1949, cited in W. Albig, *Modern Public Opinion*, 1956, p. 230.

21. *Am. Sociol. Rev.*, **13**, 1948, 552–4.

22. G. Gallup and S. F. Rae, *The Pulse of Democracy*, 1940, quoted from Key, op. cit., p. 681. Gallup also writes, 'In a democracy such as ours the *incontrovertible* fact remains that the majority of citizens usually registers *sound* judgment on issues, even though a good many are ignorant or uninformed', and 'A member of the law faculty at the University of California, Max Radin, analysed the popular vote in California, on 115 referendum propositions put before the people in State elections between 1936 and 1946. He found that in a substantial majority of cases the voters took the same attitude toward the propositions as was taken by two of California's *conservative* institutions, the Commonwealth Club of San Francisco and the Town Hall of Los Angeles, after extensive study of the issues by their legislative committees. Dr Radin concludes from the evidence of these 115 referenda that the voters not only displayed *caution* and *good judgment* but that they rejected *crackpot* suggestions with greater firmness than their elected representatives in the State legislature.' He says: 'one thing is clear. The vote of the people is *eminently* sane'. Gallup, op. cit., p. 85. (My italics.)

23. 'Sampling Public Opinion', *J. Am. statist. Ass.*, **35**, 1940, 325–34.

24. *News Chronicle*, Sept. 30, 1960. See also Albig, op. cit., pp. 26–7.

25. For example, H. Cantril, *Gauging Public Opinion*, 1944; Q. McNemar, 'Opinion-attitude methodology', *Psych. Bull.*, **43**, 1946,

289–374; D. Katz, 'Do interviewers bias poll results?', *Pub. Opin. Q.*, **6**, 1942, 248–68.

26. H. J. Parry and Helen M. Crossley, 'Validity of Responses to Survey Questions', *Pub. Opin. Q.*, **14**, 1950, 61–80, in D. Katz *et al.*, *Public Opinion and Propaganda*, 1954.

27. S. B. Withey, *Consistency of Immediate and Delayed Reports of Financial Data*, Unpubl. Ph.D. thesis, cited in A. A. Campbell and G. Katona, 'The sample survey', in L. Festinger and D. Katz (eds), *Research Methods in the Behavioral Sciences*, 1954, pp. 43–4. Similar effects are familiar in other fields. For example the very high validities possible in the use of group intelligence tests for secondary school selection can still mask substantial individual errors. See P. E. Vernon (ed.), *Secondary School Selection*, 1957, pp. 75–7.

28. Cantril, op. cit., pp. 44–6. See also D. Katz, 'The Interpretation of Survey Findings', *J. soc. Issues*, **2**, 1946, 33–44.

29. Hyman, *Interviewing in Social Research*, 1954.

30. Ibid.

31. Parry and Crossley, op. cit. The figure of half or more is derived from Table II, p. 747. Since the 31 per cent who reported not contributing were not checked on, they should be ignored for purposes of validity. Of the remainder, 49 per cent were proved invalid and a further 12 per cent presumed to be so. Hyman found similar cases – such as that 17 per cent of a sample of people who had cashed government bonds during the war denied doing so. H. H. Hyman, 'Do They Tell the Truth?', *Pub. Opin. Q.*, **8**, 1944–5, 557–9. See also Hyman, 1954, op. cit.

32. For example, D. E. Butler and R. Rose, *The British General Election of 1959*, 1960, p. 99; also D. E. G. Plowman, 'The public and the polls', *The Listener*, Jan. 14, 1960.

33. Notably in market research in industry, where the generalisation from election successes may be a proper one, since both involve sampling a mass population.

34. Gallup, op. cit., p. 69.

35. See the follow-up polls after the 1959 British general election for some evidence, for example *Daily Telegraph*, Nov. 27, 1959, and *News Chronicle*, Sept. 26–30, 1960. In the *Telegraph* survey, for example, over half the Don't Knows actually voted, in a ratio of roughly three Conservatives to two Labour. This was sufficient to affect the prediction by about 1 per cent. Also a minority of expressed intentions was carried out differently or not at all. The effect of the time-lag was dramatically shown in the notorious American election of 1948.

36. See the references in note 19. See also A. A. Campbell *et al.*, *The American Voter*, 1960; Sir Ivor Jennings, *Party Politics. I: Appeal to*

the People, 1960; and R. Rose, 'How the Party System Works' in *Must Labour Lose?*, Penguin Books, 1960.

37. Political discussion may continue. But the part of the process involving the formation of intentions does not.

38. In fact, the judicious use of opinion-questions may sometimes improve the forecast, as in the use of questions like 'Do you think it makes any difference which party is returned?' to help forecast turnout between rival parties. In this case, inferences about action are being drawn from opinions. But this can be done only because the inferences can be validated – and they are validated against the actions of voting. The principle is not altered. Such actions for use in validation are usually absent with opinion-questions.

39. Gallup, op. cit., p. 69.

40. Ibid., p. 70.

41. It might produce, say, more 'safe' or 'responsible' replies. See note 72, in which it is pointed out that the meaning of a vote in a by-election, and therefore of a poll, is rather different from that in a general election. If this is so, then an 'opinion' in the absence of any vote at all might be even more different.

42. This is sometimes in doubt in actual referenda. Commentators on the Algerian referendum of January 1961 questioned whether the result recorded views on policies or a personal vote for de Gaulle.

43. Cf. Katz, 1942, op. cit.

44. Cantril, op. cit.

45. Katz, op. cit.

46. Hyman, 1954, op. cit., pp. 217–19.

47. B. F. Green, 'Attitude Measurement', in G. Lindzey, *Handbook of Social Psychology*, **I**, 1954, p. 340.

48. Hyman, 1954, op. cit.

49. See the discussion on p. 334 above of the 'equal weight' of opinions.

50. Cf. the expectations of some interviewers both that opinions will be held and that they will be consistent. Hyman, 1954, op. cit.

51. Cantril, op. cit., pp. 24–7. The apparent majority for intervention varied from 78 to 8 per cent. As Cantril says, it is doubtful to what extent the ten questions involved even appear to measure the same thing; and some of the questions might now be thought technically inadequate; but any estimate of actual interventionist sentiment remains impossible on these data. In any case, it is not the extent of the variation so much as the fact of it that creates problems in estimating the validity of poll findings.

52. R. S. Crutchfield and D. A. Gordon, 'Variations in respondents' interpretations of an opinion-poll question', *Int. J. Op. Att.*

Res., **I** (**3**), 1947, 1–12, cited by D. Krech and R. S. Crutchfield, *Theory and Problems of Social Psychology*, 1948, 280–1.

53. M. Abrams, 'The *Socialist Commentary* Survey', in *Must Labour Lose?*, op. cit., p. 35. This survey is open to criticism on technical grounds. See, for example, R. Samuel, 'Dr Abrams and the End of Politics', *New Left Review*, Sept.–Oct., 1960, no. 5, pp. 2–9. But the point at issue is how such a poll can be validated, and this is not affected by the detailed criticisms of methodology.

54. Dr Abrams was primarily studying reasons for voting in the 1959 general election, rather than public opinion as such. But his use of phrases such as 'the public's lack of interest in nationalization' (op. cit., p. 37) suggests that he does not draw a clear distinction.

55. See, for example, H. J. Eysenck, *The Psychology of Politics*, 1954.

56. Abrams, op. cit., p. 34. Indeed, if this were known to be the case, the question would be redundant. Anyway, Abrams uses the results to demonstrate truths about the beliefs of party supporters, so that this form of validation is logically unavailable.

57. Hyman, 1954, op. cit., p. 22.

58. The lack of controversy, except on certain topics such as sport, in say normal British working-class pub conversation is shown by, for example, J. M. Mogey, *Family and Neighbourhood*, 1956, and N. Dennis, F. Henriques and C. Slaughter, *Coal is our Life*, 1956. P. H. Rossi ('Four Landmarks in Voting Research', in Burdick and Brodbeck, op. cit., p. 28) cites the Elmira study (Berelson *et al.*, op. cit.) to show that political discussions consist mainly of 'mutually agreeable commentaries'. Under such social pressures, a man may well fail to utter his real opinions.

59. For example, R. T. LaPiere, 'Attitudes *vs.* actions', *Social Forces*, **13**, 1934, 230–7. These are properly intentions. R. L. Schank, 'A study of a community and its groups and institutions conceived of as behavior of individuals', *Psychol. Monogr.*, **43** (**2**), 1932, 1–133.

60. Green places 'action attitudes' on the same logical level as 'elicited' and 'spontaneous verbal attitudes' (op. cit., p. 340), and Murphy, Murphy and Newcomb have pointed out that attitudes can be concealed quite as effectively through actions as through words (G. Murphy, L. B. Murphy and T. M. Newcomb, *Experimental Social Psychology*, 1937, p. 912).

61. For example, the recent California work on ethnocentrism. T. W. Adorno *et al.*, *The Authoritarian Personality*, 1950.

62. For example, R. Christie and M. Jahoda, *Studies in the Scope and Method of 'The Authoritarian Personality'*, 1954.

63. See P. E. Vernon and J. B. Parry, *Personnel Selection in the British Forces*, 1949.

64. For example, E. L. Kelley and D. W. Fiske, *The Prediction of Performance in Clinical Psychology*, 1951.

65. M. B. Smith, J. S. Bruner and R. W. White, *Opinions and Personality*, 1956.

66. See D. E. G. Plowman, W. E. Minchinton, and M. Stacey, 'Local Social Status in England and Wales', *Sociol Rev.*, **10** (2), 1962, pp. 161–202.

67. For example, Benney *et al.*, op. cit.; J. Bonham, *The Middle Class Vote*, 1954; A. H. Birch, *Small Town Politics*, 1959; Rose, op. cit., pp. 78–9.

68. See, for example, Hyman, 1954, op. cit.; also Campbell and Katona, op. cit., p. 47.

69. Hyman, 1954, op. cit., p. 22.

70. Ibid., pp. 182 ff., 201 ff.

71. There are small differences between the standard polls, largely the result of differences in Don't Knows, themselves probably resulting in part from differences in wording, interviewer-technique or treatment of data; perhaps also the result of different ways of filtering the Don't Knows. For data, see Butler and Rose, op. cit., pp. 101, 105.

72. Even here, the 'protest vote' at by-elections suggests that the meaning of the standard question may vary slightly between general elections and other times. Durant maintained that many of the Conservative abstainers of 1957–8 would return to the fold at a general election.

73. Abrams, op. cit., p. 37.

74. Gallup data show a change from 6 per cent of a national sample in 1951 to 17 per cent in the spring of 1959 who identified the Labour Party with nationalisation. See Butler and Rose, op. cit., pp. 241 ff.

75. See Butler and Rose (op. cit., pp. 244, 246), who say that the extensive technical criticisms at the time were never properly established.

76. There were differences in wording and possibly interviewer technique; an interval of two months between the two surveys; and a possible sampling error of the order of 5 per cent in Abrams' small sample. On the other hand, the fact that the Hurry survey was a referendum rules out sampling error in that case, other than the probably small error introduced by the selection of marginal constituencies.

77. Abrams, op. cit., pp. 31–6.

78. Gallup, op. cit., pp. 40 ff.

79. As it did for the *Daily Telegraph* in the 1959 British election and for the Gallup Poll in earlier elections but not in 1959.

80. See F. Mosteller *et al.*, *The Pre-election Polls of 1948*, 1949, p. 12, for a discussion of these matters.

81. See the quotations on pp. 102–3.

82. Dr Abrams' survey suggests that only a small proportion of his sample gave much weight to nationalisation. Op. cit., p. 36.

83. For a contrary view, see W. H. Morris Jones, 'In defence of apathy', *Polit. Stud.*, **2**, 1954, 25–37.

Chapter 5

1. A. F. Wells, *The Local Social Survey in Great Britain*, published for the Sir Halley Stewart Trust by Allen & Unwin, London, 1935, p. 13.

2. Mark Abrams, *Social Surveys and Social Action*, London, Heinemann, 1951, p. 2.

3. The distinction between facts, values and theories is an analytical one made to facilitate the discussion. In practice they are typically entangled and interrelated, and may not easily be separable, but this does not affect the general argument. 'Theory', here and subsequently, is used in the sense of causal proposition(s) about empirical states of affairs rather than in any of the alternative senses.

4. 'State of affairs' is chosen as the most general available term; it is intended to cover both specific targets which may be reached once and for all, and continuing situations which endure over long periods.

5. Some policies may be felt to be *inherently* desirable, autotelic, valuable expressively rather than as instruments to some ulterior end. In such a case the distinction between the policy and the state of affairs which it is designed to produce loses meaning. This, however, does not affect the argument; a value-judgement is still implied in the expression of a preference for one course of action over others.

6. For a discussion of this, see Gunnar Myrdal, *Value in Social Theory*, London, Routledge & Kegan Paul, 1958, chapter 10.

7. In what follows a consistent distinction will be maintained between 'attitude', meaning a general orientation with consequences for many particular issues, and 'opinion', meaning a specific opinion about a relatively precise issue. Thus an opinion could refer directly to a possible policy, while an attitude would be too general to do so, although particular opinions would spring from it.

8. Ann Cartwright, *Human Relations and Hospital Care*, London: Routledge & Kegan Paul, 1964. This example is drawn, as are most of the rest, from the published work of the Institute of Community Studies. This should not be understood to imply that their work is unusually vulnerable to any of the possible criticisms implied. It merely reflects the fact that this article arose out of the work done for a book on the Institute (*Social Research in Bethnal Green*, Macmillan,

1971) and that their books are well known and so a convenient source to draw upon.

9. Severyn T. Bruyn, *The Human Perspective in Sociology*, Englewood Cliffs, New Jersey, Prentice-Hall, 1966, p. 250.

10. Charles Booth, *Life and Labour of the People of London*, vol. I, London, Macmillan, 1904, pp. 4–5.

11. On this subject, see Robert K. Merton, *Social Theory and Social Structure* (revised edition), Glencoe, Illinois, The Free Press, 1957; 'The Bearing of Empirical Research on Sociological Theory', pp. 103–8.

12. Barney G. Glaser and Anselm L. Strauss, *The Discovery of Grounded Theory*, London: Weidenfeld & Nicolson, 1968.

13. This exemption would be on the assumption that experts would, by definition, already have tested their theories adequately; of course this assumption could not always be justified.

14. The exception to this generalisation arises from the importance of the resource factor in practical decision-making. When policy must be decided quickly, or the resources of other kinds than time that can be committed to the decision process are limited, it may be necessary to sacrifice comprehensiveness to other considerations. Such a sacrifice must itself, however, if it is to be rational, be guided by criteria which specify what aspects can most safely be ignored, and so the problem cannot be escaped. Thus although our analysis in the text may appear to refer to an ideal rather than the real world, it is relevant even to the latter.

15. Percy Cohen, 'Social Attitudes and Sociological Enquiry', *Br. J. Sociol.*, **17** (4), Dec. 1966, pp. 341–52.

16. For a discussion of ways in which this has occurred in explanations of juvenile delinquency, see Albert K. Cohen, *Delinquent Boys*, Glencoe, Illinois, The Free Press, 1955.

17. If questions at a high level of generality are put to respondents ('do you believe in free speech?') it is not clear what specific policies are implied by the answers, and so the type (1) relationship is impossible. For this reason we do not distinguish here between general value-judgements and particular policy preferences.

18. This whole discussion of the use that can be made of respondents' opinions assumes that the opinions ascertained are about possible future policies, since only on that assumption does it make sense to talk of acting on them. In practice, however, it is common for researchers to ask only for opinions of the present state of affairs, and then treat them as though they amounted to the same thing, which clearly they don't. To be dissatisfied with the way things are now does not, unfortunately, in itself constitute a policy for change nor even a preference for one policy among the available alternatives.

19. A special case of this occurs when the fact that the survey takes place is the circumstance that changes opinions. First, the mere fact of answering systematic questions whose form may draw alternative possible views to one's attention may bring about a reconsideration; this sort of change, which responds so much to the immediate situation, is probably very volatile. Secondly, when the results are known they can have consequences; one may feel sensitive to social pressures on discovering that one is in a minority, or even in the majority may have one's perceptions of the facts of the situation changed by evidence that there are other groups with equal sincerity who think differently.

20. Or it may sometimes happen that the researcher/research sponsor/policy-maker *is* the respondents acting collectively; in that case this particular problem does not arise.

21. D. V. Donnison, 'Education and opinion', *New Society*, October 1967, pp. 583–7.

22. A possibility not mentioned earlier, but which seems to belong in this category, is that the survey should elicit general attitudes and value-judgements which the researcher then attempts to devise policies to fit. Conditions (*a*) and (*b*) would remain relevant, (*c*) and (*d*) not. The chief difficulty about this, however, is that the respondents might not recognise the policies as their own, thus depriving the procedure of its rationale. This could come about either because there are many different policies which could follow from a given general principle, and which of these was preferred might depend on the extent to which they affected *other* principles, or because respondents simply had inconsistencies between their general and particular views. (For examples of the latter in relation to beliefs, see Joan Huber Rytina, William H. Form and John Pease, 'Income and stratification ideology: beliefs about the American opportunity structure', *Am. J. Sociol.*, **75** (4), pt. 2, Jan. 1970, pp. 703–16.

23. For a discussion of some ways in which this may happen, see Jennifer Platt, 'Some problems in measuring the jointness of conjugal role-relations', *Sociology*, **3** (3), Sept. 1969, pp. 293–5.

24. This point refers to wishes for the future. It is not clear, however, that even views on the present were studied systematically; no questions about this appear in the formal interview schedule.

25. The allusion is, of course, to the data which led to the development of reference group theory. See Robert K. Merton, *Social Theory and Social Structure* (revised and enlarged edition), Glencoe, Illinois, The Free Press, 1957: 'Contributions to the Theory of Reference Group Behaviour' (with Alice S. Rossi).

Chapter 6

1. The discovery of consumer opinion is the major concern of the following studies: P. M. Voelcker, 'Juvenile courts: the parents' point of view', *Br. J. Criminol.*, **1** (2), 1960, pp. 154–66; J. Mayer and N. Timms, *The Client Speaks*, London, Routledge and Kegan Paul, 1970; A. McKay, E. M. Goldberg and D. J. Fruin, 'Consumers and a social services department', *Social Work Today*, **4** (16), 1973, pp. 486–91; J. Triseliotis, *In Search of Origins*, London, Routledge and Kegan Paul, 1973; D. Marsden, *Mothers Alone*, Harmondsworth, Penguin, 1973; P. Morris, J. Cooper and A. Byles, 'Public attitudes to problem definition and problem solving', *Br. J. Social Work*, **3** (3), 1973, pp. 301–20; O. Gill, *Whitegate: An Approved School in Transition*, Liverpool, Liverpool University Press, 1974; E. Sainsbury, *Social Work with Families*, London, Routledge and Kegan Paul, 1975. It is a partial concern in the following: Z. Butrym, *Medical Social Work in Action*, Occasional Papers on Social Administration, London, Bell, 1968; A. Cohen, 'Consumer view: retarded mothers and the social services', *Social Work Today*, **1** (12), 1971, pp. 39–43; E. M. Goldberg, *Helping the Aged*, London, Allen and Unwin, 1970; M. Bayley, *Mental Handicap and Community Care*, London, Routledge and Kegan Paul, 1973; see also N. Timms, *The Receiving End*, London, Routledge and Kegan Paul, 1973; M. Shaw, *Social Work in Prison*, London, H.M.S.O., 1974.

2. R. Holman, 'Client power', *New Society*, **31**, November 1968; A. Sinfield, *Which Way for Social Work?*, London, Fabian Society, 1969.

3. Mayer and Timms, op. cit., pp. 15–16.

4. E. Goffman, *Asylums*, New York, Anchor Books, 1961, pp. 367–8.

5. J. Platt, *Social Research in Bethnal Green*, London, Macmillan, 1971, Introduction. Working-class people still form the bulk of social service clients, although the elderly and chronically sick and handicapped probably cut across class lines.

6. Footnote 1.

7. This review is concerned with the sociological or methodological contributions made by the literature only in so far as these impinge on the way in which policy recommendations are formulated.

8. Mayer and Timms, op. cit., p. 1.

9. Butrym, op. cit., pp. 69–82.

10. Goldberg, op. cit., pp. 171–82, 189–90.

11. In the light of our earlier comments, it is worth recalling that Marsden has been associated with the work of the Institute of Community Studies for some years.

12. Triseliotis, op. cit., p. 2.

13. This section is indebted to ideas outlined by Noel Timms in his Introduction to *The Receiving End*, op. cit.

14. McKay, *et al.*, op. cit., p. 490.

15. Goldberg and McKay, op. cit., p. 74.

16. Cohen, op. cit., pp. 39–40.

17. McKay, op. cit., pp. 488–9.

18. Bayley, op. cit., p. 302.

19. Voelcker, op. cit.

20. Cohen, op. cit., pp. 42–3. The element of bargaining was found in the studies by Cohen and Mayer and Timms.

21. Voelcker, op. cit.

22. Ibid., pp. 73, 76–7.

23. Ibid., pp. 2–3.

24. Platt, op. cit., p. 35.

25. For instance, the studies by Butrym, Gill, and Mayer and Timms.

26. This point is discussed in Platt, op. cit., and in P. Marris and M. Rein, *Dilemmas of Social Reform*, Harmondsworth, Penguin, 1972, chapter 8.

27. Ibid., p. 142.

28. Cmnd. 4683, London, H.M.S.O., 1971.

29. Bayley, op. cit., chapter 19.

30. Ibid., p. 37.

31. J. Platt, chapter 5 of this volume.

32. Platt, op. cit., 1971, p. 96.

33. Triseliotis, op. cit., pp. 139, 142, 160.

34. Mayer and Timms, op. cit., pp. 22–3, 136–48.

35. Gill uses participant observation, but attempts no independent assessment of the setting.

36. Cf. Morris *et al.*, op. cit.; G. Smith and R. Harris, 'Ideologies of need and the organisation of social work departments', *Br. J. soc. Work*, **2** (1), 1972, pp. 27–45.

37. As an example of this, using life histories, see A. J. Manocchio and J. Dunn, *The Time Game: Two Views of a Prison*, Beverley Hills, Sage, 1970.

38. Butrym, op. cit.

39. Cf. J. E. Neill, D. J. Fruin, E. M. Goldberg and R. W. Warburton, 'Reactions to integration', *Social Work Today*, **4** (15), 1973, pp. 458–65.

40. Gill, op. cit., chapters 2 and 6.

41. Marsden, op. cit., pp. 8–10, chapter 12. Sainsbury's recent research with Family Service Unit Families (*Social Work with Families*, op. cit.) is a significant advance on earlier studies in that he sampled agency–client relationships.

42. O. Stevenson, Editorial, *Br. J. soc. Work*, **3** (3), 1973, p. 299.

43. R. Holman (ed.), *Socially Deprived Families in Britain*, London, Bedford Square Press, 1970, pp. 191–5; *Report of the Committee on Local Authority and Allied Personal Social Services*, Cmnd. 3703, London, H.M.S.O., 1968, paragraphs 491–4, 628.

44. The criticism of conservatism can be modified by distinguishing, as does Rein, between 'needs-resource' research, 'distributive' research and 'allocative' research. Much social work research in the past has been of the 'needs-resource' kind, aimed at identifying disparities between needs and services, and leading almost inevitably to a demand for more services of the kind already existing. The research reviewed here is mainly 'distributive' in character, aimed at the reallocation of existing resources within the social services. As such, it is less conservative, in that the existing form of services does not remain unquestioned. Its conservatism lies in leaving aside the possibility that alternative programmes are needed to reach the stated objective. (M. Rein, *Social Policy*, New York, Random House, 1970, chapter 22.)

45. A weakness of Bayley's careful study is that recommendations are drawn largely from the 53 intensive visits to the homes, and the extensive analysis carried out of records of all cases of mental handicap in Sheffield is largely overlooked.

Chapter 7

1. D. P. Moynihan (ed.), *On Understanding Poverty*, New York, Basic Books, 1969, p. 28.

2. For a general account of the three-year Educational Priority Area projects in London, Birmingham, Liverpool and the West Riding, see A. H. Halsey (ed.), *Educational Priority*, London, H.M.S.O., 1972.

3. In P. Lazarsfeld *et al.*, *The Uses of Sociology*, New York, Basic Books, 1967, p. 454.

4. Ibid.

5. J. Bainbridge, 'Race Relations and racial friction', unpublished Diploma thesis, University of Oxford, 1969.

6. S.S.R.C., *Research on Poverty*, London, Heinemann, 1968, p. 9.

7. See the essays by P. H. Rossi and Z. D. Blum, Oscar Lewis, H. J. Gans, L. Rainwater and W. Miller in Moynihan, op. cit. See also H. Gans, 'Urban Poverty and Social Planning' in Lazarsfeld, *The Uses of Sociology*.

8. Gans, 'Urban poverty and social planning'.

9. S. M. Miller, 'Invisible Men', *Psychiatric and Social Science Reviews*, vol. 2, 1968, p. 14.

10. See Oscar Lewis, 'The culture of poverty' in Moynihan, op. cit.

11. Thus in presenting the case for the Economic Opportunity Act to Congress in 1964, Sargent Shriver argued that 'being poor . . . is a rigid way of life. It is handed down from generation to generation in a cycle of inadequate education, inadequate homes, inadequate jobs and stunted ambitions. It is a peculiar axiom of poverty that the poor are poor because they earn little and they also earn little because they are poor.'

12. Otis Dudley Duncan, 'Inheritance of Poverty or Inheritance of Race' in Moynihan, op. cit., p. 88.

13. See Margaret Stacey, 'The Myth of Community Studies', *Br. J. Sociol.*, **20**, 1969.

14. See Edward Shils, 'Of plenitude and scarcity', *Encounter*, **32**, 1969.

15. Peter H. Rossi, unpublished paper at an Anglo-American conference on the evaluation of social action programmes at Ditchley Park, October 1969.

16. Jonathan Steele, 'Multi-million attack on twilight areas', *Guardian*, 15 January 1969.

17. The Community development projects will eventually cover ten or twelve slum areas or 'communities' of between 3000 and 15 000 population. Inter-service teams are being set up, addressing themselves in a co-ordinated way to the total personal needs of families and of the community as a whole by bridging the gap between the street and the offices of the various departments of welfare.

Chapter 8

1. R. Rapoport, 'Three dilemmas in action research', *Hum. Relat.*, **23** (6), pp. 499–514, reviews much of the literature.

2. J. C. Spencer, *Stress and Release on an Urban Estate*, Tavistock, London, 1962.

3. The title of the Educational Priority Area project has been abbreviated to E.P.A. throughout this chapter.

4. The title of the Community Development Project has been abbreviated to C.D.P. throughout this chapter.

5. Central Advisory Council for Education, *Children and their Primary Schools*, London, H.M.S.O., 1967.

6. Ibid., paragraph 117.

7. Home Office, *Community Development Project: Objectives and Strategy*, unpublished mimeo, London, 1969.

8. J. Greve, *Community Development Project Research Strategy*, unpublished Home Office mimeo, London, 1970.

9. See P. Marris and M. Rein, *Dilemmas of Social Reform*, Tavistock, London, 1967; and D. P. Moynihan, *Maximum Feasible Misunderstanding*, Collier-Macmillan, New York, 1969.

10. A. B. Cherns, 'Social research and its diffusion', *Hum. Relat.*, **22** (3), 1969, pp. 210–18.

11. A. B. Cherns, 'Models for the use of research', *Hum. Relat.*, **25** (1), pp. 25–36.

12. The Home Office funds the Community Development Project.

13. Such a change in policy did in fact follow the presentation of the E.P.A. projects' reports, although it is open to debate how far it was as a result of E.P.A. projects in particular, rather than of the more widespread swing in favour of pre-school education which has taken place generally in recent years.

14. E. Jacques, *The Changing Culture of the Factory*, Tavistock, London, 1951.

15. Rapoport, op. cit.

16. C. Sofer, *The Organisation from Within*, Tavistock, London, 1961.

17. A. K. Rice, *Productivity and Social Organisation*, Tavistock, London, 1968.

18. R. K. Brown, 'Research and consultancy in industrial enterprises', *Sociology*, **1** (1), pp. 33–60.

19. Rapoport, op. cit., p. 503.

20. In his introduction to Jacques, op. cit., pp. xiii–xvii.

21. For example, M. Foster, 'An introduction to the theory and practice of action research in work organisations', *Hum. Relat.*, **25** (6), pp. 529–556.

22. K. Thurley, 'The organisation and sponsorship of action research', *S.S.R.C. Newsletter*, No. 14, pp. 18–21; J. S. Henley, 'Action research in public housing organisations', paper presented to the S.S.R.C. Conference on Action Research, York, July 1970.

23. For example, D. Silverman, *The Theory of Organisations*, Heinemann, London, 1970.

24. A. H. Halsey, *Educational Priority*, London, H.M.S.O., 1972, p. 57.

25. S. W. Town, 'The Limits on Change in an EPA', in C. M. Morrison (ed.), *EPA: A Scottish Study*, London, H.M.S.O., forthcoming.

26. The interim report of the Liverpool project underlined this forcibly: 'so pressing is the need, both for the practical purpose of avoiding permanent social dislocation, and for the moral purpose of ensuring an elementary system of social justice, that it would have been preferable to have come up with an answer in three weeks', quoted in Halsey, op. cit., p. ix.

27. Halsey, op. cit., chapter 13.

28. It should be pointed out that some of those involved had always been sceptical of the value of this approach.

29. Halsey, op. cit., chapter 12.

30. As Halsey makes clear in this preface to his book, and in the general discussion of Part One, the sorts of policy and practices which E.P.A. projects promulgate represent a political position.

31. Halsey, op. cit., chapter 14.

32. Greve, op. cit.

33. Ibid.

34. R. Holman, *Socially Deprived Families in Britain*, London, Bedford Square Press, 1970, pp. 178–183.

35. Halsey, op. cit., chapter 13, esp. pp. 178–9.

36. Written reply to a parliamentary question by Reginald Maudling (Home Secretary) on 28 April, 1972. *Parliamentary Debates* (Hansard), Vol. 835, No. 106, Col. 371.

37. Recent changes in the structure of the project suggest the future course of the project may in any case be smoother. Many of the organisational difficulties which the lack of central co-ordination created have now been resolved, largely through a process of attrition. A new Information and Intelligence Unit has been set up in association with the Centre for Environmental Studies to provide a serving function for the local teams as required; this, together with the consultative council which comprises representatives of the various local projects, has replaced the Central Team of the Home Office and Central Research Unit as the co-ordinating bodies for the project. In most of the surviving local teams some sort of understanding appears to have been reached between action and research teams as to interpretation of their respective roles in that particular project, although these changes do not solve the fundamental problems of this sort of action research.

38. E. A. Suchman, *Evaluative Research*, New York, Russell Sage Foundation, 1967.

39. See, for example, the studies reported in L. A. Zurcher and C. M. Bonjean, *Planned Social Intervention*, Scranton, Chandler Publishing, 1970.

40. Halsey, op. cit., p. 175.

41. Marris and Rein, op. cit.

42. B. G. Glaser and A. L. Strauss, *The Discovery of Grounded Theory*, Weidenfeld and Nicolson, London, 1967.

43. The total spending on C.D.P. *research* will exceed £400 000, while the amount allocated for *action* from central government funds will exceed £2 million; the majority of the latter sum is spent on action projects in the community rather than on project staffing, etc.

Chapter 9

1. For example at the Anglo–American conference on the evaluation of social action programmes, Ditchley Park, October 1969.

2. In the process, they have at times apparently inherited form without understanding its purpose. Research is seen as a central part of innovation, but which part nobody is quite sure. In some of the later C.D.P.s, the desire to preserve action-research harmony has meant that evaluation of action, originally a central role, has been pushed to one side and become almost a taboo subject.

3. A. H. Halsey, 'Social science and government', *Times Literary Supplement*, 5 March 1970; and Halsey, chapter 7 of this volume.

4. Halsey, op. cit.

5. J. Bradshaw, 'Welfare rights, an experimental approach', in R. Lees and G. Smith (eds), *Action Research in Community Development*, London, Routledge, 1975, pp. 106–18.

6. M. Mayo, 'The history and early development of CDP', pp. 6–18, and J. Bennington, 'The flaw in the pluralist heaven: changing strategies in the Coventry CDP', pp. 174–87, in Lees and Smith (eds), op. cit.

7. Halsey, op. cit.

8. This approach was recommended in the discussion sparked off by the Westinghouse study of Head Start. See R. J. Light and P. V. Smith, 'Choosing a future: strategies for designing and evaluating new programmes', *Harvard Educ. Rev.*, 1970, pp. 1–28.

9. R. G. A. Williams, 'Consequences for the community', in A. E. Bennett (ed.), *Community Hospitals: Progress in Development and Evaluation*, Oxford Regional Hospital Board, 1974.

10. C. Wright Mills, *The Sociological Imagination*, New York, Oxford University Press, 1959.

11. M. Mayo, op. cit.

12. G. A. N. Smith and J. Barnes, 'Some implications of action-research projects for research', unpublished paper given at the 7th World Congress of Sociology at Varna, 1970; S. Town, chapter 8 of this volume; R. Lees, 'The action-research relationship', in Lees and Smith (eds.), op. cit., pp. 59–66.

13. For the American experience, see H. Spiegel and V. Alicea, 'The trade-off strategy in community research', in L. A. Zurcher and C. M. Bonjean (eds), *Planned Social Intervention*, San Francisco, Chandler, 1970. For recent British experience there is the Community Relations Commission's survey of black teenagers and academic studies of the black groups which have met strong resistance.

14. M. Mayo, op. cit.

15. G. Green, 'Towards community power', in S. Hatch and H. Glennerster (eds), *Positive Discrimination and Inequality*, London, Fabian Research Series 314, 1974.

16. J. W. Evans and J. Schiller, 'How preoccupation with possible regression artifacts can lead to a faulty strategy for the evaluation of social action programs', in J. Hellmuth (ed.), *The Disadvantaged Child*, vol. 3, New York, Brunner–Mazel, 1970.

17. Ibid.

Chapter 11

1. Elaine Carlisle, 'The conceptual structure of social indicators', in A. Shonfield and S. Shaw (eds), *Social Indicators and Public Policy*, London, Heinemann, 1972.

2. B. Cazes, 'The development of social indicators: a survey', ibid.

3. For example, *Towards a Social Report*, U.S. Department of Health Education and Welfare, Washington, U.S. Government Printing Office, 1969; and in Britain *Social Trends*, London, H.M.S.O., annually since 1970.

4. J. Craig and A. Driver, 'The identification and comparison of small areas of adverse social conditions: a study of social indicators and social indices', *Appl. Statist.*, **21**, (1), 1972 discusses with examples from 1966 census data the usefulness and reliability of small area census data as indicants, gives examples of applications, and discusses methods of combining index scores.

5. For example, Liverpool City Planning Department, *Social Malaise in Liverpool: Interim Report on Social Problems and their Distribution*, no date; Glasgow Corporation, *Areas of Need in Glasgow*, Glasgow Planning Department, 1972.

6. A very simple and easily interpreted form of cluster analysis is that devised by L. L. McQuitty, 'Elementary linkage analysis for isolating orthogonal and oblique types and typal relevancies', *Educ. psychol. Measur.*, **17**, 1957 (the title belies the simplicity).

7. The value implications of social indicators are considered among others by B. M. Gross, *The State of the Nation*, London, Methuen, 1966, pp. 136–7; B. Cazes, op. cit., p. 19; E. Carlisle, op. cit., pp. 24–5.

8. Liverpool City Planning Department, op. cit.; Southwark Community Project, *Working Paper on Methods of Analysing Need*, unpublished, October 1970; Waltham Forest, Department of Social Services and Planning Department, *Survey of Social Stress* in *Clearing House for Local Authority Social Services Research*, No. 6, 1973 (University of Birmingham); Greater London Council, Policy and Resources Committee, *London's Deprived Areas – A Comprehensive Approach*,

G.L.C., 1973; Newcastle upon Tyne Planning Department, *Housing: a Review of Current Problems and Policies*, Vol. 1, 1964.

9. *Report of the Committee on Housing in Greater London* (Milner–Holland report), Cmnd. 2605, London, H.M.S.O., 1965 contains a section on the identification of housing stress areas (at borough level); A. Little and C. Mabey, 'An Index for the Designation of EPAs', in Shonfield and Shaw, op. cit.; Greater London Development Plan, *Report of Studies* (1969).

Chapter 12

1. R. Bauer, *Social Indicators*, Cambridge, Mass., M.I.T. Press, 1967.

2. Ibid., p. vii.

3. Centre for Research on Scientific Knowledge, Ann Arbor, University of Michigan, 1972, mimeo.

4. Ibid., p. 5.

5. A. Little and C. Mabey. 'An index for designation of Educational Priority Areas', in A. Shonfield and S. Shaw (eds), *Social Indicators and Social Policy*, London, Heinemann, 1972.

6. *Children and their Primary Schools: A report of the Central Advisory Council for Education (England)*, London, H.M.S.O., 1967.

7. Shonfield and Shaw, op. cit., p. 79.

8. Ibid., p. 88.

9. See, for example, *Monitoring the Quality of American Life*, A proposal to the Russell Sage Foundation by A. Campbell and P. Converse, I.S.R., Ann Arbor, University of Michigan, 1970.

10. Ibid., p. 2.

11. See, A. Cartwright, *Patients and Their Doctor*, Routledge & Kegan Paul, London, 1967.

12. *Royal Commission on Local Government in England, 1966–1969*, vol. 1, Cmnd. 4040, London, H.M.S.O., 1969.

13. See, for example, S. P. Erie, *et al.*, *Reform of Metropolitan Governments*, Washington, Resources for the Future Inc., 1972.

14. See Bauer, p. 154.

15. *National Institute of Social and Economic Research Quarterly Review*, vol. 24, pp. 42–9.

16. C. F. Carter and A. D. Roy, *British Economic Statistics*, Cambridge University Press for N.I.E.S.R., 1954, p. 9.

17. S. Greer, *The Logic of Social Enquiry*, Chicago, Aldine, 1969.

18. Bauer, op. cit., p. 78.

19. See, for example, *Politics Economics and Welfare* by R. Dahl and C. Lindblom, Harper and Row, New York, 1953, and *A Strategy of Decision*, by D. Braybrooke and C. Lindblom, New York, Free Press, 1963.

20. 'On being an Economic Adviser', in *Factors in Economic Development*, London, Allen & Unwin, 1962, p. 227.

21. In J. H. Robertson, *The Reform of British Central Government*, London, Chatto & Windus, 1971.

22. See, for example, the Redcliffe Maud or Wheatley Reports on local government reform.

Chapter 13

1. A. H. Halsey (ed.), *Trends in British Society since 1900*, London, Macmillan, 1972.

2. In a crucial section of his book *Inequality*, New York, Basic Books, 1972, chapter 3, section 1, C. Jencks rejected operationism and emphasised the doubtful nature of the tests on which he was forced to rely (these were commercially produced group scholastic tests with few of the properties generally regarded as desirable in a well-validated, individually administered, intelligence test). This has not prevented sociologists interpreting his analyses as studies of intelligence.

3. Cf. M. L. Kohn, *Class and Conformity*, Homewood, Illinois, Dorsey, 1969; L. Rainwater, *Behind Ghetto Walls*, Harmondsworth, Penguin, 1970; L. Rainwater, *What Money Buys*, New York, Basic Books, 1974.

4. Cf. J. H. Goldthorpe and K. Hope, *The Social Grading of Occupations: a New Approach and a Scale*, Oxford, Clarendon Press, 1974.

5. R. Rose, 'The market for policy indicators', in A. Shonfield and S. Shaw (eds), *Social Indicators and Public Policy*, London, Heinemann, 1972, pp. 135.

6. Central Advisory Council for Education (England), *Children and their Primary Schools (the Plowden Report)*, London, H.M.S.O., 1967, paragraph 36.

7. This is emphatically not to endorse the metaphysical proposition that all characteristics of social collectivities are in some sense reducible to characteristics of individuals. Ecological analyses, in fact, rarely include anything but aggregated individual data. They are inadequate, not because they are peculiarly social or collective, but (*a*) because their aggregations are usually inappropriate to the analyst's interests and (*b*) because they contain no aggregation of *relations* between different characteristics of individuals.

Ecological argument is fallacious if the properties or variables which we observe at the group level are really properties of individuals rather than properties of groups. Indeed, a useful way of determining whether a property is meant to be taken as a collective rather than an individual characteristic is to ask whether an ecological argument would be fallacious or not. Debates over collective and individual properties are rendered obscure by the fact that not all individual properties can be induced from the study of individual behaviour. There are important parallels between the analysis of the concept of probability into distinct irreducible components (J. L. Mackie, *Truth, Probability and Paradox*, Oxford, 1973) and the analysis of social properties. We cannot directly observe the propensity of a biased die to fall on a certain side. Analogously, the propensity or disposition of a person to vote for a political party may be inferrable only from observations taken over a large number of relatively homogeneous people.

The argument from group behaviour· to (average) individual propensity is of course clumsy and wasteful but, properly conducted, it has the advantage of employing public, replicable, procedures. In contrast, the quick flash of personal insight which is characteristic of the good clinical psychologist or literary critic is more powerful, but also more error-prone because it involves assimilating the object under investigation to a very particular group which it matches at several points, and inferring its properties by analogy.

Because so many analyses are now being carried out on characteristics of areas or 'outputs' of local authorities, it would seem to be useful to give here as clear and simple an account as I can achieve of the fallacies which can and do arise when characteristics of aggregates are related to one another.

In social area analysis it is very often the case that the correlation between two variables has the property of being an 'ecological' correlation and also the property of being a 'spurious' correlation. Although a single coefficient may, and often does, possess both of these characteristics they are in fact conceptually distinct and their implications must be distinguished.

An *ecological* correlation is a correlation between summary statistics (for example, means, percentages or rates) of aggregates such as institutions, organisations, constituencies or wards. It is in general true to say that a non-zero correlation between two sets of summary statistics cannot be interpreted as showing that any individual possesses both the characteristics in question. For example, a correlation between proportion of persons in a particular ethnic group and mean degree of prejudice against that group cannot be interpreted as showing that the members of the group are prejudiced against themselves. The obvious absurdity of such an interpretation should stand as a warning of the dangers of ecological inferences which are, on the face of them, much less absurd, for example, the inference that a positive correlation between the mean age of electors and the proportion of votes cast for a particular party entails that older voters are giving their support to that party. The conclusion may or may not be true, but its credibility is in no way affected by the computation of an ecological correlation.

Conversely, one cannot argue from a zero ecological correlation to the absence of any correlation for individual persons. A *social malaise* report on the city of Liverpool, which took wards as its unit of analysis, found only low correlations between census indices of quality of housing and the malaise variables which were subjected to principal component analysis. One cannot legitimately infer from this that housing is not strongly related to malaise variables. For example, there were 380 children taken into the care of the Children's Department in the financial year 1967–8. It is quite possible that all of these children came from physically low-grade housing scattered among several wards of the city, but that the mean quality of housing in the wards is relatively little affected by the few houses from which these children come, and so the ecological correlation between quality of housing and children taken into care is near zero. This is statistically and logically quite possible; its plausibility may be assessed by child care officers who are familiar with the individual cases, and the extent of its truth may be objectively ascertained only by a study of individuals and households, rather than wards.

Whereas an ecological correlation is a correlation between characteristics of aggregates, a *spurious* correlation is a correlation between rates or indices. It is because characteristics of aggregates are often expressed as ratios or indices that correlation coefficients which are ecological are often also spurious.

A ratio or index consists of one number (the numerator a) divided by another number (the denominator n). Our purpose in computing a ratio is, usually, to standardise the numerator in terms of a measure of size of population 'at risk'. The value of such indices in making comparisons among aggregates or populations of different size cannot be doubted. It is only when we begin to treat indices as if they were ordinary uncompounded numbers, and in particular when we calculate correlations among them, that the problem of spuriousness arises.

In the Liverpool malaise data there are two variables – school absenteeism and physically handicapped children – which share the same population at risk, namely number of children aged 5–14 years. If the number of children in the ith ward who absent themselves from school is a_i, and if the number of children from that ward who attend schools for the physically handicapped is b_i, and if the population at risk in the ward is n_i, then we may compute the two ratios

$$\frac{a_i}{n_i} \text{ and } \frac{b_i}{n_i}$$

and treat the indices, taken individually, as a useful measure of the prevalence of absenteeism and physical handicap. However, if we proceed to correlate the two indices over the wards of the city it is evident that the resulting coefficient must in part reflect the fact that the two ratios have a common denominator.

In his original paper on spurious correlation Karl Pearson (1897) in effect showed that even if the a_i and the b_i for the various wards are jumbled up and then assigned to wards at random, the two indices will tend to display a fairly substantial degree of correlation simply by virtue of division of the randomly-assigned values by a common value. The precise strength of the tendency depends on the relative variances of the terms of the indices, but it is often strong (K. Pearson, 'Mathematical contributions to the theory of evolution', *Proc. R. Soc.*, **60**, 1897, pp. 489–502).

Pearson also showed that even if the denominators of the two indices are not identical but are merely correlated the same law holds, though in a lesser degree. Thus if the population 'at risk' varies from one variable to another, the phenomenon of spurious correlation will still be present, inflating the values of positive correlations between the numerators of indices in so far as there is a tendency (as is usually the case) for large wards to contain many of both types of person and small wards to contain few. If the elements of a correlation table have, in the absence of spuriousness, a general tendency to be positive, the effect of introducing spuriousness by correlating indices will be to inflate the proportion of the variance of the variables that can be accounted for by the first principal component, which is virtually a simple sum or average of the variables. In the analysis of the malaise data the first component accounts for nearly half the total variance whereas no other component accounts for more than 9 per cent.

Spurious correlations are computed because administrators are accustomed to the practice of correcting for population or size by the process of division. An alternative correction procedure, which gives promise of avoiding the inbuilt bias of spurious correlation, is to fit lines for the regression of each variable on the appropriate population at risk and to apply social area analysis to the deviations from regression which are sometimes called 'residuals'. Hope and Skrimshire ('The multivariate search for hospital efficiency', *Social and Economic Administration*, **6**, 1972, pp. 85–112) have explored the feasibility of this approach in a study of hospital ward-departments of varying size. We found that the advantages of indices may be retained by re-incorporating them in the analysis after the stage of the computation of correlations.

These technical considerations are fairly widely appreciated in a disembodied sense, but the average research worker does not get sufficient practice in applying them to be confident that he will see the need to resort to them when it arises. Spurious correlation has proved to be particularly confusing to research workers because the name has been applied by American social statisticians to a quite different, though superficially similar, concept. According to this the correlation between variables A and B is spurious if it becomes zero when variable C is partialled out. This is a rather silly use of the term 'spurious'. It was introduced at a time when there was a widespread though not quite explicit belief that statistical manipulation could save us the trouble of preliminary specification of models of social processes. I advise every research worker who ever thinks of calculating a correlation between percentages to read Pearson's original paper. Even then he must remember that a 'spurious' correlation is not necessarily spurious. As Yule and Kendall say,

> It does not follow of necessity that the correlations between indices or ratios are misleading. If the indices are uncorrelated, there will be a similar 'spurious' correlation between the absolute measurements $\zeta_1 X_3 = X_1$ and $\zeta_2 X_3 = X_2$, and the answer to the question whether the correlation between indices or that between absolute measures is misleading depends on the further question whether the indices or the absolute measures are the quantities directly determined by the causes under investigation. (G. U. Yule and M. G. Kendall, *An Introduction to the Theory of Statistics*, 14th edn, London, Griffin, 1950, pp. 330 ff.).

8. Cf., for example, R. Roberts, *The Classic Slum*, Manchester, Manchester University Press, 1971.

9. Cf. K. Coates and R. Silburn, *Poverty: the Forgotten Englishmen*, Harmondsworth, Penguin, 1970.

10. The recognition that this field of inquiry constitutes a social and intellectual *movement* is due to O. D. Duncan, *Towards Social Reporting: Next Steps*, New York, Russell Sage Foundation, 1969.

11. J. D. Watson, *The Double Helix*, London, Weidenfeld & Nicolson, 1968.

12. I refer thus sketchily and dogmatically to the origins of what I conceive to be the dominant schools in the respective countries. So far as university-based research is concerned the native tradition of social arithmetic is moribund, and where it still lives it is largely detached from recent mathematical and statistical developments.

13. L. Rainwater, *What Money Buys*, op. cit.

14. The following quotation from Cox and Dyson's introduction to *The Black Papers on Education* may help to explain why the debate did not develop in the way it has done more recently in the United States.

The nastiest feature of the reaction to Black Paper Two was the personal attack on Professor Burt. In the *Sunday Times* (October

12th) a full page attacked Black Paper statistics, relying heavily on Professor Pedley's surveys. The article referred to Professor Burt's claim in Black Paper Two that 'the average attainments in reading, spelling, mechanical and problem arithmetic are now appreciably lower than they were 55 years ago'. The *Sunday Times* stated that Professor Burt had written in a scholarly article that his statistics supporting this claim would be published in the *Irish Journal of Education*, but 'the editor of that journal says he has neither published nor received any article from Professor Burt which would substantiate his remarkable claim.' The implication that he had made it all up was frequently repeated and accepted by many teachers, as Black Paper contributors discovered when they addressed public meetings. The story was repeated in letters in the *TES* and the *Observer*.

The report in the *Sunday Times* was untrue. Dr Thomas Kellaghan, editor of the *Irish Journal of Education*, immediately (October 15th) wrote a letter to the *Sunday Times* saying that Professor Burt's article did exist and was about to be published. This letter was not printed. Eventually in December the *Sunday Times* published a letter from Professor Cox giving the truth, and the Personal Assistant to the Editor wrote to him: 'Our information about non-publication of Professor Burt's article came from two very reliable sources in the educational world and our correspondent did not think it necessary to check with him directly. He agrees now he should have done so.' When after Christmas the article was published with the statistics, it was well reported in the *TES* and *The Times*. But the damage had been done. The story had been told everywhere, and the idea that Black Paper statistics had been falsely made up is still being repeated (C. B. Cox and A. E. Dyson (eds), *The Black Papers on Education*, London, Davis-Poynter, 1971, pp. 14 ff.)

At first sight the oddity of this occurrence is that the contents of the Black Papers do not seem very far removed from one's expectations of the prejudices of an average reader of the *Sunday Times*. The clash is not, however, treated as a clash of ideologies, still less as a clash of arguable theory and evidence, but as a clash between what is 'in' and what is 'out'. To understand the power of intellectual fashion in English cultural life one must listen to a 'senior' official who is by every token of upbringing, norms and character a high Tory, mouthing the platitudes of egalitarian, social democratic, welfarism.

There is nothing odd or suspicious about the fact that sociology and social policy research are the stamping ground of ideologues.

What is unfortunate is that institutions such as newspapers should be able to block an intellectual contest before it gets fairly going, and insufficient pressure should build up to remove the obstacle. The institutional framework is lacking which might, in policy matters, *parcere subiectis, et debellare superbos.*

I do not go as far as Popper in supposing that institutions are sufficient in themselves to keep a scientist within the normative bounds. In the social sciences particularly, where replication is often costly and may be impossible, we must look for that process of internalisation of standards which constitutes integrity. Only within a fairly tight status group does the concept of integrity have any determinate reference. Like Tocqueville's fellow aristocrats, we academics have assumed the titles and emoluments of our predecessors, but have we inherited their spirit?

15. It is, surely, the universal experience of anyone who has done empirical work and published a report that the imagination continues to roam over the material and to find implications – and errors – which were not apparent at the time. Often these processes can be abridged by someone who has not had to toil at the minutiae of checking computer routines and making sure that tables are the right way round. These observations are, I think, relevant to the vexed question of how best to convey the lessons of empirical research to policy-makers. This is sometimes treated as a matter to be decided by pedagogic expediency. It is often said, for example, that a brief report for immediate consumption will suffice to convey the gist of the matter, while the main report can be written later for an academic audience. I seriously doubt whether a social researcher can, in general, know what he should, and can legitimately, put into a summary document until he has fought his way through the 'academic' complexities of his major report. And even if he can, I doubt whether, in any particular case, we can know that he can. Except in very simple cases, no social inquiry is complete until the evidence has been thoroughly chewed over by competent critics.

16. We must not, of course, exaggerate the similarities between planning and research. So far as I am aware bribery and graft have not yet invaded the field of social policy research. If ever they attempt to do so we shall know both that research has achieved a quality which makes it relatively impregnable to purely intellectual criticism, and that its content and institutionalised acceptability give it powerful redistributive implications. As one who has a firm belief in the value of the services which good planning, good research and good statistics can offer to the community I trust that the emergent profession of social researchers will not be allowed to evade that degree of intellectual accountability which is due to the society into whose entrails

they peer. If, however, research workers succeed in outflanking the political process the consequent intellectual corruption of political debate will be at least as serious as the direct effects on particular policies.

17. Lord Rothschild, 'The organisation and management of government research and development', in *A Framework for Government Research and Development*, Cmnd. 4814, London, H.M.S.O., 1971.

Chapter 14

1. P. A. Sorokin, *Fads and Foibles in Modern Sociology*, London, 1958, chapters 7 and 8.

2. E. B. Schumpeter, *English overseas trade statistics 1697–1808*, Oxford, 1960, Introduction by T. S. Ashton.

3. D. E. C. Eversley, 'The Great Western Railway and the Swindon Works in the Great Depression', (1956), in M. C. Reed (ed.), *Railways in the Victorian economy*, London, 1969, p. 111 ff.

4. D. E. C. Eversley, 'A survey of population in an area of Worcestershire from 1660 to 1850, on the basis of parish registers' (1957), in D. Glass and D. E. C. Eversley (eds), *Population in History*, London, 1965, chapter 16.

5. R. T. Vann, *The Social Development of English Quakerism*, Cambridge, Mass., 1969, chapter 11.

6. Compare series of articles entitled 'Thinking by numbers' in *Times Literary Supplement*, 6 August 1971 *et seq.*, covering such subjects as music and linguistics. Many of the themes in this chapter are in the issue of 24 September 1971: D. E. C. Eversley, 'Demography, the limits of quantification'.

7. For both the historical origins of political arithmetic and the best of Glass's own work, see: Glass and Eversley (ed.), op. cit., chapters 8 and 9. Also D. V. Glass and R. Revelle (ed.), *Population and Social Change*, London, 1972, p. 275 ff.

8. The literature of the extreme overpopulation scare phase is large, and we can give only a few samples of the misuse of numbers here: Claire and W. M. S. Russell, *Violence, Monkeys and Man*, London, 1968. Paul and Anne Ehrlich, *Population, Resources, Environment*, San Francisco, 1970. W. and P. Paddock, *Famine-1975!*, London, 1968. Almost all the publications of the Conservation Society; Paul Ehrlich, *The Population Bomb*, London, 1971.

9. J. Maddox, *The Domesday Syndrome*, London, 1972. He uses the expression 'numbers game' as the title of his second chapter. The whole book is an excellent refutation of the more extreme views now prevalent, but unfortunately his statistical apparatus is scarcely much better than that of his opponents.

10. B. Smithies and P. Fiddick, *Enoch Powell on Immigration*, London, 1969.

11. Smithies, op. cit.

12. D. Eversley and F. Sukdeo, *The Dependants of the Coloured Commonwealth Population of England and Wales*, London, Institute of Race Relations, 1969.

13. See review by Ceri Peach, in *Race*, **XI** (2), pp. 244–7.

14. B. Wootton, *Testament for Social Science*, London, 1950, especially chapter 8.

15. D. Eversley and D. Keate, *The Overspill Problem in the West Midlands*, Birmingham, 1958.

16. *Higher Education: report of the committee . . . under the chairmanship of Lord Robbins*, 1961–63. Cmnd. 2154, London, H.M.S.O., 1963. (Also 6 vols of appendices.)

17. For examples of the new directions, see *Social Trends*, London, H.M.S.O., annually since 1970.

18. *Report of the Royal Commission on the distribution of the industrial population* (Chairman, Sir Montagu Barlow), Cmd. 6153, London, H.M.S.O. 1940–42.

19. *The Intermediate Areas: report of a committee under the chairmanship of Sir Joseph Hunt*, Cmnd. 3998, London, H.M.S.O., 1969.

20. W. B. Reddaway, *et al.*, *Effects of the Selective Employment Tax: first report in the distributive trades*, London, H.M. Treasury, 1970.

21. Hunt, op. cit. Dissenting report by A. J. Brown.

22. Greater London Council: Greater London Development Plan inquiry. *The Development of Personal Incomes within the G.L.C. area compared with the Rest of the South-east Region*, Support Paper S 11/153, 1971. Also Margaret Harris and John Lyons, 'Some aspects of social polarization', (*Inner City Conference Papers*, to be published for the Centre for Environmental Studies, London, in 1973). D. E. C. Eversley, 'Rising costs and static incomes: some economic consequences of regional planning in London', *Urban Stud.*, **9** (3), October 1972.

23. G. Myrdal, *Objectivity in Social Research*, 1971 (The Wimmer Lecture, St Vincent College, Latrobe, Pennsylvania, 1967.)

24. G. Myrdal, *An American Dilemma: the Negro Problem and Modern Democracy*, New York, 1944. (Especially introduction, sections 1 and 2; and appendices 1 and 10.) Also in *Value in Social Theory*, London, 1956, chapter 5.

25. Myrdal, op. cit., for the call to bring value premises into the open.

26. The same point is made by Max Weber, who, however, thinks this is an advantage: *Theory of social and economic organization*, trans A. M. Henderson and T. Parsons, T. Parsons (ed.), London, 1964, pp. 88–120.

27. The same may occasionally of course be true in the natural sciences, though the stories about the geniuses who derived laws or inventions from everyday experience are mostly untrue (for example, Archimedes' bath, Newton's apple, and Watt's kettle).

28. G. Cherry, 'Overcrowding in cities', *Official Architecture and Planning*, March 1969, **32**, (3), p. 287.

29. D. M. Fanning, 'Families in flats', *Br. med. J.*, **4**, 1967, pp. 382–6.

30. P. Willmott and M. Young, *Family and Kinship in East London*, London, 1960.

31. H. Orlans, *Stevenage: a Sociological Study of a New Town*, London, 1952.

32. N. Dennis, *People and Planning: the Sociology of Housing in Sunderland*, London, 1970.

33. H. E. Heughan, *Pit closures at Shotts and the Migration of Miners*, Edinburgh, 1953.

34. E. J. B. Rose (ed.), *Colour and Citizenship: a Report on British Race Relations*, Oxford, 1969, chapter 12, pp. 120–48. Also E. Burney, *Housing on Trial*, London, 1967. J. Rex and R. Moore, *Race, Community and Conflict*, London, 1967. E. Radford, *The New Villagers: Urban Pressure on Rural Areas in Worcestershire*, London, 1970.

35. C. M. Lock and R. Glass. *Middlesbrough: a Plan*, Middlesbrough Corporation, 1947.

36. P. Willmott, *The Evolution of a Community: a Study of Dagenham after Forty Years*, London, 1963.

37. A. Carey. 'The Hawthorne Studies: a radical criticism', *Am. sociol. Rev.*, **32** (3), 1967, p. 403.

38. See note 29 above.

39. For a discussion of the dangers involved in the selection of variables, see: C. A. Moser and G. Kalton, *Survey Methods in Social Investigation*, London, 1971, pp. 244–54. Also J. H. Madge, *The Tools of Social Science*, London, 1953; and Jennifer Platt, 'Survey data and social policy', chapter 5 in this volume.

40. It should be noted that the selection of independent variables is in itself not always a very scientific process: it depends on the investigator's hunches as to what is and what is not important, which may often be a matter of the depth of his imagination.

41. For a sketchy first account of this investigation, see D. E. C. Eversley and K. Gales, 'Married women: Britain's biggest reservoir of labour', *Progress*, **53** (301), 1969.

42. See also the reference to G. Cherry's work, note 28.

43. D. E. C. Eversley and Valerie Jackson, 'Problems encountered in forecasting housing demand in an area of high economic activity: headship rates in relation to age structure, fertility, education and

socio-economic groups', *Proceedings of World Population Conference, 1965*. United Nations, New York, 1967. vol. 4, section A8, p. 418 ff.

44. D. E. C. Eversley, 'Urban problems in Britain today', *Quarterly Bulletin of the Intelligence Unit*, London, Greater London Council, no. 19, June 1972, p. 47.

45. Wootton, op. cit.

46. This point is further developed by W. G. Runciman who shows that highly refined techniques may be mis-applied to quite unreliable evidence. See *Times Literary Supplement*, 6 August 1971, p. 943.

47. C. V. Kyser and P. K. Whelpton (eds), *The Social and Psychological Factors Affecting Fertility*, New York, Millbank Memorial Fund, 1943–58.

48. *Studies in Family Planning*, **2** (3), March 1971; **2** (12), December 1971. Also B. Berelson (ed.), *Family Planning and Population Programs*, Chicago, 1966, chapters 4–5, 6 and 54.

49. Rex and Moore; op. cit., note 34.

50. See note 9 above.

51. For an example of the problem of multiple causation, and the dangers involved in failing to recognise that many social factors are not susceptible to mathematical or statistical analysis, see: P. O. Olusanya, 'The problem of multiple causation in population analysis, with particular reference to the polygamy-fertility hypothesis', *Sociol. Rev.*, **19** (2), pp. 165–78.

52. Rex and Moore, op. cit.

53. *Notting Hill Summer Project 1967, Interim report*. University of Sussex: Social Research Unit, for Notting Hill Housing Service. Published by Shelter, 1969.

54. Institute of Race Relations, *Colour and Citizenship*, E. J. B. Rose (ed.), Oxford, 1969, chapter 13.

55. L. White and M. White, *The Intellectual Versus the City*, New York, 1964.

56. J. Maddox, op. cit., p. 115.

57. D. Huff, *How to Lie with Statistics*, London, 1954.

58. Drapers' Company research memoirs: *Studies in National Deterioration*, F. Galton and K. Pearson (eds), London; from 1906.

59. A 1971 report by the Washington Centre for Metropolitan Studies expressed a fear of nil population growth in the United States, the initial symptom being declining sales within the toy industry. The principal danger was felt to be that neither the labour force nor the market required by the nation's growth-orientated economy would be provided. (See report in *Daily Telegraph*, 8 September 1971.)

60. G. Myrdal, op. cit., p. 40.

61. To cite just one or two examples: it is widely believed in Britain today that there are large sections of the population whom it pays better to be unemployed than to work; that inflation is caused by trade union wage demands, and that the population is doubling itself every twenty-five years because of the hyper-fertility of the poor and the blacks.

62. H. J. Eysenck, *Race, Intelligence and Education*, London, 1971.

63. Poor Law Commissioners, *Report on the Sanitary Condition of the Labouring Population of Great Britain*, by Edwin Chadwick, M. W. Flinn (ed.), Edinburgh, 1965.

64. F. Zweig, *Labour, Life and Poverty*, London, 1948.

65. O. Lewis, *The Children of Sanchez*, London, 1961. And *Pedro Martinez*, London, 1964.

66. Rex and Moore, op. cit. But even here we must remember (and Rex would be the last to deny this) that his own value system is the principal determinant of his approach to the Sparkbrook problem.

67. *Commission on the Third London Airport* (Chairman, The Hon Mr Justice Roskill), London, H.M.S.O., 1971.

68. T. Harrison, *Britain Revisited*, London, 1961, p. 20.

69. For a good example in this particular case of how two different surveys can come to diametrically opposite conclusions, see: British Road Federation, *Roads in London: the Public View*, 1970. P. Willmott and M. Young, 'How urgent are London's motorways?' *New Society*, 10 December 1970.

70. Committee on comparative studies of fertility and family planning of the International Union for Scientific Study of Population, *Variables for Comparative Fertility Studies*, Liege, 1967.

71. See 'No job for Herod yet', *The Economist*, 29 July, 1972, for a summary of a report of a new group, 'Population Stabilisation', which also believes that if people had no money worries they would have far more children – and a criticism of this argument.

Chapter 15

1. A. B. Cherns, 'Uses of the social sciences', *Hum. Relat.*, **27** (4), 1968.

2. A. Shonfield, 'Research and Public Policy', in A. B. Cherns *et al.*, *Social Science and Government*, London, Tavistock, 1972.

3. P. A. Samuelson also makes this point in his 'What economists know' in D. Lerner (ed.), *The Human Meaning of the Social Sciences*, New York, Meridian Books, 1959, as does Y. Dror somewhat more obscurely, in *Design for Policy Sciences*, New York, Elsevier, 1971, p. 8.

But at least in the British context, it is not a view that has received universal acceptance even among economists. See, for example, T. W. Hutchinson, *Economics and Economic Policy in Britain, 1946–66*, London, Allen & Unwin, 1968.

4. *The Social Sciences and the Policies of Governments*, Paris, O.E.C.D., 1966.

5. Cf. T. S. Simey, *Social Science and Social Purpose*, London, Constable, 1968, chapter 3.

6. D. K. Price, *Government and Science*, New York, New York University Press 1954, p. 4. Edward Shils also emphasises the importance of the 'lay culture' of the United States in enhancing the status of social sciences. See his *Torment of Secrecy*, London, Heinemann 1956, pp. 40–1.

7. H. D. Lasswell, 'The policy orientation' in D. Lerner and H. D. Lasswell (eds), *The Policy Sciences*, Stanford, Stanford University Press 1957, p. 15.

8. G. H. Hardy, *A Mathematician's Apology*, as quoted in I. M. D. Little, *A Critique of Welfare Economics*, 2nd edn, Oxford, Clarendon, 1957, p. 1.

9. For example, the Donovan Commission on trade unions and the Redcliffe-Maud Commission on local government.

10. For example, the Seebohm Committee on the personal social services, the Fulton Commission on the civil service and the Kilbrandon Commission on the constitution.

11. C. Cunningham, 'Research funding in the United States', *S.S.R.C. Newsletter*, no. 13, November 1971.

12. See Simey, *Social Science and Social Purpose*, chapters 4 and 5 for a discussion of this debate.

13. C. Wright Mills, *The Sociological Imagination*, New York, Oxford University Press 1959, chapters 3 and 10.

14. R. K. Merton, 'Social Scientists and Research Policy' in Lerner and Lasswell (eds), *The Policy Sciences*, op. cit., p. 293.

15. Ibid., p. 306.

16. Cunningham, op. cit. p. 19.

17. D. P. Moynihan, 'The role of social scientists in action research', *S.S.R.C. Newsletter*, no. 10, November 1970, p. 2.

18. Ibid., p. 2.

19. Personal communication to author from Professor Peabody.

20. For a succinct account of the main features of the federal civil service as compared with the British, see *The Civil Services of North America*, London, Civil Service Department, H.M.S.O., 1969.

21. G. M. Lyons, *The Uneasy Partnership*, New York, Russell Sage Foundation, 1968, p. 14.

22. K. Hope, p. 250.

23. This comment on New Deal legislation is attributed to Norman Thomas by Michael Harrington in his introduction to J. Newfield, *A Prophetic Minority*, London, Blond, 1967, p. 14.

24. R. E. Lane, 'The Decline of Politics and Ideology in a Knowledgeable Society', *Am. Sociol. Rev.*, **31**, 1966, p. 659.

25. H. W. Reicken, 'Federal Government and Social Science Policy in the United States' in Cherns *et al.*, *Social Science and Government*, op. cit., p. 176.

26. Ibid., p. 189.

27. The most notorious of these was Project Camelot. This was a very large-scale study sponsored by the Army with a budget of $6 million designed to help the United States cope with internal revolutions in South America. See G. Sjoberg, 'Project Camelot: selected reactions and personal reflections' in G. Sjoberg (ed.), *Ethics, Politics and Social Research*, London, Routledge, 1967. This book also contains a number of other examples of the way in which social scientists have been used for questionable ends both in the United States and elsewhere. For a more detailed discussion and criticism of Project Camelot see I. L. Horowitz (ed.), *The Rise and Fall of Project Camelot*, Cambridge, Mass., M.I.T. Press, 1967.

Index